POLITICAL AND LEGAL OBLIGATION

NOMOS
XII

N O M O S

NOMOS XII
Yearbook of the American Society for Political and Legal Philosophy

POLITICAL
AND LEGAL
OBLIGATION

Edited by J. ROLAND PENNOCK

Swarthmore College

and JOHN W. CHAPMAN

University of Pittsburgh

ATHERTON PRESS   New York   1970

PREFACE

With this volume *Nomos* counts up to a dozen. The American Society for Political and Legal Philosophy, of which it is the Yearbook, is an intentionally small but inevitably growing organization. Its meetings attract growing numbers of attenders from our interdisciplinary membership. The formation, recently, of the Conference on Political Thought, focusing on the development of regional discussion groups bears further testimony to the fact that political theory, as Sir Isaiah Berlin has assured us, is far from dead. In fact, it appears to be taking a new lease on life, as the recent survey of the profession by the American Political Science Association also indicates.

The Society's meetings that gave rise to *Nomos XII* were held in Detroit, in December 1967, immediately following those of the American Association of Law Schools. Harry W. Jones, Cardozo Professor of Law at Columbia University, served as chairman of the Program Committee. The chapters of this volume by John Ladd, Jeffrie G. Murphy, Mark R. MacGuigan, Gray L. Dorsey, Gerald C. MacCallum, Jr. (Chapter 9), Stuart S. Nagel, and James Luther Adams are based upon papers delivered or comments made at the annual meetings. To these men the editors of this volume are indebted as they equally are to the other authors whose contributions are included in these pages.

Our topic, "Political and Legal Obligation," is one of those permanent human concerns, perhaps more pressing today than at any time since the early days of the modern state.

J. Roland Pennock
John W. Chapman

CONTENTS

OBLIGATION AND THE CONDITIONS
OF OBEDIENCE

CIVIL DISOBEDIENCE

CONTRIBUTORS

JAMES LUTHER ADAMS
Social Ethics, Andover Newton Theological School [*Professor Emeritus, Harvard Divinity School*]

KURT BAIER
Philosophy, University of Pittsburgh

JOHN W. CHAPMAN
Political Science, University of Pittsburgh

GRAY L. DORSEY
Law, Washington University

RICHARD E. FLATHMAN
Political Science, The University of Chicago

ALAN GEWIRTH
Philosophy, The University of Chicago

KENT GREENAWALT
Law, Columbia University

NANNERL O. HENRY
Political Science, Swarthmore College

JOHN LADD
Philosophy, Brown University

WAYNE A. R. LEYS
Philosophy, Southern Illinois University

GERALD C. MacCALLUM, JR.
Philosophy, University of Wisconsin

MARK R. MacGUIGAN
Law, Member of Parliament for Windsor-Walkerville, House of Commons, Canada [formerly, University of Windsor, Canada]

ALFRED G. MEYER
Political Science, The University of Michigan

JEFFRIE G. MURPHY
Philosophy, University of Arizona

STUART S. NAGEL
Political Science, The University of Illinois

P. S. S. RAMA RAO
Philosophy, Miami University

DAVID C. RAPOPORT
Political Science, University of California, Los Angeles

MICHAEL WALZER
Political Science, Harvard University

INTRODUCTION

Like political theory itself, the theory of political obligation has had a checkered career. While it has often been said that it constituted the heart of political theory or comprised its most fundamental category, a moment's reflection will point to a contrary view. The *Crito* to the contrary notwithstanding, neither Plato nor Aristotle was primarily concerned with the problem of political obligation. The same can be said of many, perhaps most, other major figures in the history of political thought. How then account for the prevailing impression?

Two explanations, closely related, suggest themselves. Prior to the Reformation, political theory tended to be organic rather than mechanistic, collectivist rather than individualist. Occasional writers speculated about the right of tyrannicide. Others, including Thomas himself, discussed the possibility of justified resistance, not to mention the invalidity of "laws" that were contrary to Natural Law. Yet such topics tended to be treated as peripheral and not to be thoroughly analyzed. But once the individual ceased to be only a cell in the body politic and became in a sense a moral sovereign, all that was changed. The great problem for political theory, especially for a period of over two centuries after the Reformation, was to explain how any man, born "free and equal," could be rightfully under the dominion of any other man. The Great Chain of Being had been broken. If not new fetters, at least new bonds, new "ligations," had to be provided.

To this task the great contractualists of the seventeenth and eighteenth centuries devoted themselves, not to the exclusion of all else, but in overshadowing measure. This fact is the second, not-so-very-different explanation adverted to above. Hobbes, Locke, and Rousseau, to name only the greatest, so dominated the scene not only in their own day but for long afterwards that to think of political theory without political obligation seemed indeed like *Hamlet* without the Prince of Denmark.

Still a third explanation is perhaps the most relevant to our contemporary concerns. The foundations of modern political theory were laid in revolution. The name of each of the great theorists just enumerated is attached to a revolution. Whether the men wrote to justify or to condemn is of no moment; their concern was about the metes of political obligation. As memories of the most recent great revolution of the western world recede, however, the theory of political obligation gradually figures less importantly in political theorizing.

But times have changed again. A topic proposed for discussion and voted down on several occasions by the American Society for Political and Legal Philosophy suddenly carried the day. And small wonder. With draft resisters and other civil disobedients burgeoning, and with the word "revolution" (cf. *Nomos VIII*) ringing in all our ears if not tripping off our tongues, it would be both strange and unfortunate if the whole subject of obligation to the state and to law was not coming in for renewed examination. We notice that the *Institut Internationale de Philosophie Politique* devoted its 1969 meetings to this subject. Two recent collections of contemporary articles dealing with political philosophy further testify that the subject is very much alive, especially by the attention given the subject in the editors' introductions.[1]

Theories of political obligation can of course be classified in many ways and looked at from a number of points of view. One question that can always be raised, one which is perhaps peculiarly relevant for a volume devoted to the subject of political and legal obligation, is whether the obligation to obey and support the state and its laws is in any way distinctive or special. Or is it, as E. F. Carritt argued years ago, merely a set of moral obligations as they happen to apply to law and the state in a particular instance?[2] Utilitarians, whether of that particular school for whom the capital *U* is generally reserved or not, tend to fall into the latter category. For Bentham the question of obligation to obey a command of the state was simply a matter of calculating the "mischiefs" entailed by obedience and weighing them against the "mischiefs" of disobedience. For Burke, a utilitarian within certain limits, a similar calculation must be made. The presumption against disobedience, much less an act of rebellion, would for him be very strong; yet in the final analysis the kind of judgment involved would be no different from a judgment, let us say, as to whether to obey a command of one's father.

Whether the calculation relates only to consequences is perhaps not entirely clear in Burke's case. But then, if it does not, this fact merely makes it clear that the category

---

[1] See Alan Gewirth, ed., *Political Philosophy* (New York: Macmillan, 1965) and Anthony Quinton, ed., *Political Philosophy* (London: Oxford University Press, 1967). Gewirth deals with the subject more fully in the present volume. Recent works on the subject are too numerous to list.

[2] E. F. Carritt, *Morals and Politics* (Oxford: The Clarendon Press, 1935).

under discussion is not confined to utilitarians. The inclusion of Carritt himself would make that point. For him the question would be determined largely by judging the bearing of a number of self-evident prima facie rights on a consideration of the consequences of obedience or disobedience. For men like Carritt as for utilitarians of all sorts, political obligation tends to blend imperceptibly into the general class of moral obligations.

The contractualists are the most prominent and obvious example of those who place political and legal obligations in a special category. For them the obligation to obey the state is derived from some sort of promise or contract — indeed from a series of contracts obligating each member of a society to every other member and to its properly constituted government. Similarly, the political idealists — especially Green, Bosanquet, and William Ernest Hocking — set apart political obligation; they explain it in terms of individual will, cumulated and integrated as a "General Will."[3]

More generally, it may be observed that those who tend to place political obligation in a special category do so not only because of the ideas of contract and of General Will but also because they visualize the state as an institution performing distinctive functions that generate obligations. These are moral obligations. They go beyond the legal not only in that they bind apart from the law but also in that they extend to matters like voting, and voting for the general welfare, that often transcend the limits of what law can accomplish. These moral obligations — whether at the minimum level of obligations to obey the law or at the level of providing all kinds of support for the good state — are sufficiently distinctive to enjoy a special status. Since they relate to and are

---

[3]It is true that in the works of most of these writers, whether contractualists or idealists, it is not always clear how fundamentally different their explanation of other kinds of obligation would be from what they say about political obligation, but for the latter they do invent these special concepts of contract and will. The contractualists attempt to resolve the problem of one man's right to govern another by reference to a putative agreement; the idealists' strategy is to use the concept of "real" wills and to rely on the socializing influences of society to make a generalization of real wills realistic both as a goal and as a source of obligation.

supportive of institutions, they cannot properly be considered without reference to these institutions and the values they embody. It is sometimes argued that a theory about obligation to "the state" has little relevance to the question of obedience to a particular law or even a particular government. But it does have a great deal of relevance to just such questions; for it is the nature of particular institutional complexes to establish standards of behavior (even though they may not be completely effective) and to perpetuate certain values and tested ways of achieving or protecting them. This point is being made or relied upon by all the papers that stress obligation to a system, and perhaps especially by John Chapman and Nannerl Henry.

Apart from what has just been said, it would appear that there are at least two respects in which obligations to the state are unique. To point them out will do no harm and may serve to put the subject in useful perspective. First, the obligation to obey law (whenever it exists, that is to say, without reference to the argument about whether there is always an obligation to obey the law) derives much of its force from the fact that it supports other obligations. Thus Hobbes argues that the "laws of nature" do not bind in the state of nature (except in the case of contracts where one party has fulfilled his obligation), that is, in the absence of positive law backed up by the force of the state, because it would be unreasonable to expect men to fulfill their obligations to others when they have no ground for assuming that others will fulfill their obligations to them. The state, with its sanctioned laws, reverses the presumption. Latent obligations become binding (or, if one prefers, potential obligations are actualized) once the justified fear of nonreciprocity is removed.

A modern defense of essentially the same idea may be found in Stuart Brown's argument that the highest institutional good is a political and legal system that provides general protection to all high-order goods and permits each individual member of the community to place the burden of proof upon those who would deny him his good or interfere with his pursuit of it.[4] Men enjoy an unconditional and inalienable right to no particular good, he argues, but they do have such a right to the institutions that will best protect their goods. It follows, of course, that all have duties to support such institutions.

It is at least arguable that there is yet another way in which obligation to obey the law of the state is rather special. This reasoning derives from an examination of the nature of law. That subject is clearly not one on which I can now embark. But it might be worthwhile to refer to the theory of law that I have in mind. It is the theory — widely held, in slightly varying forms — that law achieves its "legitimacy," its claim to our obedience, and at least part of its morally obligatory force from a peculiar recognition that it receives from those, or the bulk of those, to whom it is supposed to apply. This recognition comes into being, I would argue, as a result of a combination of factors, about which it is impossible to be absolutely precise. But one can say that in addition to widespread obedience and agencies to encourage that obedience as well as to define and apply the law, other ingredients are normally present and essential. They may include the belief that a particular rule is right, or that the regime that supports it is good and should be supported; they are almost sure to include also the knowledge that most other people obey the law and recognize it as having a certain morally rightful claim upon their behavior, or at the very least that they behave as though they felt this way.[5] To avoid misunderstanding, I should stress, however, that I am contending that the peculiar nature of law does provide a special obligation to obey it. The fact that other people obey it *because they think they ought to* is one reason why I am obligated. I am not, of course, suggesting that this obligation is absolute.

[4]Stuart M. Brown, Jr., "Inalienable Rights," *The Philosophical Review*, 64 (1955), 192–211, at p. 211.

[5]See my "Law and Sovereignty," *The American Political Science Review*, 31 (1937), 617–637. And see Alf Ross, *Towards a Realistic Jurisprudence; a Criticism of the Dualism in Law*, transl. by Annie I. Fausboll (Copenhagen: E. Munksgaard, 1946).

As has already been noted, the discussion in this volume tends to go along lines rather different from those sketched above. The issue is less whether political and legal obligations are in any way different from other obligations as it is whether any such thing as a generalized obligation to obey law and the state can be said to exist. John Ladd, in the opening chapter, takes the provocative view that no such obligation exists. He accomplished this *tour de force* by defining obligation in a narrow sense, one that places many ought statements in a different category, and does not admit of degrees. Although he contends that (by his definition) political obligation is logically impossible, he is perhaps even more concerned to argue that the concept of political obligation is morally unsound. It lays too much stress on the legal order as a whole rather than on individual laws. Moreover, the argument that law is especially binding in a democracy because of its procedures tends to make us overlook the areas in which those procedures are mere façades.

Of the other essays in Part I, none accepts Ladd's narrow definition of "obligation" or reaches his rather unusual conclusion. Jeffrie Murphy takes direct issue with him. He holds that Ladd's analysis of the concept of "obligation" is faulty and that, even given Ladd's moral paradigm, he has not been resourceful enough in looking for political analogues. Mark MacGuigan is in accord. He argues that the relations between law and morals are highly complex and that the narrow concept of obligation offers little assistance toward clarification of these relations.

Alan Gewirth discusses many kinds of obligations. He places more emphasis on obligation to a political and legal system, especially if it is a constitutional democracy, than does Ladd. He also points to the importance of assessing the possible negative effects of disobeying a law as well as to the possible negative effects of allowing the law to rule. Richard Flathman, too, believes that obligation may be general as well as specific; but he is primarily concerned to argue, leaning heavily on linguistic analysis, that obligation is a highly complicated matter, depending upon rational delib-

eration in specific contexts for its substance. Finally, Kurt
Baier's paper is from one point of view at the opposite
extreme from Ladd's. After examining what he considers to
be the four most important theories of political obligation,
he finds three of them — those of Austin, of H. L. A. Hart,
and of the Contractualists — faulty, and concludes that only
the fourth is acceptable. To be obliged to do something, he
holds, is to fall under a rule such that not obeying that rule
would be wrong. This broad sense of the word, he argues, is
the morally and politically important one; and according to
it, he continues, there is a prima facie obligation for one
living in the territory of a given state to obey its commands.

John Chapman regards political obligation as a special
kind of moral obligation, more general and more institutional than are either moral or legal obligations as ordinarily conceived. He considers and compares the moral foundations and psychological processes that enter into liberal and
Marxian thinking about obligation. Modern Kantians would
recommend institutional arrangements more consistent with
human dynamics than does Marx, although all are in debt to
Rousseau's concept of human perfectibility.

Part II of this volume is perhaps less closely knit and its
subject matter less easily classifiable than is true of the other
Parts. Yet it is by no means a catch-all. Each paper deals, in
part at least, with what are the conditions of either obedience or obligation, that is to say, with "constitutional morality," the procedural as distinguished from the substantive
aspect of political obligation. Gray Dorsey opens the discussion with a consideration of the conditions for "felt obligation." Drawing widely upon materials from history —
English, Chinese (both Revolutionary and Nationalist),
and American—he contends that "a constitutional principle
that is expected to stimulate and sustain the flow of power
from people to government must have its apparent foundation in generally held belief" (p. 212). A general pragmatic
attitude will not suffice for the development of a sense of
obligation.

Gerald MacCallum's immediately following critique points to some of the difficulties of substantiating Dorsey's position. "Felt obligation" is not easy to ascertain, and it is even more difficult to ascertain empirically what behavior results from "felt obligation" and what does not. Stuart Nagel pursues the same general point and also refers to a sizable amount of literature relating to the subject of compliance to the law, and especially to court decisions, that could be used for further refining and testing of Dorsey's argument.

David Rapaport provides a fascinating case study of a city (Rome) that for seven centuries had no police force, and of the political attitudes and feelings of obligation that accompanied, and presumably conditioned, that experience. But he does not attribute the experience entirely to the reigning belief system. The law-making institutions were such as to insure the maximum of consensus, the minimum of resentment. Yet the system ultimately broke down; and changes in the belief system were intimately related to the systemic decay.

Nannerl Henry's discussion of "Political Obligation and Collective Goods" might be said to be the only paper in the volume, with the exception of Chapman's, that discusses the subject of political obligation in terms similar to those of the traditional "Greats" of political theory. Yet her discussion appears to belong in this Part more properly than in Part I. She considers the theories of Hobbes and Hume, of Aristotle and Rousseau, from the point of view of developing a theory of obligation based upon collective good and self-fulfillment, and also to show the special value of Aristotle's theory for this question. Aristotle recommended a form of government and society most likely, she argues, to have a valid claim upon our obedience. The upshot of her chapter, then, is to argue for a particular form of government as a condition for maximum allegiance. Not surprisingly this position is rather close to a Rousseauean or Kantian statement of the conditions for maximum allegiance.

In Part III we return to ethical questions, this time more narrowly directed to questions of civil disobedience. James Luther Adams opens with a careful, and somewhat restrictive, definition of "civil disobedience," and then performs the interesting and, at first thought, improbable exercise of applying the traditional tests for just war to the subject of civil disobedience, arguing that in large measure the same norms are applicable to the just use of violence in war as apply to authentic or justifiable civil (nonviolent) disobedience. It should be noted that a goodly portion of Mark MacGuigan's paper, included in Part I, is devoted to a discussion of this subject.

Here, as in Part I, an initial restrictive definition is followed by discussions that refuse to be bound by the limitations it implies. Such is the case with Kent Greenawalt's completely act-utilitarian and contextual approach to disobedience. He is unwilling, for instance, to confine justifiable disobedience entirely to cases of nonviolence or to make willingness to be punished a *sine qua non*. Nor need the desire to change the law be the motivating force (cf. the violators of the Fugitive Slave Law). At the same time, Greenawalt's test in terms of probable consequences for the social good lays great emphasis upon considerations likely to militate against the justifiability of disobedience.

If Kent Greenawalt is unwilling to be bound by a constrictive conception of civil disobedience (or perhaps by *any* defintion), Gerald MacCallum, in his second appearance in this volume, elaborates on the great variety of things that "civil disobedients" may be up to. The use of violence (itself a word of many meanings), adherence to any one of various suggested aims, fundamental respect for the law on the part of those who disobey it — these and various other possible tests are shown to be inadequate. Over-simple views may hide issues that need to be explored, among them, for example, the question of precisely when a person who obeys a law is *not* acting on his own judgment and in an integrity-damaging way, as some simplifiers would assume is always the case.

Michael Walzer is concerned specifically with the draft. Borrowing Locke's notion of tacit consent, melding it with the international lawyers' conception of the duties of resident aliens, and seasoning the blend with the notion of "alienation," he develops a theory of limited obligation for political "drop-outs." "Alienated residents (or those of them sufficiently self-aware to make claims on account of their alienation)," he concludes, "should probably be treated as conscientious objectors are at present. . . ."

Alfred Meyer's contribution adds a new dimension. Not only is he dealing with behavior and not with its justification but he is also discussing the subject of civil disobedience in the unusual context of Communist regimes. Not all that he treats would be subsumed under civil disobedience by most people's definition of that term; but some of it would, and the rest might well be thought of as the functional equivalent for civil disobedience under a totalitarian or semi-totalitarian regime.

Finally, Wayne Leys and P. S. S. Rama Rao bring the volume to a suitable conclusion with an examination of Gandhi's ideas and of their possible relevance to Western politics, a large and important subject indeed, when, in so many contexts, both domestic and international, we badly need to transform political confrontation into moral and legal debate.

J. ROLAND PENNOCK

LEGAL, MORAL, AND
POLITICAL OBLIGATION

.

1

LEGAL AND MORAL OBLIGATION

JOHN LADD

The problem of political and legal obligation is a facet of the more general problem of the relationship of the individual to the political and legal order, for the main function of the concepts of political and legal obligation is to provide an answer to the question: "Why ought one to obey the political authorities and the laws of the state?" The purported obligation, ostensibly a moral obligation, is invoked to explain not only why one ought to obey but also the limits of that obedience. If there is such an obligation, then we would have a pretty good answer to the general question of political and legal obedience.

It should be observed, however, that an alleged obligation to political and legal obedience is not the only possible kind of moral basis of obedience. Indeed, as I shall argue, the use of the concept of *obligation* in this connection has many significant moral implications that, when examined carefully, we might not wish to accept. Inasmuch as the whole question of civil obedience and disobedience has become a critical practical issue, it seems well worthwhile to re-examine the traditional and accepted view that from the moral point of view the question is one of obligation and the limits to that obligation.

The question that I want to discuss in this paper is not the usual question concerning the basis and limits of this alleged obligation or even the question concerning when this obligation, as a prima facie obligation, is overridden by other more pressing obligations. Rather I want to consider the prior question, namely, whether or not the concept of obligation itself is the proper one to use in explaining why we should obey the political and legal order.

Obviously we cannot begin to understand and assess the use of the concept of political and legal obligation until we have a clear idea of what we mean by the term *obligation* and until we have some notion of how it differs from other related concepts, e.g., justice, the common good, political duty, expediency, and the like. Part of our initial task is, of course, fixing on a terminology. Basically, however, we require a detailed logical analysis; for once we have decided on a certain usage for the term "obligation," e.g., the sense in which it is used in ordinary, common talk about obligations, our chief concern will be to explore the logical implications, presuppositions, and consequences of having an obligation in that sense. I shall argue that if we agree to use the word in the ordinary and strict sense, then it will become quite clear that the concept of political obligation or of an obligation to obey the law is not only inapposite but morally objectionable as well.

Since the word "obligation" has several different meanings in English, it will be necessary at the very beginning to settle two matters of terminology. Once we have noted the ambiguities in "obligation" and have made the required distinctions, we may, I hope, avoid unnecessary disputes simply over words and be able to proceed at once to more substantive issues.

Obligation: Abstract vs. Concrete Sense

Like many other words in English ending in "ation," "obligation" is used in both an abstract and a concrete sense. In the abstract sense, it stands for the state or condition a person is in when he has an obligation, i.e., the state or condition of *having* or *being under* an obligation. We use "obligation" in an abstract sense when we speak of the feeling of obligation, the sense of obligation, the grounds of obligation, theories of obligation, and so on. Thus, for instance, the "feeling of obligation" means the feeling of being under an obligation. (In German, obligation in the abstract sense is referred to as *Verpflichtung.*) [1]

In the concrete sense, the word stands for concrete obligations, i.e., the products or results of the condition of obligation (abstract sense). In this sense, "obligation" can be pluralized and given articles. A person can have obligations or an obligation, e.g., to his family, to his employer, or to his country. Here "obligation" is used to refer to particular moral requirements in much the same way grammatically as the word "duty" is used to refer to particular duties. (Again, in German, the concrete sense of "obligation" is captured by a different word, *Pflicht,* often translated "duty.")

The ambiguity of "obligation," as between the abstract and the concrete sense, is reflected when we try to describe kinds of obligation, for when "obligation" is used abstractly "kinds of obligation" means "ways of being under an obligation" or "ways of being bound or tied morally." Thus, when a person refers to kinds of obligation in this sense, he is talking about kinds of ties. For convenience we may call them *forms of obligation.* (German: *Art der Verpflichtung.*) Accordingly, legal, social, and moral obligation represent different forms of obligation.

There is a considerable body of philosophical writing on the nature of obligation (abstract sense) and its forms. It is sometimes held that, for instance, legal obligation and social obligation represent entirely different forms of obligation from moral obligation. Legal obligation, for example, might be said to differ

---

[1] The distinction referred to here is one adopted by Kant in his philosophy of law, where he uses the terms *Verpflichtung* and *Pflicht* to mark off the two senses of "obligation." See Kant, *The Metaphysical Elements of Justice,* trans. J. Ladd (New York: Bobbs-Merrill, 1965). The term *Verpflichtungsart* is there translated as a "way of being bound to a duty."

in form from moral obligation in that it involves sanctions. Sometimes it is held that there is only one form of obligation, e.g., moral or legal. I shall not discuss these questions. When "obligation" is taken in the concrete sense, however, kinds of obligation are differentiated in terms of their content rather than their form. In this sense, we speak of family, financial, or military obligations. There are several ways in which kinds of obligation so construed may be specified: by reference to the persons to whom the obligation is owed, e.g., family obligations; by reference to the kind of performance required, e.g., financial obligations; or by reference to the basis of the obligation, e.g., contractual obligations. I shall call these kinds of obligations *varieties of obligation* in order to distinguish them from what I have called *forms of obligation.*[2]

It is clear at once that in speaking of political and legal obligation in the same breath, we are confusing descriptions based on the concrete and the abstract senses of "obligation." For political obligation represents a variety of obligation, namely, an obligation to obey the government; whereas legal obligation represents a form of obligation, i.e., the form of obligation created and enforced by law. Political obligation is contrasted with, say, a family obligation, while legal obligation is contrasted with moral or social obligation.

A great deal of confusion has resulted from the failure to distinguish the forms from the varieties of obligation. Unfortunately the expression "legal obligation" has been used to describe both a form of obligation and a variety of obligation. In this paper, I shall use it only for a form of obligation, to be contrasted, say, with moral obligation.

"Political obligation" will be used for a variety of obligation, namely, the obligation to obey the political authorities and to obey the law of the land. Since our question is one of ethics, the form of obligation with which we shall be concerned is moral obligation. Hence our question becomes: is political obligation one of our moral obligations, i.e., do we have a political moral

---

[2] It is obvious that many different classifications can be developed by combining ways of describing obligations. Thus, under one form, e.g., of legal obligation, we have many varieties of obligation, e.g., financial, military, and family legal obligations.

obligation? (Henceforth, unless designated otherwise, I intend to use "political obligation" to refer to this alleged kind of moral obligation.)

Obligation: Extended vs. Strict Sense[3]

A second matter of terminology that has to be settled before we begin is to determine whether we shall use "obligation" in an extended sense or in a narrow, strict sense. Moral philosophers are prone to use "obligation" in an extended sense so as to cover almost the whole, if not the whole, of morality. Thus, "moral obligation" is accepted as a synonym for "duty," "right," "wrong not to do," or, in general, "what ought to be done." Obligation is taken to be equivalent to moral oughtness, and ethics is described as the inquiry into the principles of moral obligation.[4]

Philosophically the net effect of adopting the extended usage of "obligation" is to submerge the traditional problem of political obligation in the more general problem of the moral basis of the individual's submission to political authority and to law. The distinctive claims of a theory of political obligation are lost and the theory easily becomes confused with, for instance, utilitarian theories. (Hume's theory of political obligation is a case in point.) In this regard one suspects that proponents of the extended usage are making a philosophical point in the guise of a terminological decision.

There is, of course, a much more restricted use of "obligation" which covers not the whole of morality but only one relatively specific kind of moral requirement. A narrower usage seems more in accord with the way the term is actually used in ethical and political discourse; for when we say that someone has

---

[3] The distinction discussed in this section has been examined in some detail by R. B. Brandt, "The Concepts of Obligation and Duty," *MIND*, vol. lxxiii, no. 291 (July 1964). The position that I defend here resembles in some important respects the views presented by H. L. A. Hart, "Legal and Moral Obligation," in A. I. Melden, *Essays in Moral Philosophy* (Seattle: University of Washington Press, 1958). As will soon become evident, however, I differ with Hart on many key issues.

[4] I must personally plead guilty to having used "obligation" in this philosophers' sense in my book, *The Structure of a Moral Code* (Cambridge, Mass.: Harvard University Press, 1957), 441 n.1.

an obligation to do X we intend something much more specific and perhaps stronger than when we say that someone ought to do X. (It makes perfectly good sense to say that Jones ought to do X but has no obligation to do so.) Thus obligation in the ordinary sense carries with it certain implications and nuances that specifically differentiate it from other kinds of moral requirements. What these specific features are will be the subject of the main part of this paper. My thesis will be that to ascribe to a person an obligation to do an act is to single out him and his act for special moral consideration, to stress something very special and peculiar about the person and his act, and to call attention to the special stringency of the moral requirement so described. The special character of obligations becomes clear in the case of obligations created by promises, and so we shall take such obligations as paradigmatic of obligations in general, although it will be assumed that there are other kinds of obligation to be considered as well.

In this chapter, I intend to restrict my discussion of political obligation to the narrow and strict sense of "obligation." It should be emphasized that this decision does not rest on any essentialistic presuppositions; rather it is made for purely pragmatic reasons, namely, to help focus our attention on a certain characteristic and traditional kind of answer to the question of political obedience. In order to join the issue with most historical and contemporary theories of political obligation, I therefore propose as a matter of strategy that we adopt the narrow and strict sense of "obligation."

My procedure will be to spell out in some detail what is generally understood and implied by the term "obligation," when used narrowly and strictly, and then to ask with regard to obligation, so construed, whether or not there is such a thing as political obligation. If our answer should turn out to be no, then I submit that the burden of showing what he means by "obligation" will be shifted to anyone who claims that there is such an obligation.

There are, of course, many dangers in following this procedure and, as Aristotle warned us long ago, we should not expect more exactness than the nature of the subject permits. My intent is admittedly speculative and, hopefully, provocative.

The rest of this chapter falls into three parts. In Part I, I shall set forth six formal features of obligations in general that seem to me characteristic of ordinary kinds of obligation, e.g., those resulting from promises. In Part II, I shall illustrate this analysis by showing how these features apply in playing a game. And, finally, in Part III, I shall discuss whether or not the concept of obligation so delineated, and in particular as it is applied to playing a game, is relevant to the issues of obedience to the political and legal order.

In order to forestall any possible misunderstanding of my argument, I want to emphasize once more that I am not concerned with the problem of when and under what conditions political obligations are overridden. Rather, I am interested in the question to whether or not there is such a thing as political obligation, to begin with. Only if it is assumed there is such an obligation, i.e., a prima facie obligation,[5] does the question arise concerning when it must give away to other demands of morality. My object here is to scrutinize this assumption.

I. SIX CHARACTERISTICS FEATURES OF OBLIGATIONS

Wittgenstein and others have taught us not to search for exact definitions of fuzzy and multifunctional concepts. It is clear that the concept of obligation is a kind of family-resemblance or open-textured concept. Hence the six features that I shall present should not be taken to provide the necessary and sufficient conditions of something's being an obligation. They are merely characteristic or typical in a loose sense; they serve as marks or criteria that can help us to decide when it is proper to say that someone has an obligation to do something.

1. The first thing to note about obligations in the strict sense is that they can be created and terminated. They come into being through being assumed or incurred, and they go out of being through being discharged or dissolved. An obligation typically makes an act (or attitude) that was previously morally indifferent or optional into something that one is required to do or not to do. The implication of saying that a person is under an

---

[5] The subject of prima facie duties and obligations and the question of how they are overridden will be discussed in a forthcoming paper entitled "Moral Dilemmas."

obligation to do or not to do something is that his doing of it is per se neither right nor wrong, but has become right or wrong for him to do solely on account of the obligation that has arisen with respect to it.[6] This morally creative side of obligations can be easily seen in the case of promises. If I promise to do *A*, e.g., go for a walk, then that act, walking, is no longer something that I may choose to do or not, but has become something that I am required to do, i.e., an action that would be wrong for me not to do.[7] Or if I promise not to tell Jones something, then my act of telling Jones, which was previously morally indifferent or optional, now becomes something wrong for me to do. Insofar as legislative and judicial acts create obligations, the same point obtains, for they make acts that are per se indifferent or optional into acts that are right or wrong.

In sum, in connection with obligations, acts become right or wrong for a person to do by virtue of his having an obligation, rather than becoming obligations for him by virtue of their being right or wrong. It follows that one cannot have a general obligation to do acts that are right in themselves, e.g., to save a life; or to refrain from doing acts that are wrong in themselves, e.g., to refrain from murder or from lying; for these acts are already right or wrong, as the case may be.

Obligations are, in a sense, superadded to the ordinary requirements of morality. This is because they characteristically impose new and special requirements on particular persons in particular circumstances. They make what was previously indifferent or optional for a particular person into something he *must* do. In this sense, they add a new kind of moral reason for doing or refraining from doing something.

---

[6] Here I am using "right" in a strong sense to mean something like "wrong not to do." It should be noted that there are other moral terms, besides "right" and "wrong," that are weaker, for example, "good to do," "desirable," or "meritorious." The latter are used for what are sometimes called "acts of supererogation," i.e., acts that are good to do but not wrong not to do. Such acts are good but also optional. I do not mean to exclude such acts from becoming the subject matter of an obligation. On acts of supererogation, see my *Structure of a Moral Code*, pp. 125-30. Also, Joel Feinberg, "Supererogation and Rules," *Ethics*, vol. 71 (1961) and R. M. Chisholm, "Supererogation and Offence," *Ratio*, vol. 5 (1963).

[7] *Ceteris paribus*, for there might be some other, unmentioned moral reason for not doing it which overrides the obligation in this case.

2. Every obligation must have come into being through some fact, occurrence or circumstance, specifically related to the agent-obligor.[8] In other words, obligations are attached to particular people on account of particular facts, which are, as it were, unique to them. I shall call this fact the *basis of the obligation.* Promising provides a good example of this aspect of obligation, for the act of promising, the factual occurrence, provides the basis of the obligation that it creates. The basis explains how the obligor came to have the obligation.

It is often held that the basis of an obligation must be a voluntary act of the obligor, e.g., a promise, a commitment, or an acceptance of a benefit. That is, it is assumed that obligations are always incurred voluntarily and freely.[9] The appeal of this voluntaristic conception of obligation is that it permits us to invoke the principle *volenti non fit injuria* to justify the keeping of obligations that are ostensibly or immediately contrary to our self-interest.

It seems unnecessarily restrictive, however, to limit the basis of obligations in this way. There seems no reason to exclude obligations that are based upon a person's involuntary acts; for instance, the obligation that a person may have to repair the damage he has caused completely involuntarily to another's person or property. We might, indeed, wish also to allow for obligations arising from the acts of others, e.g., servants or children. And, of course, we want to allow for the possibility that legislative and judicial acts can create obligations quite independently of any voluntary acts of our own.

For our purposes, then, all we need assume is that the basis of an obligation be some special fact about the person (the obligor) that places him under an obligation.

It should be observed that the basis of a particular obligation explains not only why there is an obligation in the first place but also why the obligation attaches to one particular person rather than another. This is clear in the case of promising, for Jones has the obligation, rather than Smith, because he, Jones, was the one

---

[8] Henceforth I shall use the term *obligor* for the person-agent who has the obligation and the term *obligee* for the person-subject to whom it is owed.

[9] Thus Rawls writes: "obligations are normally the consequence of voluntary acts of persons," in "Legal Obligation and the Duty of Fair Play," *Law and Philosophy*, ed. S. Hook (New York: New York University Press, 1964), p. 4.

who made the promise. The basis thus functions as a kind of
principle of individuation by putting the person's name, as it
were, on the obligation.

Since every obligation must have a basis, we are always justified in asking for the basis of an alleged obligation. We can ask:
what special fact is there about the agent-obligor that places him
under an obligation? If no basis can be given, we may conclude
that the person in question has no such obligation.

We see now why there can be no general obligation binding on
everyone to save lives or to refrain from murdering. There could
be no basis for such an obligation, i.e., special facts about
particular agents that require them to do these things. In contradistinction to obligations, the rightness of saving lives and the
wrongness of committing murder arise from facts about the
persons affected, e.g., their needs, rather than from facts about
the particular persons who might perform these acts.

3. Obligations are interpersonal, that is, they involve not only
a particular person who owes the obligation but also a particular
person to whom the obligation is owed. Obligations, in other
words, involve both an obligor and an obligee. (We may have to
admit that collective persons, composed in some way or other of
individual persons, can be obligors or obligees; for example, a
family may owe an obligation or have an obligation owed to it.)

The existence of an obligee is as essential to an obligation as
the existence of an obligor; for the obligee, as it were, holds the
other end of the rope and can determine whether or not the
performance owed must take place. To begin with, the obligee
can release the obligor from his obligation. Moreover, he can
refuse the performance owed. The right of refusal is evident
when we consider the absurdity of an utterance such as: "I am
under an obligation to do this for you, whether you want me to
do it or not!" (Such an utterance would make sense only if the
obligee were different from the beneficiary, e.g., in a situation in
which one has promised parents he would look after their
children.) The voluntary acquiescence of the obligee seems
necessary to the bindingness of an obligation, for an obligation
cannot be performed against his will.

The obligee also has, under certain conditions, the power to
require the performance owed and to invoke sanctions or repara-
tions for failure to perform. If the obligee insists, then the
obligor must perform or else suffer the consequences.

Other things being equal, then, the will of the obligee is not only necessary but also sufficient for binding the obligor to the performance owed. The obligee is thus in many respects more important than the obligor as far as the obligation itself is concerned.

Here again, the crucial logical function of the basis can be observed. For the basis determines not only who has the obligation but to whom it is owed. Both obligor and obligee are particular persons related to each other through a particular fact that creates the obligation. It follows that we cannot know about a person's obligations or about persons to whom obligations are owed, unless we know something about them personally, i.e., some part of their personal history. This feature is quite evident in the case of obligations arising from promises, because we can know nothing about such obligations without knowing an historical fact about the obligor and the obligee, namely, that the one made a promise to the other.

In this respect, obligations represent a very personal sort of moral requirement, i.e., obligations are always individualized. That is, they attach to persons by virtue of the historical situations they find themselves in, rather than by virtue of, say, a role or office, or even by virtue of simply being a human being. This might be one way of distinguishing obligations from duties, which are often attached to roles or offices. It should be noted, however, that an individual, Mr. Smith, may, through a commitment of some kind, place himself under an obligation to his clients or constituents to fulfill the duties of a certain office.

The fact that obligations are personalized in this sense may explain, in part, why obligations are among the most stringent moral requirements. Since they come with "names on them," they cannot be so easily avoided. They are not like other kinds of moral requirements, which are relatively anonymous.

At this point, it is worthwhile pointing out that there is what might be called a hyperbolic sense of obligation, that is, the concept of obligation is sometimes used in an extended, hyperbolic sense in order to accentuate the extreme stringency of a moral requirement. Thus we find statements like: "We all have a moral obligation to work for peace," or "Everyone has a moral obligation to vote." Such statements receive their forcefulness precisely from the fact that obligations are individualized, for they imply that the obligations referred to attach to every individual as an individual. He, as an individual, no longer has any option. Nevertheless, the use of "obligation" in such contexts is, I submit, hyperbolic, for it is parasitic on the more usual use already noted, which individualizes obligations in a more specific way.

4. Another typical feature of obligations in the strict sense is that they authorized the use of sanctions in the case of nonfulfillment. (By "sanctions" I mean to include not only punishment but also various forms of social condemnation and the so-called "internal sanctions" of conscience.) I have just mentioned the fact that the obligee can require the obligor to perform what is owed. Another way of stating this is to say that obligations confer certain rights on the obligee, not only the right to the performance but also the right to enforce and the right to remedy in case of nonfulfillment. Thus, obligations and rights represent two sides of the same coin.[10]

I want to stress that obligations justify many different kinds of measures that would otherwise be morally objectionable, e.g. (in some cases) the use of force. The reason for this is that where there is an obligation, the nonperformance of the required act is morally wrong and blameworthy. There is no merit in performing one's obligations, only demerit in not performing them. That is why writers like Kant say of obligations that they are "perfect duties."[11]

Because of the intimate logical connection between obligations and sanctions, many philosophers, e.g., Hobbes, Bentham, and Austin, have tried to define "obligation" in terms of sanctions rather than the other way around. Their attempt may partly be explained by the fact that they took "obligation" to mean "being obliged." This identification is, of course, gratuitous, not to say misleading; for one can be obliged to do many things where no

---

[10] It is no mere coincidence, I submit, that in Roman Law the term *obligatio* refers to "a legal relation between two ascertained persons, in virtue of which the one is entitled to claim an act or forbearance from the other. The one, or creditor, has a right in personam, the other, or debtor, owes to him a relative duty, etc." Quoted from *Imperatoris Iustiniani Institutionum*, edited with commentary by J. B. Moyle (Oxford: The Clarendon Press, 1955), pp. 345–46 *et passim*.

[11] Kant's distinction between perfect and imperfect duties is set forth in his *Metaphysics of Morals:* Part I, *The Metaphysical Elements of Justice* (see note 1) and Part II, *The Metaphysical Principles of Virtue*, trans. J. Ellington (New York: Bobbs-Merrill, 1964). It is also discussed in Paul D. Eisenberg, "Basic Categories in Kant's *Tugendlehre*," *American Philosophical Quarterly*, vol. 3, no. 4 (October 1966).

obligation is involved and vice versa. (One may be obliged to jump off a burning ship, but that does not mean that one is under an obligation to jump.) [12] The positivist reduction of obligation to sanctions can be seen to be mistaken as soon as it is noted that obligations are logically prior to sanctions, for obligations are used to justify the application of sanctions rather than vice versa.

5. Another interesting feature of obligations is that to be morally binding they must conform to the limits set by other general moral principles (and perhaps even positive laws). By this I mean that the moral validity of an obligation is automatically nullified if what it requires conflicts with these principles. Obligations supplement the ordinary requirements of morality but cannot contradict them.

Ordinary practices (including legal practices) relating to promises and contracts illustrate this aspect of obligations, for promises and contracts are considered binding only if they do not require acts that are immoral. One cannot through a promise or contract acquire an obligation to commit murder or even to lie. Such promises and contracts would ipso facto be rendered null and void. This does not simply mean that, e.g., a promise to do something (known to be) wrong is overridden by other moral demands. The question of such an "obligation" being overridden does not arise, since it is not morally binding to begin with. Thus "obligations" to do something immoral are not prima facie obligations; rather they are not moral obligations at all, although they may, of course, be obligations of another kind. One way of seeing the difference between a morally binding obligation and one that is not is to note that in the case of nonfulfillment of an immoral "obligation" the obligee has no moral recourse, i.e., no moral right to enforce or to be compensated, and sanctions are not properly applied for nonfulfillment.

I should hasten to add that what I have said applies only to moral obligations, i.e., morally binding obligations, and not to other forms of obligations. As Plato pointed out, there is honor among thieves. Murderers and thieves often scrupulously honor

---

[12] As any quick reference to a dictionary will attest, "to be obliged" means to be compelled or forced, including by natural forces. There is, of course, a usage, "to oblige," which means to do a favor or a service of, e.g., "I am obliged to you for helping me." This point is brought out clearly in K. Baier, "Moral Obligation," *American Philosophical Quarterly*, vol. 3, no. 3 (July 1966), 220 n.

their obligations in defiance of the precepts of morality. We all know how strong these obligations can be, especially when they involve keeping promises; witness the Salome story. But such obligations, however powerful, cease to be moral obligations and become institutional obligations of another sort. That is, they no longer can provide moral reasons for doing what is demanded by the obligation. To say that I murdered because I promised is not even an extenuating circumstance! At this point we face the whole issue of whether or not obligations are part of morality, e.g., whether obligations are moral or, say, only institutional.[13] If it is admitted that there can be immoral obligations, in the same sense of obligation in which one can have a moral obligation, then it would appear that obligation is a nonmoral concept. In that case, it would be of no interest in connection with the moral problem of political obedience. On the other hand, if we want to allow for moral obligations as at least a subspecies of obligation, we would have to adduce moral principles of some kind over and above the principle of honoring one's obligations to substantiate the claim that a particular obligation is a moral obligation. If we choose the latter course, then we will have to accept proposition 5 as a necessary feature of moral obligations.

6. Finally, within the moral limits just pointed out in 5, obligations have what I shall call the qualities of being *opaque* and *totalistic*. In calling them *opaque* I mean that obligations bind us to actions quite independently of the intrinsic nature or other interesting properties of those actions themselves. That is, if a person is under an obligation to do something, then, other things being equal, he should (or must) do it whether or not what is required is in itself a good, desirable, or worthwhile thing for him to do, i.e., apart from the obligation. In other words, an obligor may not inquire into the merits or demerits of the action in question when determining whether or not it should be done; having an obligation is of itself a sufficient reason for performing the action.

Opaqueness is obvious in the case of obligations arising from

---

[13] I do not intend to imply, however, that obligations cannot be both. The relationship between morality and institutions (conventions, customs) is, in my opinion, a subtle and complicated one. See my article "Custom," the *Encyclopedia of Philosophy*, ed. Paul Edwards (New York: The Free Press, 1967), Vol. 2, pp. 278-80.

promises: if I promise you that I will do something, then I am
required to do what is promised and whether or not I want to do
it is no longer relevant. Having promised, I can no longer have
regard to whether doing what I have promised is unpleasant,
tedious, difficult, onerous, disadvantageous for me, or even
whether or not there are other things that I could do instead that
would be better for you or for others.

In calling an obligation *totalistic* I mean that when one
undertakes or is placed under an obligation to do something, one
is *eo ipso* required to do the whole of it. In a sense, obligations
come as wholes. If one has promised to do *A*, which comprises a
set of parts, say, subactions *a,b,c,d,e,* one is bound to do all five of
these subactions, i.e., the totality of the parts, and is not permitted to choose which ones he will do. If I am engaged as a
gardener, I cannot choose to weed the flowers and neglect the
vegetables and cleaning up. I cannot pick and choose which
parts of an obligation to perform any more than I can pick and
choose which parts of a promise to keep. The obligation has to
be taken as applying to the whole.

Both the opaqueness and the totalism of obligations follow
from the fact already frequently alluded to, that an obligation
creates a new kind of reason for acting that is logically independent of the nature of the acts themselves. An obligation typically
provides per se not only a sufficient reason for doing something
but also a reason that automatically excludes other considerations not related to the obligation from determining whether
the action, or any part of it, should be done. (One must, of course,
specify "under normal conditions," in order to allow for those
unusual cases in which an obligation is overridden or invali-
dated.) The opaqueness and totalism of obligations thus explain,
in part at least, why obligations have such a high degree of
stringency, one of the striking characteristics of obligations already mentioned.

II. APPLICATION TO THE PLAYING OF A GAME
The six characteristic features of obligation that I have
just set forth are readily apparent in the kind of mutual obligation that exists between people engaged in playing a game, e.g.,
softball or chess, for when a group of individuals plays a game
together, they mutually bind themselves to obey the rules of the
game.

There are several reasons for choosing game-playing to illustrate the points that have been made about obligation. First, the obligations found in connection with game-playing differ in some interesting ways from obligations arising from promises and contracts. Thus I hope to achieve greater generality for the analysis presented here by using a somewhat different type of example from the ones already used.

Second, and more important, the game-playing model has already received considerable attention in political philosophy as an alternative to the older contractual model; for it has many advantages over the latter as a way of analyzing the traditional problems of political obligation. To begin with, the game model makes it possible to avoid having to postulate an *actus contractarius*, which has always been a source of embarrassment to contractarians. Furthermore, it enables us to conceive of the political and legal order as a body of rules, practices, and roles, rather than as a simple personal relationship between a sovereign and his subjects analyzed in terms of commands and obedience. Recent studies of the logic of rules and of the different types of rules provide a much more useful model of analysis than the traditional command model.[14]

Nevertheless, I shall try to show that the game model cannot, in the final analysis, give us a completely satisfactory account of political obligation. Before we can judge the merits or shortcomings of this particular model, we must first see how the six features described earlier appear in the obligation to obey the rules when playing a game. Let us examine each of these features in turn.

1′. Upon entering into a game certain actions that are per se indifferent or optional become for the player actions that are

14 The literature on rules and games is by now quite extensive. For general discussions involving this type of analysis, see Max Black, *Models and Metaphors* (Ithaca: Cornell University Press, 1962), ch. 6 ; Newton Garver, "Rules," in *Encyclopedia of Philosophy*, vol. 7, pp. 231–33. The game analogy was used with great skill by Rawls in his well-known essay, "Two Concepts of Rules," *Philosophical Review*, vol. lxiv (1955) and by John Searle in his "How to Derive 'Ought' from 'Is,' " *Philosophical Review*, vol. lxxiii, no. 2 (January 1964) and "What Is a Speech Act?" in *Philosophy in America*, ed. Max Black (Ithaca: Cornell University Press, 1965). The approach has also been adapted for political philosophy by Hannah Pitkin in her "Obligation and Consent," *American Political Science Review*, vol. 59, no. 4 (December 1965) and vol. 60, no. 1 (March 1966).

right or wrong, required or forbidden. For instance, although previously Jones was free to throw the ball to anyone or to arrange the men on the board in any way he chose, once he started to play the game these actions became circumscribed for him: certain actions must be done and others must not be done. The rules of the game now determine what acts are right or wrong for him to do, and the obligation to adhere to the rules now makes what the rules prescribe mandatory for him.

2′. The basis of a person's subjection to the rules is the simple fact of joining the game and continuing to play it. A kind of consent is implied by the mere fact of participation.[15] This fact of participation is what differentiates the agent-obligor from others who are not bound to obey the rules because they are not playing. In this case, as in the earlier ones, we see how the basis determines who does and who does not have the obligation.

3′. Who has the obligation and to whom is it owed? Obviously, both obligor and obligee must be participants in the game. No one outside the game is bound by the rules and no one outside the game has the right to demand that another obey the rules.[16]

It is interesting to observe the role of players as obligees, for it is in this capacity, rather than as obligors, that players are able to abrogate or change the rules or institute new ones. Thus, when playing softball in the backyard, certain special rules have to be agreed upon (e.g., because of the greenhouse next door, every hit in that direction must be counted an out). Since every player is an obligee as well as an obligor, the assent of all the players is considered both a necessary and a sufficient condition for changing the rules, i.e., the content of the obligation (unless the game itself contains some special rule for changing rules).

4′. The obligation to play according to the rules also justifies the application of sanctions in the case of noncompliance with them, i.e., cheating. For game-playing, the usual sanctions are social sanctions, e.g., a reprimand ("That's unfair" or "That's

---

[15] Rawls writes: "the obligation to obey the law . . . (is) an obligation in the more limited sense that it depends upon our having accepted and our intention to continue accepting the benefits of a just scheme of cooperation. . . ." "Legal Obligation and the Duty of Fair Play," in Hook, *Law and Philosophy*, p. 10.

[16] It is obvious that the basis, i.e., participation, determines who is the obligee as well as who is the obligor. The obligation describes a relation only between players.

cheating") or, in the extreme case, being thrown out of the game altogether. The punishment involved here is directly related to failure to comply with the rules, i.e., it is for violation of the obligation to heed the rules. As such, it should not be confused with the various penalties provided within the framework of the rules of the game themselves for particular acts, such as for being offside in football or not jumping in checkers. Logically speaking, rules setting forth such penalties can be construed as presenting options, e.g., if you don't do X, then Y will happen, and, as such, they are a regular part of the game comparable to, for instance, a sacrifice hit.[17]

Penalties, in contrast to sanctions, are part of the game itself; and, in a sense, a person is not indeed hurt by the penalties except in the context of playing the game. Thus, penalties obtain within the system, whereas sanctions obtain with regard to the system (and in this sense are outside the system).

5'. The moral limitations on the obligation to submit to the rules of the game one is playing are obvious. If some act is required by the obligation that is patently immoral, e.g., killing or maiming someone, the obligation is simply dissolved. There is, for instance, no longer any obligation to continue if a player is injured or if someone else's rights are violated. It should be noted that in such cases the obligation is nullified, i.e., extinguished, and not merely overridden.

It is interesting to note that often within games and as long as one is playing them there is a sense in which certain general moral principles are suspended. For example, the Christian precept to turn the other cheek is an inappropriate one to follow if you happen to be boxing, or the precept to help the poor is not a necessary guide for action if you are playing Monopoly. Indeed, lying, cheating, and physical assault are often accepted parts of a game. And generosity, kindness, solicitude, and even courage are often not virtues in games, whereas rational egoism, on the other hand, which is normally frowned upon by moralists, is taken for granted by most interesting competitive games.

---

[17] It is interesting to observe that lawyers often talk as if the penalties set forth in the law are to be construed as options: you have a choice between doing X or paying a penalty Y, e.g., "Walk or pay $2.00" or "File your tax return on time or pay 6 percent interest." The game model has its abuses as well as its proper uses!

The obvious point is that although there are many otherwise morally objectionable actions that are permissible within a game, this permissibility, like the prescriptions and prohibitions of the game, holds only within the bounds of the game. It is a severely limited permissibility, for we usually explain the actions in question as "being done in play" or as "not being serious." The main point of this section still holds, therefore, namely, that the obligation to obey the rules of the game is limited by what is antecedently right or wrong.

6'. The opaqueness and totalism of the obligation to obey the rules while playing a game are obvious. The obligation is opaque because the intrinsic properties of the acts required or proscribed, e.g., even whether they are acts of kindness or of courage, are completely irrelevant to the question of whether or not they should be done *while playing the game.* Indeed, as has often been observed, many acts are quite meaningless apart from the rules of the game, e.g., moving a piece of wood a couple of inches.[18] Acts that are per se insignificant or even meaningless become right or wrong as the result of the obligation to obey the rules.

The obligation is also totalistic, that is, it applies to all the rules; for a player is bound to obey all the rules all the time he is playing. He cannot pick and choose which rules he wants to obey or even which rules he thinks ought to be obeyed. As soon as an individual, for whatever reason, becomes selective about which rules he will obey, he has simply stopped playing the game.[19]

General Comments on the Game-Playing Model

It is hardly necessary to point out the advantage of the game model over the contractual model as a tool for analyzing political obligation. It provides us with a model of consent through participation rather than through contract. It also provides us with a much more satisfactory answer to the question: to whom is the political obligation owed? In determining that the obligees be the other players, i.e., the other participants in the political process, the game philosopher has found a way of

---

[18] Such rules are called "constitutive rules" by Searle. See footnote 22.

[19] "The notion of somebody breaking the rules constantly but yet playing chess does not make sense," Black, *Models and Metaphors,* p. 123.

relating political obligation to the individual's role as a citizen-subject rather than leaving it hanging as an external, accidental feature, say, of his birth.

Above all, the use of the game model suggests important analogies between rules in games and rules in politics and law. One of the most important of these, at least for democratic theory, is the property of *reversibility*, namely, that every rule applies to a person regardless of whether he is at the giving or receiving end. For when playing a game, a player is committed to abiding by a rule if and when the players' roles are reversed, e.g., the same rule holds when he plays defense as when he plays offense. When it is the other player's turn, then I must grant him the same advantage (benefits, rights) as I have when it is my turn, and when it is my turn, I must do what he has to do when it is his turn.[20]

The reversibility of the rules of a game, or at least of typical competitive games, provides a seductive model for the moral-political concepts of fairness and justice, equality and impartiality. Justice is thought to require that laws be made and applied impartially and equally to everyone alike. This means that they must be accepted and obeyed by each one of us without regard to whether he is, or will be, at the giving or receiving end. To agree

[20] The term "reversibility" is used by K. Baier in *The Moral Point of View* (New York: Random House, 1965), pp. 108, 135. Baier believes that reversibility is essential to rules regarded from the moral point of view. Substantially the same property of rules is stressed by Rawls when he proposes a "procedure . . . to let each person propose the principles upon which he wishes his complaints to be tried with the understanding that, if acknowledged, the complaints of others will be similarly tried . . . (and) no one (will) be given the opportunity to tailor the canons of a legitimate complaint to fit his own conditions and then to discard them when they no longer fit his purpose," in "Justice as Fairness," reprinted in *Philosophy, Politics and Society*, second series, eds. P. Laslett and W. G. Runciman (Oxford: Blackwell, 1962), p. 138. In another article, Rawls secures this reversibility by stipulating that "the initial situation (in which people decide about their conception of justice) one of the significant features of which is that no one knows his position in society, etc. . . . A veil of ignorance prevents anyone from being advantaged or disadvantaged. . ." from "Distributive Justice," in *Philosophy, Politics and Society*, third series, eds. P. Laslett and W. G. Runciman (Oxford: Blackwell, 1967), p. 60. These features, regarded by Baier as descriptive of the moral point of view and by Rawls as part of the procedure for establishing the rules of justice, are, I submit, taken in the first instance from the model of playing games. In their application to morality and politics, they are open to the same criticisms as the game-playing model in general.

to rules of this sort means to be ready and willing to abide by
them even if the roles are reversed or, to put it in another way,
on the supposition that one does not know whether he, personally, will be at the giving or receiving end.

In the case of games it seems eminently reasonable for an
individual to assent to reversible rules of this kind, because it is
quite possible that sometime in the course of the game he (or his
partners) will be in a position to play the role of the giver as
well as that of the receiver: he will have his turn, his innings,
and so on. Therefore it is to his long-term advantage, as a player,
to accept certain rules even though he knows that they will
sometimes work to his disadvantage. As far as games are concerned, we can agree with Rawls that "the system of cooperation
consistently followed by everyone else itself produces the advantages generally received."[21]

It should be quite clear that the game analogy provides a nice,
plausible rationale for many of the practices and ideals of a
democracy like ours. For example, it applies to the relations
between the majority and the minority: the majority respects the
rights of the minority because the individuals who are in the
majority today may be in the minority tomorrow; and the minority accepts and obeys the decrees of the majority because some
day those who are in the minority will be in the majority and
will want the others to obey them in turn. The possibility,
indeed probability, of the roles being reversed sometimes makes it
easy to accept reversible rules. Similarly, in judicial proceedings,
the adversary system is based on a system of reversible rules that
assure to each party that it will have its turn in court, so that he
who is the accuser today will play under the same rules when he
is the defendant tomorrow. Accordingly, in many of our institutions, we regard it as fair to accept and obey rules granting rights
to others because we may sometime be in their position and want
them to respect our rights in turn. The question, of course, is
whether this is a dream or a reality.

The fact that reversible rules like those found in competitive
games are also to be found in political and legal institutions, or if
not found there, ought to be there as a requirement of justice (or
fairness), still does not prove that the game model provides a

---

[21] Rawls, "Legal Obligation and the Duty of Fair Play," *op. cit.*, p. 16.

satisfactory answer to the question: why should we obey the law? For, as we shall see, joint acknowledgment of reversible rules is neither a necessary nor a sufficient condition justifying obedience to the political and legal order as a whole.

In addition to reversibility, there are, of course, other properties of rules in a game that are useful in the analysis of political and legal concepts. For example, we find in games what have been called "constitutive rules," that is, rules that define moves, roles, penalties, goals, and even the game itself. Such rules function not so much to tell us what or what not to do as what is to "count as," for instance, a move, a strike, a checkmate.[22] Obviously many laws, or parts of laws, are constitutive in this sense. Perhaps, indeed, the whole political setup or the judicial system can only be defined by reference to the rules under which they operate. Furthermore, the game model may be useful in explaining the function of roles like that of umpire and leader, which find their counterparts in the political and legal order. Finally, of course, the concept of strategies, taken from formal game theory, has many applications within the sphere of politics and law. Thus, even if we reject the game model as a model for understanding political obligation, we may find it useful for other, more limited purposes.

III. APPLICATION TO THE
POLITICAL AND LEGAL ORDER

Let us now turn to the question of whether or not there is such a thing as political obligation, that is, a special moral obligation to obey the political authorities and the law, say, under a democratic form of government and constitution. (It would, of course, have to be a prima facie obligation.) I have proposed as one way of answering the question that we examine the individual's relation to the political and legal order and see

22 See Rawls' definition of "practice" as "any form of activity specified by a system of rules which defines offices, roles, moves, penalties, defences, and so on, and which gives the activity its structure," from "Justice as Fairness," *op. cit.*, p. 132n. The expression "constitutive rule" is used by Searle in the two articles mentioned above in note 14. Searle distinguishes between "regulative rules," which he says can be paraphrased as imperatives, and "constitutive rules," which define moves, and so on, and determine what is to "count as," e.g., a touchdown or checkmate.

whether any or all of the six features that seem to characterize obligations in the ordinary sense are found to be present in that relation. In order to maintain plausibly that the individual does have a political obligation of the sort mentioned, it is not necessary that all six of these features be present. However, if none of these features seems to characterize an individual's political and legal relationships we should hardly be justified in asserting that an obligation exists. It would have to be a very curious kind of obligation indeed, and the burden would be on the proponent of such an obligation to explain what he has in mind in asserting there is such an obligation and to give us some reason for supposing that it exists.

Our next task, then, is to examine each of our six features with a view to finding out whether or not they are to be found in the individual's relation to the political and legal order.

1″. There is no doubt that the political and legal authorities can, through various decrees and legislative acts, make acts that are per se morally neutral or optional into acts that are right or wrong. As in the case of games, therefore, the political and legal order can, through its own rules, create new moral demands and restrictions on our behavior. The acts that are thus made wrong are known as *mala prohibita*.

Mala prohibita and, in general, rights and wrongs created by law constitute only a part of the political and legal order; for a large part of that order is concerned with actions that are already, antecedently, part of morality, e.g., *mala in se*. Without entering into the question of the difference between law and morality, it seems obvious that a considerable part of the law is concerned directly or indirectly with enforcing the standards of morality, taken in the broad sense to include the demands of public interest and justice. Therefore, unlike typical obligations, the requirements proceeding from the political and the legal order follow from the antecedent requirements of morality.[23]

The question therefore naturally arises: does the alleged political obligation apply only to *mala prohibita*, or to *mala in se* as well? The assumption of the state of nature vs. civil society dichotomy made by many traditional contract theories gives aid

---

[23] I have explained this at greater length in my "Law and Morality: Internalism *vs.* Externalism," in *Law and Philosophy*, ed. S. Hook (New York: New York University Press, 1964).

and comfort to the view that civil (or positive) law creates a new obligation supplemental to the requirements of the natural law. But this position presupposes that a clear-cut and meaningful distinction can be made between *mala prohibita* and *mala in se*. More generally, if, as I have argued, obligations do not apply to actions that are antecedently right or wrong, then, in order to save the notion of political obligation, we would have to assume that positive law and its requirements are in themselves morally neutral (or optional). This seems, on the face of it, a gratuitous assumption and one that it is as difficult to defend as the distinction between *mala prohibita* and *mala in se*.

In any case, the first feature on our list raises some questions about the proper applicability of the concept of obligation with respect to the law.

2″. The question of the basis of political obligation has always been a source of embarrassment to political theorists who believe in political obligation. The older contract theory has given way to the idea of consent through participation. Accordingly, Rawls writes that political obligation "depends upon our having accepted and our intention to continue accepting the benefits of a just scheme of cooperation that the constitution defines. In this sense it depends on our voluntary acts."[24] To someone who is not especially enamored of the contractarian approach, it does not seem that benefits received constitute either a necessary or a sufficient condition for the duty to obey the law.

Apart from the difficult question of determining what kind of facts could serve as the basis of the alleged obligation to obey the law, it will suffice here to point out that the assertion of any sort of basis whatsoever of the alleged obligation is a logical impossibility. It is logically impossible to have such a basis, simply because the logical function of any basis is to tie down an obligation to one particular individual or set of individuals rather than another, whereas the purported intent of the notion of political obligation is to impose a requirement on everyone in the state. Obligations are individual, whereas political obligation, if there were such a thing, would have to be universal.

Another way of putting the same point is to say that the moral requirement that we obey the political order and the state is

---

[24] Rawls, "Legal Obligation and the Duty of Fair Play," *op. cit.*, p. 10.

contingent not upon benefits received, acts of consent, or other hypothetical facts, but on the nature and intent of the laws and the acts and procedures of the political order itself. Unless benefits and consent are construed so loosely and generally as to make the fact of their occurrence not really an empirical issue at all, it is clear that these "facts" apply only to a restricted segment of the population. Accordingly, it would follow that only a restricted segment of the population has the moral obligation to obey the political authorities and the law. Only the élite is under such an obligation![25]

The obligation theorist is thus presented with a dilemma. If he claims that there is such a thing as political obligation, then he must admit that there is some basis in fact that creates the obligation which is thereby binding only on some, but not all, members of the society. If, on the other hand, he wants to preserve the notion that there is a universal moral requirement binding on everyone in the society to obey the law, then he has to abandon the notion of a general moral obligation to obey the law and the state.

Since the two purposes of the obligation theorist are logically incompatible, the only way for him to save his theory is to move into the realm of mythology, the land of impossible facts, where so much of political philosophy has traditionally found its home.[26]

3″. The traditional answer to the question, to whom is the political obligation owed, is that it is owed to the other members of the society, just as our obligation to play a game according to the rules is an obligation owed to the other players. The consequence is that political obligation, being a kind of moral obligation, is a personal obligation owed to other persons linked together through the factual basis of the obligation.

[25] Some consent theorists do, of course, allow some "shrinkage," i.e., limitation on the class of individuals who are bound by the obligation to obey. See, for example, Joseph Tussman, *Obligation and the Body Politic* (New York: Oxford University Press, 1960), p. 37, "non-consenting adult citizens are, in effect, like minors who are governed without their own consent."

[26] For an illuminating discussion of the function of pictures invented by political philosophers, see Margaret MacDonald, "The Language of Political Theory," in *Logic and Language*, first series, ed. A. Flew (Oxford: Blackwell, 1952).

If the obligation is a kind of mutual obligation where obligors are at the same time obligees, as in games, then it follows that we owe the obligation of political obedience only to that restricted segment of the population who are plausibly considered obligors. We have a kind of in-group élite of individuals who are bound by mutual political obligation; the citizenry, like players in a game, are the only ones bound to observe the rules. Outsiders, i.e., those who have not placed themselves through some act under an obligation, are not bound, nor is anyone bound to them.

It would be absurd to deny that within a society such mutually obligated groups do exist and, indeed, have some validity. It would be perfectly correct to describe moral relations between members of particular political groups in terms of moral obligation. But the positive moral aspects of political obedience and obedience to the laws is not at all adequately described in such terms, at least under a constitutional or democratic regime, for we want also to be able to say that we ought to obey the law for general moral reasons and not for personal reasons, even if the personal reasons are also moral ones. This is what we intend when we say metaphorically that our moral obligation is to the laws or to the constitution, rather than to individuals. (That is not to say, of course, that, e.g., under a totalitarian regime, political obedience cannot be construed as a personal obligation owed to an individual, e.g., the *Führer*.) [27]

4″. It would appear that when we turn to the role of sanctions in the concept of obligation we have at last discovered something that is essential to both obligation and to the political and legal order; for the power of sanctions has always been regarded as one of the perquisites of this order. Nevertheless, when we look closer, we see that the obligation model's way of construing sanctions does not strictly apply to the way that sanctions operate (logically) within a modern political and legal order. The disanalogy is illuminating.

With regard to obligations, sanctions, as we have seen, come into play when a moral obligation is violated, and they may be justified by reference to the obligation alone. Pursuing the analogy in the case of an alleged political obligation, sanctions would

---

[27] See H. Arendt, *Eichmann in Jerusalem* (New York: Viking Press, 1963) for vivid illustrations of this point.

come into play and be justified solely on the basis of the failure to comply with that obligation, e.g., disobeying the law. In the game model, the analogous condition of a sanction would be cheating.

As was pointed out earlier, sanctions, which hold with regard to observing the rules of a game, must be distinguished from penalties, which are provided for within the rules of the game. Penalties are provided for specific breaches; whereas sanctions, as referred to here, apply to the violation of a rule as a rule. A cheater is, as it were, an outlaw rather than a criminal.

Sanctions, insofar as they are imposed by law and government, are more like penalties for specific breaches than they are like sanctions brought against players who cheat or, more generally, individuals who renege on their obligations. For legal sanctions, i.e., legal punishment and other coercive measures, are provided for and governed by the rules of the legal order itself. They are sanctions within the system rather than sanctions with regard to the system. Legal sanctions are always for specific crimes, specific breaches. There is, as far as I know, no sanction for the general disregard of the law, i.e., for reneging on one's "political obligation."

Once more the basic analogy upon which the notion of political obligation is founded breaks down. The underlying reason for the breakdown is that sanctions, and obligations, for that matter, are part of the legal order, i.e., exist within it, and do not bind the individual to that order from the outside. Thus we cannot have an obligation, say a political obligation, to perform our other obligations, e.g., our legal obligations, which arise out of and are defined by the political and legal order itself.

5″. The principle that moral obligations are limited to what is not incompatible with the moral law is, of course, part of the traditional contract theory; for according to the usual versions of that theory the political contract is limited by the natural law. Political obligations are supplemental to, but not contradictory of, the moral (or natural) law.

The consequences of taking this position on the relation of morality to the political and legal order have already been touched upon under 1″, and will be discussed further later in this chapter. In the meantime, two remarks on the question may be in order here. First, the idea that our moral relationships to the political and legal order are, in some way, supplemental or added to our other moral relationships, say, by means of an obligation, tends to trivialize the moral aspects of the relationship, making them extrinsic rather than intrinsic to the relationship and to the political and legal order itself.

Second, the requirement that obligations are rendered null and void if they conflict with the moral law hardly represents an accurate rendering of the type of moral dilemma that political and legal issues often present us with. If, as Locke would presumably hold, our political obligation is valid only as long as it requires nothing contrary to the natural law and does not exceed the bounds of the powers delegated by the contract, then no great moral issues can arise within the political framework. The moral issues of politics are, as it were, apolitical. Once again, then, it appears that the obligation model requires us to separate politics from morality in the wrong way and at the wrong place.

6''. The distorted picture of the relation of politics and morality forced on us by the obligation model becomes even clearer when we turn to the opaqueness and totalism of obligations.

The opaqueness of an obligation requires us to do the required actions without regard to the intrinsic merits or desirability of the actions themselves, excepting the conditions mentioned under 5. When applied to political obligation this means that we ought to do anything at all that is prescribed by the political authorities and the law, regardless of its content, providing only that it is not incompatible with the moral law. The mere fact that something is prescribed by them is not only a sufficient reason for doing it; it is the only relevant consideration. For obligations as such function logically so as to exclude other considerations. That is the main force of attributing an obligation to a person. Consequently, given such an obligation, it is quite irrelevant to ask whether the decree or law to be obeyed is good or poor, well- or ill-considered, trivial or momentous, foolish, capricious, or simply a nuisance. It is the law, we are bound to obey the law, and so no further questions are in order— excepting, of course, those covered under 5. As far as our obligation is concerned, all laws and decrees of the proper authorities are on the same level. We must be blind to their content.[28]

---

[28] Sometimes, of course, one must take account of the content and what is the "best thing to do," namely, when the obligation itself specifies what is to be done in those terms. If, e.g., the orders are to solve a problem as

The totalism of the alleged political obligation leads to the same result, for it requires us to do everything that is prescribed by the authorities. We cannot pick and choose which laws to obey and which ones to disregard. Our obligation binds us to the totality of them. Our obligation to obey all the laws is as binding as our obligation to obey any particular law; for, indeed, it is the same obligation.

These are the logical consequences following from the obligation model. Needless to say none of us, even the authorities themselves, would ever contemplate fulfilling them completely and to the letter. There are many well-known cases in which law and order have broken down simply because all the laws on the books were being scrupulously executed. That is why the injunction to obey the law as a whole and "blindly" is more a piece of propaganda than it is a serious moral demand.

The analogy with games, which is so popular these days, makes the consequences just noted quite clear. The game model provides a good illustration of the implicit logic of obligation that is assumed here: through the very act of participating in a game we accept the system of rules of that game *in toto,* and without regard to their content, and are thereby placed under an obligation to obey every particular rule without questioning it.

On closer inspection, it should become obvious that the game model describes the individual's relation to the rules in a way that is exactly opposite to the way in which they are related in the political and legal order. Within a game it makes no sense to challenge a particular rule; for example, I cannot ask "Why should I obey the rule that I have to stop batting when I have three strikes?" The answer is simply "Because that is one of the rules of the game. You have to accept that rule if you want to play." On the other hand, it makes perfectly good sense to challenge the enterprise as a whole: "Why should I play that game?"

When we examine the political and legal order we find that exactly the opposite holds, namely, that it makes sense to challenge a particular rule (decree or law) but not the order as a

---

expeditiously as possible, then one would have to consider the qualities of the alternative acts open to one. But such qualities would be relevant only because they are elements involved in executing the obligation. I am indebted to Oskar Wood for pointing out this difficulty to me.

whole. The difference between games and law is not simply a moral difference but a logical one; for the logical presuppositions that make one set of questions, e.g., with regard to games, meaningful are absent in the case of the political order and law. We cannot challenge the political order and law as a whole simply because we would not know what we are challenging.

Underlying the notion of political obligation is the notion, exemplified in games, that the political and legal order comprises a *system* of rules (laws, norms, and so on). The notion of obligation would make no sense if law could not be conceived as a system. Indeed, it would have to be a system which could provide us with a determinate decision-procedure by means of which it could be determined what falls under the law and what does not. Presumably this condition is what Hart and Kelsen intend by their doctrine of the Rule of Recognition and the Basic Norm, respectively. It hardly needs to be observed that one of the principal objectives of the legal positivists is to reduce law to a system of some kind or other, in order, of course, to be able to define it independently of morality.

The whole notion of a legal system is, however, an obscure one. It is impossible, I submit, to supply the necessary and sufficient conditions for determining whether or not a rule belongs to the system.[29] The legal system and the political system, insofar as they are properly regarded as systems at all, are not closed systems like the systems we find in highly structured games. (The notion of a "dynamic system" presented by Kelsen merely substitutes another way of closing the system, for in principle it provides a decision-procedure for determining what is law.)

Indeed, for reasons that need not be detailed here, the concepts of law and the state are open-textured and multifunctional concepts. At the very least they are "family-resemblance" concepts, in Wittgenstein's terms. They might, indeed, even be what W. B. Gallie calls "essentially contested concepts."[30] For it will suffice to point out that only if they are so regarded will we be able to explain why law and politics provide an arena of controversy and debate quite unlike anything that takes place in

[29] This, I take it, is the underlying issue in the famous Hart-Fuller debate, "Separation of Law and Morals," *Harvard Law Review*, lxxi (1958).

[30] See W. B. Gallie, "Essentially Contested Concepts," *Philosophy and the Historical Understanding* (New York: Schocken Books, 1968), ch. 8.

connection with the rules of a game. (I do not want to deny that some parts of law are systematized or systematizable. Here, however, I am speaking of law and the political order as a whole.) My point can be put in another way by once more examining the concept of obligation. Obligation, it will be recalled, makes sense as a moral category only if we can contrast an individual's being under an obligation to do something with his not being under that obligation, or with others' not being under the obligation. The logical function of the basis is precisely to explain why one individual does and other individuals do not have an obligation to do a certain thing. It follows that we can make sense out of the notion of a person's having an obligation to do something only if we can make sense out of the notion of his not having the obligation, i.e., its not being wrong for him to do the thing in question if he so desires.

When we come to the alleged obligation to obey the political and legal order as a whole, the condition just mentioned does not seem to obtain; for it is not possible to conceive what it would be like not to accept or not to obey the order as a whole, i.e., in its entirety. The philosophers who invented the concept of a state of nature intended to conceptualize that possibility, but Plato is more likely to be right in holding that any society whatsoever involves a kind of political and legal order, however minimal. Especially today, however, it is impossible to say what it would be like to refrain from accepting the political and legal order as such. (Of course, we can refuse to accept and obey parts of it. But that is a different question and, needless to say, a perfectly legitimate one if we reject the obligation theory.)

The logical point here is that the obligation model and the game model require us to conceive of ourselves as placed outside the political and legal order altogether, as if we were watching a game and deliberating whether or not to join. But, as I have argued, we simply cannot place ourselves outside or even conceive of ourselves as outside these orders.[31]

But perhaps even more important than the logical objections to the notion of political obligation are the moral objections to it. A final word on this aspect may be in order.

---

[31] I have argued this point in more detail in my "Law and Morality: Internalism *vs.* Externalism," *op. cit.* Theories that I have called "externalist" are those that involve placing or conceiving oneself outside the legal system.

It should not be thought that because I have rejected the notion of political obligation that I deny that we ought to obey the political authorities and the law. For there are many other kinds of moral requirements and moral relations besides those created by obligations.

Whitehead used to ascribe many of the difficulties of modern philosophy to what he called the "fallacy of misplaced concreteness." With apologies to Whitehead, I should like to coin a phrase, the "fallacy of misplaced morality," to stand for a similar source of many of our difficulties in political and legal philosophy. The notion of political obligation provides an exemplary illustration of this fallacy, for what it does is to place the moral emphasis in the wrong place and by implication take it away from the right place.

By placing the moral emphasis on the political and legal order as a whole, e.g., on the constitution, it deflects our attention from the moral aspects of particular decrees, rules, statutes, codes and procedures. It says that, e.g., as long as we have a "just" constitution, then, other things being equal, we must obey all its decrees and laws regardless of their content. By the same token, if the constitution is "unjust," we have no obligation at all to obey the government and the law. In the latter case, we should have regard only to the content and consequences, etc.

This seems an odd way to have to "cut" our moral relations to the law and the state, for it forces us to buy many things wholesale without examining them, as well as to reject other things without examining them. Lest it be thought that the difference between the two approaches, which I have elsewhere labeled externalism (e.g., obligation theory) and internalism, let me point out some practical differences between them.

If we assume that the basis of political obedience is an obligation, then the onus is on an individual who is inclined to disobey a particular legal or judicial prescription to defend his doing so. And he can do so only by showing either that what is required is immoral in itself and therefore the prima facie obligation should be overridden or else that the constitution is unjust.[32] The Establishment, on the other hand, does not *ab initio* have to justify its claim that we ought to obey any particular decree

---

[32] Or else, of course, that the requirement is not part of the legal system.

issued by it; for the notion of political obligation has, as it were, given it a blank check for our obedience. In sum, if any of its laws are challenged, the burden of proof devolves upon the challenger to show why it should not be obeyed. The net effect of the logic of the situation is that the rulers of a constitutional democracy are invested with a certain kind of immunity to being challenged. This immunity, it is obvious, tends to relieve them of the moral responsibility of making their decrees worthy of being obeyed by the people.[33]

Part of the mythology that justifies this misplacement of morality is the picture of democracy as a kind of game, with reversible rules, umpires, moves, and penalties.[34] Therefore, its procedures are "fair," for "someday we will have our turn. We will be in the majority and they will be in the minority, and they will have to obey us. So let us play according to the rules now." That is a very fine argument for those who have some genuine prospect of being in the majority in the not too distant future. But it is not an argument that has any appeal for individuals who are members of a permanent minority, which in our society comprises not only Negroes but also intellectuals. The liberal mythology should not blind us to the facts about how things work and, as I have argued, the notion of political obligation is based on this mythology.

My conclusion, then, is that the theory of political obligation permits and, indeed, requires the separation of law and morality at precisely the level where they should come together, namely, at the level of the concrete actions and choices of individual people. It is about time, I submit, that we should try to bring law and morality together again.

---

[33] It is interesting to note that today the contract theory is employed for precisely the opposite purpose from that for which it was originally framed. Under Locke and his followers it was a revolutionary doctrine. Today it represents the position of the Establishment, for the reasons just mentioned.

[34] This model of democratic decision-making is brilliantly portrayed in J. M. Buchanan and G. Tullock, *The Calculus of Consent* (Ann Arbor: University of Michigan Press, 1967).

2

IN DEFENSE OF OBLIGATION

JEFFRIE G. MURPHY

The concept of obligation, used broadly to denote all the moral relations in which an individual might find himself entangled, has been the workhorse of moral philosophy. And, as Professor Ladd rightly notes (Chapter 1), its broad use has been more productive of confusion than clarity, blurring as it does the important differences in kind between the various moral demands we all face. In this way the concept is like the Platonic concept of justice used as a general concept for all that is good, and it is in need of its own sober Aristotle to make some relevant distinctions and to map for us its limited and proper use.

These comments on John Ladd's paper were written on the basis of a version of that paper delivered at the meetings of the Society. They do not, therefore, take into account any alterations he may have made in preparing his manuscript for publication.

Professor Ladd seeks to provide such restriction and clarification for the concept of obligation, particularly in so far as this concept has played a role in attempts to outline what moral reasons, if any, there are for obedience to law. Political theorists have pretty generally assumed that the reasons are of such a nature that they make it appropriate to speak of the moral relation obtaining between a citizen and his legal government as one of obligation, and so if there are confusions here, they have a venerable history. Professor Ladd's strategy, then, is to map the concept of obligation, illustrate its clear use in certain paradigms like promising and game-playing, and then hold his map up to the political terrain and see how the two match. And his conclusion is that they do not match well at all. For it appears that the characteristic features which must be noted for a proper mapping of the concept of obligation have no interesting analogues in the political sphere. Thus, whatever the moral relation between a citizen and the law, it is not one of obligation.

Now important as this sort of inquiry is, I believe that Professor Ladd fails to establish the conclusions he wants to draw from his conduct of it. This is so, first, because his analysis of the concept of obligation is in certain respects defective and, second, because he has not been sufficiently resourceful in looking for political analogues to the features present in his paradigms. I shall not, of course, attempt to conclude from this that obligation is the proper concept for the illumination of moral fidelity to law. My limited purpose here is simply to argue that if it is not, Professor Ladd's arguments have failed to show this to be the case.

It will be useful to begin by listing briefly, and I hope fairly, the conditions Ladd takes to be characteristic of the paradigm use of the concept of obligation, the "strongest" of all our moral concepts. There are six such conditions.

1. Obligations are morally creative. They "make acts that are per se indifferent into acts that are right or wrong, as the case may be. . . . It follows that one cannot have an obligation to do something that is right in itself, e.g., to help others, and one cannot have an obligation not to do something that is wrong in itself, e.g., not to murder."

2. Obligations have a basis. That is, their existence depends upon some formal (usually institutional or conventional) relation obtaining between the obligator and the obligatee—e.g., a promise.

3. Obligations are personal. That is, both the obligator and the obligatee are nameable individuals. "One can always ask: *who* has the obligation and to whom does he have it? If both questions cannot be answered, then we must conclude that there is no obligation."

4. There is no merit in honoring one's obligations, rather demerit in failing to do so. For this reason sanctions are at least prima facie appropriate for violations of obligation.

5. Obligations, to be morally binding, must conform to the limits set by moral and positive laws and are automatically nullified if they conflict with these laws.

6. Obligations are opaque and totalistic. They are opaque in that they bind us quite independently of the intrinsic merits of the actions themselves. They are totalistic in that they demand that we do the whole of what we are obligated to do exactly when we are obligated to do it. In this way obligations are unlike Kant's imperfect duties (e.g., benevolence) which allow the agent latitude in the time and manner of their fulfillment.

It is important to keep in mind that "throughout this discussion the obligations we are discussing are prima facie obligations." The only hope we have of getting clear about any kind of moral requirement is if, at least at first, we discuss it in isolation from all the features which might in particular circumstances void or override it. Indeed, one way to put Ladd's worry would be as follows: When we decide, for moral reasons, not to obey the law, is this properly described as overriding our prima facie obligation to obey the law? And Ladd's ultimate answer to this question is No.

Why is Ladd led to embrace this negative answer? In the main, it is because he believes that the six conditions characteristic of obligation simply do not present an accurate picture of the moral reasons that can be given in defense of fidelity to law. And so obligation, so productive of illumination for institutions like promising and game-playing, is productive of confusion and even immorality in the political sphere. It is productive of confusion because there is always confusion when a concept is used outside the sphere of its clear application. It is productive of immorality because it loads the moral case too strongly in favor of obedience to law and thereby discourages a discriminating and selective response to particular laws and their particular merits and the allegiance that each deserves.

Now, Ladd's case for regarding obligation as an improper concept for the illumination of the moral response to law rests upon two factors: the extent to which his analysis of the concept of obligation is accurate and the extent to which he is correct in believing that the characteristic criteria for the application of this concept are not satisfied in the political sphere. It will be useful to consider both.

First, what about Ladd's own analysis of the concept of obligation? Unfortunately, it seems to me that the analysis is quite basically defective and, even worse, that its defects are of such a nature as to undermine the ultimate purpose to which the analysis is to be put—namely, to show that there is no moral obligation to obey the law as such. My main worry is about conditions 1 and 5: that we cannot be obligated to do that which it is good in itself to do and that obligations must conform to the limits set by moral and positive laws. These claims are inconsistent with condition 6 which argues for the opacity of obligations. Also, they are false.

The inconsistency, I am afraid, is blatant. Ladd cannot consistently say that obligations are opaque—that is, bind us irrespective of the intrinsic merits of the actions—and say also that obligations cannot violate moral demands. For if we cannot be obligated to do what is immoral (condition 5) and cannot be obligated to do what is good in itself (condition 1) then there is an important sense in which obligations are not opaque, since quite clearly these conditions tell us that some actions, because of their intrinsic qualities, are ruled out as obligatory. Ladd simply cannot have it both ways. (He tries to have it both ways by suggesting that condition 6 is subject to the limitations set forth in his previous conditions, but this buys verbal consistency at a high price. If condition 6 is really so limited, then—as I suggest—there is an important sense in which obligations are not opaque. Thus opacity is going to have to be narrowly construed, and this makes condition 6 much less interesting than it looks on its face.)

Conditions 1 and 5 are not merely inconsistent with the rest of Ladd's analysis, however. They are also false. Obligations quite clearly can bind us to the immoral or to the moral. They are creative, but they do not have to be creative *ex nihilo*. It is, for example, morally good to read to your invalid aunt. If you promise to read to her, however, it is not merely good that you do so but also obligatory. Similarly, if Ned promises Ed that he shall murder Ted, then surely the promise to Ed makes Ned's situation more morally complicated than it otherwise would have been—because, in (hopefully) not murdering Ted, Ned shall now be violating an obligation to Ed. Ladd fails to see this, I think, because he quite forgets that he is supposed to be talking about prima facie obligations, not total obligations. Of course one's total obligation cannot be to do something which is morally wrong.[1] This is a tautology. But surely one can have a prima facie obligation to do something which is morally wrong or right in itself. Ladd's confusion on this point is very deep:

1. One cannot have an obligation to do something right in itself, e.g., to help others, and one cannot have an obligation not to do something that is wrong in itself, e.g., not to murder. 2. Obligations are, in this sense, superadded to the other requirements of morality. They add a new kind of moral reason for actions to the other kinds of moral reason.

I do not think that Ladd appreciates how very different these two claims are. Point (2) is surely correct. An obligation presents a new kind of moral reason for acting. Obligations are superadded. But what this shows is that one can have a prima facie obligation to do what is wrong or right in itself—that is, that 1 is false. Though helping others is good in itself, by obligating myself to do it (through promising, say) I have added another reason for performing the action over and above its intrinsic merits.

It would be nice if Ladd could simply drop these conditions and make his case on the basis of the remainder. This will not work, however, because these conditions are specifically appealed to at important points in the succeeding argument. For example, Ladd wants to argue that the concept of obligation cannot be applied vis-à-vis the legal and political order in part because it cannot comprehend the distinction in law between *mala prohibita* and *mala in se*—things wrong because prohibited and things wrong in themselves. Obligation will work for the former but not, because of conditions 1 and 5, for the latter.

---

[1] Though one could, it seems, have a total obligation to violate the *positive* law. Presumably this is how one might justify cases of civil disobedience or even revolution. Thus I do not see what inclines Ladd to include the notion of "limits of positive law" in his condition 5.

> Unlike promises and games, much of the political and legal order relates to acts and rules that are already part of morality. . . . As we press on, it becomes more and more evident that the concept of political obligation is principally, if not exclusively, concerned with *mala prohibita;* for if, and to the extent that it relates to *mala in se,* it adds nothing to what we are morally required to do or even to our understanding of the relation of morality to law. For the concept of obligation, if applied to conduct that is antecedently moral, becomes redundant, pointless, or, in Wittgenstein's words, it is "idling."

This seems confused. First of all, Ladd has not noted here any crucial difference between the legal order and games. It is intrinsically wrong to push and shove people about (i.e., always stands in need of justification), but this becomes my obligation in the context of certain contact sports. Second, it is important to see the following: that murder is wrong and that I have (in Ladd's strict sense) an obligation not to murder are different claims. The latter is not, as Ladd seems to think, redundant in principle— even if it is sometimes redundant in practice. It is true that it "adds nothing to what we are morally required to do"—in that it does not require that we do some additional thing—over and above not murdering—but it does add one more reason for not murdering. For in saying that I have (because perhaps of a general defense of fidelity to law) an obligation not to murder because murder is illegal, I am saying that I have a moral reason against murder over and above the intrinsic wrongness of murder.[2]

---

[2] For most of us, of course, the intrinsic wrongness of murder is a sufficient reason against acting, and so there is no practical need for another reason. But this is also just the kind of situation where talk about the obligation to obey the law as such would not arise, since such a consideration is generally raised when someone is contemplating disobedience. Consider, then, an example where the cards are not quite so heavily stacked: Smoking marajuana is taken by most people to be *mala in se,* but I am sure that these people are wrong. However, since there is a law against its use and since I feel a prima facie obligation to obey the law, I find this at least a relevant reason against my using the drug. After all, there is (except for the most obvious cases like murder) notorious disagreement over just what is *mala in se.* And it is when this kind of disagreement arises that one is tempted to talk about the obligation to obey the law as such—as when, after *Brown* vs. *Board of Education,* many of us appealed to Southern citizens to put aside their belief that integration is immoral and to instead respect the law of the land.

This leads me to my second worry about Ladd's attack on the concept of obligation in politics: his lack of resourcefulness in looking for political analogues to the features he notes in promising and game-playing which, in his view, make the concept of obligation an appropriate one to apply. Since I have, I believe, already raised enough doubts about conditions 1, 5, and 6, I shall now pass on to other matters. In particular I want to consider Ladd's notion of the basis for an obligation (condition 2) and the correctness of his judgment that a basis is lacking for political obligation.

Ladd's main interest is in attacking John Rawls' notion that the basis for political obligation is participation in a system of benefits made possible as a result of reciprocal sacrifice. As Rawls says, political obligation "depends upon our having accepted and our intention to continue accepting the benefits of a just scheme of cooperation that the constitution defines."[3]

But this, according to Ladd, is plainly wrong. For it makes the obligation too individual in that it restricts it solely to those people who do receive benefits (or satisfy some other restrictive condition) in the system in which they live.

> This individualization of obligation is precisely what we do not want in political theory. We do not want to say that the "obligation" to obey the government and the laws holds only for people fulfilling certain requirements; rather, we want to say that it holds for everyone (within the jurisdiction) no matter whether he has consented, received benefits, or has "played the game," or not.

These remarks are troublesome. For who constitutes the "we" here who want political obligation to hold for everyone? Certainly not Ladd himself, since he does not believe that there is any such thing as political obligation. I, for one, take it to be a virtue of Rawls' analysis, and of social contract theory in general, that it reminds us that government exists to serve each individual fairly and that the obligations of each individual depend upon the extent to which government performs this proper function. Thus I am inclined to think that those people who are systemati-

---

[3] "Legal Obligation and the Duty of Fair Play," in S. Hook, *Law and Philosophy* (New York: New York University Press, 1964).

cally excluded from the benefits of a society do not have any moral obligation to obey that society's laws as such (though they may have moral reasons of a nonobligational variety and many prudential reasons). Consider, by way of example, the case of black people in urban American ghettos. These people have been systematically excluded from the benefits of our society, and yet our government calls upon them (by drafting them in great numbers for military service) to make sacrifices required to insure these benefits for others. To say that they have any moral obligation to serve is to say that they have an obligation to become slaves, and that is absurd.

It seems to me, therefore, that the general kind of position that Rawls seeks to defend does not fall to Ladd's attack. It seems initially reasonable to say that we have an obligation to obey the law to the extent that the law functions to support a system of benefits made possible only by reciprocal sacrifice (and obedience is a sacrifice). Its basis: participation in the system. Who has the obligation? Each citizen who derives benefits.[4] To whom is the obligation owed? To other members of the society. It is owed to them as an obligation of fairness because the system necessarily involves a modification in the expectations of the participants. I expect others to obey when their turn comes and thus it is only fair, since they have similar expectations, that I do likewise. The recognition of such an obligation is surely a necessary condition for the workability of any social decision procedures. What sanctions are there? Though there are no formal sanctions against disobedience to law as such, there are the informal sanctions (as in a game) of ostracism and condemnation. Also, one earns no praise for obeying the law, rather demerit for disobeying in the absence of a good justification. If all this is wrong, Ladd has not shown why.

Ladd's basic motivation, I think, is similar to Bentham's in opposing natural law theory: a fear that the view supports the status quo by assuming a presumptive moral case in favor of the law.

---

[4] There are, of course, some serious problems here. As Hume observed, many citizens are simply unable (perhaps because of educational and financial reasons) to leave a society and stop receiving whatever benefits they do receive. It is a very strained sense of "voluntary" to call this voluntary participation. Also, just what benefits does a citizen have a right to expect in exchange for his obedience? These considerations are, I think, much more worrisome than many of those raised by Ladd.

From the opaqueness of the obligation to obey the political
authorities and the law, it follows that we ought to do
anything at all that is prescribed by the authorities and the
law. . . . [But] every intelligent and responsible citizen has
to take a much more discriminating and selective attitude
toward the laws. We do not, cannot and should not obey
blindly any and every law.

Ladd's worry here is a real one and the attitude of slavish
obedience to law is indeed a danger. However, this attitude can
hardly be attributed (either causally or logically) to the analysis
Ladd seeks to attack. For if we remember that the obligation to
obey the law is simply a prima facie obligation, then we will be
on our moral guard in each particular case to see if those
considerations that would justify our overriding that obligation
are present. If we do not do this, this is our fault and not the
fault of any philosophical analysis. [5]

In closing, I should like to make one positive observation: It
does not seem to me an accident that discussions of political
obligation grew up in conjunction with the question of the
proper function of government and with a certain Enlightenment answer to that question. This answer was that government
functions primarily, through its "rule of law," to provide a
binding way of resolving (nonviolently) conflict between individuals—to provide a social decision procedure consisting of rules
for the authoritative determination of conflict and policy. Now it
seems clear that if we are committed to such a system (for
Hobbesian or Lockean or Kantian reasons) we are also prima
facie committed to obey the laws of that system even when, in
our own judgment, they are not for the best. For if one is going
to decide each case solely upon its own merits as one sees them,

[5] I cannot help feeling that much of Ladd's discussion is purely verbal.
Rawls, I gather, would want to claim the following: When I participate in a
system based on general obedience, and when my acceptance of benefits from
that system gives rise to expectations on the part of others, then it is morally
incumbent upon me to obey when my turn comes *unless I have a good moral
justification for not doing so.* We normally expect that reasonable people, if
they violate a law, will at least be prepared to offer what they take to be a
good reason for so doing. Now if Ladd would not describe the situation of one
who violates a law as "violating a moral or political obligation," would he still
agree that the burden of moral proof is upon the violator to supply a good
justification? If he would, then Rawls' point is made and the worries about
the appropriateness of the term *obligation* are beside the point. If Ladd does

then there is no sense to the notion of social rules or of the rule of law as a social decision procedure. And it is this realization, I think, which is at the heart of the belief that there is such a thing as political obligation—a prima facie obligation to obey the law as such.

---

not believe that the violator bears the burden of moral proof, then I do not think he has really defended such a claim in his paper—however correct he is about the proper use of the term obligation.

3

OBLIGATION AND OBEDIENCE

MARK R. MacGUIGAN

Professor Ladd has made a genuine contribution to legal philosophy by raising the question of the appropriateness of the concept of obligation as an explanation of obedience to law and by effectively demonstrating in the detail of his argument the inadequacy of the narrow sense of that concept. He might have gone even further and brought into question the appropriateness of the concept for morals as well as for law, since antiobligationist moralists take the position that there is a fundamental opposition between the true ethics—the ethics of love—and the ethics of obligation. In their view obligation that is a consequence of law (as in the case of *mala prohibita*) and a legalistic ethics, an ethics in which the basis of morality is conformity to rules imposed by a lawgiver, is an extrinsicism unworthy of the name of ethics. The narrow concept of obligation is drawn primarily from the area of commutative justice, the one-to-one relationship which characterizes contractual arrangements, and the further it is extended from this core meaning, the less adequately it can explain normative conduct. Truly, it cannot serve either law or morals.

But while Professor Ladd's general endeavor, which I take to be an attempt more adequately to define the close interrelationship which he discerns between law and morals, is advanced negatively by his argument respecting obligation, it is hard to see that his undertaking is one of fundamental importance. He is probably right in thinking that the substitution of moral concepts like "justice" or "the common good," which have a content of their own, would produce a different analysis of obedience to law, but I venture to say that the same would not be true of mere moral copulas like "duty" or "oughtness." Moreover, if we have a heightened awareness of its latent ambiguity, the broad concept of obligation would still seem to allow an adequate explanation of the relationship of law and morals, even if it be granted that the concept of oughtness expresses the same reality with fewer difficulties. In either case, it seems to me, the substantive investigation is the same, viz., the kind of necessity involved in the moral "ought," which in my view is prior to the legal "ought."

Professor Ladd's new approach to law and morals is characterized by his strong feeling against the opaqueness and totalism of obligations as a suitable model for the legal order. I believe he has overstated the importance of particular decrees and rules in contrast to the value of the whole system. To my mind it is essential that emphasis should remain on the legal order as a whole, even though a judgment must still be made as to the moral force of each law.

First, this makes possible the most integrated and adequate theory of the legal ought. How otherwise could we explain *mala prohibita,* which are wrong not in themselves but only because the legislature has decided to render their performance illegal! Although morals provide the principal content of legal norms which are *mala in se*, it affects *mala prohibita* only by controlling the process by which they are made.

In other words, the effect of morals upon legal rules varies according to the derivation of the rules. If the rules are derived from morals, i.e., if they are *mala in se,* then their content may be said to be derived from morals and their binding force may be ascertained by weighing them individually. But although it is true that *mala in se* constitute the underlying substructures of positive law, by far the greater number of legal rules are not moral precepts or logically necessary deductions from them, but are rather legislative determinations of what is otherwise morally indifferent. Even when the source of a particular legal rule is an antecedent moral one, its expression will usually be distinctively juridical and not mere idling. As Lord Atkin put it in *Donoghue* v. *Stevenson:*

> The rule that you are to love your neighbor becomes in law, you must not injure your neighbor: and the lawyer's question, Who is my neighbor? receives a restricted reply. ... The answer seems to be—persons who are so closely and directly affected by my act that I ought reasonably to have them in contemplation as being so affected when I am directing my mind to the acts or omissions which are called in question.[1]

The legal rule, then, may be such a circumscribed version of the moral precept that it cannot reasonably be judged only as a moral statement.

When we add to this consideration the fact that by far the greater number of explicit legal rules are not logically necessary conclusions from moral precepts (i.e., they are in the category of *mala prohibita*), but are legislative determinations of what is morally neutral, then we must come to the conclusion that most laws derive their oughtness from their role in the system rather than from their own intrinsic value. Of course, it remains to consider whether or not they are in themselves reasonable exercises of legislative power, but usually an answer is possible only in relation to other aspects of the system. The focus in the legal order, then, is on the whole corpus and process of law and not on the individual elements. While I do not suggest that this precludes judgment of the elements, in my opinion such individual judging is not characteristic of the legal order and I therefore do not accept Professor Ladd's "fallacy of misplaced morality."

---

[1] *M'Alister (or Donoghue)* v. *Stevenson* [1932], A.C. 562, 580.

My first reason for emphasizing the legal order as a whole instead of its particular components arises from situations of compliance with the law. My second reason comes from the area of disobedience to law. The question of whether or not to disobey a particular law is in most philosophies a separate question from the judgment that it is an immoral or bad law. A decision to disobey a particular law will be made after weighing (1) the worth of the whole legal order, (2) the role of the particular law in the legal order, (3) the degree of iniquity of the law, and (4) the seriousness of the consequences of disobedience. The internal incoherence of the Nazi legal system, as described by Professor Fuller in his dialogue with Professor Hart,[2] would be an important factor in the decision whether or not to obey a particular Nazi edict. On the other hand, a bad law might be morally binding on a particular person at a particular time for the sake of the preservation of the whole system, if the degree of iniquity were not great and the degree of potential scandal (bad example) through disobedience were great.

Perhaps the most difficult case of disobedience is where the citizen does not regard the law which he disobeys as illegal, but takes the view that he may nevertheless disobey it in good conscience as an incident of his protest against some other law. Such indirect disobedience, as it may appropriately be called in contradistinction to direct disobedience where the law disobeyed is the very one against which the protest is being made, frequently involves trespass against land, and is sufficiently controversial to be worth separate consideration below.

A third reason for taking an overall view is that the validity of the whole legal system is a highly relevant factor in the determination of what means are morally right for the purpose of disobeying a particular law. Potential means of disobedience range from purely passive nonresistance through demonstrations, noncooperation, and physical confrontations to outright revolution. The more violent means are less likely to be justifiable, not only in small matters, but also in democratic societies where there are legally established methods of changing public policy.

Consequently, even though he adopts a position of the primacy

---

[2] Lon L. Fuller, "Positivism and Fidelity to Law—A Reply to Professor Hart," *Harvard Law Review*, 71 (1958), 630.

of morals over law, the citizen is not, in such a situation, compelled to choose between showing that the whole system is unjust or that the particular prescription is not part of the legal system; his most likely alternative is simply to say, "Despite the presumption in favor of the legitimacy of legislation, this rule is morally wrong and I will not obey it." In that case, of course, he may be subjected to certain sanctions by the state, but this is a price which a morally sensitive and courageous citizen will be prepared to pay.

The orthodox legal position is that disobedience to law, however justifiable it may be on moral grounds, cannot have a legal justification, for it manifests an express refusal to conform to the commands of the law, through reliance on an appeal to nonlegal norms.[3] The classical natural-law tradition would take sharp issue with legal orthodoxy on the question of what constitutes legality,[4] and it is apparent that the orthodox legal position is nothing other than the legal expression of the philosophical doctrine of legal positivism. Natural-law thought recognized a legal justification for disobedience to bad laws. Not even natural-law theory, however, required disobedience to every unjust law, but left this determination to an ultimate practical judgment, so that there is a certain indefiniteness even in a natural-law context about the legality of disobedience. Few have gone so far as Professor Harrop Freeman in arguing that disobedience is completely legal if it is nonviolent,[5] but many would agree at least that civil disobedience is not opposed to the spirit of the law. If we define civil disobedience as a public, nonviolent act of illegality, performed for a moral purpose, with a willingness to accept the legal penalty attached to the breach of the law, perhaps it would be useful to think of it as *paralegal* rather than as either legal or illegal. Civil disobedience is directed toward justice and is not oriented so much against law as beyond the letter of the law. The facts that the violation of the law is open, that only

---

[3] The orthodoxy is illustrated by *Walker* v. *Birmingham* (1967), 388 U.S. 307.

[4] See, for example, St. Thomas Aquinas, *Summa Theologiae*, I-II, q. 90, a. 1, ad 3.

[5] Harrop Freeman, "Civil Disobedience and the Law," *Rutgers Law Review*, 21 (1966), 17; "The Right of Protest and Civil Disobedience," *Indiana Law Journal*, 41 (1966), 228, 238.

nonviolent means are used, and that legal penalties are willingly accepted express a fundamental respect for the legal system even while demonstrating a refusal to accept a particular law. Civil disobedience is thus neither fully legal nor completely illegal. It is a benign illegality marked by a concern for the legal order. But whatever the legal status of disobedience to law, its moral status is secure provided that it is a proportionate response to injustice. Even violence may be a proportionate response to some injustices, though within a framework of democratic government it is hard to conceive of circumstances, short of direct governmental compulsion of a minority to perform unconscionable acts, in which violent action would be an apt reaction to inadequacy or injustice in the laws. Direct civil disobedience, on the other hand, appears to be almost universally accepted as an appropriate moral response to governmental iniquity, even by authors who deny it legal validity. There may even be general agreement respecting its moral bounds as delimited by Dr. Adams' norms of civil disobedience, on the analogy of the norms of a just war.

But there is no such unanimity with regard to indirect civil disobedience. Dr. Mortimer Adler, for example, has forcefully declared: "Breaking laws for the sake of making public demonstrations against general injustice in society—against segregation or an unjust war—is criminal, not civil disobedience. . . . Those who act in this way cannot claim any of the protection that is and should be accorded to civil disobedience."[6] Mr. Fortas has taken a similar position: "In my judgment civil disobedience—the deliberate violation of law—is never justified in our nation, where the law being violated is not itself the focus or target of the protest."[7] Such disobedience is "morally as well as politically unacceptable."[8]

Such a limitation on civil disobedience would disallow the possibility of symbolic means of resistance. Gandhi, for example, distilled salt from the sea, thus violating a specific law, in order to show the injustice not of that law but of the whole British rule of India. He justified such disobedience where the breach of law

[6] Mortimer Adler, "Is There a Jurisprudence of Civil Disobedience?" *Illinois Continuing Legal Education*, 5 (1966) 71, 86.
[7] Abe Fortas, *Concerning Dissent and Civil Disobedience* (New York: Signet, 1968), p. 124.
[8] *Ibid.*

"does not involve moral turpitude and is undertaken as a symbol of revolt against the State."[9] It would indeed seem that a necessary condition of the justification of indirect disobedience would be the closeness of the relationship, whether symbolic or conventional, between the object of protest and the law disobeyed, over and above the requisites for moral standing in the case of direct disobedience. A symbolic relationship might take its significance from its location (an appropriate government office) or its time (an anniversary) or its nature or purpose (a draft card). The more remote the relationship, the weaker the moral justification. If the connection is purely arbitrary, it will be entirely without justification.

To take a hypothesis which Mr. Justice Fortas himself cites, based upon *Brown v. Louisiana*,[10] we can see an unreasonableness in resting the morality of an act upon the resolution of a marginal illegality. In the Brown case five Negroes sat in, in a public library to protest against the fact of its segregation and were arrested, tried, and convicted of disorderly conduct under a Louisiana statute. On appeal the United States Supreme Court decided by a 5-4 vote to set aside the conviction. The majority judges apparently took the view that a peaceful protest held in a library is protected by the First Amendment if it does not interfere with others and if it takes place when the protesters have a right to be present; whereas the minority judges believed that the Negroes were expressing their protest in an inappropriate and unauthorized place. Mr. Justice Fortas suggests that a majority of the court might have held against the protesters on the hypothesis that they had stayed in the library after its regular closing hour; possibly there might again have been dissenting opinions.

Now, just as it is reasonable that the judicial judgment should relate back to the library sit-in to determine the legality of that action, it is equally reasonable that such relation back should not determine the morality of the protesters' action, which surely falls to be determined at the time of their action according to the best objective perception of the circumstances, including the

---

[9] M. K. Gandhi, *Non-Violent Resistance* (New York: Schocken, 1961), p. 175. It should be noted that Gandhi himself thought such resistance justified only in a corrupt or tyrannical state.
[10] (1966), 383 U.S. 131.

relevant law. The law in existence at the time of the act, even if it is crystal clear, may be subsequently changed by the court through its power of reversal, but surely the morality of act cannot thus be reversed by a judicial change of mind. The point is that some acts of disobedience to law (e.g., minor forms of trespass) involve such marginal disobedience that the decisive question should not be whether or not they are in fact illegal—with the consequence that if they are illegal, they turn the act into one that is morally wrong—when even the courts may have difficulty in deciding their illegality. Of course, not all acts of indirect disobedience are of such marginal illegality, but I would suggest that the proper test ought to be whether such acts are on balance more coercive than persuasive.

Violence is a form of coercion, but coercion is a broader concept than violence, since it includes types of nonviolent action. The concept to be contrasted with coercion is persuasion, with the essential difference between the two indicated by the reaction of the opponent. If the opponent is induced to act favorably because he has become convinced by the disobeyer's case, he has been persuaded; but if he acts favorably only in order to avoid trouble, while continuing to hold a contrary position to the disobeyer, he has been coerced rather than persuaded. Coercion, even when nonviolent, is analogous to violence, for it employs force even if it is of the nonphysical variety. Coercion manipulates the opponent as an object, while persuasion respects him as a person. In a democratic society, with its commitment to rationality in government and in political dialogue, persuasion must be the moral technique, since it makes its appeal to reason and to love.

Almost all techniques of civil disobedience combine both persuasion and coercion. Often the coercive aspect is the more arresting, but it is also the more socially disruptive. In my opinion, unless a particular tactic inconveniences only the people heavily involved in the injustice, it passes beyond the permissible limits of civil disobedience when the coercive aspect assumes more importance than the persuasive aspect. Ideally it should put the major burden of the suffering it causes upon the shoulders of the protesters themselves and not upon innocent bystanders. It will not always achieve the ideal, but it must achieve a due proportion.

Thus disruptive tactics like bridge stall-ins or building sit-ins which prevent the normal flow of traffic are invalid means of civil disobedience because of the inconvenience they cause to innocent members of society, in addition to the fact that they have a purely arbitrary relationship to the injustice whose correction is sought. There is no doubt that in concrete circumstances it may be difficult to decide whether the persuasive or the coercive element is predominant (or is likely to be, if the decision is being made in advance), but I believe this must be the ultimate test of indirect disobedience in a democracy. As an example of the principle of persuasion, it is an acceptable form of the political process which is the heart of democracy. But as a tool of violence, it has no place in a society dedicated to the rule of law.

Legal obligation involves an interplay not only between law and morals but also between particular laws and the whole legal system ("law" in the collective sense). If law were merely morals writ small, the relationship between moral and legal oughtness would be universal and particular. But the relationship of law and morals is an immensely rich and subtle one marked by both reciprocal causality and a distinction between obligation and obedience.[11] The delineation of the narrow concept of obligation is of only negative assistance in translating this complex relationship into conceptual terms.

Today there is difficulty both in gathering together the diverse threads of a modern legal system and in achieving some certainty as to moral truth at a time when apparent absolutes seem to disintegrate before the impact of the new morality. An adequate conception of obligation requires that all elements of the problem be taken into account; thus laws and law, formal and felt obligation, obedience and disobedience must all be terms of the legal equation from which an understanding of obligation will emerge.

---

[11] I have developed this notion of reciprocal causality in "Positive Law and Moral Law," *Current Law and Social Problems*, 2 (1961), 89.

4

OBLIGATION: POLITICAL, LEGAL, MORAL

ALAN GEWIRTH

There is a puzzling complexity in the concept of obligation. It seems tautologically obvious that obligations are obligatory, that "A is under an obligation to do x" entails "it is obligatory for A to do x." Since the obligatory is the most stringent of deontic modalities, corresponding to the necessarily true in the sphere of alethic modalities, it follows that fulfillment of one's obligations is normatively unescapable or mandatory. On the other hand, there seem to be obligations which do not have this eminently stringent quality. For example, when two obligations conflict, both cannot be fulfilled; hence, one must either contradict one's previous conviction that both of them were obligations or else give up the idea that all obligations are obligatory, since it seems absurd to regard what is impossible as mandatory. For another example, there are "social obligations" involving various amenities of polite society; since many of these are relatively trivial, their fulfillment can hardly be regarded as mandatory. Still a third kind of case is found in the Fourteenth Amendment to the Constitution of the United States, where, referring to "any debt or obligation incurred in aid of insurrection or rebellion against the United States," it is solemnly declared that "all such debts, obligations, and claims shall be held illegal and void." Here, so far from its being obligatory to fulfill one's obligations, it is instead made obligatory not to fulfill them.

An initial question, then, is: How can obligations be not only obligatory but also trivial, escapable, and even prohibited? Obviously, distinctions must be drawn between kinds or concepts or contexts of obligation. And indeed philosophers have distinguished between perfect and imperfect obligations, between prima facie and actual obligations, between hypothetical and categorical obligations, and so forth. While each of these distinctions is relevant to the contrasts indicated above, I wish to call attention to another distinction which is especially pertinent to the understanding of political and legal obligation.

INSTITUTIONAL OBLIGATIONS

One important concept of obligation is logically tied to the concepts of an institution and a rule. An institution is a standardized arrangement whereby persons jointly pursue or participate in some purposive activity which is socially approved on the ground of its value for society. This arrangement may be solely functional in that it is concerned only with the purposive activity itself, or it may also be organizational in that it is concerned as well with structured groupings of persons associated for pursuing and regulating the activity.[1] Thus if education, religion, and buying and selling are institutions in the functional sense, the corresponding organizational institutions are, among others, schools, churches, and corporations. Indeed, we some-

---

[1] See such discussions of institutions as B. Malinowski, *A Scientific Theory of Culture and Other Essays* (Chapel Hill: University of North Carolina Press, 1944), pp. 52 ff.; S. F. Nadel, *The Foundations of Social Anthropology* (London: Cohen and West, 1958), pp. 107 ff.

times refer to the latter groups as "organized education," "organized religion," and the like; and we sometimes ask whether a given (organizational) institution has lost its function. In any case, institutions are constituted by rules which define what men are required to do if they are to participate in the respective functions or activities; and these requirements are the obligations which men have qua such participants. Thus, in virtue of the requirements set by the rules constitutive of the institutions mentioned above, men have obligations to teach, to pray or worship, to pay for what they buy, and the like, just as, in connection with such other institutions as promising and marriage, we speak of the obligations persons have to keep their promises and to be faithful to their spouses. I shall refer to such requirements as *institutional obligations*.

It follows from this that institutional obligations are "objective" in that persons who are to participate in institutions must take on the corresponding obligations. This "must" is not moral but logical. It is analogous to the requirements for participating in rule-governed games: if one is to play tennis, for example, then one must hit the ball with one's racket, not with one's bare hands, and so forth. This logical status of institutional obligations should not be obscured by the reference to "purpose" or "function" in the definition of an institution, nor by the fact that institutional obligations operate as constraints or demands on individuals, tying them to performances of acts of certain kinds even in the face of contrary inclinations. Despite these features, the relation of the purpose or function of an institution to its institutional obligations is not primarily a contingent one of end to means but rather is a conceptual one of a definition to its logical components or logical consequences. It is not that action in accordance with institutional obligations comprises the most efficient means to achieving the purpose or goal of some institution, but rather that the obligations are logically required by the very concept of that institution as contained in its constitutive rules. It is in this logical sense that we may say that institutional obligations rest (logically) on reasons which consist in the function or purpose and the corresponding constitutive rules of the institution in question.

Institutions may, of course, change, so that at certain points it may be unclear just what are their constitutive rules and corresponding obligations. Consider, for example, the various changes in religious practices, or in American marriage as depicted in the Kinsey reports. This flexibility does not, however, affect the logical relation indicated above between institutions and obligations. For at such transitional periods questions arise as to whether it is still the same institution, or indeed whether it is then an institution at all, since the aspects of standardization and of social approval are sharply reduced. It remains the case, then, that so long as an institution is defined by constitutive rules, the relation between it and its corresponding obligations is a logical one.

It must also be noted, however, that there is nothing in the concept of an institution, as such, which necessitates either that participation in it be voluntary, or that all participants in it have rights correlative with their obligations, or that the obligations involve equal sacrifices on the part of all. For example, Negro slavery in the Southern United States, sometimes described by its adherents as "the peculiar institution," was an institution in the sense defined above. But while it imposed extreme obligations on the slave, the obligations of the master were minimal, and were in any case sharply curtailed by his ownership relation to the slave.[2] Other examples of such one-sided institutions are suttee, apartheid, the Inquisition, and the jus primae noctis.

The use of the word "obligation" in connection with such institutions may be challenged. It may be contended that "obligation," like "ought," presupposes both "can" and "may not," so that it is illegitimate to speak of a person's having obligations where he has not freely accepted the requirement or status in question and where he is not free to refrain from fulfilling it except at a prohibitive price. Thus it may be urged that the slave, like a man accosted by a gunman, was *obliged* to accede but not that he had an *obligation* to do so. In this connection, however, it is important to note not only the distinction between institutional and moral obligations (to be discussed below), but also the distinction between institutionalized and noninstitutionalized relationships. Since a gunman's domination of his victim, unlike the master's domination of his slave, is not part of a

---

[2] See K. M. Stampp, *The Peculiar Institution: Slavery in the Ante-Bellum South* (New York: Alfred A. Knopf, 1956), pp. 192 ff.; S. M. Elkins, *Slavery: A Problem in American Institutional and Intellectual Life* (New York: Grosset and Dunlap Universal Library, 1963), pp. 52 ff.

standardized, socially approved arrangement, it does not have the aspects of alleged justification and of formal, stabilized allocation of responsibility that underlie the use of "obligation" to describe the institutional relationship.[3]

DESCRIPTIVE AND PRESCRIPTIVE OBLIGATION-STATEMENTS

The consideration of such institutions suggests the following consequence: one may, with full consistency, describe and even participate in an institution and fulfill its obligations, without holding that one *ought* to fulfill those obligations. To put it schematically, from "*A* has an obligation to do *x*" there does not logically follow "*A* ought to do *x*."[4] The reason why it does not follow is that the obligation-statement may be a purely descriptive one about what is required by some institution; but the person making the statement may not himself accept the institution or its purposes as right or justified. He may therefore admit that the obligation does in fact exist as part of an institution and yet deny that the obligation ought to be carried out.[5]

We must therefore distinguish between *descriptive* and *prescriptive* obligation-statements. Both kinds of statement as

[3] See, for example, Stampp, *Institution, op. cit.*, p. 206. The slave codes of each slave state "held slaves, as thinking beings, morally responsible and punishable for misdemeanors and felonies."

[4] Such logical disconnection between "obligation" and "ought" has been emphasized, among others, by H. L. A. Hart. See "Are There Any Natural Rights?" *Philosophical Review*, 64 (April 1955), 186; *The Concept of Law* (Oxford: Clarendon Press, 1961), p. 83. Hart does not, however, tie this point to institutional obligations.

[5] See the use of "obligation" in such passages as: "In the British West Indies the achievement of manumission merely involved a release from the obligation to serve a special master. It did not carry with it any new rights. . ." (F. Tannenbaum, *Slave and Citizen: The Negro in the Americas* [New York: Vintage Books, 1946], pp. 93–94).

"The existing Hindoo written law, which is a mixed body of religious, moral, and legal ordinances, is pre-eminently distinguished by the strictness with which it maintains a number of obligations plainly traceable to the ancient despotism of the Family. . ." (H. S. Maine, *Lectures on the Early History of Institutions* [London: John Murray, 1875], pp. 322–23).

"A Henry County, Alabama, landlord required two Negro laborers to sign the following contract before giving them employment: 'That said Laborers shall not attach themselves, belong to, or in any way perform any of the obligations required of what is known as the Loyal League Society. . .'" (K. M. Stampp, *The Era of Reconstruction, 1865–1877* [New York: Vintage Books, 1967], p. 204).

uttered by a speaker S may have the form, "A has an obligation (or is under an obligation) to do x." In its descriptive sense, however, the statement is used by S to indicate that A's doing x is required by certain institutional rules, but S does not himself endorse or advocate A's doing x. There are two possibilities here. One is that S in general accepts the relevant institution and its requirements but holds that in this particular case the requirement should not be fulfilled because it conflicts with a more important obligation. The other possibility is that S does not accept the relevant institution at all. As an example of the first case S, while recognizing that A has the obligation to repay on a certain date a sum of money he borrowed, may yet hold that A ought not to repay the money on that date because he needs it to buy medicine for his sick child. As an example of the second case S, while recognizing that A, a South African black person, has certain obligations under apartheid, may yet hold vigorously that the obligations ought not to be fulfilled.

In its prescriptive sense, on the other hand, the obligation-statement is used by S to endorse or advocate A's doing x; and insofar as S regards A's doing x as a requirement deriving from the rule of some institution, S endorses that rule and institution as well. He may, indeed, endorse the act because of the rule; but then his attitude toward the rule is not merely a descriptive or reportive one but rather one of advocacy or endorsement. In addition, however, S may use the statement to endorse A's doing x without regard to the act's being required by an institutional rule. For example, he may say to A, with solemn emphasis, "It was your moral obligation to come to that poor man's rescue when he was being attacked; in failing to do so, you fell down on your obligation." Here, "obligation" is used as equivalent to "ought," in the sense of what one was required to do as determined by strong justifying reasons.

The failure to take account of this distinction between prescriptive and descriptive obligation-statements has led some philosophers to hold that the correct use of "obligation" is exclusively restricted to what I have called institutional obligations.[6] This view, however, overlooks the fact that "obligation"

[6] For a useful corrective, see R. B. Brandt's distinction between "paradigm" and "extended" uses in "The Concepts of Obligation and Duty," *Mind*, 73 (July 1964), 384 ff. The failure to note the distinction between descriptive and prescriptive obligation-statements underlies many attempts to deduce a

may be used in a prescriptive way which lacks the tentativeness or conditionalness characteristic of the concept of an institutional obligation as such. To restrict "obligation" to the institutional context is to make unintelligible both its connection with "obligatory" and the features which are common to descriptive and prescriptive, institutional and moral uses of "obligation." What all uses of "obligation" have in common is the idea of a practical (or task-setting) requirement based on some general alleged justifying reason which can be understood as such, even if not accepted as successfully justificatory, by those who are subject to the requirement. This reason may be some institution with its purpose and rules; but the reason may also consist in quite different considerations, including moral ones.

TENTATIVE AND DETERMINATIVE OBLIGATIONS

The distinction between prescriptive and descriptive obligation-statements leads us to recognize a related distinction between what I shall call *tentative* and *determinative* obligations. A tentative obligation is one that obtains only within a context which has not itself yet received successful justification; it hence does not determine what one's "real" obligations are, that is, what is justifiably required of one, or what one ought to do. A determinative obligation, on the other hand, determines what is justifiably required of one, what one ought to do. Unlike a tentative obligation, it is already justified, and hence does not need to await justification (or disjustification) from some further set of considerations. Determinative obligations, in turn, are of two kinds, *prima facie* and *conclusive*. A prima facie obligation

---

moral ought-statement from a factual is-statement. Such attempts begin from premises which are descriptive obligation-statements (is-statements) to the effect that some person has an institutional obligation; they conclude with a prescriptive obligation-statement to the effect that he ought to fulfill that obligation. This conclusion is a *non sequitur* because it contains an endorsement of the institutional obligation, whereas the premise according to the argument as presented contains no such endorsement. For a recent noteworthy instance of this attempt, see J. R. Searle, "How To Derive 'Ought' from 'Is,' " *Philosophical Review*, 73 (January 1964), 43–58; see also the critique by A. Flew, "On Not Deriving 'Ought' from 'Is,' " *Analysis*, 28 (1964). For a related attempt in connection with the justification of legal obligation, see note 14 below.

is one that ought to be fulfilled unless some other determinative
or justificatory obligation has a higher priority in the particular
case in question. A conclusive obligation is one where this
question of competing priority either does not arise or has
already been resolved in favor of the obligation in question;
hence, a conclusive obligation determines what one ought to do,
decisively and without further question.

In these terms, what is the status of institutional obligations?
While a full answer to this question must wait on an explicit
discussion of the criteria of justification, the following preliminary considerations can be presented here. We may distinguish
two aspects of any institution, its form and its content. Its form is
what it has in common with any institution, as indicated by the
definition of an institution given above. Its content is the specific
kind of institution that it is. Now in respect of its form, the
relevant question is: If we consider an institutional obligation
simply qua institutional, is it a tentative or a determinative
obligation? To answer this question, we must ask another: Do
institutions, as such, perform justifiable functions in society? Let
us assume that there may be both institutionalized and noninstitutionalized ways of pursuing or participating in the same purposive activities and let us assume also, for the present context,
that those activities are themselves justified ones. Does the fact of
their being institutionalized itself contribute an important element relevant to justification? One obvious answer to this question is that since the aspect of standardization common to all
institutions involves acting in accordance with rules, this provides an important stabilizing element. On the other hand, such
stabilization may operate to reduce or even remove spontaneity
and innovation, so that an activity which was itself a justified one
might be diminished rather than augmented in relevant valuable
respects by the fact of institutionalization. We must add to this
the consideration that the contents of institutions may themselves be unjustifiable or evil, and a stabilized evil is still an evil.
I conclude, then, that institutional obligations, as such, are only
tentative, not determinative: the mere fact that an obligation
derives from some institution does not, as such, determine what
one ought to do. In other words, institutions with their rules and
obligations are not, as such, self-justifying; if their obligations
are to determine what is justifiably required of persons, the
institutions must be justifiable by other considerations.

This question of the justification of institutions may take two different forms. One is the general question: Why should there be such an institution at all? Another is the specific question: Granted that there should be such an institution, why should it involve such and such a particular arrangement, have such and such a particular rule? Whether there is any point to asking the specific question depends on whether or not the general institution admits of variation. In the case of promising, for example, it seems that only one arrangement is possible: that one keep one's promises. But in the case of marriage, defined in general terms as the contractually established and socially recognized cohabitation of persons of opposite sex, many arrangements are possible, such as monogamy, polygamy, polyandry, endogamy, exogamy, and so forth. Both forms of the question of justification can be construed as questions about second-order obligations. For both forms ask, in the terms presented above, why is there a determinative obligation to have the obligations which, simply as deriving from some institution, are tentative. The determinative obligation derives from reasons which justify that one fulfill the institutional obligations.

MORAL REASONS

An obvious move at this point is to say that these justifying reasons must be moral ones. Now I think this is true; but it is important to be clear about its meaning and status in order to avoid question-begging assumptions. For one thing, men have often tried to justify institutions and their rules and obligations by an appeal to such considerations as the national interest, or the interests of some race, class, or other group, or tradition, or religion, and so forth. Are all, or any, of these considerations moral ones? If we answer in the affirmative, then to call a reason a moral one will mean merely that it is any reason appealed to in justification of an institution, so that the assertion that institutions must be justified by moral reasons will be an unilluminating tautology. In addition, the question will still remain as to why *such* reasons should be accepted as succeeding in the task of justification. If, on the other hand, we say that considerations like those listed above are not moral ones, then the question will remain as to what we mean by the considerations or reasons that we do call moral, and why these should be accorded greater justificatory weight over the others and over institutional obligations generally.

To deal with these questions we must first note that "moral" can be used either in a descriptive sense (in which it is opposed to "nonmoral") or in an evaluative sense (in which it is opposed to "immoral"). Initially, I shall be concerned with the former sense. Now nonmoral rules as well as moral ones may be practical or "action-guiding"; but two differences between them have been held to be especially important. One difference is "formal": a person who upholds a rule or a reason as a moral one regards it as supremely authoritative or of overriding importance, such that it should, in his view, take precedence over all other rules or reasons. The other difference is "material": a person who upholds a rule or a reason as a moral one regards it as being affected with a social interest, in that it bears importantly on furthering the welfare of persons other than himself.[7]

Now there is, of course, no assurance that these two differentiating criteria will always coincide. But even if we were to take them jointly as the criteria of the moral as opposed to the nonmoral, it would still remain the case that considerations of the national interest and the others mentioned above could qualify as moral reasons. Hence, if we hold that institutions must be justified by moral reasons, these considerations would, so far, pass muster as such reasons. There would still remain, then, the question of how we are to choose among them: Which of these moral reasons is morally right or justified?

There is a further difficulty in our project of justifying institutions by moral reasons. It may be contended that morality is itself an institution parallel to such other institutions as law and religion, in that it is a very extensive, socially endorsed arrangement for participating in and regulating a broad range of purposive activities. On this view, moral obligations would them-

---

[7] See W. K. Frankena, "Recent Conceptions of Morality," in H. N. Castaneda and G. Nakhnikian, eds., *Morality and the Language of Conduct* (Detroit: Wayne State University Press, 1963), pp. 1-24; N. Cooper, "Two Concepts of Morality, *Philosophy*, 41 (January 1966), 19 ff. I have discussed the relation between moral and nonmoral "oughts" in "Must One Play the Moral Language Game?" *American Philosophical Quarterly*, 7 (April 1970).

selves be a kind of institutional obligation, and moral obligation-statements, far from representing justificatory reasons superior to those of institutions, would themselves be conditional upon one's acceptance of an institution, morality. Moreover, just as specific legal or religious rules may or may not be accepted as right or justified, so too with specific moral rules.

Now it is true that there are and have been different "positive" or "conventional" moralities in the sense of informal systems of social regulation. But it is also true that these moralities can themselves be evaluated in respect of their moral rightness. This might be interpreted as meaning simply that one code of positive morality is used to evaluate another. Such an interpretation, however, would still leave open the question of which of these positive moralities is right or justified. What this shows is that the concept of morality in the sense of moral rightness is distinct from the concept of morality in the sense of what is upheld as supremely authoritative and welfare-furthering by the rules of one or another institution of positive morality. It is to the former concept, and not to the latter, that appeal is made when the question concerns the evaluation and justification of institutions, including those of the various positive moralities.

By what kinds of considerations of moral rightness, then, are institutions and their rules and obligations to be justified? Let us put the question in the negative: How do we show (or try to show) that an institution is not justified? That is, how do we criticize institutions? We do so, I suggest, by appealing to one or more of three main kinds of consideration: first, that the institution does no good, or does harm, or does more harm than good; second, that even if the institution does good, it is at others' expense, or is wrongly discriminatory, so that the goods which the institution fosters or the harms which it removes are distributed unjustly or unfairly; third, that even if the institution does good and distributes that good fairly, still the institution and its obligations were imposed on the persons subject to them without those persons' consenting or participating in the decision. These three considerations involve reasons, respectively, of welfare, justice, and freedom. The first two considerations are substantive ones bearing on the content of institutional obligations, whereas the third consideration is a procedural one: it concerns the decision-making process whereby men came to be subject to the institution with its rules and obligations.

THE INHERENT RATIONALITY
OF MORAL REASONS

Many questions may, of course, be raised about each of these considerations and about the relations between them. But first I must supplement the above a posteriori approach with an a priori one. The reason for this is that the a posteriori approach still leaves unanswered the question of why these considerations should be accepted as the ones that are to be used in evaluating institutions. After all, the considerations have competitors, such as the national interest and the other grounds mentioned above. What must be shown, then, is that the considerations of freedom, welfare, and justice, as adumbrated above, are superior to their competitors in terms of rightness.

Let us try to make this point more precise. As we have seen, institutional obligations, as such, are not self-justifying, since when the question is raised whether they ought to be fulfilled it must be answered by an appeal to considerations other than the fact that they derive from an institution. Now we seem to have seen the same thing in relation to the competing basic reasons or principles of moral obligation-statements. The question, then, is whether there are any moral principles which are self-justifying. Since moral principles are advanced as basic reasons, another way to put this question is whether any moral principles are inherently rational. For if a principle is inherently rational, then it needs no further reason to justify it and is hence self-justifying.

But what does it mean for a principle to be inherently rational? One traditional answer has been that the principle must be self-evident, in the sense of being seen to be true or correct by immediate inspection or intuition. Such a criterion, however, is open to well-known and well-founded charges of psychologism and dogmatism. The "inherent rationality" which is here in question must be understood in a logical rather than in a psychological sense. Now a necessary condition of all rationality is freedom from self-contradiction. If a principle is self-contradictory, then, entirely apart from any other considerations, it is inherently irrational and self-disjustifying, since it can be shown to refute itself: it denies what it affirms. If, on the other hand, a principle is such that its denial is self-contradictory, then it is inherently rational and self-justifying, since its denial refutes itself, so that the original principle must stand unchallenged by any reasons that may be brought against it.

Can any moral principle be shown to be inherently rational in this sense? The most famous example of such an attempt is Kant's categorical imperative, according to which the test of the rightness of a moral rule or maxim is that when generalized it not be self-contradictory. This test, however, has important difficulties; it would not, for example, rule out the maxim that deformed children should be left unprotected to die. I wish to sketch here an argument for a somewhat different principle. Thus far I have discussed rationality in the logical sense of freedom from self-contradiction: this is the formal requirement of rationality. There is also, however, a material requirement, in that reason takes account of the necessary features of one's subject matter. Now the subject matter of morality is, primarily, human action. When human agents act, they do not merely engage in bodily movements; their action has certain necessary features which may be summarized as voluntariness and purposiveness. For insofar as men are agents, they initiate and control their movements (voluntariness) in the light of their intentions and purposes (purposiveness). This is why human agents can be held responsible both for their acts and for the consequences of the acts.

These features of voluntariness and purposiveness are the maximally general, constitutive conditions of all human action. I shall refer to them as the *categorial rules* of action, since they descriptively pertain to the category of human action as such, and not merely to one kind of act as against another. Whenever a human agent acts, he necessarily applies to himself these categorial rules: that is, he necessarily acts voluntarily and purposively.

Now suppose one person (the agent) acts on another (the recipient). I shall refer to this situation as a *transaction*. In transactions, the agent may or may not apply to his recipient the same categorial rules that he applies to himself. That is, while the agent necessarily acts voluntarily and purposively, he may act toward his recipient in such a way that the latter does or does not himself participate in the transaction voluntarily and purposively. If the recipient's participation is not voluntary, this means that the agent has coerced him; if it is not purposive, this means that the agent has harmed him, in that the recipient's own purposes or aims have not been considered or have been frustrated by the agent's action. It is at this point that the formal aspect of rationality makes connection with the material aspect. If the agent does not apply to his recipient the same categorial rules that he applies to himself—that is, if the agent coerces or harms his recipient—then the agent contradicts himself. For since the recipient, as a potential or prospective agent, is similar to the agent in respect of the categorial rules of action, the agent would be in the position of saying that what is right for him—to participate voluntarily and purposively in their joint transaction—is not right for a relevantly similar person. And this is self-contradictory. Hence, on pain of self-contradiction, the agent logically must accept a principle which may be stated as follows: Apply to your recipient the same categorial rules of action that you apply to yourself. I shall call this the *Principle of Categorial Consistency (PCC)*, since it combines the formal consideration of consistency with the material consideration of the categorial rules of action. The *PCC* fulfills the requirement mentioned above, that the principle of moral rightness must be inherently rational or self-justifying.[8]

It will be noted that the *PCC* contains the same three components as emerged in my brief a posteriori discussion above of how we justify and criticize institutions. We may now put those components in terms of obligation. According to the *PCC*, men have three basic moral obligations: they must refrain from coercing other persons (freedom); they must refrain from harming other persons (welfare); and they must be impartial as between themselves and other persons when the latter's freedom and welfare are at stake (justice). Indeed, the *PCC* as a whole may be explicated in terms of justice, in that it requires an agent to respect his recipient's freedom and welfare as well as his own. As I have stated them, these obligations are, of course, quite gener-

---

[8] I have presented this argument in somewhat more detail in "Categorial Consistency in Ethics," *Philosophical Quarterly*, 17 (October 1967), 289 ff. For a discussion of the related question of whether the "criterion of relevant similarities" can be so individualized that its application is restricted to a single person, see my "The Non-trivializability of Universalizability," *Australasian Journal of Philosophy*, 47 (August 1969). In my forthcoming book, *Reason and Ethics*, I attempt a full-scale development of the whole argument.

al. The important point, however, is that while their specific application in various contexts must inevitably involve many complexities, this application can nevertheless be made, so that it can be ascertained whether or not the criteria set by the obligations are fulfilled. Because these obligations have been justified by reasons which are inherently rational, they are not only determinative of what men ought to do but are the basis of all other determinative obligations. Hence, if the tentative obligations deriving from institutions are to be determinative, they must meet the criteria set by the *PCC*.

The basis of these determinative moral obligations differs, in respects which are both theoretically and practically important, from that espoused in a pervasive tradition of moral and legal philosophy. This tradition upholds the following interrelated theses: that moral obligations must be "self-imposed";[9] that the only legitimate way to indicate the content of one's moral obligations is to say that one ought to do what one thinks right ("subjective obligation"), not what is right ("objective obligation");[10] that what one ought to do, including whether one ought to obey a law, must be determined by one's own conscience. These theses are often put into a context of "agent morality" rather than "act morality." The former is concerned primarily with the moral goodness of the agent, including the quality of his motivations and their relation to his character,

---

[9] See, e.g., P. H. Nowell-Smith, *Ethics* (Baltimore: Penguin Books, 1954), p. 210: "The feature which distinguishes moral obligations from all others is that they are self-imposed." This position goes back in modern times at least to Hobbes. See *Leviathan*, ch. 21, ed. M. Oakeshott (Oxford: Basil Blackwell, n.d.), p. 141: ". . . there being no obligation on any man, which ariseth not from some act of his own; for all men equally, are by nature free." The idea that obligations are "self-imposed" is highly ambiguous, it can mean at least three different things: (a) one has no moral obligations until one performs voluntary acts toward other persons; (b) whether one has moral obligations depends on one's voluntary agreements with or promises to other persons; (c) whether one has a moral obligation (including the content of the obligation) depends on whether one accepts it as an obligation, and not merely on what one says or does to other persons.

[10] See H. D. Thoreau, *Civil Disobedience*, in *Selected Writings on Nature and Liberty*, O. Cargill, ed., (Indianapolis: Bobbs-Merrill, 1952), p. 11: "The only obligation which I have a right to assume is to do at any time what I think right." On the distinction between "subjective" and "objective" obligation, see A. C. Ewing, *The Definition of Good* (New York: The Macmillian Co., 1947), pp. 118 ff., and K. Baier, *The Moral Point of View* (Ithaca, N.Y.: Cornell University Press, 1958), pp. 143 ff.

while act morality is concerned rather with the moral rightness of external acts themselves, including within "acts" the agent's intention, his knowledge of relevant circumstances, and his ability to control what he does in the light of his intention and knowledge.[11]

The *PCC* is directly concerned with act morality rather than with agent morality, although it can also be used to evaluate in part the agent's moral character. According to the *PCC*, an agent has basic moral obligations toward his recipient whether the agent agrees to have them or not, and they are obligations to do what is right as determined by the *PCC*. The appeal to conscience leaves unanswered the question whether there are any moral reasons or criteria for the guidance of conscience itself. If there are no such reasons, then there is an obvious danger of arbitrariness and anarchy. But if there are such reasons, then conscience is at most a secondary rather than a primary determinant of moral obligation, since conscience must itself conform to these reasons if it is to be morally right.

The two interrelated ideas of the self-imposition of moral obligations and guidance by one's own conscience are somewhat similar to the freedom criterion adduced above as a component of the *PCC*: that if transactions are to be morally right, then their recipients must participate in them voluntarily. The similarity arises especially when we think of institutions as imposing obligations; for the freedom criterion requires that those who are subject to such obligations accept them freely. Even in this case, however, there are some important differences. The freedom criterion of the *PCC* is advanced not as a definition of moral obligation but rather as a basic theorem about moral obligation, which must itself be proved. Moreover, the freedom criterion, of itself, sets prima facie rather than conclusive moral obligations; as a procedural criterion, it must be supplemented by the substantive criteria of welfare and justice. Hence, whereas exclusive reliance on conscience as the determinant of moral obligations

---

[11] For a good discussion of this distinction, see J. Laird, "Act Ethics and Agent Ethics," *Mind*, 55 (April 1946), 113-132. I have discussed the bearing of the tradition discussed in the text on the relation between legal and moral obligation, in "Some Misconceptions of the Relation between Law and Morality," *Proceedings of the Seventh Inter-American Congress of Philosophy* (Quebec : Les Presses de l'Université Laval, 1967), I, 208-222.

might be used (and has been used) to justify harmful and unjust acts and institutions, this is not the case with the freedom criterion. While the individual's conscience must be respected, then, because of its relation to his freedom and its importance to his feelings, it should not of itself determine the content of moral obligations.

Another aspect of the basic moral obligations must be briefly considered at this point. It may be objected that the welfare criterion as stated above, requiring merely that one refrain from harming other persons, is too negative, for one might fulfill it by sheer inaction or passivity, and this would make no positive contribution to welfare. The justice criterion, however, puts this point in proper perspective. Specifically, two replies must be made to the objection. First, to refrain from harming other persons requires action rather than inaction whenever one's voluntary or deliberate inaction is harmful to others. The "duty to rescue" is an obvious example of this, but there are also many other such cases in a mass society of interdependent persons.[12] Second, to put the welfare criterion in positive terms, as the obligation to do good or to advance the welfare or interests of other persons, would yield an unmanageable proliferation of obligations. The moral obligation to obey the law is sometimes upheld by such a criterion: law ought to be obeyed because it does great good. But this argument would similarly go to prove

---

[12] See G. A. Coe, "What Is Violence?" in M. Q. Sibley, ed., *The Quiet Battle* (New York: Doubleday, 1963), p. 48: "For mere non-intercourse, mere refusal to buy and sell, can produce hunger and death just as surely as an embargo by means of warships. . . . For certainly, given the present interdependence of men, we can weaken, distort, and destroy the bodies of our fellows by merely doing nothing." Cf. from a different perspective, the comments of A. Tunc, "The Volunteer and the Good Samaritan," in J. M. Ratcliffe, ed., *The Good Samaritan and the Law* (New York: Doubleday, 1966), pp. 45–46: "From a philosophical point of view, it does not appear possible to distinguish between the man who does something and the man who allows something to be done, when he can interfere. Such a distinction would disregard the liberty of man, his freedom of choice, his creative power, his 'engagement' in the world and among other men. A stone does not bear any liability if a murder is committed beside it; a man does. By his decision not to interfere or to intervene, he participates in the murder." In order to keep clear the distinction between the morally obligatory and moral athleticism or supererogation, this position would have to specify many factual matters about knowledge, ability, and consequences. Nevertheless, when properly interpreted, the position does indicate an important positive application of the welfare and justice criteria.

that men have a moral obligation to support garden clubs, madrigal-singing groups, and the like. If it were replied that the law does more good than any of these, this would subject the obligation to obey the law to a calculus which would jeopardize the stability often alleged as a chief argument for obeying the law. Some of the familiar problems of utilitarianism involved in this issue will be touched on below in connection with legal obligation.[13]

THE MORAL JUSTIFICATION OF INSTITUTIONS

Let us now consider how the *PCC*'s criteria of moral obligation are to be applied in ascertaining whether an institution's obligations are determinative of what men ought to do. To begin, we must note that while the *PCC*'s criteria refer directly to how an agent, a human individual, is to act toward his recipients, there is also a sense in which an institution is an agent. For it operates by imposing obligations on the persons who participate in it, so that the latter are in the position of recipients of the institution's operations. If this seems too metaphorical, however, the same point can be made in terms of human agents. For although many institutions are the results of organic growth rather than of human contrivance, each institution has persons who profit from it or who at least uphold it. Hence, they can be asked the questions set by the *PCC*'s criteria. It must also be noted that individuals and groups often act on other persons in accordance with the rules of institutions. Hence, we can ask whether these actions are in accord with the criteria set by the *PCC*. This is to ask whether the tentative obligations which derive tautologically from the constitutive rules of an institution are also determinative or moral obligations. The application of the *PCC* to test the moral justification of institutions, then, may be made from two different perspectives: from that of the institu-

---

[13] It is not always easy, of course, to distinguish among refraining from harm, preventing harm, and doing good. Formally, it may be said that all cases of preventing harm are cases of doing good, although not conversely. Also, when one is able to prevent harm to other persons and is aware of this, to refrain from harming them requires that one prevent that harm. Further qualifications are needed, however, especially concerning the cost aspects of "able."

tion as agent and from that of the persons who participate in the institution as agents. Let us consider each of these in turn.

From the first perspective, the following questions set by the *PCC* are addressed to an institution or to its upholders: Was the institution freely accepted by the persons subject to it? Would its absence be harmful to their interests or welfare? Does it respect the freedom and welfare of all equally? If these questions are answered in the affirmative, they establish that the institution's obligations are determinative, whereas if they are answered in the negative, then the institution's obligations remain only tentative. But what if one question is answered in the affirmative and another in the negative? With respect to the freedom and welfare criteria which enter, respectively, into the first two questions, one of their underlying assumptions, based on the categorial structure of human action as sketched above, is that men in acting voluntarily intend to fulfill their own purposes and hence to obtain something that seems good to them. In this broad sense, which is the one that figures in the *PCC,* there is no conflict between what men freely choose to do and their interests or welfare, except insofar as the latter may involve means to what men want rather than the wants themselves as ends. As for the justice criterion which enters into the third question above, this may well conflict with the freedom and welfare criteria, in that an institution may be unequal or discriminatory in its relation to persons' freedom and welfare. In such a case, however, it is important to ask whether the inequality is instrumental or final, that is, whether the inequality is used as a means toward increasing freedom and welfare to a point where they come closer to equality for all who are affected or whether, on the contrary, the inequality is accepted as an end of the institution. In the former case, the institution's obligations are determinative; in the latter case, they are not.

Let us now turn to the other perspective from which the *PCC* is to be applied to institutions, that of the individuals who act in accordance with the institutions. Whereas from the first perspective all the individuals who participate in an institution were regarded as recipients of the institution's operations, from this second perspective some of these participants are agents and others recipients, each fulfilling the role set for him by the institution's rules. In this perspective, the specific questions set by the *PCC* are addressed to the agents: Do they, in fulfilling their institutional obligations, coerce or harm other persons or favor the freedom and welfare of some persons at the expense of others? If the answer to any part of this complex question is affirmative, then the persons involved have no prima facie determinative or moral obligation to fulfill their institutional obligations. The significance of this prima facie qualification is related to the reason for distinguishing between the institutional and individual perspectives in asking the questions set by the *PCC*. For it is possible that institutions satisfy the requirements of the *PCC* while individuals who act in accordance with those institutions do not. For example, insofar as a teacher gives a failing grade to a college student, the teacher may be said to harm the student and to act on him against his will; but in so doing, the teacher is acting in accordance with institutional rules (for example, the rules of the college) which are themselves accepted by, and are beneficial to, the students as a whole insofar as they are involved in the functioning of the institution. Hence, the relation of the *PCC* to the acts of individuals and to institutional rules must be put as follows. The obligations which the *PCC* sets for the particular acts of individuals are prima facie rather than conclusive, in that any particular act must be in accord with the *PCC* unless the act is in accord with an institutional rule which is itself in accord with the *PCC*.

The above paragraphs provide, of course, only a very general sketch of the criteria involved in the moral justification of institutions. A fuller account would have to analyze in much greater detail both the criteria themselves and the complex ways in which they may or may not be satisfied by various institutions. Apart from the fact that I attempt such an analysis elsewhere (see note 8), I have tried at least to suggest the logical basis and the general features of the relevant criteria.

THE INSTITUTION OF LAW

Our next step must be to consider how these criteria for the moral justification of institutions are to be applied to law. To begin with, we must note that "law," in the sense in which it is restricted to municipal law, is used with three different kinds of reference. It is used to refer, first, to a general social institution ("law₁") common to all societies which have even minimal legal systems; second, to one or another specific legal system ("law₂") which may differ from other legal systems in its contents and procedures; and third, to particular legal rules ("law₃") which may exist within the same or different legal systems. (These rules are called particular only with respect to their being restricted parts of a legal system; they are general insofar as they deal with classes of acts and persons.) Thus, in the first reference we talk of law as against, for example, religion, as a kind of social institution and as a method of social regulation; in the second reference we talk of United States law, Soviet law, and the like; and in the third reference we talk of the United States income tax laws, and so forth.

When law is called an institution, the reference may be either to law₁ or to law₂. I shall call these, respectively, the general and the specific institutions of law. And when the question is asked, "Why should one obey the law?" the word "law" may be used with all three kinds of reference. As we shall see, serious confusion is generated by not distinguishing these.

In its most general form, law₁ is a second-order institution, in that it provides a certain kind of regulation of other institutions as well as of noninstitutionalized activities. This regulation is concerned with guaranteeing the peace and order or stability which are the necessary conditions—logically and not merely causally—of men's living together in an organized society. To secure these conditions, violence must be controlled and conflicts resolved by antecedently known general rules carrying coercive sanctions, and there must be recognized officials to make, interpret, and execute the rules.

As a general institution, law₁ is defined by constitutive rules which determine what is to count as a legal system in general and what men are required to do if they are to participate in such a system and in any society which is regulated by it. In a parallel way, law₂ as a specific institution is also defined by more restricted constitutive rules (sometimes called a "constitution") which determine the nature of the specific legal system and what men are required to do if they are to participate in that system and in the particular society which is regulated by it. In both cases, the requirements in question are men's legal obligations, that is, their obligations to obey, respectively, the rules of any legal system as such (law₁) and the rules of a specific legal system (law$_2$). According to our previous analysis, however, these legal obligations, insofar as they are institutional obligations entailed by the constitutive rules of a certain kind of institution, are only tentative, not determinative (let alone conclusive). For legal obligations to be determinative of what men ought to do, they, or the institution from which they derive, must be morally justified.

THE MORAL JUSTIFICATION
OF LEGAL OBLIGATION

From failure to distinguish kinds of obligation and kinds of law, it has sometimes been held that it is pointless to ask for a moral justification of legal obligation. Now it is true, but insufficient, to say that an institutional obligation to obey some law$_3$ in a particular society follows from membership in that society with its specific legal system, just as the obligation to obey the rules of some game follows from playing that game.[14] This is insufficient, for since one does not voluntarily undertake membership in a political society in the way in which one undertakes participation in a game, there still remains the question whether there is a rational justification for accepting that the society's legal system should determine what one is to do, either in general or in a particular case. This latter question requires something other than the reiteration of the institutional obligation to obey the law, for it asks about the moral justification of the institution itself or of some part of it. As such, the question may refer to the particular law$_3$ or to the whole legal system (and the society constituted by it); and it may even refer to the general institution of law$_1$. Let us consider each of these in turn.

The moral justification of the general institution of law$_1$ is

[14] Cf. T. D. Weldon, *The Vocabulary of Politics* (Baltimore: Penguin Books, 1953), p. 57: "Suppose however the objector goes on to say 'Even if it is the law, I don't see why I should obey it.' The only further comment possible is 'Well, this is Great Britain, isn't it?' The position is indeed exactly parallel to that of the cricketer who asks 'Why should I obey the umpire? What right has he to give me out?' One can answer only by expounding the rules of cricket, the position of the M.C.C., and so on. Beyond that there is nothing to be done except to say 'This is a game of cricket, isn't it?' " For similar positions, see J. R. Carnes, "Why Should I Obey the Law?," *Ethics*, 71 (October 1960), 14 ff., and T. McPherson, *Political Obligation* (London: Routledge and Kegan Paul, 1967), 59 ff.

suggested by the moral overtones of traditional expressions like the "rule of law" and "due process of law," as well as by repeated references to law_1 as a "minimum ethic,"[15] a "minimum limit of morality,"[16] having the "minimum content of natural law,"[17] and so forth. We may explicate these expressions in terms of the criteria of the *PCC*. With respect to justice, law_1 contains general rules which apply uniformly to all cases falling under them. With respect to welfare, human life would be difficult or impossible without law_1's stabilizing influence, including its regulation of violence and conflict. With respect to freedom, law_1 enables men to determine their conduct with intelligent foresight by its curbing of violence and by making publicly known ahead of time those areas of conduct to which coercive sanctions are attached.

To the extent to which law_1 contains these general features, there is a prima facie moral obligation to obey it. It must be noted that law_1 here occupies a different status from that which pertains to institutions generally. I said above that institutional obligations, as such, are only tentative, not determinative, because the mere fact of institutionalization (which I called the "formal" aspect of institutions) might be harmful as well as beneficial to the activities standardized by it. Now law_1 corresponds to the formal aspect of institutions insofar as it comprises simply what is common to all law. But the legalization provided by law_1 has a much stronger justification, especially in terms of the welfare criterion of the *PCC,* than the institutionalization provided by all institutions as such. One obvious reason for this is that law_1's regulation of violence and conflict is more indispensable to human life than are the kinds of stabilization given by institutions as such. In addition, however, law_1 is unique among institutions because of the other ways in which it is necessary to

---

[15] G. Jellinek's phrase; see R. Pound, *Law and Morals* (Chapel Hill, N.C.: University of North Carolina Press, 1926), p. 103.

[16] J. Dewey, in Dewey and J. H. Tufts, *Ethics* (1st ed., New York: Henry Holt, 1908), p. 467.

[17] Hart, *The Concept of Law*, pp. 189 ff. As I have argued elsewhere, even such a positivist as Hans Kelsen is unable to avoid attributing to law as such a basic moral content. See my essay "The Quest for Specificity in Jurisprudence," *Ethics,* 69 (April 1959), 172 ff., and Kelsen, *General Theory of Law and State,* trans. A. Wedberg (Cambridge, Mass.: Harvard University Press, 1945), pp. 22 ff., 54 ff., 69; also *What Is Justice?* (Berkeley and Los Angeles: University of California Press, 1957), pp. 238, 241, 248 ff.

the existence of an organized society, including its provisions for the making of particular laws₃ and its enforcement of legal "certainty" or "predictability." Hence, the moral obligation to obey law₁ attaches not only to those of its contents which prohibit *mala in se;* it attaches also to those which prohibit *mala quia prohibita* insofar as the latter contents, even though not independently objects of moral obligation, are generically necessary to stabilize an organized society.[18]

The moral obligation to obey law₁ is, nonetheless, only prima facie and not conclusive because of considerations deriving from the specific contents of laws. The general features of law₁ which justify obedience to it may be specified in immoral ways, and the moral obligations violated by these ways may override the general obligation to obey law₁.

It will have been noted that the freedom criterion met by law₁ as I stated it above diverges from my earlier statement of that criterion as applied to institutions. Whether persons subject to an institution have freely accepted it is not the same consideration as whether they are enabled to have a degree of freedom by the operation of the institution. The two considerations are, of course, related: they refer to men's effective free choice as figuring, respectively, in the cause and in the effect of institutions. Nevertheless, the issue of freedom in the former respect, that of free acceptance, is insistently raised by the fact that law₁, unlike other institutions, does not merely impose obligations but attaches coercive physical or economic sanctions to them. Hence, men are not free to disobey law₁ except at the price of punishment. It would be insufficient to try to meet this issue by saying that law is coercive only toward those who want to coerce others, for this would not account for many other coercive contents of law₁. There are even more obvious inadequacies in the answer of traditional consent theory that coercive law does not remove freedom because each individual has freely consented to obey the

---

[18] See in this connection the two ways in which, according to Thomas Aquinas, human laws can be derived from natural law: as deduced conclusions and as specifications, the latter being morally indifferent except insofar as they provide a particular, legally determined way of carrying out the general requirements of natural law (*Summa Theologica*, II, I, Question 95, Article 2).

law$_1$.[19] The most that can be said on this score is, perhaps, that for any legal system to exist there must be some degree of acquiescence in it by a large proportion of the persons subject to it.

Law$_1$, with its coercive sanctions, provides an important example of the distinction drawn earlier between the fulfillment of moral criteria by an institution itself as agent and by individuals who act in accordance with the institution. A judge who punishes a criminal in accordance with law harms him, yet the institution of criminal law itself fulfills the criterion of welfare.

Let us turn to specific legal systems (law$_2$). Every legal system shares the general features and hence the general justification of law$_1$, but adds its own specific features. These, however, can markedly affect the moral quality of the system. With respect to justice, the general rules of the system may be heavily discriminatory against certain groups. With respect to welfare, law$_2$ may stabilize a society to the point of stagnation and promote inefficiency in many other ways, and it may regulate violence by making it legally available to some groups at the expense of others. With respect to freedom, law$_2$ may be dictatorially imposed and may be severely repressive.

It is clear that such a legal system and the society constituted by it do not meet the moral criteria of the *PCC*. It is also clear that insofar as men act in accordance with such a system, their acts too do not meet the moral criteria. Do these points, then, settle conclusively the question of legal obligation, of whether men ought to obey such a legal system in those of its features which are morally wrong? In order to answer this question, we must also take into account the relation of disobedience to the criteria of welfare, freedom, and justice for all the persons affected. Suppose, for example, that one group's disobedience predictably leads to savage reprisals against other groups, or to revolutionary upheavals that disrupt the lives of many other persons. In such a case, the disobedient group might well stand accused of doing harm and injustice, especially if the other groups were themselves not willing to incur the risks involved.

---

[19] I have previously discussed the principle of consent in "Political Justice," in R. B. Brandt, ed., *Social Justice* (Englewood Cliffs, N.J.: Prentice-Hall, 1962), pp. 128 ff.

On the other hand, where persons and groups are able to ward off an immoral society's harms and injustices without such prohibitive costs, the criteria of welfare and justice make it their moral obligation to do so. To this extent, the persons involved have no moral obligation to obey the laws$_3$ of such a system.

POLITICAL OBLIGATION

It is in connection with questions of this sort that we must come to political obligation in the respect in which it is not the same as legal obligation. Political and legal obligation coincide insofar as the former is the obligation to obey the government or the legitimate political authority; for since this authority rests on law$_2$ and operates through laws$_3$, obedience to the authority is also obedience to law$_{2,3}$. Two plausible redefinitions of political obligation, however, remove this coincidence with legal obligation. One is where political obligation is viewed as referring specifically to the obligations of the governors or rulers of a state. While their regular, official obligation is to act in accordance with the law$_2$, a crisis might arise in which, in order to save the state, they might have to act outside the law.[20] A second, related redefinition of political obligation would refer to the "policy" obligations of all the citizens, rulers and ruled alike, in respect of making or influencing the contents of laws, as against obeying the laws already made. It is this policy sense of political obligation that becomes especially important when we confront the problems of immoral legal systems and the laws$_3$ deriving from them. But as we shall see, such political obligations of active citizenship are also incumbent on citizens of constitutional democracies.

In the general sense in which "policy" is here used, it emerges in the "political life" of individuals and groups who try to influence legislation and government in accord with their self-regarding or public-regarding objectives. Such political life is frequently institutionalized in many formal or informal ways, ranging from political parties and clubs to various other kinds of pressure groups. And, as with the other institutions discussed

---

[20] Cf. L. Legaz y Lacambra, "Political Obligation and Natural Law," *Natural Law Forum* 2 (1957), 119 ff.

above, these institutions have their constitutive rules and institutional obligations. One kind of political obligation in the policy sense, then, refers simply to these institutional obligations of political groups, that is, the requirements set by the constitutive rules of such groups for the persons who participate in them. For example, the political obligations of lobbyists for the NAM or the AFL-CIO derive from the roles assigned to them by the policies of the respective organizations. Insofar as these political obligations are institutional ones, however, they are only tentative, not determinative; whether they determine what the persons in question ought to do depends on whether the respective institutions and their purposes can meet the rational criteria of moral justification. Thus the basic question of political obligation, as also of legal obligation, is whether or not it satisfies the criteria which would make it a moral obligation. In this context, "moral" refers to the reasons or criteria which are brought to bear in evaluation or justification, while "legal" and "political" refer to the institutions or activities which are adjudged by the criteria. Hence, talk of legal or political obligations may consist in either prescriptive or descriptive obligation-statements, depending on whether or not the speaker is endorsing the acts, policies, or institutions in question. As I have argued above, the correct basis for endorsement is provided by the *PCC*.

LEGAL OBLIGATION IN
A CONSTITUTIONAL DEMOCRACY

The issues of political and legal obligation are sharpened when we consider law$_2$ in a constitutional democracy. Such a democracy has two main features relevant to its law$_2$. In its democratic aspect, the legislative officials are elected by universal suffrage, with each person having one vote and the majority vote being decisive; in its constitutional aspect, there are certain constitutionally prescribed restrictions on the contents of the laws$_3$. the civil liberties of speech, press, assembly, and so forth are guaranteed equally for all. These two features constitute what I have elsewhere called the "method of consent,"[21] for they

21 "Political Justice" (see note 19 above), pp. 137 ff.

provide that each sane, noncriminal adult has the legal right to participate freely in the process which determines who shall have political authority, including the authority to make the laws$_3$. The freedom to participate at this level is the closest that any legal system can attain to the freedom criterion of the *PCC*. For the freedom to participate in determining who shall have political authority must be distinguished from the freedom to determine whether there shall be any political authority or law$_1$ at all, as well as from the freedom to determine whether one shall oneself be subject to that authority. It is sometimes plausible to assume, however, that a person who uses the first of the three freedoms just listed has implicitly given an affirmative answer to the questions accompanying the two other freedoms, which figured centrally in the theory of the social contract.

In addition to this degree of fulfillment of the freedom criterion of the *PCC*, the legal system of a constitutional democracy also fulfills the criterion of political justice, for it gives each person an equal vote and equal rights and liberties for participating in the political process. It has also been a traditional claim of democratic theorists that the system progressively fulfills the criteria of both socioeconomic justice and welfare. For laws$_3$ which emerge through the method of consent will reflect the purposes or interests of those who participate in the method, and since all men have an equal right to participate, this will tend toward an equalization of welfare. The equal protection of the laws, in one interpretation of it, requires, or at least encourages, such equalization. From these considerations it follows that persons who live under the legal system of a constitutional democracy have a moral obligation to obey it.

The actual workings of the system, of course, often fall short of these moral criteria. Great inequalities of social and especially economic power make for drastic inequalities in the ability to participate effectively in the method of consent. Conflicts of actual or perceived interests, based on racial, economic, or ideological grounds, lead some groups to perceive others as enemies and hence to try to deny them important components of welfare and justice. There are also strong differences of opinion, partly based on ideological differences, about the causes of socially important phenomena. As a result of all these factors, the policies which become legalized are sometimes regarded as drastically immoral by sizable groups in the society.

The problem of legal obligation raised by these conflicts may be put in the form of a dilemma. If one obeys certain laws₃ of a constitutional democracy, then one does what is morally wrong; if one disobeys those laws₃, then one violates the law₂ of a constitutional democracy with its relations to freedom, justice, and welfare, and this too is morally wrong. Thus there are two opposed moral obligations, each ultimately based on the same moral criteria: the moral obligation to obey the laws₃ not merely because they are laws but because they conform to the law₂ of a constitutional democracy, and the moral obligation to disobey laws₃ which are harmful, unjust, or violative of the method of consent. To take a current example, many persons have held that there is a moral obligation to disobey the various laws₃ accompanying the Vietnam war, especially the draft laws, for the following reasons: (1) the war, with its use of napalm and other lethal weapons, subjects countless numbers of innocent persons to terrible suffering and death, and it does so needlessly, since the United States has no important interest at stake in Vietnam (*welfare criterion*); (2) the draft laws discriminate against those young men who cannot afford to go to college and also against those who seek exemption because of their objection to a particular war for nonreligious reasons, since the draft laws admit as valid ground for exemption only religiously based objections against all wars (*justice criterion*); (3) the war policy was imposed on the American people by deception and manipulation, and without giving the people or their elected representatives a chance to vote on the issue (*freedom criterion*).

CIVIL DISOBEDIENCE

How is this opposition of moral obligations to be resolved? One purported resolution is that of civil disobedience, and I wish to consider some of its claims and problems in the light of the concepts presented in this essay. According to the usual definition, civil disobedience consists in intentionally disobeying some law₃ on the ground that it, or a policy related to it, is morally wrong, the manner of disobedience being public, nonviolent, and accepting of the legally prescribed penalty for disobedience. It is to be noted that by this definition civil disobedience purports to resolve the dilemma presented above. For it claims both to disobey the morally wrong law$_3$ and at the same time to obey the law$_2$ of constitutional democracy; for in accepting, and not trying to evade, the legally prescribed penalty the civil disobedient shows that he wishes to accept the whole legal order as moral while rejecting one part of it as immoral.[22]

Now if such joint acceptance and rejection are to be rational or coherent, then two kinds of relation between law$_{1,2}$ and law$_3$ must be excluded. One relation is logical: the relation of the whole legal system to a particular law within the system cannot be a deductive one analogous to the relation between primitive axioms and the theorems they entail, for the denial of any of the theorems logically entails the denial of the axioms and hence of the whole system. The other excluded relation is causal: the existence of the legal system as a viable, effective institution cannot depend on the efficacy of the particular law, that is, on its being universally or generally obeyed. For if the relation were of this kind, then disobedience of the particular law would undermine, or would at least tend to undermine, the existence of the whole legal order. And if this were so, then it would not be rational or coherent to hold that one can both disobey a particular law and accept, let alone respect, the whole legal order.

The first possibility, that of a logical or deductive relation between the whole legal system and a particular law, may seem too far-fetched to merit serious consideration, especially in the light of critiques of the kind made by legal realists. Suppose, however, that we adopt a procedural rather than a substantive interpretation of such a logical relation. Our focus would then be not on the content of the particular law in relation to the content of the whole legal system or of its constitutional principles; rather, it would be on the methods which the system

---

22 See M. L. King, Jr., *Why We Can't Wait* (New York: New American Library, Signet Books, 1964), pp. 83-84: "I submit that an individual who breaks *a law* that conscience tells him is unjust, and who willingly accepts the penalty of imprisonment in order to arouse the conscience of the community over its injustice, is in reality expressing the highest respect for *law*" (my italics). See also M. K. Gandhi, *Non-Violent Resistance* (New York: Schocken Books, 1961), p. 60.

requires one to use if one is to be faithful to the system or to operate within it. Clearly, these methods cannot be extralegal ones. Hence, one cannot break a particular law and at the same time claim to be faithful to or respectful of the legal system as a whole. To put it generally, even if one accepts the legally prescribed penalty, one cannot consistently look to a whole legal system to provide one with a justification for disobeying any part of that system, whether the relation of part to whole be conceived substantively or procedurally.[23]

Two partial qualifications of this general point must be noted. First, the legal system as a whole must itself be consistent. For if a legal system *S* contains two inconsistent rules R*a* and R*b,* then one may appeal to R*a* to justify disobeying R*b*. Now in the American legal system there are at least two kinds of inconsistencies which give rise to actual or potential conflicts. One is within the federal Constitution itself, as when the First Amendment's guarantee of freedom of the press conflicts with the Sixth Amendment's guarantee of trial by an impartial jury of the district. The other conflict is when local or state laws are inconsistent with federal laws and ultimately with the Constitution, as was the case with Southern segregation laws. But this latter conflict involved an inconsistency between law_3 and law_2; hence, in such a case to violate a particular law while appealing to the whole legal system was a possibly rational procedure.

If such law-violation is to be called "civil disobedience," however, then a distinction must be drawn between two types, which

---

[23] A doctrine found in various ways in Blackstone, Bentham, and Holmes might be thought to support the position that by accepting the legally prescribed penalty one can violate a law_3 and still respect the law_2. This doctrine assimilates the law_2 to an economic system in that particular $laws_3$ are conceived as having as part of their contents the "prices" attached both for obeying and for disobeying them, punishments of one sort or another being the price of disobedience. This doctrine has the paradoxical result that a person who breaks some law_3 and accepts the penalty (whether willingly or unwillingly) is operating within "the law" just as much as the person who obeys the law. There is, however, a crucial difference in this respect between an economic and a legal system: the alternative of buying or not buying is not analogous to the alternative of obeying or not obeying, for the latter alternative, unlike the former, involves violating a norm based on moral criteria. Hence disobedience, unlike the economic concepts, connotes wrong and guilt. Consequently, the proponent of civil disobedience cannot use this doctrine to support his claim that violation of a law_3 is compatible with respect for law_2.

I shall call *absolute* and *relative*. Absolute civil disobedience consists in disobeying some law$_3$ simply on the ground that it, or a related policy, is morally wrong, without claiming in addition that this law$_3$ or policy is itself illegal or unconstitutional because it violates the law$_2$, that is, some constitutional principle of the whole legal system. Relative civil disobedience consists in disobeying some law$_3$ on the ground that it, or a related policy, is in violation of the law$_2$. Most of the famous cases of civil disobedience over racial issues in the early sixties were of this relative kind—the sit-ins, the freedom rides, the demonstrations for voting rights, and so forth. Hence, scholars have debated whether these cases have been true instances of civil disobedience at all, since they lacked the condition of intentionally disobeying a law; for the protagonists denied that what they were disobeying was legally valid. Whatever one's position on this partly verbal question, it must be noted that relative civil disobedience would not be an issue unless it were in important respects reducible to absolute civil disobedience. For the reason why disobedients objected to certain city or state laws$_3$ as being in violation of law$_2$ was that they regarded the latter as itself morally right, so that ordinances in violation of it were morally wrong. As was suggested above, moral norms are embedded in the constitutional system of American law$_2$ in the guise of concepts like due process, the general welfare, and the equal protection of the laws. Hence, to appeal to one's constitutional rights is at the same time to appeal to one's moral rights of justice, welfare, and freedom.

Even relative civil disobedience, however, still leaves unsettled the question of procedural consistency. Since the legal system itself provides intralegal means both for testing the legal validity of rules and for working to change them, it is not *logically* necessary to violate the rules for this purpose; indeed, it may still seem logically inconsistent to use the procedure of violating the law while claiming to respect it. At this point, however, we must note a second qualification of the general point made above. The inconsistency in question vanishes when not only are alleged laws$_3$ or legal procedures used for ends which are in palpable violation of the law$_2$ of the Constitution, but in addition the legal procedures made available to remove the violations are in fact ineffective because of the prejudice of the authorities and other realities affecting the distribution of power.[24] In such cases it may well be argued that the procedure of civil law violation shows respect for the Constitution by opposing the unconstitutional procedures.

This consideration of effectiveness, which is an empirical matter, brings us to the other, causal relation indicated above as having to obtain between law_2 and $laws_3$ if the claims of civil disobedience were to be coherent. The civil disobedients' violating of $laws_3$ cannot be such as to cause general disrespect for and violation of law_2. The ascertainment of causal relations in social phenomena is, of course, a highly complex affair. It has frequently been claimed that causal responsibility for the riots and other racial violence and lawlessness of the late 1960s rests in

[24] Cf. King, *Why We Can't Wait*, p. 70: "The injunction method has now become the leading instrument of the South to block the direct-action civil-rights drive and to prevent Negro citizens and their white allies from engaging in peaceable assembly, a right guaranteed by the First Amendment. You initiate a non-violent demonstration. The power structure secures an injunction against you. It can conceivably take two or three years before any disposition of the case is made. The Alabama courts are notorious for 'sitting on' cases of this nature. This has been a maliciously effective, pseudo-legal way of breaking the back of legitimate moral protest." For parallel examples of misuse and unequal distribution of political power in the North, see the five part series of articles by M. W. Newman, "Chicago's Voiceless Ghetto," *Chicago Daily News*, April 29–May 3, 1968. In the first article, Newman writes: "The West Side is a community without real power of any kind—except the power to destroy. The population is overwhelmingly Negro, but absentee white politicians have the power, the votes, the patronage. White businessmen hold the economic reins. . . . Challenging this political system of 'taxation without representation' is dangerous. 'It can get you killed,' said the Rev. Mr. Doss. 'They can hire a black man to do it.' He did not identify the 'they.' "

See, on the other hand, Abe Fortas, *Concerning Dissent and Civil Disobedience* (New York: New American Library, Signet Books, 1968), p. 19: "The events of the past few years in this nation dramatically illustrate the power of the ordinary citizen, armed with the great rights to speak, to organize, to demonstrate. It would be difficult to find many situations in history where so much has been accomplished by those who, in cold realism, were divorced from the conventional instruments of power. Negroes and the youth-generation . . . have caused great events to occur." Mr. Fortas here refers primarily to the advances in civil-rights legislation, and to a lesser extent to the agitation about the Vietnam war. Whether the "ordinary citizen" can obtain the power to effect by legal means corresponding changes in his economic and social conditions is the great question of constitutional democracy in the United States.

important part with the civil disobedience of the earlier 1960s.[25] To the extent to which this claim can be supported by empirical inquiry, it casts further doubt on the doctrine that civil disobedients can coherently violate laws$_3$ while respecting law^2. The conclusions suggested by these considerations are the following. Civil disobedience can never be completely excluded as a morally justified procedure, either in its absolute or its relative form. But a crucial question in ascertaining its justifiability in a constitutional democracy is whether legal methods are actually and effectively available to those who suffer injustices in society. This question is crucial because it asks whether the method of consent which is definitive of constitutional democracy is effective or merely formal. If it is merely formal for the persons who most need its aid, then the institutional legal obligations of constitutional democracy can hardly be made out to be determinative or moral obligations for such persons. Hence, a prime moral obligation of those who uphold the morally justified claims of the method of consent is to seek to make that method and its fruits available to those who are effectively excluded from it. To do this requires an acceptance of the political obligation of active, informed, reformist citizenship.[26]

---

[25] See the judicious discussion of this claim in F. A. Allen, "Civil Disobedience and the Legal Order," *University of Cincinnati Law Review*, 36 (Winter 1967), 29 ff. The commission appointed by President Johnson to investigate the riots, in listing the causes of "a climate that tends toward approval and encouragement of violence as a form of protest," included "some protest groups engaging in civil disobedience who turn their backs on nonviolence . . . and resort to violence. . . ." *Report of the National Advisory Commission on Civil Disorders* (New York: Bantam Books, 1968), pp. 10-11, 204–205. This statement, however, involves a redefinition of civil disobedience unless it is understood in the sense that groups which formerly engaged in civil disobedience (which by definition is nonviolent) subsequently resorted to violence.

[26] I have discussed some of these problems of civil disobedience more fully in "Civil Disobedience, Law and Morality," *The Monist*, 54 (July 1970).

5

OBLIGATION, IDEALS, AND ABILITY

RICHARD E. FLATHMAN

It has been a favorite project of students of politics to take the life out of their subject matter; to render static, uniform, and predictable something we all perceive to be diverse, dynamic, and maddening in complexity and changeability. The variegated character of politics results from the fact that man is a reasoning, deliberating, intention-forming, evaluation-making creature. True, these activities of man sometimes lead to agreement and even to uniform action. To the extent that they do so the possibility of identifying uniformities is created. But it is a fact that they often do not do so and, more important, it is a part of the logic of the concepts involved that we cannot determine or even predict that they will or will not do so in the ways in which we can determine and predict the consequences of the operation

Work on this article was supported by a grant from the American Philosophical Society.

of physical forces or even instincts, motives, and habits.[1] Thus in
order to carry out their project students of politics have sought
ways either to change man so as to minimize the importance of
these of his characteristics or (what might be the same enterprise
in a different guise) to change the understandings human beings
have of themselves by explaining these characteristics away, by
showing that they are superficial indicators of something deeper
and more orderly or even that they are purely fictitious. Political
philosophers have prescribed complex social and institutional
arrangements designed to alter the behavior if not the nature of
man, and more descriptively inclined investigators have deployed
industry and ingenuity in paring away differentia and showing
that man is in fact a simpler and more orderly phenomenon than
he has understood himself to be.

This tendency has been particularly marked in discussions of
political obligation. One of the major purposes of Plato's scheme
in the *Republic* is to condition and train the bulk of the
subjects of the republic to unthinking obedience. According to
Hobbes, men must reflect and choose (or so it is made to
appear) whether to agree to an obligation to obey, but once
having agreed further reflection and choice are strongly discouraged. In Bergson the argument is that in fact men do discharge
obligations in the manner that Plato contended they should
discharge them. More generally, the view is widely held that the
realm of obligation is the realm of the basic or fundamental, of
that on which everything else in politics is built and depends.
From this (correct) premise it is inferred that this realm at least
must be fixed and unchanging, that men must somehow be
gotten to act not only in a regular but in a predictable manner
in this realm, and that this is how they in fact act—or, perhaps
better, behave—in any moderately stable and successful polity.
Since deliberation, reflection, and evaluation and choice cannot
be relied upon to produce such behavior they should be discouraged and they will be found to be minimal in successful polities.

For the most part the project we have been discussing has been
a conspicuous failure. In practical councils the prescriptions of

[1] See especially Alasdair MacIntyre, "The Antecedents of Action" in B.
Williams and A. Montefiore, eds., *British Analytical Philosophy* (London:
Routledge and Kegan Paul, 1966). Recall also Hobbes' discussion of the
differences between men and ants and bees, *Leviathan*, ch. 17.

political philosophers have generally received the attention which, as prescriptions, they deserve. And as our language itself testifies, the reductionist accounts and theories of man advanced by political and other social scientists have hardly won the day outside the schools that have produced them. Men continue to think of themselves as rational, deliberative agents able to evaluate and choose and continue to frame and act upon intentions and purposes. A major purpose of this essay is to make a start toward showing that this understanding is no less appropriate or valuable in the area of political obligation than in any other realm of political life.

It has been widely thought that "*A* is under an obligation to do *X*" presupposes that *A* is able to do X. "*A* is under an obligation to live forever" is senseless; the purpose of saying it is to guide *A*'s conduct, but the "guidance" is such that *A* could not possibly act upon it. This point about "obligation" is summarized in the maxim " 'Obligation' implies 'ability.' "

Stated conceptually, a necessary condition of the use of "obligation" to guide conduct is that it be possible to use one or more of those concepts, e.g., "ability," "capacity," "capability," or any one of the lower-order concepts indicating specific capacities, to describe (in a positive way) the relationship between the obligor[2] (*A*) and the action alleged to be obligatory for him (*X*). A showing that the conditions necessary to the proper use of one or more of these concepts are not satisfied in a set of circumstances constitutes a showing that it is improper to say, in those circumstances, that *A* has an obligation to do X.[3]

[2] I am using "obligor" to refer to one who has an obligation. Compare "debtor," one who has a debt, "contractor," one who has made a contract.

[3] The statement in the text suggests that a complete analysis of " 'Obligation' implies 'ability' " would require analysis of "ability" and related concepts, as well as "obligation." We are faced here with a recurrent problem. We analyze the use of "obligation" by referring it to other concepts, the concepts that must be available if "obligation" is to be properly used. But if analysis is required to determine the proper use of "obligation," why is it not necessary in the case of the concepts to which we appeal in analyzing "obligation"? Are we not simply referring one unclear matter to another that is equally unclear?

Any concept can be used without analyzing it. (Cf. F. Waismann, *The Principles of Linguistic Philosophy* (London: Macmillan, 1965), p. 146. This is as true of "obligation" as it is of "ability." If it were not true we wouldn't

As with the more general and more common " 'Ought' implies 'can,' " " 'Obligation' implies 'ability' " might seem to be a truism in little need of analysis. But even truisms can be enlightening, and in fact "ought" does not always imply "can," "obligation" does not always imply "ability," and since obligations can be assigned and discharged only where it is appropriate to use the concept obligation, sorting out the circumstances under which the maxims hold true will tell us something about the conditions under which obligations can be assigned and discharged and about some of the problems that arise in connection with the practice of assigning and discharging them. It will also pinpoint some of the difficulties with Professor Ladd's argument that "political obligation" is at once an inapposite or even senseless notion and a morally objectionable one.[4] Our procedure will be to examine a major exception to " 'Ought' implies 'can,' " try to determine whether it holds for " 'Obligation' implies 'ability' " as well, and then pursue some of the political implications of our conceptual findings.

OBLIGATIONS AND IDEALS

A major exception to " 'Ought' implies 'can' " arises in discourse concerning ideals or aspirations. *A* might regard the life of St. Francis as an ideal to which to aspire and might

---

know where to begin in analyzing the concept. Thus in analyzing "obligation" in terms of "ability" we appeal to our preanalytic knowledge of the way "ability" is used in order to make explicit and refine our knowledge of the way "obligation" is used. If our interest was in "ability," we might reverse the procedure. This is of course not to say that examination of "ability" would be irrelevant to the study of obligation, only that a detailed examination is not essential. In particular, it is not essential that we enter into the vexed disputes concerning free-will and determinism to which study of "ability" could quickly lead us. Following Frankena, I will be using "able," "ability," and "can" in the sense of "I know how to do X and am (now) physically capable of doing it" or "I am actively (as opposed to latently) able to do X if I choose." See William Frankena, "Obligation and Ability," esp. pp. 148-49, Max Black, ed., *Philosophical Analysis* (Englewood Cliffs, N.J.: Prentice-Hall, 1963.)

[4] See John Ladd, "Legal and Moral Obligation," ch. 1, this volume. The comments herein on John Ladd were written on the basis of a version of that paper delivered at the meetings of the Society. They do not, therefore, take into account any alterations he may have made in preparing his manuscript for publication.

fervently exclaim "I ought to live as he did"; he might say this despite considerable experience that had taught him that such a life was beyond his capacities. In general, ideals set by the great religious teachers, and the religious teachings modeled upon them, often explicitly reject the idea that "ought" must imply "can." Typically these ideals hold the life and teaching of a religious leader to be the life model that ought to be imitated, but they recognize, or rather insist, that mere men are unable to do so completely. In some versions of the Christian teaching, for example, men ought to be Christlike (and they are held blameworthy, i.e., sinful, when they fail) but they cannot. Their inability to be so means that they would be lost or damned if it were not for divine love and the possibility of undeserved forgiveness and redemption. Rejection of " 'Ought' implies 'can' " is an essential part of the doctrine. (The exact interpretation placed upon this doctrine, of course, varies among the several Christian denominations. The position described here is most characteristic of Lutheranism.) It is true that men ought *to try* to be Christlike, that they have the capacity to try, and that they have the capacity to achieve limited successes. If these statements could not be made the teaching would be unattractive if not senseless. But to try and yet fail, or to try and succeed only in part, satisfies only the "ought" that says one ought to try. If this was the only "ought" involved, failure to succeed could not be accounted sin. On the other hand, if one ought to succeed, and if "ought" did imply can, the doctrine would imply that men could achieve salvation by their own efforts.[5]

This exception to " 'Ought' implies 'can' " is most clearly illustrated by but is not restricted to religious ideals. The inapplicability of the maxim is a characteristic of discourse about many kinds of ideals, and the reasons why this is the case provide

---

[5] Nor is it the case that religious ideals are concerned only with feelings, e.g., love and gratitude, that are peculiarly outside the control of the individual who experiences them. The Christian ought to act as Christ acted (or would act), not just have the feelings that Christ had (or would have).

Of course a man who thinks that "ought" *must* imply "can" might argue that these uses are somehow improper. Although he does not enter into the general questions raised by this view, Frankena has disposed of it to our satisfaction: "For we can seriously defend [uses of "ought" that don't imply "can"] just as we can seriously defend the use of "dear" in "She is very dear to his heart," if we do not *assume* that "dear" always implies "expensive." *Ibid.*, p. 151.

an enlightening contrast with discourse in which "obligation" is used. I will mention two such reasons and then draw comparisons with "obligation." First, an ideal is ordinarily something that we strive toward, something intended to inspire us to improve our present level of performance. Once an ideal has been realized it no longer serves this purpose and a new ideal is needed. Thus ideals are either set so high as to be unattainable, as in the case of "Imitate the life of Christ," or revised upward periodically so as to stay ahead of actual achievement. Second, ideals typically have a loosely specified and even open-ended character. The Christian "Imitate the life of Christ," and the Greek "Realize the highest human potential" illustrate the point. Each directs attention to a model of life that has many facets, that can be approached by many courses of action, and that develops and enlarges for the individual as he pursues it and reflects upon it. The individual is to contemplate the model, seek to become imbued with its spirit, and make choices that seem likely to bring him more closely in accord with it. The choices will not only be affected by the circumstances in which they are made but by the facet of the ideal relevant to and grasped by the actor in question.[6]

"Obligation" is one of the most forceful of our conduct-guiding words. To say that X is obligatory is to say that it "must be performed," that A is "bound" to do X (OED). As several commentators have noted, etymologically the concept traces to "ligare" which meant "to bind," perhaps physically. The suggestion of physical constraint is analogical but not inappropriate to the strong connotations that the word carries.[7] Thus to use "obligation" as regards achieving ideals would be to suggest that men must, or are bound, to achieve them. That it would be good

---

[6] In the second respect, though not in the first, ideals differ from goals. The goal of a fund-raising drive is usually set higher than the amount raised in previous drives, thus spurring the fund-raisers and the contributors to greater efforts. But the goal will be specified quite exactly so that everyone will know when the drive has been successful. An ideal fund-raising drive, on the other hand, would probably exceed its goal—by an amount not specified in advance—and would have other virtues as well, perhaps harmonious relationships among the fund-raisers and between the latter and the larger community.

[7] Cf. David Gauthier, *Practical Reasoning* (London: Oxford University Press, 1963), ch. XII.

or commendable or meritorious to achieve an ideal is analytic, but it would be inappropriate to say that there is an obligation to do so.

The same conclusion is suggested by the loosely specified and open-ended character of ideals. There is no single formula or set of rules that will tell a man how to achieve the Christian ideal or how to fulfill his highest potential as a human being. Some choices and actions promise more in this respect than others, and hence there are good choices and actions and even best choices and actions in a set of circumstances. But when we say that an action is obligatory we are saying that it is the one action that the man must do, that to do any other action would be to fail to perform the obligation. Notice that we often use the verb "discharge" with "obligation": we discharge our obligations. To be able to say that a man has or has not discharged an obligation requires a closely specified understanding of what it is that is obligatory, an understanding that allows us to distinguish performance of the obligation from other actions and that allows us to identify a terminal point at which the obligation has been discharged. Thus "The Christian is obligated to imitate the life of Christ" is odd because it is too indefinite and open-ended for obligation. By contrast, "It is your obligation to register with the selective service system" and "Having promised to meet X at 5:00 P.M. you are under an obligation to do so" are appropriate. We know what must be done and we know when the obligation has been discharged (or not).[8]

These differences between the use of "obligation" and the uses of "ought" in discourse about ideals embody a number of the differences between two segments of morality, segments that some moral philosophers have regarded as so different as to constitute distinct types of morality. The exception to " 'Ought' implies 'can' " that we have been discussing typically occurs within "moralities of aspiration," in moralities or segments of morality

---

[8] Another feature of the use of "obligation" that I will not have space to discuss is relevant here. Use of "obligatory" ordinarily implies that failure to do the action will be blamed and perhaps punished, but performance of the act will not be praised. To assign blame, and especially to punish, requires clear specification, usually in advance, of what constitutes acceptable and unacceptable conduct—again a condition not usually satisfied by ideals of discourse concerning ideals. But it is almost always appropriate to praise people for acting in a manner that brings them closer to an ideal.

that aim to elevate human beings and societies above their
present level, to spur them to achievements over and above what
they think they can achieve and over and above mere survival or
even mere satisfaction of their needs and desires as presently
conceived. It is a morality that urges men to press beyond a
satisfactory life to a life of excellence, to aspire to the achievements of saints and heroes.

There have been men for whom a morality of aspiration
constituted a sufficient guide to behavior; they genuinely sought
to make their every action accord with or bring them closer to a
very high ideal and they were prepared to sacrifice more immediate satisfaction to the ideal. There have even been societies and
groups of men within societies that sought to base all relations on
a morality of aspiration. Such men or such societies would have
no occasion to employ the concept of obligation as it is now used
in English.

For most men and most societies, however, the morality of
aspiration is built upon a morality which, if effective, contributes
to making human life tolerable, to making it possible for men to
live together in reasonable peace and order and to satisfy the
material needs and desires common among them. The requirements of this second kind or aspect of morality are typically
embodied in rules or laws that apply to all or most of the
members of the society. These rules or laws bind the members to
specified types of conduct and failure to conform to the rules
usually meets with some form of sanctions.[9]

This second kind of morality is the usual home of the concept
"obligation," and the requisites of such a morality are among the
requisites of the use of the concept to guide conduct. One of
these requisites would seem to be the existence and identification
of commonality or common denominators among all or most of

[9] Thus this second kind of morality has often been labeled "law" or
"rule-governed" morality and "social morality." On the distinction between
the two kinds of morality see for example: H. L. A. Hart, *The Concept of
Law* (London: Oxford University Press, 1961); Lon Fuller, *The Morality of
Law* (New Haven: Yale University Press, 1964); Henri Bergson, *The Two
Sources of Morality and Religion* (Garden City, N.Y.: Doubleday, n.d.); Lord
Lindsay, *The Two Moralities* (London: Eyre and Spottiswoode, 1948); J. O.
Urmson, "Saints and Heroes," in A. I. Melden, ed., *Essays in Moral
Philosophy* (Seattle: University of Washington Press, 1958); G. E. M.
Anscombe, "Modern Moral Philosophy," *Philosophy*, XXXIII (January
1958).

the members of the society. Some commonality of interest and/or need is necessary if the judgment that a type of conduct should be required of all members is to be widely accepted. More important here, for a type of conduct to be obligatory for all the members of a society, the member must share the capacities necessary to discharge the obligation.[10] Thus it would seem that a morality of obligation is built upon and emphasizes characteristics common to groups of men, minimizes individual differences and idiosyncracies. It would also seem that it discourages, or at least minimizes the importance of individual reflection and choice; in the realm of obligation proper conduct is determined for the individual by rules that the individual does not make, and the individual's task is simply to conform to them. These two implications have been accepted with alacrity by numerous moral and political philosophers from Plato to Bergson. Whether or to what extent they are validly implied by or a part of the ideals-obligation distinction will be a concern in the remainder of this essay.

POLITICAL OBLIGATION AND THE OBLIGATION TO KEEP PROMISES

The degree of commonality required, to begin with, varies according to the extent to which the obligations assigned are in fact the same for all members of the society. Among the most important sources of obligations in Western societies are practices such as promising and contracting. As Hume and others have argued there can be an obligation to keep promises only because there is a general rule in society that promises and contracts generate obligations.[11] This general rule presupposes that the members of society are able to understand and act

[10] Assigning obligations has been regarded as a way to *create* a common denominator among the members of a society, as a way to weld a diversity of men into a unity sufficient to make political life possible. At the very least, however, this practice presupposes commonality of latent or potential capacity sufficient to make it possible for men to accept and discharge the assigned obligations. In this respect, at least, the practice of assigning and discharging obligations is grounded in and limited by what is common to men as men or at least common to the members of a society qua members of the society.

[11] See David Hume, *Treatise of Human Nature*, Book III, Part II, Section V. See also H. L. A. Hart, *Concept of Law, op. cit.*, pp. 42–43; John Searle, "How to Derive 'Ought' from 'Is,' " *Philosophical Review*, Vol. 73, pp. 43 ff.

according to the rules and procedures that constitute promising, including the rule that one ought not to make promises that are beyond his capacity to keep, and to this degree it presupposes commonality. (Those who are assumed not to have the requisite capacities, for example young children and the legally insane, are excluded from the practice.) But the procedures constituting the practice place only very general limits on what, substantively speaking, one can promise or contract to do, and there are few if any actions that members are obligated to promise or contract to do. Thus the capacity required is as diverse as the substance of the promises or contracts actually made. Put another way, individual reflection and choice about action retains an important place in promising.

Some commentators have treated promising as paradigmatic of all obligation-generating practices and have argued that we only use "obligation" in situations that resemble promising contexts, at least in that the obligor must undertake the obligation and that the content or substance of the obligation will be determined by and hence will vary with the content of the agreement, promise, or undertaking.[12] It seems undeniable, however, that "obligation" is also used in situations that not only lack this feature but in fact involve assigning substantively identical obligations to a great many people who have never agreed to or undertaken the particular obligations in any meaningful sense. I see no oddity or infelicity in the statement "Christians may . . . choose to serve the cause of racial justice by disobeying a law that clearly violates their obligations as Christians;"[13] nor, to take the more immediately relevant case, in the statement "Citizens of the United States have an obligation to submit an income tax return each year." Indeed it has been widely thought that one of the distinctive characteristics of the modern nation-state is that it seeks to assign a substantial number of identical obligations to all of its citizens, obligations that many of the citizens would not undertake if left to their own devices. Whereas in

---

[12] See for example Gauthier, *Practical Reasoning, op. cit.*, ch. 12, and Alexander Sesonske, *Value and Obligation* (New York: Oxford University Press, 1964). But see also, Richard Brandt, "The Concepts of Obligation and Duty," *Mind*, 73 (1964).

[13] "Race Relations," statement adopted by the Biennial Convention of the Lutheran Church in America, 1964.

feudal societies such political obligations as there were had been defined through personal relationships of a contractual or quasi-contractual type and were adapted to local and individual conditions, in the postfeudal Western state there are obligations that are common to all members. This feature of the modern state has been thought to be one of the main sources of its strength. Common obligations bind all of the members of society together in a unity that feudal societies were unable to achieve, and thus make the massed power of the members of the state available for collective action.[14]

These points of difference between obligations undertaken by promising and political obligations, readily accepted by many political leaders as well as philosophers, have prompted others to argue that the notion of a political obligation, especially an obligation to obey the law, is not a cogent notion, that it involves an inappropriate use of "obligation."[15] They concede, by the very act of criticizing the notion of political obligation, that it has had use in the language that they have been able to understand, but they argue that it distorts the logic of the "paradigm" or "strict" (Ladd) uses of the concept and hence produces muddles. They also assert that it has implications that are objectionable on moral grounds, namely rendering individual choice irrelevant. Granting for the moment that promising contexts provide the paradigm use of "obligation," the conclusion that

[14] Note that this generalization assumes that there are concepts (concepts, not words) in French, German, Dutch, and so on, that are comparable in the relevant respects to the English "obligation." This has to be the case if we are to say that the practice of ascribing identical obligations to all members is a feature of the "modern Western nation-state." To the extent that it is the case, we are justified in generalizing from our findings concerning "obligation" and obligation in English and English-speaking societies to other modern Western nation-states. We are of course equally justified in generalizing to any other society that has a concept relevantly similar to the English "obligation." I have not made the investigations of French, German, and so on, to say nothing of non-Western languages, that would be required to verify the generalizations, (nor seen the results of such investigations by others) and hence, strictly speaking, I must regard the generalization as an assumption. But I do have some familiarity with the history, politics, and literature of modern Western civilization and with a tradition of discourse and reflection produced by men who have lived in and spoken the languages of that civilization, a tradition in which the generalization in question is commonly encountered. Hence I feel justified in regarding the assumption as more than an unsupported hunch or guess.

[15] See esp. Ladd, "Legal and Moral Obligation," ch. 1, this volume.

"political obligation" is inapposite or even without sense seems to me to be unwarranted. First, it ignores important similarities between "There is an obligation to obey the law," and "There is an obligation to keep promises," some of which I will be discussing momentarily. More generally the argument seems to presume that there is (and must be?) one and only one set of conventions governing all uses of "obligation." It is true that there must be a set of conventions governing the use of a concept, and it is true that if there are differing conventions governing different uses, e.g., as regards promising and as regards obeying the law, the *concept* differs from use to use. But it would hardly follow that one of the uses is appropriate and the others not. Finally, the argument that "political obligation" is both inapposite or even senseless and morally objectionable is somewhat hard to follow. If the use is without sense it can have no implications, morally objectionable or otherwise.

Rather than dismissing "political obligation," then, we will do better to see whether its characteristics shed light on political practice. We will begin with the differences between "obligation" in political contexts and "obligation" in promising contexts, and then turn to the (more instructive) area of similarity between the two. Obligations undertaken by promising are usually unique to the obligor, and owed to an obligee who will be inconvenienced or injured if the obligation is not discharged and who can remind the obligor of his obligation if he seems disinclined to discharge it. If I promise to drive you to the airport at 12:00 I know quite concretely the consequences of my failure to do so. By contrast, political obligations such as paying taxes are common to millions of men and are not ordinarily thought of as owed to determinate obligees (certain political philosophers to the contrary notwithstanding). The fact that my obligation to pay taxes is shared with millions of others creates a standing temptation to parasitical behavior, a temptation to think that my failure to discharge the obligation will not have serious consequences because many others will discharge an identical obligation. And even if I am aware that there will be ill consequences, my failure will rarely injure particular individuals in a direct or obvious way, and it is unlikely that I will have a personal relationship with the persons injured or with the officials whose job it is to see that I discharge my obligations. Thus political obligations, at least in large and impersonal modern states, lack sources of support that are an important part of promising. It is no doubt in part for this reason that legally imposed sanctions have been thought to be essential to the practice of political obligation.

The second point relates more directly to the theme of obligation and ability. The members of a legislature can hardly know the capacities (to say nothing of the inclinations) of the millions to whom they assign an obligation to register with the selective service system in the way that the promisor knows his own capacities. Thus there is a constant danger that obligations will be assigned which the obligors will be unable to discharge and a constant difficulty in working out classifications and exceptions on the basis of inadequate information. In addition, whereas the practice of promising is expected to produce a diversity of obligations adapted to individual capacity and circumstances, we look to the practice of political obligation to unify the society by establishing common obligations for all members. Thus political obligations meet the " 'Obligation' implies 'ability' " requirement and best serve a unifying function if they are adapted to a common denominator among the capacities of the citizenry. If this common denominator is very low in a particular respect, the society will be held down to that level insofar as it relies on obligation rules to guide the conduct of the populace. Thus a society that contains a large percentage of illiterate people will experience difficulties in assigning a general obligation to comply with complex regulations, to submit complicated forms, or perhaps even to vote. In some cases special arrangements can be made to overcome the disability, for example voting by colored cards or providing assistance in filling out forms. Such arrangements call attention to differences among the populace in what some might regard as an invidious manner, thereby having a divisive effect. In cases such as military service that require a certain minimum of physical capacity and where existing disabilities are irremediable for parts of the population, no universal obligation of a substantively identical sort can be assigned. If service is nevertheless made obligatory for those with the requisite capacities, as opposed for example to relying upon a system of voluntary service, inequalities result that have in fact been divisive and that have generated disinclination to discharge obligations.

Thus the differences between the use of "obligation" in political contexts and in promising contexts are a source of insight concerning the practice of political obligation and should not be treated as a ground for dismissing "political obligation" as an inapposite if not senseless notion. Of course this conclusion can be taken as support for the view that the notion, or rather the practice to which the notion is tied, is morally objectionable.

We turn now to the similarities between "political obligation" and "obligation" in promising contexts. We have already noted that the obligation to keep particular promises depends upon the general rule that there is an obligation to keep promises. A similar rule; namely, "There is an obligation to obey the law," lies behind the obligation to obey all particular (obligation-generating) laws and constitutes the most important similarity between the uses of "obligation" in the two contexts (a similarity that Ladd never mentions). We will approach the basis and significance of this general rule by noticing a respect in which our account of the differences between promising and political obligation must be qualified.

Mention of selective service reminds us that modern states have by no means restricted themselves to assigning universal obligations, obligations that hold for all or nearly all members of the society. Through the familiar device of legislative classification, differing obligations are assigned to people with differing capacities. "Common denominator" often means "common denominator in class A," not in the entire populace. Thus in the United States most of the provisions of the Selective Service Act apply to males between eighteen and thirty-six years of age.[16] This procedure expands the versatility of obligation as an instrument of social control and direction and it has been of the utmost importance in allowing government to deal directly and yet widely with the citizenry. It also reduces one dimension of the

---

[16] All laws apply to all residents in the society in at least the following respects: they are promulgated by an authority common to all; no one is legally permitted to interfere with their operation; and all residents can be required to support them by paying taxes and in other ways that are adapted to the varying capacities of those from whom support is demanded.

impersonality of political obligation. The citizen shares his obligation with many others in the society, but he does not share it with all others and he is encouraged to think that he is a part of a distinct group with special capacities.

As important and valuable as the use of classification undoubtedly is, it is also the source of strains in the practice of political obligation. To understand these we must draw the elementary but important distinction just mentioned, a distinction masked by the notion that citizens have an obligation to obey the law. Most of the obligations we would call political are defined by law. The citizen or subject has an obligation to do those actions required by law and to avoid those actions prohibited by law.[17] But while statutes often state that X must be done, they rarely if ever state that there is an obligation to do X. Nor do legislatures enact laws stating that citizens or subjects are obligated to obey the law. Whence, then, the idea of an obligation to obey laws? If the man in the street commands me to stop at a red light or not to carry a pistol concealed in my pocket I will not think that I am under an obligation to obey his "command." I may think his advice good and decide to act upon it, but I will rarely if ever think I am under an obligation to do so. Why then are the "must" and "must not" of a statute treated as the source of an obligation?

Conceptually speaking, a large part of the answer to this question is bound up with the fact that laws are authoritative commands whereas imperatives issued by the man in the street are not. When we can say that a command is authoritative we have thereby said that there is a (prima facie) obligation to obey it.[18] Thus to answer our question completely we would have to examine the use of "authority" and "authoritative." We will note only that to say that a particular command is authoritative, to say it is a law in the relevant sense of "law," presupposes a system or structure of authority. There is no sense to the notion of an authoritative command in isolation from an authority. Now if

---

[17] It is by no means the case that all laws either require or prohibit behavior. Thus it is not the case that all laws ascribe obligations. On this point see H. L. A. Hart, *Concept of Law, op. cit.*, chs. 3, 5, and *passim*.

[18] On the relation between "obligation" and "authority" see especially Hanna Pitkin, "Obligation and Consent" II, *American Political Science Review*, LX:1 (March 1966).

there is a (prima facie) obligation to obey authoritative commands, it follows that behind the particular statement or rule
(A) "Citizens of the United States have an obligation to submit
an income tax return," there lies the general rule (B) "Citizens
of the United States have an obligation to obey the authoritative
commands, of which laws are one species, of their government."[19]
When we state A we contextually imply B. In the same way,
when we say "You promised to do X and therefore you have an
obligation to do it," we contextually imply "To make a promise
is to undertake a (prima facie) obligation" or "There is a
(prima facie) obligation to keep promises."

POLITICAL OBLIGATION, INDIVIDUAL
REFLECTION, AND THE CONTAGIOUS
EFFECTS OF DISOBEDIENCE

It is of course impossible to obey or disobey a particular
rule—e.g., "Stop at red lights," "Do not transport women in
interstate commerce for immoral purposes"—without violating
the general rule as well (and the converse). But the standing of
and justification for the general rule is very different from the
standing of and justification for any particular rule, and it is
quite possible to act in the manner required by both while
accepting the justification for only one. Thoreau might have
refrained from carrying concealed weapons because he believed
it a good rule of conduct and despite being unconvinced by the
argument for the general rule. Abraham Lincoln might have
been entirely unconvinced by the arguments for not carrying
concealed weapons and yet have obeyed the rule because it was a
legal rule which he could not disobey without disobeying the
general rule.[20]

Even Lincoln's argument concerning the importance of legal
rules leaves open the question of whether there should be a legal
rule on this point or that and whether it should be this rule or

[19] I am assuming that we can use "government" and "authorities"
interchangeably in the present context.

[20] For Lincoln's view see especially "Address to the Young Men's Lyceum
of Springfield." This remarkable speech is available in T. Harry Williams, ed.,
Abraham Lincoln, Selected Speeches, Messages, and Letters (New York:
Rinehart, 1957).

that. Thus one cannot infer from the argument for the general rule the importance of any particular rule as such. But it is more plausible to infer from the argument for the importance of the general rule the importance of *obeying* particular rules. This is the use to which the argument for the general rule is most often put. The man who objects to a particular rule and is inclined to disobey it is told that he must not do so because, even if his objections are sound, to disobey the particular rule is necessarily to disobey the general rule, and disobedience to the latter threatens the system of authority and the legal rules promulgated through that system. In large, diverse political societies that promulgate many laws, some of which almost inevitably affect some members of society adversely, the general rule has been thought to be of great importance. If the argument for obedience rested entirely on the argument for each particular rule, there would be a higher incidence of disobedience and a larger number of cases in which disobedience would be justified than is now the case.

Reliance upon the argument for the general rule, however, has some disadvantages that have not been given sufficient attention. These are perhaps most obvious in the case of unstable regimes, regimes that have not won the loyalty or firm support of their members. Emphasizing the general rule has the effect of making the question of obedience to a particular rule a question of supporting or undermining the regime itself. If a group of men objected to a particular rule, and if they had no great respect for or attachment to the regime, emphasizing the general rule might raise the question most dangerous for the regime. In such a regime, the greater the importance attached to the particular rule, the greater the danger of relying upon the argument for the general rule to win obedience to the particular rule.

In a well-established, stable regime enjoying strong support from its members, reliance upon the general rule is not likely to create the problem just mentioned. In appealing to the general rule the regime can appeal to loyalty to the regime and to the whole array of benefits and advantages generated by the system of authority and law. When *A* evidences disinclination to obey a particular rule he can be reminded of the benefits he has received and, more important, can expect to continue to receive if the regime persists, and he can be led to weigh those benefits and

advantages against the disadvantages he expects from the particular rule he finds objectionable. At the same time, other members of the society will be reminded of the benefits generated by
the regime and may be moved to express disapproval of A's
disobedience or contemplated disobedience.

The considerations just summarized form the nucleus of a
standard argument for obedience to laws the individual finds
objectionable. This argument has been widely accepted not only
by political philosophers and leaders but by large parts of the
citizenry of many states. But does the argument provide a cogent
prima facie case for obedience to particular rules? Granting that
I cannot disobey particular rule X without disobeying the general rule as it applies to X (which is the indisputable logical point
at the core of the standard argument), why should I expect that
my disobeying X will influence others to do so or will influence
myself or others to lose respect for the general rule or the
regime? The argument that I should not disobey X because
doing so will lead to disobedience to X or Y or Z obviously
involves an extension of the logical point just mentioned. Most
of the attempts to defend this extension have made use of some
version of the assertion that disobedience is contagious. A difficulty common to many of these attempts is that they treat
disobedience as a single thing which either is or is not contagious. Some kinds of disobedience are contagious and some are
not, and those that are contagious are contagious under some
circumstances and not under others. The conceptual points that
we discussed above suggest some distinctions among types of cases
in which men may be inclined to disobey particular rules, distinctions that may shed some light on the question of when and
why disobedience is likely to be contagious in stable regimes.

Insofar as particular legal rules are widely agreed to be good
rules and addressed to matters thought to be of importance to
society, the relationship between particular rules and the general
rule is not a source of difficulty. The law against homicide, for
example, serves one of the most fundamental objectives of virtually all societies and when the law is broken society has, to that
degree, failed to achieve one of its basic objectives. Breaking the
law can be condemned without showing that one homicide will
lead to another or that breaking the law against homicide will
lead to violations of other laws. One should respect and obey this

law because doing so contributes to the achievement of the basic objectives of society. In conceptual terms, one of the most important conditions requisite to the use of the strong language of "obligation" is satisfied.

In short, legal rules approved and widely thought to be important can be defended against the attacks of the occasional disobedient without relying upon the case for the general rule in isolation from the case for the particular rule in question. The general rule remains logically essential because without it (or some substitute for it) particular rules would not generate obligations, but there may be little need to appeal to it in order to persuade most men to obey the particular rule or to justify compelling obedience or punishing disobedience on the part of the occasional disobedient. If the case for the general rule is used for the latter purpose, it can be argued that it (the rule) should be respected because it provides ancillary support for particular rules extremely important to society.

In a stable regime these points hold even for laws addressed to what are agreed to be important matters but to which some members have strong and principled objections. The sense of importance of the matter covered by the law increases the likelihood that men will be concerned about it and that those who support the law will consider it worthwhile to try to meet the objections to it and in other ways to try to discourage disobedience. Since the matter is both important and controversial, a case can be made that it is essential that there be a law, even an unsatisfactory law, regularizing behavior concerning it. If there was no law, or if the law was widely disobeyed, the members of society would be acting at cross purposes and conflicts and inequities might result. Thus once again the argument for obedience need not depend on a showing that disobeying a particular law will influence men to disobey other laws as well. Disobedience to this law is itself productive of undesirable consequences. The availability of the latter arguments (and corresponding social pressures) constitutes a significant bar to a contagion effect and thus renders the argument from contagion not so much false as irrelevant.

The second type of case involves the use of law to require or prohibit types of conduct not thought to be of great import or thought to be important only by small segments of the populace.

As the conception of the function of the state has enlarged, the statute books have been swollen by measures that may be well drafted and useful, but are hardly essential to an ordered society or to the achievement of the basic objectives of society. Moreover, much of this legislation is directed to problems special to limited segments of society. The segments of the populace directly affected by it may think it important, but large parts of the population may not even be aware of it and may not support it.

Noticing these facts, H. L. A. Hart has argued that one of the differences between moral and legal obligations is that rules defining moral obligations "are regarded as . . . of great importance to maintain," while "importance is not essential to the status of all legal rules."[21] But if a law is not important to maintain, why should I obey it? And why should others who observe my disobedience disapprove of it? More urgently perhaps, if a law is unimportant what is the justification for punishing my failure to obey it?[22] Perhaps even comparatively unim-

---

[21] H. L. A. Hart, *Concept of Law, op. cit.,* pp. 170, 171. Hart recognizes that many legal rules are thought extremely important to maintain. In addition, however, we should note certain complexities and qualifications that Hart does not discuss. Hart's argument applies most clearly to the case of laws that have fallen into desuetude, laws that remain on the statute books only because the legislature has never had occasion to repeal them. Such laws are certainly not thought to be important. Other laws, for example parking regulations, are a general matter not thought very important—as indicated by the fact that while violations are penalized they do not prompt other forms of disapproval. But in some circumstances, for example where there is very heavy use of available parking space, the rules are taken seriously and violations are strongly disapproved. Again, the man who persistently violates parking regulations, who incurs many parking tickets each year, might meet with expressions of disapproval that would be unusual and even thought inappropriate in the case of the person who receives an occasional ticket. In the first case Hart is right but his argument is uninteresting. In the second it is certainly true that parking regulations are thought less important than, say, laws against homicide, but there is nevertheless a social purpose that is served by them and in some circumstances they take on considerable importance. Presumably this would be true of almost any law that had not fallen into desuetude. Thus the sort of justification that would be appropriate for violating even the less important legal rules would vary according to the circumstances in which the violation was committed, as would the sort of disapproval appropriate to violations. The third case illustrates the connection between particular rules and the general rule that we discuss immediately below. Persistent and willful violation of even an unimportant law is thought to flout and show lack of respect for law in general.

[22] In the case of laws that have fallen into desuetude, of course, the answer given by all but the most insistent legal absolutists is that I need not obey and that disapproval and punishment are neither required nor appropriate.

portant laws should be obeyed because it is important to obey the law. The apparently paradoxical character of this reply vanishes when we draw the distinction between the general and the particular rule. The latter may be unimportant, but the former is of great importance; and the latter cannot be disobeyed without disobeying the former and without influencing others to disobey the former as well. But if there is no paradox in the relationship between the general rule and particular rules, the peculiarities of the relationship in the type of case in question might mean that reliance on the argument for the general rule will actually contribute to the likelihood of contagious disobedience. Whatever abstract arguments can be made for accepting the general rule, if the behavioral significance of doing so is that men are regularly required to act in ways they think unimportant, commitment to the general rule might be expected to weaken. Reliance upon the general rule to support the demand for obedience to particular rules not thought important can be expected to weaken the sense of the importance of the general rule itself. *A* perceives that the general rule requires him to do *X, Y,* and *Z,* all of which he considers trivial. He generalizes from these cases and draws the conclusion that the general rule is unimportant. He then brings this conclusion to his deliberations concerning all cases that fall under the general rule.

We can give this speculation greater cogency by stating it more explicitly in terms of the conceptual points discussed earlier. We say there is an obligation to obey the law, an obligation to conform to the general rule. As noted above, "obligation" and "obligatory" are typically used of types of actions thought to be of great importance to the society or social group and they are especially forceful conduct-guiding concepts because they are used in connection with types of actions thought to be of great importance. Thus a sense of the importance of the allegedly obligatory action is one of the conditions the presence of which makes it appropriate to use "obligatory" and "obligation" with their implication that the actions "must be performed." Occasional use of the concepts in the absence of those conditions, as when "obligation" is made to do for the whole range of moral action-guiding concepts, is not likely to alter the conventions governing or the implications of "obligation." In the type of case in question, however, the relationship between the general rule and primary rules creates a pervasive and continuing tension among the conventions governing the use of "obligation." The availability of "authority" and "authoritative" to characterize particular rules makes it appropriate to use "obligation" in conduct-guiding discourse about them. But the sense of the unimportance of the conduct required by many particular rules deprives "obligation" of sources of support that makes it ("obligation") cogent and forceful. Use of the concept under these conditions violates or at least strains the ordinary logic of the concept and weakens its conduct-guiding force as compared with its use under conditions according more completely with its usual logic. Continued violation of the logic of a concept is likely to change its logic, at least for the class of uses in question. In this case the change is almost certain to be in the direction of reducing if not eliminating the implication that obligatory actions are actions that must be performed. The *word* will remain the same but the *concept* will have undergone a change. Thus members of the society may continue to use "obligation" in connection with particular rules but the inference that particular rules must therefore be obeyed would no longer follow from its use.

There is indirect evidence that such a development has in fact occurred in the case of legal rules such as parking and traffic regulations, antilitter ordinances, and regulations of a more specialized kind, for example those governing profit reporting by corporations, antitrust legislation, and regulations concerning contracts with the government. These laws are often violated and disapproval of violations is less than uniform or insistent; one should pay the penalty if caught but to disobey without being caught is sometimes thought a kind of achievement or success. Strictly speaking, the disobedience is criminal but the disobedients are not thought of as criminals. Yet the belief that one should pay the penalty tacitly concedes that these regulations are authoritative and hence that it is linguistically appropriate to say there is an obligation to obey them. Thus it would seem that the logic of "obligation" in these contexts is not always thought to include "must be performed." In its application to such rules the general rule can be said to be obligatory, but the concept does not have the same conduct-guiding force it has in other contexts.

Linguistic developments of the sort we have been discussing are more symptomatic of changes in attitudes and patterns of behavior than they are causes of the latter. Despite what we said above, it is not likely that the tension between the general rule and particular rules would itself constitute a sufficient explanation for a significant number of acts of disobedience. At best the explanation could account for the comparatively uninteresting case of disobedience to laws not thought to be important· in society. It would be implausible to argue that the sense of the unimportance of the general rule as it applied to unimportant particular rules would carry over to its applications to laws agreed to be important. Such an argument, sometimes encountered in the writings of legal absolutists, would rest on a mistake similar to the one of which we accused Ladd, namely thinking "obligation" must work exactly the same way in all its uses.

Aside from clarifying the relationship between the general rule and particular rules (and perhaps casting some light in a small corner of the practice of political obligation), our discussion of important and unimportant legal rules directs attention to a related but different class of cases; that in which men obey particular rules out of habit or in some other unreflective or uncritical manner, that is, in just the manner that the distinction between ideals and obligation might suggest they should and do. Here the particular rule might in fact be important, but it is not thought to be important; it is not thought to be important because it is simply not thought about. Men obey it, or rather the behavior of men conforms with it, but they do so unreflectively or uncritically.[23] Because men do conform to the rule (and hence to the general rule as it applies to the particular rule in question) it would seem that the question of explaining their disobedience simply would not arise in a practical way, a situation that many would think difficult to improve upon. Despite its apparent virtues, however, habitual, unreflective conformity with particular rules on the part of any very sizable segment of a populace can be a source of difficulties. Law, after all, is an instrument that human beings use to serve their purposes, to

---

[23] On the differences between following a rule and acting habitually see, among many other recent discussions: Peter Winch, *The Idea of a Social Science* (London: Routledge and Kegan Paul, 1958), esp. pp. 57–65; H. L. A. Hart, *Concept of Law, op. cit.*, esp. pp. 54–59; and Max Black, "Rules and Routines," in R. S. Peters, ed., *The Concept of Education* (London: Routledge and Kegan Paul, 1967), esp. pp. 97–98.

assist them in achieving their objectives. Particular legal rules are ordinarily passed to solve some problem or meet some need. The sense that they do so is what lies behind the sense that they are important and should be obeyed. When men conform to them in an unthinking manner this sense is lost. One result of such a development is that a sense of the importance of a law cannot be conveyed to new generations. Since the latter may find the habits of their elders unattractive, and since the elders have lost the capacity to defend their own behavior, conflict may develop between generations. Similarly, technological and other types of change may take place that render the laws inappropriate. Since conformity to the laws has become unthinking, these changes and/or their implications for the laws may go unnoticed and neither the laws nor the behavior patterns associated with them will be changed to adapt to them.

The most general and most dangerous outcome of such a situation is the accumulation of social problems until a crisis is reached. The crisis may be sufficient to jar people out of their habitual modes of behavior but it is apt to do so in a costly and unpleasant manner. Restricting ourselves to the narrower concerns of the present discussion, such a situation could strain the relationship between the general and the particular rule in a manner not unlike (but much more significant than) the strain created by parking regulations and antilitter ordinances. Those who are skeptical of the established modes of behavior and the particular rules that correspond with them, whether members of a younger generation or not, will find a defense of those rules hard to come by from those who conform to them and will find it difficult to initiate a dialogue concerning them. It is a conceptual point that a habit is not something that is defended. So long as a mode of behavior remains habitual for a group of men they will be puzzled if not irritated by requests that they defend it, and they will be unable to respond to them. (If they are in fact forced to defend it the habit will thereby have ceased to be a habit, at least for the time being.) But the unavailability of a defense of the particular rule will not alter the fact that the rule remains a legal rule which there is a (prima facie) obligation to obey. Indeed, if the mode of behavior in question is habitual for a large segment of the populace, the fact that no defense is forthcoming and no discussion is possible will increase the likelihood that the rule will remain a legal rule. Thus unless those skeptical of the rule satisfy themselves concerning its value they will be thrown back on the case for the general rule as a ground for obeying it. (I deliberately pass over the possibility that they will decide to obey the particular rule simply to avoid inconvenience or punishment.) Thus once again the case for the general rule will not be supported by the case for the particular rule to which it applies in the case at hand. Unlike the case of parking regulations, however, in this situation the skeptic is not likely to dismiss the matter as insignificant; "obligation" will be attenuated in its application to important cases.

Once again there is evidence of such a process in this and other countries in recent years. Consider the case of laws on such subjects as relationships between races, the use of drugs, and sexual behavior. Many people accepted these laws under conditions that no longer prevail and continue to conform to them (and the nonlegal norms and rules concerning the same subjects) in what, judging from their response to critics, is often an habitual manner. Thus for conceptual as well as sociological reasons it is difficult for critics of the laws to initiate meaningful discussion concerning them, and criticisms of the laws (to say nothing of tendencies to depart from the modes of behavior prescribed by the laws and the related social norms) meet with hostile and sometimes repressive responses. Of course large numbers of people have continued to obey these laws despite skepticism concerning their value. This fact may be testimony that the general rule can be effective even when it receives little or no support from arguments for the particular rules to which it applies. But disobedience has been widespread and approval of disobedience (or at least refusal to express disapproval) even more so. Moreover, such disobedience has often been accompanied by expressions of generalized doubt concerning the importance of obeying the law (concerning the general rule).

Whether or to what extent any of the cases of disobedience alluded to can be explained in the terms of the present discussion is a question that could not be decided without making an investigation of the attitudes, opinions, and arguments of those who have disobeyed and supported disobedience. Our purpose in mentioning them has been less to comment on some fairly obvious social phenomena than to suggest examples of the conceptual relationships that have been our major concern. Stated in the most general terms, the point suggested by the foregoing discussion is that the attitudes of the citizenry toward particular legal rules influence in an important way their attitude toward the general rule. This is hardly surprising and is worth emphasizing largely because it has been denied or, where its existence has been recognized, condemned as unfortunate by some of the most influential theorists of political obligation. These theorists, for example Plato (especially in the *Republic*), Hobbes, Hume, Bergson, Lincoln, and many contemporary legal absolutists, have argued that political obligations are in fact or should be discharged without reflection about or even concern with the content of the obligation, perhaps habitually or even "sonambulistically" (Bergson). Our discussion of habitual obedience and its relation to the general rule is intended to suggest that it is so far from being appropriate to "obligation" that it is systematically at odds with the logic of that concept; and it is so far from contributing to the order and stability craved by the theorists just mentioned that it can contribute to an increase in disobedience.

Stated somewhat more specifically, we have tried to suggest that the citizen's views concerning the importance of particular rules influence his attitude toward the general rule as it applies to those rules, affect the manner in which "obligation" is used in connection with the general rule, and is sometimes predictive of whether the obligation to obey particular rules will be discharged. It is, of course, not our intention to suggest that the question of whether the citizen thinks a particular rule good or bad is of no significance. But very few people have strong pro or con attitudes toward parking or antilitter ordinances, yet they are regularly disobeyed. Similarly, laws that are strongly disapproved are more likely to be obeyed when the actor himself or large numbers of his fellow citizens think it is sufficiently important that there be a law on the subject in question to take the trouble to defend the law against critics and to urge obedience to it. The conceptual considerations we have discussed suggest that the likelihood that disobedience will be contagious increases as the sense of the importance of the law decreases (and vice versa).

From a more explicitly evaluative perspective, it follows from the foregoing that there is an important sense in which those who obey laws habitually or mechanically share a part of the responsibility for the contagious effects of disobedience on the part of those who disobey the laws because they disapprove of them and think the matter important enough to take the risks involved in disobedience. It also follows that the argument that one should not disobey rule X because doing so will undermine the general rule and regime—that this argument is least cogent where the law is regarded as important and where criticism and disobedience of it prompt vigorous discussion and controversy. Contrary to what seemed at first to be the implication of the distinction between ideals and obligations, it now appears that critical awareness, reflection, and evaluation are no less important in the practice of political obligation in a stable society than in any other aspect of politics in such a society. Such reflection takes place in a more restricting context than does reflection concerning ideals and the pursuit of ideals, but in its absence acting out of a sense of obligation degenerates into acting habitually, out of fear, or in some other mechanical manner.[24] A political society nourished by reflection and discussion concerning its obligation rules is not likely to be brought down by epidemics of disobedience. In such a society a measure of disobedience might be a symptom of and might even contribute to a healthy, adaptive body politic. By the same token, persistent reliance upon arguments for obedience grounded in the importance of the general rule as such may be symptomatic of a stagnant or stagnating political process and political society, a society in which political obligation is degenerating into something else.

[24] I hope to develop these distinctions and their significance for political obligation in a larger work on political obligation now in progress.

6

OBLIGATION: POLITICAL
AND MORAL

KURT BAIER

Traditionally, the problem of political obligation has been construed as the problem of whether there is any such thing.

Let me first say what this problem is not. It is not the problem of whether certain people, in virtue of certain special conditions, which apply to them but not to others living in a given state, have what are ordinarily called "political obligations." Thus, a candidate for office may incur so many political obligations (that is, obligations to special interest groups that help him get elected) that on taking office he is unable to keep his election promises; a citizen living abroad may have certain political obligations or duties (that is, obligations to engage in certain political activities), such as posting his absentee ballot or defending the policies of his country; someone who has received special governmental benefits, such as a scholarship, grant, or pension may be under a political obligation (that is, under obligation to do something for his country). Clearly, the traditional problem of political obligation is not the problem of determining who has what political obligations in this ordinary sense.

Again, it is not the problem of whether there are in fact territorial states which have, as opposed to merely claiming to have, de facto or even de jure (constitutional) authority—for this is not a problem but a plain fact.

Lastly, it is not the problem of whether a given person ought on a given occasion to obey a given directive of a given government. It is, rather, the problem of whether one ought, prima facie, to obey any and every government actually having political authority. The import of this is that if there is no political obligation, then each person living in the territory of such a state in reason may and should consider each directive of such a government on its own merits: he can please himself whether to obey or disobey, follow his inclination, or weigh his own best interest—unless, of course, he has some special moral obligation to obey such directives, e.g., special favors received or a freely given oath of allegiance, and so on. By contrast, if there is such an obligation, then he should obey such directives—unless, of course, there are overriding considerations to the contrary; but the fact that he is inclined not to follow a given directive or that following it would not be in his own best interest would not be adequate overriding reasons.

The traditional problem of obligation is thus the problem of whether anyone and everyone, simply in virtue of the fact that he lives in the territory over which a given state has political authority, is prima facie obliged, or has a prima facie obligation to do a certain sort of thing, namely, obey the directives (laws) of that state, whatever (within certain limits) they may be. Knowing the solution to the traditional problem of political obligation would not thus get us very far. It would merely enable us to make a correct start in that process of reasoning whose conclusion yields an answer to the important question of whether a given person on a given occasion ought to obey a given directive of a given political authority. But, of course, even making a correct start is not unimportant.

How, then, can we hope to solve this problem and thus ensure a correct start? Clearly, we must determine what it is to be obliged or to have an obligation to do something, what constitutes grounds for saying that someone has such an obligation, and whether living in the territory of a given state constitutes such grounds.

I shall now examine what I take to be the four most important theories of obligation and their answers to these questions. These four theories maintain that to be obliged to do something is (1) to be commanded to do it; (2) to fall under a social rule imposing an obligation; (3) to be under obligation to someone; (4) to fall under a rule such that not obeying that rule would be wrong. The outcome of my examination is that only the last theory can hope to give a tenable account of obligation and that, on that theory, we can indeed say that there is such a thing as political obligation.

1. The classical exposition of this first theory is found in John Austin's *The Province of Jurisprudence Determined.* Austin there says that "*command, duty,* and *sanction* are inseparably connected terms: . . . each embraces the same ideas as the others, though each denotes these ideas in a peculiar order or series. . . . Each of the three terms *signifies* the same notion; but each *denotes* a different part of that notion, and connotes the residue."[1] And he explains the part of the notion denoted by obligation in this way: "When I am talking *directly* of the chance of incurring evil, or (changing the expression) of the liability or obnoxiousness to the evil, I employ the the term *duty,* or the term *obligation*: the liability or obnoxiousness to the evil being put foremost, and the rest of the complete notion being signified implicitly."[2]

If Austin's account of obligation as liability to some evil for disobeying some directive were correct, there clearly would not be such a thing as political obligation. On Austin's view it does not follow that a person is obliged, in his sense, to do what he is by law *required* or directed to do. A person may know that

[1] John Austin, *The Province of Jurisprudence Determined* (reprint edition; London: Weidenfeld and Nicolson, Library of Ideas) pp. 17, 18.
[2] *Ibid.,* p. 18.

though he is by law required to do a certain thing, he is not liable or obnoxious to the sanction, and so has no duty or obligation, in Austin's sense, to do that which the law requires, i.e., no duty or obligation to obey the law. It may be objected on Austin's behalf that, by his definition, one is commanded by law to do something if and only if one is obliged to do so, hence no one can be commanded by law to do something without being obliged to do it. We need not contest this point, for it implies only that one may fall under a given law without, in Austin's sense, being commanded by it. Hence it can establish only that to be commanded by law is necessarily to be obliged by it and conversely, to be obliged to obey is to be commanded, but this cannot show that there is such a thing as political obligation. For being obliged (as we ordinarily understand it) to obey the political authority involves not merely being obliged when not obeying the law can be expected to lead to punishment, but being obliged whenever the law applies to one. Otherwise anyone who broke a law that applied to him and got away with it could then claim that this was a law he was (i.e., turned out to be) not obliged to obey.

However, this conclusion is insecurely grounded in as far as it depends on Austin's account of obligation, for that account is quite implausible. Thus, H. L. A. Hart argues that Austin misconstrues the kind of nonoptionality involved in obligation. Austin takes as his model the gunman situation, in which someone is ordered at gunpoint, and so is obliged to hand over his money. But, Hart argues, a person in such a situation does not have an obligation, though he is obliged to hand over his money. Hart lists two respects in which being obliged differs from having an obligation. Firstly, a person who (reasonably or unreasonably) believes that he has nothing to fear from disobedience, is not obliged, but may well have an obligation to obey. Secondly, whereas one cannot be said to be obliged to do something unless one does it, this is not true of having an obligation to do something.[3] According to Hart, Austin may have given a correct account of what it is to be obliged to do something but not of what it is to have an obligation to do it. But the problem of political obligation relates to what it is to have a political

---

[3] H. L. A. Hart, *The Concept of Law* (Oxford: Clarendon Press, 1961), pp. 80–81.

obligation, not to what it is to be politically obliged. Hence the implication of Austin's theory of obligation, that there is no such thing as political obligation, can be ignored.[4]

2. I now turn to a theory which treats obligation as what is imposed by a certain sort of social rule. Such an account differs from Austin's in that it derives the obligating power not from coercive orders but from the social rule which confers on people in certain social positions the authority to bind obligatorily by their commands. On such an account, the gunman's orders, though coercive, do not obligate because the gunman does not hold the appropriate position of authority, which only an appropriate social rule could confer.

Hart, in *The Concept of Law,* develops such a theory. According to him, one has an obligation when one is correctly said, by someone who himself accepts it, to fall under a generally accepted obligation-imposing social rule. Thus, two conditions must be satisfied for someone to be correctly said to have an obligation: (a) He must fall under a generally accepted obligation-imposing rule, and (b) he must be said to fall under that rule by someone who accepts it. Incidentally, it is important to note a feature (whose soundness I have not the space to discuss) of this account: having an obligation differs from having other possessions, such as an appendix or a wart, in that one cannot have it without being said to have it; having an obligation and

---

[4] In a highly interesting article, "On Being Obliged to Act," *The Human Agent,* G. N. A. Vesey, ed. (New York: St. Martin's Press, 1968), which might be thought to undermine Hart's refutation of Austin's theory of obligation, Alan White rejects Hart's contention that "having an obligation" and "being obliged" are different notions. His thesis is, on the contrary, that when one has an obligation one is obliged, and is obliged in exactly the same sense in which one is obliged when one does not have an obligation, as in the gunman case, the difference being that it is a rule, not a circumstance, which obliges one. Limitations of space prevent me from taking up any of the interesting points made by White, but it should in any case be clear that even if White's thesis is correct, it does not affect Hart's point against Austin. For even on White's account there are important differences between being obliged when one has, and being obliged when one does not have, an obligation, in particular that it is a rule which obliges one, not any other obliging factor. Austin's analysis fits the case of being obliged when one does not have an obligation, but the problem of political obligation relates to the case of being obliged when one has an obligation. Austin's account of being obliged thus does not accommodate the important features of being obliged which are relevant to obligation. Hence even if White is right, Austin's account of obligation can be ignored.

being said to have one cannot be separated in the way in which having an appendix and being said to have one can be. This deserves closer attention than I can give it here. The first condition is comparatively unproblematic. Hart characterizes the class of obligation-imposing rules as that subclass of rules imposing requirements (as opposed to those permitting or empowering someone to do something), which satisfy six criteria.[5] And a rule is generally accepted if the bulk of the group, but not necessarily the whole group, accepts them, provided there is an adequate level of acceptance to make the rule system in question efficacious.[6] I shall not here take up this first condition.[7]

Condition b, however, is important for our present discussion. For it implies that whether someone has an obligation is not a question of straightforward empirical fact. At first sight, it looks like the empirical question of whether someone falls under a social rule of a certain sort, but it is not so. An affirmative answer to that question would be merely a statement "from the external point of view,"[8] the point of view which would be taken by sociologists or by those who, though living in the society, "reject its rules and are only concerned with them when and because they judge that unpleasant consequences are likely to follow violation." From that point of view, the fact that someone falls under such a rule, according to Hart, would be expressed not in terms of obligation, but only in terms of being obliged or related terms. "That point of view will need for its expression, 'I was obliged to do it,' 'I am likely to suffer for it if. . . ,' 'You will probably suffer for it if. . . ,' 'They will do that to you if. . . .' But they will not need forms of expression like 'I had an obligation' or 'You have an obligation' for these are required only by those who see their own and other people's conduct from the internal point of view."[9] Looking at the social rules from the external point of view is looking at them merely as guides to

---

[5] Hart, *Concept of Law, op. cit.,* pp. 55, 83–85.
[6] *Ibid.,* pp. 100, 101.
[7] For a critical discussion, see White, "On Being Obliged to Act," *op. cit.,* pp. 69, 70; also, Frederick Siegler, "Hart on Rules of Obligation," *Australasian Journal of Philosophy* (December 1967); my own account in "Moral Obligation," *American Philosophical Quarterly* (July 1966).
[8] Hart, *Concept of Law, op. cit.,* pp. 86–88.
[9] *Ibid.,* p. 88.

other people's behavior. Looking at them from the internal
point of view is looking at them as guides to how one should
behave oneself.[10]

Supposing that Hart's account of obligation claims and of the
underlying concept of obligation is correct, what answer can we
give to our main question? From the external point of view that
question cannot be raised, for from that point of view we can ask
only whether everyone everywhere is obliged (i.e., compelled) to
obey the government of the territory in which he lives, or
whether he is deemed by his fellows to have an obligation to
obey. Obviously, neither of these questions is the one which
troubles political philosophers, for theirs is a normative, not a
sociological question.

To be able to raise the traditional problem of political obligation, we must not, then, adopt the external point of view. But do
we manage to raise that question even if we adopt the internal
point of view? It seems not. For according to Hart, it will be
remembered, an obligation claim does two things. It says that a
person falls under a certain obligation-imposing rule which is
generally accepted in the society in question, and it implies or
expresses the speaker's own acceptance of that rule. Thus, saying
there is such a thing as political obligation amounts to claiming
that everyone has an obligation to obey the government, and
this, on Hart's analysis, involves two things: (1) asserting that
everyone falls under the generally accepted rule of universal
political obedience, and (2) implying or expressing the speaker's
own acceptance of that rule. However, this formulation conceals
the ambiguity of the expression "the government." For obeying
the government here may mean *this* government, that is, the
government of the state in regard to which the speaker has
adopted the internal point of view; or it may mean *his* government, the government of the state in whose territory whoever is
referred to by the speaker happens to reside. On the first inter-

---

[10] Actually, once people do have the internal point of view and the terms
needed by it, claims made from the external point of view can also be
formulated in terms of obligation. However, from the external point of view,
the fact that someone falls under an obligation-imposing rule cannot be
expressed by saying that he has an obligation, but can be expressed merely by
saying that he is deemed, in that society, to have an obligation. Put in this
way, the claim implies general acceptance of that rule in that society without
implying the speaker's acceptance of it.

pretation, "There is such a thing as political obligation" would amount merely to "In my society, there is such a thing as political obligation" or "In my society, people have an obligation to obey the government." On the second interpretation, it becomes "Everyone has an obligation to obey his government," that is, the government of the territory in which he resides.

Clearly, the first interpretation does not correctly render the traditional question of political obligation. That question is not about some one, particular society, but is about all and any societies that can be called political.

But the second interpretation is still ambiguous. For it does not make clear the scope of "everyone, everywhere." On one interpretation, it would amount to the claim that literally everyone, everywhere falls under the rule of universal political obedience which is generally accepted in his society, together with the implication or expression of the speaker's own acceptance of all these various rules (if indeed this makes sense). Since such a claim presupposes that the rule of universal political obedience is generally accepted everywhere, in all societies, whether there is such a thing as political obligation would then depend on a matter of empirical fact, namely, whether that rule is in fact everywhere generally accepted. If it is not thus accepted, then either the claim that there is such a thing as political obligation is false or the very question of whether there is such a thing cannot arise. Obviously, this, too, is not the claim that troubles political philosophers.

On a second interpretation, our claim that there is such a thing as political obligation would amount to a double-barreled remark consisting of (1) the claim that there is, in the speaker's society, a second-order rule analogous to "When in Rome, do as the Romans do," which directs people in the speaker's society, whenever they happen to reside in a society in which the rule of universal political obedience is generally accepted, to obey the government of that society, and (2) the implication or expression of the speaker's own acceptance of that second-order rule. But, clearly, this too is not the problem that troubles political philosophers. For that problem is not whether to obey foreign governments when such obedience is required by a second-order rule generally accepted in one's own society and by a first-order rule in the foreign society. The problem is simpler but more fundamental. It is whether the rule of universal political obedience is sound; whether societies which lack such a rule lack something it would be better for them to have; whether one ought to obey one's government even when such a rule is not generally accepted in one's society.

As far as I can see, Hart's analysis of obligation allows of no other interpretations of the claim that there is such a thing as political obligation. But if I am right in what I have just said, then none of these interpretations correctly renders the traditional claim, hence Hart's analysis must be false.

It might be argued that Hart is offering a rational reconstruction of the claim; that in its traditional form the claim raises illegitimate or insoluble problems concerning the soundness of the rule of universal political obedience; and that one of the advantages of Hart's analysis is that it precludes the very arising of these problems. But this defense of a "noncognitivist" analysis along Hartian lines will not stand scrutiny. For such an elimination of the epistemological problems concerning the soundness of the rule of universal political obedience could be accomplished only by a certain positivist interpretation of the idea of the speaker's acceptance of the rule expressed or implied by him every time he makes an obligation-claim. But such a positivist interpretation of acceptance involves absurdity. Let me explain this point.

Hart rightly insists on distinguishing between the observer's (external) and the agent's (internal) points of view. But in characterizing the internal point of view, he runs together two quite different things: the point of view of a person who in fact accepts, that is, is guided by a given rule, and the point of view of a person who is set on being guided by sound rules and who takes the rule in question to be sound. The former uncritically accepts and is uncritically guided by the rule. The latter accepts the rule only critically, that is, he is guided by it only as long as he believes it to be sound. Hart must assume that obligation-claims express the former, uncritical, acceptance of the rule. If he did not assume this, he would not have bypassed the epistemological problems concerning the soundness of the rule of universal political obedience. But this assumption is mistaken.

For in the first place, a person who does not yet accept the rule could not on Hart's analysis ask whether he has an obligation to do what the rule requires him to do. Yet he clearly can ask that question. The reason why he can ask that question is, of course, that asking it is tantamount to asking whether that obligation-imposing rule is sound.

Second, and this is a much more important point, one could not, without absurdity, simply ask oneself whether one accepted a given rule quite irrespective of its soundness. To do so would be as absurd as asking oneself whether one believed a certain statement irrespective of its truth. One may ask whether one has, in the past and up to now, accepted a certain rule, in this purely positive sense. But when one comes to the present, when one asks whether one still accepts it, one cannot, without absurdity, exclude the condition of soundness. Thus whenever someone says that someone, including himself, has an obligation, then if such a claim implies or expresses the speaker's acceptance of a certain rule, the acceptance must be critical and not just positive acceptance. And if someone asks whether someone, including himself, has a certain obligation, then that question, if it involves the question of whether he accepts a given obligation-imposing rule, must concern his critical, not just his positive acceptance of that rule.

Lastly, if actual acceptance were involved, a person who did not accept a given rule could not ask whether he had an obligation to do what that rule required him to do, and a person who claimed that he had such an obligation could not then be answering any such question. Hence the remark, "You have an obligation to do X" would have a different status, depending on whether or not the person to whom it was addressed accepted the relevant rule. But this is surely quite implausible. If, instead of actual acceptance, we mean critical acceptance, then we avoid this duality of status.

I believe that Hart has been led to this theory of obligation by his concern to maintain a logical gap between the claim that *N has an obligation*, whether legal, customary, or moral, to do *X*, and the claim that *N ought* to do *X*. Thus, in *The Concept of Law*[11] Hart argues that from the fact that someone has a legal obligation to do *X*, it does not follow that he does (or that he does not) have a customary or a moral obligation to do *X*, let

[11] Hart, *Concept of Law, op. cit.,* pp. 194, 195.

alone that he ought to do X. In this respect, all types of obligation are on a par, according to Hart. To qualify an obligation as legal, moral, customary, and the like, is simply to point to those different institutions which constitute the relevant obliging factor: a law in the case of a legal obligation, a moral rule in the case of a moral obligation, a custom in the case of a customary obligation, and so on. The connection between such different types of obligations is purely contingent. Hart admits that there will of necessity be certain rules which form a part both of law and of morality, but he claims that this is not a matter of a logically necessary connection. Similarly, it is a purely contingent matter whether one of these systems contains a rule which "backs" another in its entirety. Thus, in a given society there may or may not be a generally accepted moral rule of universal political obedience, or conversely, a law to the effect that whatever is morally wrong is also illegal. And the question whether there is such a thing as political obligation, like the question of whether one has a legal obligation to be moral, depends on whether one lives in a society which has these relevant rules. We have already mentioned objections to this sort of interpretation of the traditional question of political obligation.

Now, the interesting point about Hart's analysis is that, when qualified by "legal," "customary," "contractual," or "conventional," obligation is perhaps quite naturally used in this positivist way. Thus, the members of a certain minority group may be said to have (not just "to be deemed to have") a legal obligation to carry identity papers, report to the police every morning, and occupy only the rear of a bus. If we object to such laws, we need not express our objection by denying the existence of such legal obligations; but we can merely claim, with Hart, that it does not follow that they ought to do what they have such legal obligations to do, or that they ought not to have such legal obligations.

However, "moral" obligation does not seem to be naturally used in this positivist way. We would not at all naturally express our criticism of a positive morality in this manner. For the positive morality of a group is a system of rules embodying certain beliefs, the moral convictions of the community; much as the conventional wisdom of a group is a system of rules which embodies certain widely held beliefs. We can express the rules of conventional wisdom in terms of what one, prudentially speaking, ought to do. These rules are therefore based on certain beliefs about how following them will favorably, not following them, unfavorably affect one's life. If these beliefs are false, then contrary to what is generally accepted, one has no good reason to do what the rules prescribe. Thus, if rising and retiring early does not have the favorable effects on one's life it is believed to have, then the claim that one ought to rise and retire early is without foundation. If moral rules are also based on beliefs relating to the good life, and if these rules can therefore be said to state what one (prima facie) morally ought to do, and if moral obligations are imposed by such moral rules, then, if some of the beliefs on which these rules are based are false, it follows that though it be generally believed that someone has a moral obligation to do X, he may not really have one.

If, as I believe, there is such a parallel between the prudential and the moral ought, then there is good reason for not using moral obligation in the same positive way in which we perhaps quite naturally use legal obligation. And if this is so, then there is good reason for saying that "N has a moral obligation to do X" implies "N (prima facie) morally ought to do X" rather than (as Hart claims) "N actually accepts a social rule imposing an obligation to do X." If I am right in this, then we can accept the part of Hart's theory of obligation which says that obligation-claims, such as "N has an obligation to do X" are to be explained as claims to the effect that N's case falls under a social rule directing people in such circumstances to do X, without having to accept that part of his theory which implies that the speaker actually accepts this rule, while implying nothing about its soundness or otherwise. And if this is correct, then we have no reason for accepting the corollary of Hart's theory mentioned before, namely that the traditional problem of political obligation does not arise.

In the next two sections, I examine two theories of obligation which accept the points just made, with a view to determining whether, on these theories, there is such a thing as political obligation.

3. The third general type of account treats having an obligation to do something as having a certain type of morally sanctioned task or burden which can be discharged only by doing the

thing in question. Other comparable types of task or burden
would be duties, responsibilities, and commitments. What distinguishes these not necessarily incompatible types from one another are not necessarily differences in the same respect. Thus duties
are recurring specific tasks which have become one's tasks owing
to one's station or position or role. Responsibilities are tasks in
whatever manner acquired, whose performance involves initiative, forethought, and care. Commitments are tasks of whatever
sort which one has come to have as a result of what one has
actually said or has through one's behavior given others to
understand. Obligations (of which commitments may be regarded as a species) are tasks which one has come to have as a result
of one's entering into certain sorts of relations to others, of which
the prime examples are someone's doing something for one, or
one's doing something to someone. Commitments are the most
specific and the most will-dependent kinds of obligations. By my
words I can spell out precisely, and as I decide, what my
obligation shall be. When I promise to the organizers to give $20
a month to the United Fund, the promise is both the ground of
my being under an obligation to the organizers, and the specification of what that obligation is, i.e., how it can be discharged.
By contrast, when someone has done something for me, then I
cannot spell out as I decide what I shall be obligated to do: I am
under an obligation to that person to do something for someone,
usually but not necessarily the same person who obliged me. If I
do some harm or damage to another, I have an obligation to him
to repair the harm or damage or to pay compensation. In these
cases, the ground of the obligation determines its content only in
a vague way. Custom or law, not my own decision, fills in the
details. But although there are many differences between duties,
obligations, commitments, and responsibilities, they are all morally sanctioned tasks or burdens, i.e., tasks or burdens whose
nondischarge would be prima facie morally wrong.

Unlike the first two types of account, this type may treat
political obligation as a moral concept. On this account, that
there is such a thing as political obligation means (a) that it is
morally wrong to disobey the relevant political authority; (b)
that there is a certain kind of ground for saying so, namely, that
any person living in the territory in question is ipso facto under
an obligation to someone; and (c) that this obligation cannot be

discharged except by obeying the government, that is, its laws. On this view, "there is such a thing as political obligation" is like "there is such a thing as filial, marital, teaching obligation" which indicates, without fully specifying, the content of the obligation, and not like "there is such a thing as promissory, contractual, legal, moral obligation" which indicates the ground but not the content.

If this account of political obligation is acceptable, there could indeed be such a thing as political obligation, and there would be if there were an adequate ground. The most popular theory about the ground of political obligation in this sense is, of course, that offered by the contract theory. On that theory, everyone inside the territory is actually committed to obeying the political authority. Here I can do no more than run quickly through the well-known (and in my opinion perfectly adequate) reasons for rejecting the contract theory as a theory of the ground of political obligation in the sense now under discussion.

The first reason is that for most people living in a given territory, the ground simply does not apply. Few people have committed themselves explicitly or implicitly. Only those who swear an oath of allegiance do so explicitly, e.g., soldiers, or aliens at naturalization ceremonies. Only a few states were created by an original commitment and these commitments can of course bind only the original participants. Even if certain actions by all those living in a given territory could be interpreted as giving others to understand that they are thereby committing themselves to obeying the government (and this is not a plausible assumption), there nowadays are many who explicitly disavow any such commitment. Since anyone can in principle do so, anyone can by such a deliberate disavowal disprove the claim that there is such a thing as political obligation. If this is the ground, then there is no such thing as political obligation.

It is now often argued that the original contract or the current explicit or implicit undertakings should not be interpreted as actual historical occurrences. But unless so interpreted, they cannot be the ground of actual commitments. All mothers may have an obligation to look after their children. Even an unmarried girl whose child is the product of rape may have such an obligation. But if so, the ground of that obligation can hardly be a commitment she made in having the child. She did not thus commit herself to it in the marriage ceremony, or in the act of intercourse, or in allowing the child to be born, if abortion is illegal or beyond her means. Being in the territory of a given state need be no more of an explicit or implicit commitment to anything than is being the victim of a rape. If maternal or political obligation must be grounded on commitment, explicit or implicit, then there is no such thing as (universal) maternal or political obligation.

Another version of this type of account is sketched very briefly in Hart's paper "Legal and Moral Obligation."[12] He suggests there that the ground of political obligation may be "that particular members of our own society have obeyed the law and expect it to be obeyed. Where obedience to the law is motivated by such considerations, there is no recognition of a moral obligation to obey. . . . " If I understand him correctly, he suggests that the ground of my obligation to obey the law is that other people have done so, that they have thereby benefitted me by contributing to conditions of security, freedom to plan my life, and the ability to lead a life enriched by the rewards of civilization, and that they have thus put me under an obligation to them, which I can discharge only by obeying the law myself.

It is a corollary of this theory that since some people benefit more than others from the law-abidingness of other people, they have a stronger obligation to obey the law than those who benefit less, and have perhaps an obligation to obey more of the laws and obey them more often than those others. But this is a rather objectionable consequence. For suppose a given society has two classes benefiting very unequally. Then the ruling class is under an obligation to the ruled class to obey these discriminatory laws which will further exploit and suppress the ruled class. Those among the ruling class who find these laws unjust and work for their repeal or modification would be guilty of failure to discharge their obligation to the ruled class to obey the law. But what a strange way of discharging their obligation to them upholding the law would be!

Another difficulty for this version of the theory is that the proposed ground of obligation is very vague, thus covering a

---

[12] *Ibid.*, p. 105.

wide range of levels of law-abidingness. Must the bulk of the population obey the law? Would a minority suffice? Would one person? Must all the laws be obeyed or only some? Must they always be obeyed, by and large, or only once? I waive altogether the difficulty of devising a measure for different levels of conformity and of applying that measure to a given political society. But there is still the difficulty of giving a good reason for pointing to a given level as the minimum sufficient to constitute a ground of political obligation. It might be argued that the very existence of a political society implies such a minimum level, but without further argument that would be quite arbitrary; quite as arbitrary as fixing the minimum level elsewhere say, lower or higher than what is implied by the existence of a state. Yet the question of whether there is such a thing as political obligation (on this version) depends on exactly where the minimum level of obligation is fixed. If it is fixed no higher than the minimum level required for the very existence of a state, then wherever there is a state, there is adequate ground for saying that everyone living in its territory has a moral obligation to obey the law, i.e., that there is such a thing as political obligation; otherwise, there is no such thing. But since, in the absence of additional reasons based on different factors, any specification of the level of conformity would be arbitrary, we must conclude that this version of the theory does not yield a definite answer to our question.

The whole discussion has brought to light the essential weakness of this account of obligation. Like the two earlier accounts, it attempts to find purely nonevaluative criteria for telling what are the grounds of obligation. It arrives at what are a person's obligations (and incidentally also his duties, responsibilities, or commitments), and so what he prima facie ought to do by simply looking at the social or institutional arrangements prevalent in a given society. It therefore attempts to arrive at moral conclusions in much the same way in which the other two accounts arrive at positive obligations: by derivation from some "privileged will" (the sovereign, the people accepting the social rules, and so on). But whereas the previous theories (insofar as their exponents manage to be consistent) regard talk of obligations as no more than shorthand ways of saying that there are directives of a certain content issued by the privileged will, the present theory attaches moral implications to this fact. It does, in other words, commit itself to the view that one (prima facie) morally ought to follow the directives of such a privileged will. But for this commitment it offers no reasons at all. I am not, of course, saying that no such reasons could be given.

4. I turn now to the last major account of obligation. It holds that in the sense relevant to our main question, *obligation* is the noun logically correlative to morally ought. When we say things such as "It is your obligation (or duty) to pay for her education" or "I have an obligation not to divulge this piece of information" we mean simply that the person in question (prima facie) morally ought to do the things in question. This theory can acknowledge that this use of obligation is wider than some ordinary uses; even that, as Hart puts it, "It is absurd to speak of having a moral *duty* not to kill another human being, or an *obligation* not to torture a child."[13] But it must maintain that the wider sense is the morally and politically important sense. If, in asking whether there is such a thing as political obligation, we resolutely stick to the narrow sense, then, since there appears to be no plausible ground for holding that there is such a thing, in the narrow sense, we are simply ignoring an important possibility: that being in the territory of a given state may be sufficient ground for saying that one (prima facie) morally ought to obey that state, or putting it differently, that it would be (prima facie) morally wrong for one not to obey it.

In any case, the main attraction of the ordinary, narrow sense of obligation rests on a mistake. It is simply not the case, as is widely thought, that the grounds for obligations in the narrow sense conclusively establish the existence of such obligations, and that such grounds are readily ascertained. Thus, it is often assumed that when a contract has been concluded, a point which is easily established empirically, then there is no question but that the contracting partners have obligations to do what they have in the contract undertaken to do and (prima facie) morally ought to do it. In this respect, it may be thought, moral ought judgments based on obligations are more easily proved than other moral judgments, such as that one (prima facie) morally ought not to harm others or ought to promote their good. But this confidence rests on a failure to separate obligation in the

[13] *Ibid.*, p. 82.

narrow and the wide senses. From the proof that a contract has been concluded, it does indeed follow that the contracting partners have an obligation (legal or customary) in the narrow, positive sense, to carry out the provisions of the contract. But it does not follow that they have an obligation in the wider, normative sense, the sense in which having an obligation implies that one (prima facie) morally ought to do what one has an obligation to do. In order to establish the latter and more important point, it is not sufficient to establish that they have an obligation in the positive sense, based on the criteria of the institutions of their society. We would need a further normative premise. We would need some premise such as that one (prima facie) morally ought to discharge his positive obligations. This additional normative premise is no doubt extremely plausible, but no more so than the premise that one ought not to harm others, and no less in need of proof than it.[14]

A further complication is introduced by the existence of presumptive implications and defeating or rebutting conditions of such implications. Thus we can say that although signing on the dotted line does not imply that the signatory has a (normative) obligation to carry out what he undertook to do, there is a presumption that he has such an obligation. It has therefore seemed to some philosophers that the logical gap between is and morally ought can be empirically closed by reliance on the recognized presumptions which connect the criteria for the existence of positive obligations with normative conclusions. But this is to run together two quite different gaps which must be kept apart. The first is the gap between the establishment of presumptive positive obligations (such as the presumptive obligation to do certain things one has solemnly declared one's intention to do), and the demonstrated positive obligation to do these things when all possible defeating or rebutting conditions have been

---

[14] Cf. John Searle, "How to Derive 'Ought' from 'Is,'" *The Philosophical Review*, 73 (1964), 43–58; Roger Montague, "'Ought' From 'Is,'" *Australasian Journal of Philosophy*, 43 (1965), 144–67; Evan K. Jobe, "On Deriving 'Ought' From 'Is,'" *Analysis*, 25 (1965), 179–81; W. D. Hudson, "The 'Is-Ought' Controversy," *Analysis*, 25 (1965), 191–95; Antony Flew, "On Not Deriving 'Ought' From 'Is,'" *Analysis*, 24 (1964), 25–32; James E. McClellan and B. Paul Komisar, "On Deriving 'Ought' From 'Is,'" *Analysis*, 24 (1964), 32–37; James and Judith Thomson, "How Not To Derive 'Ought' From 'Is,'" *The Philosophical Review*, 73 (1964), 512–16.

eliminated. Closing this gap shows, e.g., the contract to be valid. The second is the gap between an already established positive obligation (which a sociologist might correctly formulate by saying "N is indefeasibly deemed to have an obligation to do X" which does not entail that N (prima facie) morally ought to do it), and the normative obligation to do X, having which entails that one (prima facie) morally ought to do it. That is, there is still the question, "Ought I to keep this valid contract?" The empirical closure of the first gap does not ipso facto close the second. In order to move from the closure of the first gap to that of the second, we would need two further premises. The first is that the recognized (positive) rebutting conditions (grounds of invalidity) include all and only legitimate rebuttals, and this would have to be demonstrated by some normative argument, not just by reliance on some recognized practice. For one can always ask whether the rules of a given practice (think of selling oneself into slavery, of indentured labor, or of suttee) are unobjectionable. There may, of course, be a further positive presumption to the effect that the actually recognized rebutting conditions include all and only legitimate rebuttals, unless there are good reasons to the contrary. But this presumption, too, would have to be established by some normative argument. (I am not, of course, denying the possibility of some such argument. On the contrary, I believe it to be possible. Here I am only insisting that it is necessary.) The second premise is that the whole institution as thus defined is desirable and unobjectionable and this is not necessarily true of all social practices.

Supposing, then, that there are no insuperable objections to the present use of obligation, we can return to our main question: Is there such a thing as political obligation? As interpreted by the present account, the question is whether a person's being in the territory of a given state is an adequate ground for the claim that he (prima facie) morally ought to obey the government of that state. An examination of this question requires us to elucidate claims to the effect that someone (prima facie) morally ought to do something, or what comes to the same thing, that something is (prima facie) morally wrong. To this question I now offer my own answer.

To say that some course of action is morally wrong is to make two claims: (i) the weightiest reasons of a certain kind, those we normally call moral reasons, oppose this course of action; (ii) because this course is opposed by reasons of this kind, the question of whether someone enters on it is not solely his business. An examination of claim ii will throw light on the contentious claim i. I therefore begin by examining ii.

That whether or not someone enters on a course opposed by reasons of a certain kind is not solely his business implies two things. The first is that it is desirable and important that everyone should follow reasons of that kind, and that it is therefore legitimate for a society to ensure by appropriate steps that its members know these reasons and follow them. It is a plausible hypothesis that appropriate steps to this end would be the formulation and promulgation of social rules of behavior which would constitute such reasons; also, if necessary, the creation of practices designed to ensure a high level of conformity, including possibly practices such as the widespread expression of approval and disapproval, commendation and condemnation, reward and punishment for following or disregarding these rules.

The second implication of such a claim is that reasons of the kind in question, those we normally call moral reasons, must be such as to justify us in making the important claim that it is not solely the agent's business whether he follows these reasons or not. The principles underlying the content of these reasons must justify other people's concern with our conformity to them.

The concept of moral wrongness thus confronts us with two tasks of justification. The first is this. The claim that something is morally wrong implies the justifiability of ensuring conformity with certain social rules; if necessary, by enforcing them, that is, by practices which are prima facie undesirable, because they involve the curtailment of some of the most fundamental human values—spontaneity, autonomy, and the freedom to do as we please. Therefore even the employment of the concept of moral wrongness requires justification. It requires, in other words, a demonstration of its indispensability, or at least its helpfulness, in protecting other equally fundamental human values, and of its capacity also to safeguard, to a significant extent, those values which it curtails.

The second task of justification involves two things: (1) the explanation of the principles underlying a certain mode of reasoning, the mode we usually call moral, and (2) the demonstration that the employment of reasons of this type as superior to, and overriding reasons of other types, particularly reasons of self-interest, satisfies the criteria required by the first task of justification, the justification of having the concept of moral wrongness. In other words, the needs which justify the practices of enforcement must be satisfied by the selection of an appropriate content for the rules to be enforced. If, for example, in the absence of an enforced rule against killing human beings, the incidence of killing would be such as to make human life unbearably insecure, then the treatment of the rule "Thou shalt not kill" as a moral rule and the consideration "It would be a case of killing" as a moral reason, superior to and overriding other kinds of reason, would be justified.

We can perform the first task of justification in three steps: the justification of regulating human behavior at all; regulating it by the promulgation of social rules and by the inculcation in people of respect for, and willingness to abide by, these rules; sanctioning these rules for the purpose of attaining desirably high levels of conformity which would otherwise be unattainable.

Let me sketch briefly a set of assumptions by which we could justify the regulation of human behavior. Such a set would include at least the following: it is rational for an individual to allocate his resources in such a way as to make his life as good as possible. No individual can hope for as good a life for himself outside the framework of a society as within it—that is, as good as within a rule-governed way of life which provides for the division of labor, the cooperative production and distribution of the goods and services which make life worthwhile. The most rational policy for all members is for each to aim at everyone's obtaining these advantages (this is perhaps the most contentious assumption). If all are to obtain them, society (through its organs) must formulate and promulgate those restrictions on the inclinations and self-interest of each member without which the business of cooperative production and distribution cannot be effectively carried on. The least objectionable way of accomplishing the necessary conformity with these social rules would be a voluntary one, that is, one accomplished simply by two steps: the promulgation of these social rules and the inculcation in each individual member of an understanding of the need for, and so a respect for, and willingness to conform to these promulgated rules. Finally, the gains in the excellence of the life for each individual are worth the cost in terms of the freedom to do as one pleases. Given that these assumptions are sound, the practice of allowing society to regulate its members' behavior by compulsory rules is justified.

Let us then grant the justifiability of regulating people's behavior and the preferability, other things being equal, of regulating it solely by education and the promulgation of compulsory social rules—in particular the preferability over regulating it not solely in this way but in this way supplemented by the practice of bringing people to account. What further assumptions must we make if that additional practice is to be justified? We must assume that the existence of this practice raises the level of conformity with the compulsory social rules, that the maintenance of the higher level of conformity together with the existence of such additional practices is preferable to the lower level together with their absence, and that of all the other possible additional practices which would also raise that level, it is the least objectionable.

Given that this justification of having the concept of moral wrongness is adequate, what can we learn from it about the content of those rules and reasons which can justifiably be treated as superior to and overriding other kinds of rules and reasons, in particular those of self-interest? In other words, what can we learn about those rules we ordinarily call moral because we take them to be rules and reasons which satisfy this requirement (among others)? The justification brings to light the main reason for the need to regulate human behavior in conditions of human interaction, namely, the likelihood of frequent conflicts of concerns and interest and the desirability of determining authoritatively whose concern or interest should give way, thereby avoiding the wasteful use of resources on settling the conflict by force. Thus, rules and reasons properly called moral can have as their content the adjudication of the conflict of concerns and interests. For this will not only be a desirable and important topic for such rules to handle, but it will also satisfy the requirement that whether a person follows the rules is not solely his business. If the rule adjudicates between conflicting concerns or interests, then a person's not following such a rule will ipso facto also affect someone else's concerns and interests, and so be not solely the agent's business. For the same reason, there will be a natural tendency on the part of those whose concern or interest has been set aside not to follow the rule and so a need to regard the rule as superior to and overriding others, and as in need of enforcement.

Our sketch of justification brings to light a further point. Since it is desirable that the role of enforcement should be reduced to the very minimum compatible with a high level of conformity, it is desirable that the rules should be such as to command the highest possible respect and voluntary obedience. A rational way of achieving this is to give them a content such that it is in the interest of everyone alike that they should be followed. This does not of course mean that when such rules adjudicate between conflicting interests, then on every occasion when the interest of one person is set aside in favor of the interest of another following the rule must be equally in the interest of both, for that is logically impossible. It should be in the interest of all affected to lead a way of life such as will result from obedience to the rule rather than a way of life resulting from a general disregard of the rule. To see whether this is so or not, one may have to take into account a longish period of time and more than a single rule. In any case, this consideration brings to light a further criterion of rules and reasons which can claim to be moral: their content must be informed by the principles of justice and fairness. And a fuller examination of what justifies rules and reasons which can be called moral may bring to light further constraints on what such rules may direct people to do.

Now, among the rules which can be justified along the lines just suggested, there are not only rules which command or forbid everyone to do certain things in certain circumstances, such as "Thou shalt not kill" and "Thou shalt not lie," but also rules endorsing the social imposition of tasks in the course of socially organized cooperative enterprises involving the production and distribution of the goods and services which make up the civilized life. As we have seen, these are the tasks we call duties, obligations, and responsibilities. In addition to these, however, there are moral rules endorsing those social institutions which empower individuals to create moral ties at will, i.e., to obligate themselves or others by uttering an appropriate verbal formula: the promise, and the command of an authority. If we can give a justification along the lines suggested of these obligation-creating social devices, then there are sound moral rules to the effect that one (prima facie) morally ought to keep one's promises and that one (prima facie) morally ought to obey the commands of a properly constituted authority.

Hence, on this interpretation of obligation, the problem of political obligation becomes the question of whether there is a justification, along the lines sketched, for the existence of a political authority, i.e., for the existence of governments and the coercive apparatus which is an essential feature of such political societies.

The main ground for saying that there is such a thing as political obligation would then seem to be that the institution of government is an improvement over mere custom. If my sketch of the justification of the concept of moral wrongness is sound, then (almost) any society is preferable to none. At the same time, the advantages of political over prepolitical societies are many and great. I mention only two obvious ones: the possibility of quickly and rationally adjusting the compulsory rules by which a society lives to new and improved methods for meeting human needs and wants made possible by the increase in human knowledge; and the possibility of stimulating and organizing the search for such knowledge. If the existence of compulsory rules is justified in a prepolitical society and if the introduction of political authority is an improvement, then *a fortiori* the existence of political authority is justified, and so there is such a thing as political obligation.

Of course, the existence of political authority also gives rise to new dangers and abuses. The most obvious is the misuse of political authority for the purpose of introducing, or preventing the modification of unjust laws, especially those which violate the rules of distributive justice, and the misuse of governmental power for the purpose of preventing, by force or by subtle means, changes in the direction of greater justice in the prevalent laws or in their application to different groups in the community. Clearly, the burden of proof that there have occurred abuses sufficient to reverse the prima facie wrongness of disobeying the government must lie on the person who makes such a claim, though this does not, of course, mean that he must discharge this burden in a court of law or in accordance with the rules and procedures admissible there. This is not the place to begin an examination of what would constitute such grounds and what exactly they would entitle or require one to do; whether to disobey some specific laws, to overthrow the government, or to overthrow the constitution, and for what purpose. I can only emphasize that such a ground simply replaces the (prima facie) obligatoriness of obeying the law with the (prima facie) obligatoriness of some other specific mode of conduct, such as civil disobedience, political agitation for the repeal of the unjust law, the defeat of the government by whatever constitutional methods are available, or where none are available or the legitimate ones are effectively blocked by the government, by a coup d'état, or if the constitution itself is unjust, by a revolution. Every citizen, not only those who are unfavorably affected by the unjust legislation, but possibly everyone living in a state where there is such a ground overriding the prima facie obligation of obedience, now has such a new obligation. If those who are thus unfavorably affected regard themselves as entirely released from their obligation to obey the law and if, instead of trying to discharge their new overriding obligations, they set out to destroy the state which has discriminated against them, then they do what is wrong and, moreover, what is in all probability contrary to their best interest. But the citizens who have benefited from the unjust laws and have not discharged their own obligations to have these laws replaced are in a bad position to condemn those others who are trying to destroy the state. Morally speaking they are in much the same position as receivers of stolen goods when the robbed attempt to take revenge on the robbers by destroying them and their irrecoverable booty. At the same time, the organs of the state, the police and the law courts, have an obligation in their professional capacity to continue to enforce all of the laws, even though those living in the state no longer have an obligation to obey all of them. Of course, as citizens such officials have an obligation, like all other citizens, to work for the repeal of the unjust laws.

However, as we have seen, the argument designed to justify the concept of moral wrongness shows only that almost *any* society is better than no society. Some political societies may be so bad that it is preferable to destroy their very basis, i.e., their constitution, and return to prepolitical conditions, at least pending the creation of a new constitution, rather than go on living under the old one. Under these conditions, the obligation to obey the law is replaced by the prima facie obligation to revolution.

7

THE MORAL FOUNDATIONS OF POLITICAL OBLIGATION

JOHN W. CHAPMAN

During this century and throughout the world today, in situations of unprecedented intensity, men face, are confounded and divided by problems of political obligation. In mid-century, at the dawn of the nuclear era, J. Robert Oppenheimer asked, "What are we to think of such a civilization, which has not been able to talk about the prospect of killing almost everybody, except in prudential and game-theoretic terms?"[1] No doubt, Oppenheimer's question was rhetorical, but not entirely so. We never were so lacking in a sense of moral and political responsi-

---

[1] Quoted by Nuel Pharr Davis in his *Lawrence & Oppenheimer* (New York: Simon and Schuster, 1968), p. 330.

bility as he suggests. But in America, nearly two decades later, an unfortunate and miscalculated war and a belated revolution awaken conscience in some and drive others into desperation and defiance; over many hang the threats of civil disobedience and violence.[2] The moral worth and political relevance of liberalism seem doubtful to men who find Marxism persuasive.[3] To others, for reasons both good and bad, authority in the great institutions of church and university has lost legitimacy, and hence these become the object of contempt and disdain.[4] Clearly the West is in a condition of moral and political confusion, of impatience and psychic insecurity, if not despair. Power and prejudice block the development of human potentialities. Frustrated by social complexity and political ambiguity, those needs and capacities, in which Rousseau had seen the characteristic of "perfectibility," now generate a sense of outrage as well as obligation. Moral idealism strains against political inertia, and confidence in liberalism is shaken by the disparity between its aspirations and its achievements.

Elsewhere tensions appear even more severe. From Russia come discordant voices: An ideologically deranged traitor basks in Moscow like a moonlit mackerel; an eminent scientist calls for intellectual freedom; a General, recently arrested, and a famous author, along with younger men and women, defy censorship;

---

[2] See Ernest van den Haag, "Government, Conscience, and Disobedience," in Paul Kurtz (Ed.), *Sidney Hook and the Contemporary World: Essays on the Pragmatic Intelligence* (New York: John Day, 1968), pp. 105-20; Richard A. Wasserstrom, "The Obligation to Obey the Law," in Robert G. Summers (Ed.), *Essays in Legal Philosophy* (Oxford: Basil Blackwell, 1968), pp. 274-304; Christian Bay, "Civil Disobedience: Prerequisite for Democracy in Mass Society," and Michael Walzer, "The Obligation to Disobey," both in David Spitz (Ed.), *Political Theory and Social Change* (New York: Atherton Press, 1967), pp. 163-83, 185-202.

[3] Consult the writings of C. B. Macpherson, in particular his *The Political Theory of Possessive Individualism: Hobbes to Locke* (Oxford: Clarendon Press, 1962), and also those of Erich Fromm and Herbert Marcuse.

[4] Of speical interest, I have found the following: Edmund Leach, *A Runaway World?* (New York: Oxford University Press, 1968); *The Universities*, A Special Issue of *The Public Interest*, Number 13, (Fall 1968); Daniel and Gabriel Cohn-Bendit, *Obsolete Communism: The Left Wing Alternative* (New York: McGraw-Hill, 1969); Lewis S. Feuer, *The Conflict of Generations: The Character and Significance of Student Movements* (New York: Basic Books, 1969); Edward Shils, "Of Plenitude and Scarcity," *Encounter*, *XXXII* (May 1969), 37-57.

and oligarchs pursue strategic strength, lean into the winds of pluralism for the sake of Party, and perhaps personal, power.[5] The people of Czechoslovakia, their sovereignty and legality violated, their sense of right thwarted, are counseled to prudence by liberalizing leaders, whose fate remains uncertain.[6] Poland's sense of political obligation has been further attenuated by an immobilizing regime which drives from that country the remnant of a hapless minority. In Romania and Yugoslavia, national independence and self-determination revive against strategic and ideological coercion.

Ideological disorder seems implicit in a Yugoslav philosopher's assertion that "certain essential theses of dialectical materialism are full of difficulties and are irreconcilable with Marx's humanistic conception of man."[7] A colleague, arguing for democracy in the form of "self-management," worries about the moral impact of increasing reliance upon economic incentives and competitive practices.[8] Repeating Marx's talk about the blindness and coerciveness of economic forces, the Cohn-Bendits propose to replace economic rationality with what they call "objective logic and necessity."[9] They fail to explain the meaning of these cryptic

[5] On Kim Philby, see Hugh Trevor-Roper, *The Philby Affair: Espionage, Treason, and Secret Services* (London: William Kimber, 1968); on Andrei D. Sakharov, see his *Progress, Coexistence, and Intellectual Freedom*, trans. *The New York Times*, with Introduction, Afterword, and Notes by Harrison E. Salisbury (New York: W. W. Norton, 1968); for an appraisal of Soviet politics and prospects, Arnold L. Horelick, *Fifty Years After October: Party and Society in the USSR* (Santa Monica, Calif.: The RAND Corporation, P-3630, September 1967).

[6] Alexander Dubcek's ideas are presented in *Czechoslovakia's Blueprint for "Freedom,"* Introduction and Analysis by Paul Ello (Washington, D. C.: Acropolis Books, 1968). See also Harry Schwartz, *Prague's 200 Days: The Struggle for Democracy in Czechoslovakia* (New York: Frederick A. Praeger, 1969).

[7] Gajo Petrović, *Marx in the Mid-Twentieth Century: A Yugoslav Philosopher Reconsiders Karl Marx's Writings* (Garden City, N.Y.: Doubleday, 1967), p. 64.

[8] Mihailo Marković, "Socialism and Self-Menagement" (*sic*), I *Praxis* (1965), 178–95. He says, "The type of people who would be created by a society under such conditions would not essentially differ from the type of people created by capitalism. It would be made up of people whose entire motivation to action is directed by the single motive of acquiring and possessing material goods," p. 194. This does seem rather an exaggeration in view of that combination of material and ideal interests which has historically been the mark of liberal societies. Nor do contemporary impulses in these societies lend it support.

[9] Cohen-Bendits, *Obsolete Communism*, p. 108.

criteria. The relevance of "Leninism" as an ideology for the industrialized is questioned.[10] In the course of an historical examination of Soviet thinking, a social psychologist detects "a redefinition of the concept of man. . . . The new man was the *Party man*."[11] And he goes on to argue that "this development is not towards self-determination and freedom."[12] It would seem impossible to derive coherent principles of political obligation from this ideological flux; the doctrines of the "Party man" and "self-management" are incompatible, as are the beliefs in historical inevitability and human freedom. If both the Soviet conception of the "higher phase of communism" and the Yugoslavian and Czechoslovakian conceptions of "socialist humanism" are outcomes of "Marxism-Leninism," the claim of this body of theory to consistency seems tenuous indeed.

Ultimately, in my opinion, disorder in both the West and the East may be traced to an ideal that is shared by liberalism and Marxism, to that vision of personal and social integration implicit in Rousseau's conception of human "perfectibility." Speaking of Hegel and Marx, John Plamenatz points out that "their ideal is also, at bottom, the ideal of Rousseau and Kant: that no man should be the mere instrument of other men, and that all men should be able to live in accordance with principles they inwardly accept."[13] I do not wish to suggest that all liberal thinkers would accept Rousseau's reading of human potentialities, or that all Marxists would subscribe to Marx's optimism, which Rousseau himself would certainly not share.[14] Nor do I mean to say

[10] See James E. Connor's "Introduction" to his *Lenin on Politics and Revolution: Selected Writings* (New York: Pegasus, 1968).

[11] Z. Barbu, "Soviet Historiography and the Concept of Man," *Acta Philosophica et Theologica*, Tomus II (Rome: 1964), pp. 69–79, 78.

[12] *Ibid.*

[13] J. P. Plamenatz, *Man and Society: Political and Social Theory: Bentham through Marx*, 2 vols. (New York: McGraw-Hill, 1963), II, p. 407. According to Erich Fromm, "all Humanists have shared a belief in the possibility of man's perfectibility. . . ." *Socialist Humanism: An International Symposium* (Garden City, N.Y.: Doubleday, 1966), p. vii.

[14] Milovan Djilas says: "To speak of society as imperfect may seem to imply that it *can* be perfect, which in truth it cannot. The task for contemporary man is to accept the reality that society is unperfect, but also to understand that humanist, humanitarian dreams and visions are necessary in order to reform society, in order to improve and advance it." *The Unperfect Society: Beyond the New Class*, trans. Dorian Cooke (New York: Harcourt, Brace & World, 1969), p. 5.

that liberal and Marxist conceptions of perfectibility are identical; their differences are of profound importance, and I shall wish to bring them out. Still there is at the core of both political theories a common belief in social harmony based on equality of opportunity and moral freedom, a psychological and moral condition which men have it in them to attain. For Marx, as Eugene Kamenka holds: "Man's nature consisted of a set of potentialities; freedom allowed him to go about the task of realizing them to the full. It enabled him to subordinate nature and his environment to his will, to realize himself in work and in his intercourse with others instead of subordinating himself to demands confronting him as alien requirements, as limitations on his being and not as fulfilments of it."[15] Kamenka notices and emphasizes the influence of Rousseau and Kant, as well as that of Hegel, on Marx's thinking.

Within the communist movement itself there are special sources of friction and disorder. According to Robert Jay Lifton, the Confucian notion of "sincerity" depends upon a principle of harmony, "harmony within, permitting one to act correctly in an automatic fashion, and harmony without, enabling one to find his proper behavior in relationship to other men."[16] The ideal of perfectibility even has a Confucian equivalent, but in China obligations imposed by Maoist "psychism" are meeting with resistance from the character of those whom Lifton labels "protean men."[17] And Mao has taken over "Leninism," only to turn that ideology back against the country of its origin.

As for much of the rest of the world, the prevailing form of society is the "Praetorian," in which all inherit mutually frustrating personal and social obligations.[18] Neither personal nor social integration is attainable in this situation. In these societies the liberal relation of the moral and the political would seem to

[15] Eugene Kamenka, *Marxism and Ethics* (London: Macmillan, 1969), p. 12.

[16] Robert Jay Lifton, *Thought Reform and the Psychology of Totalism: A Study of "Brainwashing" in China* (New York: W. W. Norton, 1963), p. 391.

[17] Robert Jay Lifton, *Revolutionary Immortality: Mao Tse-tung and the Chinese Cultural Revolution* (New York: Vintage Books, 1968), pp. 151–53.

[18] On the concept of the "Praetorian Society," see Samuel P. Huntington, *Political Order in Changing Societies* (New Haven: Yale University Press, 1968). Huntington credits David Rapoport with the formulation of the concept of the "Praetorian Society."

be reversed. For ethical beliefs and objectives do not provide criteria and direction for political authority. Only through the development of a common sense of justice and of political obligation can the "Praetorian" societies hope to advance toward a genuine morality and modern personality. For them the only alternative to shifting oligarchy, stagnation, and violence is the creation of effective and rational political authority, a diagnosis on which both Machiavelli and Lenin would agree.[19] But an un-Marxian Marxist proposes that intensification of insecurity through guerrilla warfare is the way to prepare people to accept political supremacy of the Party in the name of social justice.[20]

Toward resolution of so various and so vast forms of moral and intellectual disorder, what may be expected from political theory? Practical, operational advice in the shape of strategies for political development and stability is to be had in what I have called "the political theory of pluralism," a distillation of Western thought and experience.[21] And one may try to demonstrate the theoretical and moral coherence of liberalism.[22] But people in our time seem to be asking for something more than advice and analysis. They want an end to ethical uncertainty and political ambiguity. They need a political theory that can serve as a philosophy of life, that offers moral foundations upon which can rise a common sense of the politically obligatory. Perhaps creatures such as ourselves, fundamentally purposive and moral, may not be said even to understand their situation unless they know what they should be trying to bring about, not merely what is prudent, sensible, or in their interest to do. Hence we cannot avoid asking whether anything can be said about political obligation that is rationally and empirically persuasive, that could command conceivably universal assent.

[19] On the sources of violence, see Henry Bienen, *Violence and Social Change: A Review of Current Literature* (Chicago: The University of Chicago Press, 1968).

[20] Régis Debray, *Revolution in the Revolution? Armed Struggle and Political Struggle in Latin America*, trans. Bobbye Ortiz (New York: Grove Press, 1967).

[21] "Voluntary Association and the Political Theory of Pluralism," in J. Roland Pennock and John W. Chapman (Eds.), *Voluntary Associations, Nomos XI* (New York: Atherton Press, 1969), pp. 87–118.

[22] As I have, in my "Natural Rights and Justice in Liberalism," in D. D. Raphael (Ed.), *Political Theory and the Rights of Man* (London and Bloomington: Macmillan and Indiana University Press, 1967), pp. 27–42.

I distinguish political obligation, properly so called, from those other and more narrow kinds of obligation that we recognize as moral or legal. Political obligation has to do with the moral objectives of life, and with the network of institutions essential to their achievement. This is the meaning of the concept as we find it in Western political thinking. I do not propose to examine all of its interpretations. Rather I shall wish to consider the contemporary confrontation of liberal and Marxist theories of political obligation and significant issues which bear on this debate of both a philosophical and a psychological nature.

We have already noticed—and this hint of universality is in itself encouraging—that liberalism and Marxism, although their interpretations of it are radically different, do share the ideal of human perfectibility, understood as that form of development of our potentialities, the outcome of which is an harmonious meshing of moral freedom and psychological need, in terms of both character and institutions. The idea is Rousseau's, and by it he meant also to convey an impression of human flexibility, misunderstanding of which could and did, in his opinion, result in an institutional distortion of our nature and consequent dissatisfaction. We need not and should not, however, restrict the meaning of perfectibility to Rousseau's understanding of it. Nor should we take the notion of perfectibility to imply some condition of tensionless harmony. I assume that elements of strain and challenge will be present in any progressive society, and indeed are essential aspects of a life worth living. For our purposes the important and useful thing about the concept of perfectibility is that it is a compound concept, both moral and psychological, dynamic or developmental, and institutional, implying that there is a way of life which human beings can recognize as appropriate to their nature.

I propose to begin with an examination of the experience on which the ideal of perfectibility is based, both moral and psychological. I shall then consider the Marxist interpretation of the ideal by way of a comparison of liberal and Marxist psychodynamics. On these foundations and in an historical perspective I shall appraise contemporary theories of political obligation, in particular those which depend upon Kantian metaethics. My conclusion will be that both experience and reflection show that the moral foundations of political obligation as displayed in liberalism are more firmly established than are Marxian alternatives. Uncertainties as to political direction and destiny will not, of course, be entirely resolved, and perhaps cannot be. Rather my aim is to render less perplexing that perpetual and again newly urgent problem of political obligation.

PERFECTIBILITY AND POLITICAL OBLIGATION

If we apply the plain historical method to Western experience, there has been one big shift in the moral foundations of political obligation, and that may be described as a movement from moral functionalism to moral individualism. By moral functionalism I mean the view, characteristic of classical and medieval thinking, that men are born or called to the performance of a function, to the duties of a station. There is a moral structure intrinsic to the human enterprise, and this structure, whether it be conceived in terms of the classical conception of justice or its descendant, the medieval conception of natural law, obliges each and all in a rational pattern of differentiated and hierarchically organized roles. Analytically speaking, the concept of moral functionalism is simply a way of generalizing about the ethical component of those political theories we ordinarily call rationalist.

Moral functionalism transforms into moral individualism as the concept of natural law inverts into that of natural rights, conceived initially as metaphysical attributes of men who recognize, in Locke's words, a "law of reason" as their moral and political guide. With this fundamental change in orientation the modern theory of political obligation begins to develop and to elaborate as Western thinkers have had to cope with a succession of intellectual and situational concerns. For Hobbes, faced as he was by political disorder, the first "law of nature" is to "endeavour peace," and security and prosperity are to be had by keeping one's promises, above all the obligation to obey the commands of the sovereign. Only a unified allegiance can lead men possessed of natural rights from that condition of preemptive instability that is the Hobbesian "state of nature." For such creatures the sovereign state is the means essential to that which they most value and desire, to get on with the work of life, unimpeded by mutual fear and distrust. Personal security and rationality are to be maintained by the threat of centralized coercion, a deterrent which obliges all.

Once security is achieved, however, men who have come to think of themselves as individuals demand more from their political arrangements. No government is legitimate unless it has their consent; their obligation to obey is conditional upon the performance of government, upon its protection of their natural rights, especially the right to freedom in all its various forms. Such is the somewhat ambiguous position reached by John Locke.[23] For him the legislature rather than the monarch is the locus of sovereignty, and against this government the individual retains an indefeasible right of revolution should that government fail the trust bestowed upon it.

The problem posed by these moral and political innovations is how to secure their natural rights equally to all. This can be done, Rousseau will argue, because men are "perfectible," that is to say, despite their deformation by inegalitarian institutions, men do recognize and respect one another's moral claims and potentialities. Given security and freedom, they will next call for justice and equality, demands which are really needs, and which Rousseau summarizes in his concept of a "general will." In an appropriate institutional environment, there will arise in each a will for justice that can issue in a common conception and sense of justice, and this is the guarantee of each against moral or political oppression, and the prerequisite for equality of natural right. For Rousseau, our specifically political obligation is to bring into existence and to sustain those social and political institutions appropriate to human nature, through which human development is toward the promise of integration implicit in the concept of perfectibility. His conception of a "general will," one notices, was already present in moral individualism conceived in terms of equal natural rights.

The moral pattern in our historical experience seems plain

---

[23] On the significance of consent for political obligation, see J. P. Plamenatz, *Consent, Freedom and Political Obligation*, 2d ed. (London: Oxford University Press, 1968), "Postscript to the Second Edition," pp. 162–82; Hanna Pitkin, "Obligation and Consent: I" *American Political Science Review*, LIX (December 1965), 990–99; "Obligation and Consent: II," *American Political Science Review*, LX (March 1966), 39–52.

enough. Once the transformation from moral functionalism to individualism is accomplished, is it not simply a matter of first things coming first? The course of political theory from Hobbes through Locke to Rousseau is not adventitious. Rather it contains a moral logic. Having broken out of the mold of moral functionalism, men require security against one another if their energies are to be released. But "peace" alone cannot satisfy rational and ambitious beings; they want freedom. This demand is both an expression and a recognition of moral personality, and moral personalities cannot and will not ignore the claims of justice and equality. Hence our obligation to obey the state and the law, to the degree that these embody a "general will," depends on their being essential means to the achievement of these fundamental political values. This is the modern and liberal theory of political obligation.[24] The transition from Hobbes' sovereign to Rousseau's sovereignty of the "general will" is based on the emergence of moral needs and a correlative change in the conception of political obligation. Hobbes' men are "economic men," for whom obligation and rational advantage are all but equivalent. Being what they are, mutual coercion is the price of their security. Unlike Hobbes, Rousseau is interested in moral improvement, in the development of "natural goodness." Hence for him human "perfectibility" becomes the moral foundation of the politically obligatory. Political obligation is impersonal and institutional; it goes only to that form of society and government through which self-government and self-development are possible.

THE PSYCHOLOGICAL DIMENSION

In Rousseau's work, moral individualism arrives at the "paradox" of self-government, as Bosanquet was later to call it.[25] Considered from a moral standpoint, resolution of the paradox depends on the development of a common conception of justice. But there is more to the moral psychology of liberalism

[24] The modern liberal theory of political obligation is presented in summary form by J. Roland Pennock in his "The Obligation to Obey the Law and the Ends of the State," in Sidney Hook (Ed.), *Law and Philosophy: A Symposium* (New York: New York University Press, 1964), pp. 77–85.

[25] Bernard Bosanquet, *The Philosophical Theory of the State*, 4th ed. (London: Macmillan, 1923), Chapter III.

than this. Western moral and political experience has a psychological dimension that may be phrased in terms of Robert M. MacIver's concepts of "differentiation" and "socialization," or what, more recently, Zevedei Barbu has called the processes of "individuation" and "rationalization."[26] These psychological processes help to account for the way in which an intensified sense of individuality is compatible with self-government and political unity. Individuation and rationalization are the psychological, or characterological, aspects of "perfectibility."

Moral individualism and the doctrine of natural rights need not and do not lead to social and political chaos for, as Locke argued, men so endowed also possess knowledge of a law of nature or reason, criteria of mutual respect and dealing, on the basis of which they are enabled to act rationally and fairly. The experience that individuality and rationality advance together is central to the moral psychology of liberalism. It is present in the idea of social and political contract, in the belief that men can agree rationally on the terms and purposes of their association. Hume did not have much use for the concept of contract, but his view that justice is the product of reflection upon experience, essentially an invention the purpose of which is to enable men more effectively to cooperate with one another, is also an expression of this confidence in men's capacity for self-determination. Perhaps the most striking commitment to the complementary nature of individuality and rationality is Rousseau's proposition that in free men, and only in such men, does there arise that feeling of mutual respect, that devotion to equality of treatment, he calls a "general will." The conviction that individuality does not imply anarchy reaches an extreme in Kant's virtual equation of rationality and morality. For, according to him, the truly autonomous personality is the one who acts in accordance with the dictate of reason, the categorical imperative. And even Hegel, despite his transference of reason from the human individual to a metaphysical force, may be regarded as a representative of the liberal persuasion that individuality and rationality are processes that make for social and political integration.

The institutional texture of a liberal society is to be woven

[26] See Barbu's *Democracy and Dictatorship: Their Psychology and Patterns of Life* (New York: Grove Press, 1956), and *Problems of Historical Psychology* (London: Routledge & Kegan Paul, 1960).

with these principles of moral psychology. Human welfare can be advanced through economic rationality and secured by general recognition of rationally defensible principles of justice. The state itself may be conceived as an artifact of reason, essentially a technique for ensuring that men hold fast to their real and permanent interests. The principles of political economy would convert rational self-interest into collective benefits. Although Hume and Kant might differ on the moral function of reason, and although Rousseau's conception of human nature is not that of the utilitarians, still one can see at the heart of liberalism a vision of the rational individual, capable of both competition and cooperation, a polarized and yet an integrated personality, a man who was both economic and moral. As Hegel argued, the great and contrasting institutions of family, economy, and state articulate and integrate the principles of moral individuality.

Thus the liberal conception of human "perfectibility" is based on a synthesis of moral and psychological processes. The liberal thinkers have many points of disagreement—philosophical, psychological, ethical, and institutional—and in other contexts I should not wish to minimize these. But notice that even the dour and flinty behaviorist, James Mill, kindles in the common blaze: "When the grand sources of felicity are formed into the leading and governing ideas, each in its due and relative strength, Education has then performed its most perfect work; and thus the individual becomes, to the greatest degree, the source of utility to others, and of happiness to himself."[27] For present purposes it does not matter whether we think in terms of utilitarian interests or Lockean natural rights, in terms of giving men what they are trained to want or of helping them to become what they ought to be. The doctrine of natural rights is an assertion of moral freedom, of a claim to live in accordance with one's sense of right, and while the utilitarian liberal might dispute the wording of the claim, he would not contest its spirit. All would see this expression of individuality as compatible with social unity, for since men are rational, or can be made so, they cannot but arrive at a common understanding of their mutual rights and obliga-

---

[27] Mill, *Analysis of the Phenomena of the Human Mind,* a new edition with notes illustrative and critical by Alexander Bain, Andrew Findlater, and George Grote, edited by John Stuart Mill, 2 vols. (London: Longmans Green Reader and Dyer, 1869), I, 378.

tions. Their consciences and their character, their obligations and their aspirations, mesh in a form of life that all can regard as worth living, in a "Kingdom of ends."

Implicit in Locke is the thought that protection of individual rights gives rise to political obligation; Rousseau holds that the only legitimate form of government is self-government in a classless society; the utilitarians see political obligation in the general obligation to increase happiness. Behind these doctrines are common beliefs in a new morality and a new psychology. The moral psychology of liberalism contains a new conception of both the ends and means of life, in which there is combined the moral logic of political experience and enhanced confidence in individual rationality.

THE GREAT DEFLECTION

If this interpretation of the record is in the main correct, then much of the thought and experience of the nineteenth and twentieth centuries is to be seen as a great deflection of the liberal enterprise. The liberal ways of thinking about the ends and obligations of life are challenged. Inequality and insecurity, the fruits of industrial revolution and industrialized war, unleashed massive pressures toward psychological and moral regression, pressures which have proved, temporarily at least, fatal for the fragility and rationality of liberalism. A drastic simplification, I shall argue, is the significance of Marxism and its project of displacing institutions based on political and economic rationality by ones based on emotional and moral solidarity. The liberal equipoise gives way to a new vision of human "perfectibility," in which psychological unity replaces ambivalence as the defining category of human nature.

Moral functionalism returns as the socialist reaction against liberalism begins with the Saint-Simonian proposal to replace competition with association and democracy with benevolent élitism. Not individual rationality but the "New Christianity" is to be the foundation of social unity and political responsibility. And for Marx, man in a liberal society exists in a condition of corruption and alienation. The principles of political economy, of economic rationality, are nothing but an ideology which separates men from one another and from their own communist

essence as "species-beings." Through their conditioned and enforced acquisativeness men are deformed and embittered, the
victims of their institutions. The concept of justice itself is an
ideological manifestation of alienation, not an authentic expression of human "perfectibility." Correction of maldistribution cannot save those who are warped by the competitive and specialized
organization of productivity. The whole doctrine of natural rights
is an assertion of class interest, masquerading in terms of universality. The fundamental difficulty, according to Marx, is that
men have, through the force of circumstance and institutional
arrangement, been led to misconceive the relations in which they
ought to stand to one another, and until they achieve the
appropriate relations, they cannot be other than alienated and in
the grip of ideology. Liberal institutions have no valid and
enduring claim upon their allegiance. Their basic political obligation is to understand and to bring about, in tune with natural
social and economic processes, a new form of society and government, one which recognizes their essence as free and associational
beings.

In Marx's new and functional society, the institutional criterion of rationality is to have as substitutes the criteria of
mutuality and reciprocity. "Surprisingly, Marx discovers this
paradigm of the future in the family, or, to be more exact, in the
relationship between the sexes. According to Marx, the unique
pattern of these relations has a systematic significance which
makes it possible to project them as a general model for the
structure of human relations in socialist society."[28] Marx proposes that a single structure, an "identity in difference"—to use
Bosanquet's expression for the concept of concrete universality—
underlies all human activities—sexual, social, economic, and political. Noncompetitive, associative, and ultimately aesthetic are
the only forms of human relations that are fully satisfactory and
authentically expressive of our moral psychology. In contrast to
the liberal conception of human complexity and ambivalence,
Marx's would appear to be a simplistic picture of human nature,
perhaps ultimately Platonic in the implication that the source of

[28] Shlomo Avineri, *The Social and Political Thought of Karl Marx*
(Cambridge: Cambridge University Press, 1968), p. 89. And see also Herbert
Marcuse's *Eros and Civilization: A Philosophical Inquiry into Freud* (Boston:
Beacon Press, 1955).

social unity and political obligation is love, or Augustinian. The relations between men and women, at their best, provide the key to the Marxian notion of "perfectibility." It is a vision of an equalitarian moral functionalism, Hegelian and rationalist, as Marx's early writings show, in its immediate inspiration.

There are a number of observations to be made on Marx's formulation of human perfectibility. Having depreciated rationality, particularly in his attack upon the "principles of political economy," and having chosen to treat justice as an item of ideology of the alienated, it is difficult to see where else he has to turn, except to love and emotional solidarity for the moral foundations of unity and obligation. Moreover, he holds that in his new society individuality is to be maximized as free and spontaneous creativity. And yet the anthropological and historical evidence at our disposal suggests that societies based entirely on an emotional form of unity are anything but hospitable to the flowering of individuals, to the development of resilient personalities of the kind that John Stuart Mill had in mind. Rousseau had recognized that deliberate intensification of social sentiment was inconsistent with his own analysis of the psychology of moral individualism.[29] In this light, Marx's proposal does not appear so much as an advance upon as a retreat from the complexity inherent in the liberal understanding of human nature, in which, as Barbu has shown, "individuation" and "rationalization" are experienced as concomitant processes.

These critical reflections find support in recent events. We know that Marx was addressing men in a condition of stress and frustration, incapable of rational self-direction, craving for emotional solidarity and to be rid of a feeling of impersonal and institutionalized coercion. In these circumstances, we would now expect a revulsion against the principles of moral individualism and the appearance of regressive tendencies toward less demanding, and apparently less tense, forms of social integration. And we now know that when such tendencies matured, they took the form of nationalism. If democracy is divorced from socialism, as with Lenin, and guidance of an emotionally unified mass is seen as the function of a political élite organized as a party and claiming historical insight into our moral destiny, then Marxism,

---

[29] See my *Rousseau—Totalitarian or Liberal?* (New York: Columbia University Press, 1956), Part II, Chapter 6.

in the shape of Marxism-Leninism, provides the operative political formula of the twentieth century: National Socialism. In this perspective, Soviet Communism is something else again, not a form of society approaching that which Marx envisaged, not characterized by spontaneity and reciprocity. Rather it appears to be intensely rationalist, in the sense of being centrally organized and administered; impersonality and unemotionality are offically valued to an inhuman degree. Somehow Marx's antipathy to rationality as the criterion of humanity has led to social rigidification and political oppression. Has a political theory ever so badly and so ironically miscarried? Have ever there arisen regimes less compelling in their claim to allegiance, less respectful of the moral principles that men can inwardly accept, or more unworthy as claimants to man's political obligation?

LIBERAL AND MARXIST PSYCHODYNAMICS

As we have been arguing throughout, liberalism and Marxism have in common an ideal of human "perfectibility," a conception of a way of life that exerts its claim upon men as both within their reach and consistent with their nature. In both political theories this ideal condition is the moral foundation of political obligation; to gain it is obligatory upon men as morally purposive beings. Where these types of theory differ is on human dynamics, and hence on the institutional articulation of the shared ideal.

In liberal thinking there is a persistent strain of congruence between psychological processes, on the one hand, and moral and political aspiration, on the other. For the mature individual is conceived as possessing an inner source of authority, whether we call this reason or conscience, that at one and the same time may serve to articulate, regulate, and unify human relations. Emotional processes may be conceived, as in the case of Rousseau's psychology, as functionally dependent upon, and hence supportive of, rationality in attitude and action. In Marxist as in Freudian psychodynamics, rationality and emotionality are seen as opposed; the institutional requirements of rationality are experienced as emotionally oppressive. These human characteristics are thought by Marx to offer alternative foundations for social organization, or at least one characteristic must be given the priority. Liberal emphasis on rationality is his diagnosis of the source of oppressiveness and alienation. The essential thesis of Marxism, in its classical form, is that we should and will shift to more affectively oriented forms of life.

Marx would appear to have overlooked the possibility that what he calls alienation has its roots in social complexity and the demoralization attendant upon the strains imposed by cultural change. If this be so, then he has mistaken a transient, although recurrent, craving for a permanent cure. To attempt to act on his moral psychology would hence be self-defeating. For if he wants creative individuality, it cannot be had by adopting emotional identification as the single pervasive criterion of the humanness of human relations.

In fact, it seems to me, Marx has stumbled upon and into a Freudian psychodynamic, the one that underlies much of the political experience of our time; namely, that anxiety, insecurity, and disappointment breed psychological and moral regression. And this formula exhibits itself not only in the varieties of fascism, but also in the intellectual performance and political practice of Marxists, as the latent formula emerges to devour the overt ideal. Jean-Paul Sartre constructs a theory of human relations shot through with anxiety and conflict, and then collapses his people emotionally into what he calls the "group," socialism with a Hobbist face. The imposition of emotional unity through deliberate cultivation of anxiety is the purpose of that technique of character manipulation called "brain washing." Many, of whom the latest is Régis Debray, have discovered that intensification of insecurity is a way to force people into political dependence and commitment.

Indeed, if we have in mind the difference between the latent and the manifest content of Marxism, then it is apparent that Marxism has not been so much followed, for that is impossible, as applied. As a political theory, Marxism has the remarkably dubious virtue of being able to explain its own failure. Or more prosaically, Marxism suffers from that defect, fatal to a political theory, of an incoherent moral psychology. Its psychological principles and institutional projections are imcompatible with its ethical objectives. As such a mixture, Marxism can provide no version of human "perfectibility," superior to that which is present in liberal thought. And hence no overriding principle of political obligation. For no valid political imperative can be derived from an apparently generous but decisively mistaken appreciation of human possibilities.

If Marxism, both in theory and in practice, is a deflection from the rise of moral individualism and its associated doctrines, and indeed, in many ways, a retreat or reversion to earlier and more primitive conceptions of social unity and purpose, then it cannot be taken to supersede the liberal interpretation of political obligation. In the end, the trouble with Marx's brand of moral functionalism is that it, by postulating a single ideal pattern for human relations, gravely underestimates our potentialities. The older functionalisms saw men as united for the pursuit of a single purpose, justice or salvation, and the presence of that purpose both organizes and obliges them. Marx sees not a single purpose implicit in humanity, but rather a single pattern of association inherent in human nature. The political consequences are much the same, a lack or loss of sensitivity for human rights in metaphysical fascination with the ideal pattern. In contrast to the functionalisms, moral individualism recognizes a diversity of human purposes and capacities, and the conception of "perfectibility" emerges as a belief that these can harmonize, in appropriately balanced institutional environments. This is the conviction at the heart of liberalism, and which requires further clarification.

DIVERSE INTERPRETATIONS

Moral individualism requires interpretation. We can see and appreciate the moral logic and the psychodynamics of our experience and yet look for further, ultimately philosophical, explanation of its meaning. One theorist says that the flow of political thought and activity shows that two sorts of fundamental considerations are involved, the deontological and the teleological.[30] Justice and utility or welfare are the two moral constants that permeate politics and press for institutional reconciliation. Another thinker suggests that the concept of a "com-

[30] Alan Gewirth in the "Introduction" to his *Political Philosophy* (New York: Macmillan, 1965), pp. 1–30.

mon good" is at the core of Western political thinking.[31] But still a third assures us that "value words, and intrinsic value judgments in which they occur, have expressive and directive, rather than cognitive, meanings."[32] All these writers adhere to moral individualism. Moreover, all of them probably would pretty much agree in their ethical and political judgments. Where they differ is as to the status of these judgments, whether they are cognitive, demonstrative in some sense, or not. Not to know what it is that we are doing when we engage in ethical and political deliberation is to be left in a state of metaethical uncertainty.

This uncertainty infects the very conception of political obligation. According to Thomas McPherson, obligation is a concept not properly applicable to politics, and to apply it to politics is to moralize the political, with unhappy consequences. He concludes that "we may well feel justified in dispensing with the concept of political obligation."[33] A. J. Ayer reviews Western thinking and concludes that the grounds which theorists have offered for political obligation are "persuasive," in C. L. Stevenson's sense of that term. "They amount to the advocacy of a certain form of political organization."[34] Anthony Quinton is inclined morally to defuse the concept. The real question, he says, is "what makes it a generally good or desirable thing for me, or anyone, to obey the state?"[35] Once the question is put this way, then the "rationality of political obedience is identified neither with its moral obligatoriness nor with its conduciveness to strictly personal interest and advantage."[36] McPherson, Ayer, and Quinton are all in one way or another connected with the British schools of analytic and linguistic philosophy. But even this degree of intellectual unity does not produce agreement on the interpretation and significance of political obligation. At the other end of

[31] George Kateb, *Political Theory: Its Nature and Uses* (New York: St. Martin's Press, 1968).

[32] Felix E. Oppenheim, *Moral Principles in Political Philosophy* (New York: Randon House, 1968), p. 179.

[33] Thomas McPherson, *Political Obligation* (London: Routledge & Kegan Paul, 1967), p. 84.

[34] A. J. Ayer, *Philosophy and Politics* (Liverpool: Liverpool University Press, 1967), p. 21.

[35] Anthony Quinton (Ed.), *Political Philosophy* (London: Oxford University Press, 1967), "Introduction," 1–18, p. 10.

[36] *Ibid.*

this spectrum of opinion we find Sir Isaiah Berlin, for whom the problem of political obligation is "perhaps the most fundamental of all political questions. . . . When we ask why a man should obey, we are asking for the explanation of what is normative in such notions as authority, sovereignty, liberty, and the justification of their validity in political arguments."[37]

With Berlin's statement of the question, our problem of the moral foundations of political obligation comes back into focus. If we can find in human nature and experience anchors for this concept of the "normative," perhaps then we shall have a clue to the resolution of metaethical uncertainty, to the status of our fundamental moral concepts and objectives. For so long as metaethical uncertainty persists, the meaning of moral individualism and the significance of political obligation remain problematical. What we ought to aim for as forms of government and society would continue to perplex, and political argument could not advance, as Ayer suggests, beyond persuasion and advocacy. This may be all there is to it, and even this may be enough. But men do hanker to ground their values and obligations in "reality" and feel uncomfortable with the thought that there are ultimate differences in moral and political attitude, behind which it is impossible to go. Does our moral psychology admit of variant interpretations; does the "normative" in political life and argument reduce to the "emotive" or the "prescriptive?" If so, then to ask for the moral foundations of political obligation would be mistaken. For men there are only recommendations: "Endeavor peace," and be on your guard against the "fanatical!"

WORDS AND THEIR SIGNIFICANCE

Since Bosanquet and Hocking, much of philosophical thinking about ethics and politics has been concerned with conceptual analysis and clarification and with the relations among the members of conceptual clusters. Some, including Bertrand Russell and A. J. Ayer, and perhaps many, have looked askance at this enterprise, surely an oblique and unprofitable way to go about

[37] Sir Isaiah Berlin, "Does Political Theory Still Exist?" in Peter Laslett and W. G. Runciman (Eds.), *Philosophy, Politics and Society* (*Second Series*) (Oxford: Basil Blackwell, 1962), 1–33, p. 7.

ordering the data of human experience. What could be expected from an investigation of the ordinary and unscientific uses of language: the performative, the rhetorical, the persuasive, expressive, prescriptive, and the like? The dissolution of some metaphysical puzzles, the disestablishment of universals, and beyond these not much of genuinely philosophical interest. If G. E. Moore was right about the "naturalistic fallacy," and if meaning is a matter of "empirical verifiability," then normative talk and activity must be finally "emotive" in nature.[38] Hobbes and Hume had seen the truth. Profitable thinking about ethics and politics must start from an indissoluble distinction between fact and value, between descriptive and evaluative forms of discourse.

It now seems safe to say, safer than it would have been even a decade ago, that linguistic empiricism casts real doubt on the postulates of logical positivism. For what began with Wittgenstein as a critique of metaphysical thinking has turned into a phenomenology of moral experience, into a new metaethic. Moral psychology, the very conception of which defies positivist distinctions, has reappeared as linguistic analysis.

To begin with, that logical line which positivism had drawn between the factual and the ethical does not seem to govern our use of language. As J. L. Austin liked to point out, when we call a house "squat," we not only describe it but also evaluate it. The linguistic philosophers have taught us to notice how language is laden with criteria, concepts which are both descriptive and normative, and which we use to grade, to recommend, to prescribe, and to do all sorts of things that ignore positivist injunctions. Indeed, it would seem that we inhabit a medium of evaluation; we are like fish in a sea of value. There are, as G. J. Warnock puts it, moral "facts."[39] From a positivist standpoint, the very notion of a moral "fact" is a contradiction in terms. But what Warnock has in mind seems clear enough. Language contains evaluative criteria; we do not choose these criteria; they are given. When we employ a criterion correctly and appropriately,

[38] J. O. Urmson in his *The Emotive Theory of Ethics* (London: Hutchinson University Library, 1968) analyzes the origins and development of "emotivism."

[39] G. J. Warnock, *Contemporary Moral Philosophy* (London: Macmillan, 1967), p. 60.

and the web of language is sufficiently tightly woven to control the application of specific concepts, then we may be said to be stating a moral "fact." There would appear to be an inescapably cognitive and demonstrative aspect to ethical discourse. Linguistic phenomenology is moving toward a new form of ethical naturalism. The significance of words is that they are windows on human nature and experience.

PERSISTING CATEGORIES

The full significance of linguistic empiricism does not appear, I think, until an historical dimension is brought into the analysis. This has been done by Sir Isaiah Berlin, who thinks of our inherited moral and political concepts as indicative of the fundamental "categories" of human nature, as pointing at and reflecting "permanent human attributes," or, I should wish to add, potentialities.[40] In his view, conceptual analysis not only offers insight into the moral structure of human activity and thinking but is also a way of getting at the meaning of human experience, and this meaning is intrinsically "normative." Attention to our linguistic history shows how we have come to conceive of ourselves, what it means to be "human." In the older idiom, it would be said that linguistic phenomenology is a technique for elucidating the psychology, or even the anthropology, of moral experience.

When fundamental "categories" or concepts, such as justice or freedom, are placed in an historical perspective, at once a paradoxical phenomenon comes into view; they appear both to be stable and to be afflicted with instability. As Berlin points out, these concepts are "sufficiently continuous . . . to constitute a common world which we share with medieval and classical thinkers."[41] In the West, at least, they have been with us since the beginning, and yet over time their content and their relations alter. This is, I suspect, an intelligible phenomenon, an understanding of which does not commit us to either metaethical or ethical relativism, so long as these alterations make sense in the light of human needs and psychodynamics.

[40] Berlin, "Does Political Theory Still Exist?" *op. cit.*, and elsewhere.
[41] *Ibid.*, p. 30.

There are four, and perhaps more, sources of influence on our moral conceptions, which taken together help to explain their changes of content. The first of these I would label broadly "environmental," an example of which is the way an intensely competitive situation can shape men's view of merit and responsibility.[42] Notice, too, how the concept of justice tends to enlarge as the struggle for existence becomes less severe.[43] Second, as Hume remarked, metaphysical beliefs do have a profoundly distorting, and yet rationally intelligible, effect upon moral and political thinking. Berlin reads in human nature a metaphysical craving for symmetry, to which doctrines such as Marxism strongly appeal, and which ill accords with the plurality of values which we do in fact confront. And if one thinks of values, especially of justice, as metaphysically given features of our environment, then one can be driven into an inegalitarian type of moral functionalism, in which the value of freedom becomes secondary and depreciated. In addition, as we have seen, psychological needs created by exposure to change and insecurity, or inherent in different forms of psychic structure, cannot help but influence human evaluations and conceptions of obligation. With reference to forms of psychic structure, I have in mind such things as the relation between conscience and instinct, whether there is tension or accommodation, or the comparative intensity of needs for clarity and authority in moral and political situations. These are questions of the dynamics of our moral psychology, about which we need to know a good deal more than our earlier analysis of liberalism and Marxism provides, in particular about the connections between psychological needs and ideologies. And finally ethical principles, and their relative weight, would appear to be dependent on their social and political context. In a "Praetorian" society men will conceive their purposes and obligations much more narrowly than they do in more open and more secure circumstances.

[42] See Arthur W. H. Adkins, *Merit and Responsibility: A Study in Greek Values* (Oxford: Clarendon Press, 1960). Further analysis of moral causation may be found in W. B. Gallie, *Philosophy and the Historical Understanding* (London: Chatto & Windus, 1964), and Alasdair MacIntyre, *Secularization and Moral Change* (London: Oxford University Press, 1967).

[43] See my "Justice and Fairness," in Carl J. Friedrich and John W. Chapman (Eds.), *Justice, Nomos VI* (New York: Atherton Press, 1963), pp. 147–69.

Having these sources of influence in mind, and looking at the story of our moral and political experience, one may have the almost Aristotelian sensation of "looking through" the variations to something permanent and enduring. But what can this something be? Surely it is not a matter of intuiting "essences" or "universals," metaphysically conceived, although it is understandable that men have thought this way.

A more promising interpretation of that combination of historical permanence and lawful change characteristic of Western humanity is that which Berlin derives from Kant. For natural rights are not metaphysical attributes of human beings, nor are beliefs in moral individualism and the possiblity of human "perfectibility" based on metaphysical insight. Rather I think we are seeing, or discovering, or bringing into consciousness our permanent attributes as human beings, those potentialities distinctive to us, as these are, or rather have been, given conceptual recognition and expression. Another way of putting this is to say that our moral conceptions, our evaluative criteria, are the products of evolutionary agreements, mutual recognitions that have been hammered out in our dealings with one another, and that are rational in the sense that although they may vary in content and emphasis, still these variations make sense in the light of differing circumstances, beliefs, and salient needs. Behind the phenomena of instability, moral and political conceptions seem to have a logic; that is, structure and direction, features of our experience that are given a metaphysical interpretation by rationalist thinkers, but which may be afforded an empirical interpretation, an anchor in human nature and historical experience. Indeed, these persisting linguistic "categories" are the "attributes" definitive of the "human," as Berlin, and before him Rousseau and Kant, agreed.

SOME IMPLICATIONS AND QUESTIONS

What are the implications of these linguistic reflections for the problem of the politically obligatory? I would suggest that sensitivity to conceptual considerations tends to confirm the result of our historical and psychological analyses, that human experience is morally structured. This is the implication of

Berlin's conception of "permanent human attributes." And if there is a moral structure or logic in human experience, then it would seem that it is improper to speak as though we choose what we ought to do. As Warnock affirms, we do not choose our evaluative criteria. Linguistically and phenomenologically speaking, these are given, as are values generally, and not invented, at least by individuals.

But may it not be the case that we do have to choose among criteria and values, some at least of which are to be regarded as ultimates? This would appear to be Berlin's position. He says that "respect for the principles of justice . . . is as basic in men as the desire for liberty."[44] These are fundamental or ultimate moral categories. "In the end, men choose between ultimate values; they choose as they do, because their life and thought are determined by fundamental moral categories and concepts that are as much a part of their being and conscious thought and sense of their own identity, as their basic physical structure."[45] What Berlin seems to be saying is that the obligatory is qualified by a degree of openness that forces upon us a necessity for choice, that requires of us a decision. We face ultimates, each one of which separately presses its claim upon us and stands in a relation of polarization with the others. For example, equality, as an ultimate, would oblige us to ignore the claims of freedom and of justice. And so also with these other values; each confronts us with an inner momentum of its own.

Faced with this situation, the nature of which is essentially economic, what we do is to strike a balance, or, as Berlin puts it, choose a "blend." This choosing of a "blend" is, it would appear, a rational process, although, according to Berlin, it defies a fully explicit explanation. "A part of what we mean by rationality is the art of applying, and combining, reconciling, choosing among general principles in a manner for which complete theoretical explanation (or justification) can never, in principle, be given."[46] In Berlin's opinion, there is a flexibility or range of ethical indeterminacy in the human situation that precludes

44 Berlin, *Two Concepts of Liberty* (Oxford: Clarendon Press, 1958), p. 55.
45 *Ibid.*, p. 57.
46 See his "Equality as an Ideal," in Frederick A. Olafson (Ed.), *Justice and Social Policy: A Collection of Essays* (Englewood Cliffs, N.J.: Prentice-Hall, 1961), 128–50, p. 130.

uniqueness of choice. Human rationality has to deal with a plurality of ends. The timber of humanity is crooked. Desire for ethical certainty has no empirical or phenomenological warrant; rather it indicates the presence and pressure of a metaphysical need.

The question, it seems to me, is whether Berlin has succeeded in giving a full and cogent account of the phenomenology of our moral experience. It appears correct to say that we face, or rather embody, a plurality, not a hierarchy of values. There is no single ultimate criterion available for the appraisal of human activity. And he argues from this observation to the conclusion that our very nature precludes an engineering form of solution to the problem of the politically obligatory. We cannot affirm one supreme moral objective, to which all other values are related as means or derivatives, and set our political course accordingly. Left somewhat uncertain, however, in Berlin's writings is the matter of the scope of choice, the degree to which the composition of the "blend" may vary. How many forms of satisfactory ethical integration there are, in the end only experience and experiment can tell. But may it not be that the scope for personal variation in "blend" is rather greater than that for political values? Indeed, one senses that the demands of moral individuality impose constraints upon the political "blend," that is to say, upon the moral objectives to be furthered by political and social institutions, which is but to say again that moral individualism implies a theory of political obligation.

Berlin's remark about the nature and function of rationality suggests that our ethical situation has an economic structure, by which I mean to suggest that there may be an equilibrium among the "ultimates," departures from which would tend to be self-correcting, an equilibrium which establishes the direction of political activity and obligation. This may well be the case with the liberal constellation of values: equality of freedom, justice, and welfare, understood in both material and spiritual terms. If so, this equilibrium would constitute an empirical and operational definition of the older conception of human "perfectibility," and our fundamental political obligation would be to aim for, achieve, and sustain this equilibrium. This principle of obligation is consistent with that historical experience of a direction in the development of moral consciousness, or a moral logic, as I called it earlier, based on fundamental needs as these seek satisfaction in changing environments.

These observations may imply a more strict sense of moral equilibrium than Berlin himself would perceive in human nature. For he did once assert that "human thought and language change under the impact of the factors which determine the forms and the concepts in which men think, feel, communicate—factors which seem to pursue no regular pattern of a discernible kind."[47] But more recently, he surmises that "objective patterns in history may, for all I know, be discernible."[48] Perhaps Berlin's reluctance to admit the presence of a moral logic in human experience arises from his fear that such an admission would once again open the way for metaphysical impulse to impose upon an essentially pluralistic humanity. In any event, the range of moral variation, for Berlin, is not without limits; there is, one might say, a range of the "perfectible." He says that a human being is "a being endowed with a nucleus of needs and goals, a nucleus common to all men, which may have a shifting pattern, but one whose limits are determined by the basic need to communicate with other similar beings."[49] Communication requires recognition of men as what they are. Berlin offers a descriptive metaethic, a categorial empiricism, the residual fuzziness of which is, he would argue, intrinsic to human nature.

ANOTHER KANTIAN THEME

Linguistic empiricism leads to Warnock's naturalistic doctrine of moral "facts" and to Berlin's Kantian and phenomenological vision of the "fundamental moral categories" of human nature. Both the linguistic and the historical lines of conceptual exploration lend to ethical and political thinking a characteristic of objectivity absent from emotive interpretations. In what sense objective? In the sense that ethical concepts and criteria mark human attributes, have empirical origins in human dynamics. They may be conceived as agree-

[47] Berlin, *The Age of Enlightenment* (New York: Mentor Books, 1956), p. 27.

[48] Berlin, *Four Essays on Liberty* (New York: Oxford University Press, 1969), p. xxxv.

[49] *Ibid.*, p. lxii.

ments or recognitions through which, in our dealings with one another, we have come to define our enduring features, and to discover and to recognize our emerging potentialities. In this sense a descriptive metaethic is the outcome of Berlin's image of the human as the rational accommodation to partially divergent and insistent needs.

An alternative to Berlin's categorial empiricism, one also Kantian in inspiration and equally an authentic expression of liberalism, may be found in the categorical rationalism of John Rawls.[50] Here the concept of agreement or recognition is given a rational and demonstrative, as distinguished from an historical and linguistic, interpretation. In consequence, a more tightly knit and firmly articulated moral equilibrium is envisaged. For, according to Rawls, the content of the concept of justice may be determined by a demonstration of what men could be expected to agree to rationally. What men would choose by way of a society and polity; that is, what they would regard as acceptable, assuming that they decide rationally and impartially, is the most efficient just society. Their political obligation is to the just constitution, the political framework of such a society.

Given a just constitution, legal obligation becomes a matter of "fair play." Should the "general will" prove to be mistaken and an unjust law enacted, still one should obey. "Unless one obeys the law enacted under it, the proper equilibrium, or balance, between competing claims defined by the constitution will not be maintained."[51] Through appropriate institutionalization of these conceptions, we may expect to move toward a "society of persons with the greatest talent enjoying the benefits of the greatest equal liberty. . . ."[52] Rational agreement, as Rawls derives its conceptual and institutional implications, thus displays both deontological and teleological imperatives. Justice is a primitive moral concept, an intrinsic value, that, unlike the principle of utility, is fundamental to the relations of moral

---

[50] See, in particular, his "Distributive Justice," in Peter Laslett and W. G. Runciman (Eds.), *Philosophy, Politics and Society (Third Series)*, (Oxford: Basil Blackwell, 1967), pp. 58–82.

[51] Rawls, "Legal Obligation and the Duty of Fair Play," in Hook (Ed.), *Law and Philosophy*, 3–18, pp. 10–11.

[52] Rawls, "Distributive Justice," in Laslett and Runciman (Eds.), *Philosophy, Politics and Society*, p. 76.

personalities. Rawls' moral psychology, like Rousseau's, "presupposes that type of personality which has in itself both the condition of its own independence, and the pattern according to which this freedom has to be used in order to fit into the common way of life."[53] Unlike Rousseau, however, who considered human "perfectibility" conditional upon the retention of social simplicity, Rawls conceives of the "most efficient just society" as evolving in a morally right direction, toward a condition of greatest equal talent, composed of men who can cope with complexity. It is a picture of a moving political equilibrium, not a range, but both unique and dynamic, in which human development once again displays moral direction and structure. Rationality directs rather than accommodates the ends of life, and so is presumed to demonstrate, not merely to adumbrate, a principle of political obligation.

We noticed earlier that moral and political concepts have histories, their content and relations alter in a reasonable manner according to environmental and intellectual pressures. An additional source of influence may be located in human inequality, in differences in mental and physical endowment. Rational agreement, according to Rawls, requires abstraction from these differences, the elimination of the "threat advantage" which these provide, if it is also to qualify as impartial.

If we abstract from "threat advantage" we may expect to settle upon principles of justice more equalitarian than those which we have inherited, since these we may presume to have been affected by human differentials. For especially in intensely competitive situations marginal differences in ability may be expected to pay off excessively, and market processes tend to confer upon the well-endowed a form of rent. And in fact people do appear willing to tolerate as just achieved social and economic inequalities that fail to meet Rawls' test of rational agreement; they do not hasten to install the institutional and distributional arrangements necessary to achieve and to run the most efficient just society. The going conception of justice, according to which men are entitled to hold and use wealth, regardless of the conditions under which it was obtained, the effects which it has upon equality of opportunity, or its economic rationality, is less equalitarian than the concept which Rawls entertains.

[53] Barbu, *Democracy and Dictatorship*, p. 56.

W. G. Runciman argues that "The denial of equal opportunity begins in infancy, and with it the long process of habituation to inequality without which society would be forever in a state of civil war."[54] Berlin refers to the clash between parental discretion and "the need to provide the maximum number of children with opportunities for free choice, which equality in education is likely to increase."[55] In these respects, among others, a linguistic and phenomenological treatment of the meaning of justice, one sensitive to the prevailing sense of justice, may well be insufficiently egalitarian. Partly it may be a matter, as Brian Barry suggests, that "justice is not a forward-looking virtue."[56] And partly also, one suspects, it is a matter of people being unwilling to forego passing on whatever competitive advantages they may possess.

These considerations suggest that there is a positive and prospective dimension to political obligation that does not receive adequate attention in a purely phenomenological metaethic. Rawls' metaethic of categorical rationalism does give to his theory of political obligation an appropriately imperative dimension, and so does provide a standpoint from which to criticize our moral inheritance as this is reflected in ordinary usage. It is patent that we have yet to achieve that equilibrium of institutionalized values, conceived either as a range or as unique, that seems implicit in the political history and theory of liberalism.

RATIONAL AND EMPIRICAL FOUNDATIONS

In its turn, Rawls' metaethical principle of rational agreement does seem vulnerable to criticism from the phenomenology of Berlin's categorial empiricism. Ultimately, it seems to me, what is at stake is the degree to which the realm of value is irreducibly complex and pluralistic.

For Berlin, there is pluralism to an intense degree; this is the

[54] W. G. Runciman, *Relative Deprivation and Social Justice: A Study of Attitudes to Social Inequality in Twentieth-Century England* (Berkeley: University of California Press, 1966), p. 294.

[55] Berlin, *Four Concepts*, p. liv.

[56] Barry, "On Social Justice," Number 5, *The Oxford Review* (Trinity 1967), 29–52, p. 39.

implication of his conception of the unavoidability of choice and of his reference to a "shifting pattern." Those who think of an equilibrium are concerned not so much with agonizing choice as with a balancing of values. Rawls' categorical rationalism would seem to imply—Berlin would say, to impose—a monistic solution to the problem of political obligation. There is a hierarchy of values, at the apex of which is justice, which contains a right to equal freedom, and to which considerations of utility are subordinate conceptually, although Rawls argues, and with good reason, that in practice these considerations will not seriously conflict with the requirements of justice. "In this inquiry," Rawls could say, "I shall endeavor always to unite what right sanctions with what is prescribed by interest, in order that justice and utility may in no case be divided."[57] For him, to the extent that balancing is involved in moral and political calculation, it is best conceived as a "balance of justice."[58] As compared with Berlin's descriptive metaethic, Rawls' analysis of moral and political deliberation results in a fully determinate and demonstrative conceptual equilibrium, and yet one which has a Rousseauean drift toward greater equality. Or perhaps we could say that for Rawls justice is an equilibrating concept, whereas Berlin accords it a very high but still competitive status. In fact, we notice that in certain situations, perhaps abnormal, considerations of justice do give way to claims of utility, a point on which Berlin and Pennock would agree.[59] And this does very strongly suggest that political deliberation involves more balancing, and balancing of a different type, than seems consistent with Rawls' metaethical postulate.

There is at least one point in his analysis at which may be detected an inclination on Rawls' part to overlook a necessity for choosing or balancing. He says that "equality of opportunity is a certain set of institutions which assures equally good education and chances of culture for all and which keeps open the competition for positions on the basis of qualities reasonably related to

57 Rousseau, *The Social Contract*, trans. G. D. H. Cole (New York: E. P. Dutton, 1913), p. 5.
58 Rawls, "Legal Obligation," in Hook (Ed.), *Law and Philosophy*, p. 15.
59 Berlin, *Four Concepts*, p. lx, and Pennock, "The Obligation to Obey the Law," in Hook (Ed.), *Law and Philosophy*, pp. 82–83.

performance, and so on."[60] As we have seen, Berlin would say that to opt for "equally good education" is a choice made against the liberty of some. There may also be another choice involved, not clearly subject to demonstrative resolution, since educational resources are scarce and human beings differentiated in capacity.

Think of the alternatives that must be considered in the investment of an increment of professional talent. This increment could be spent on the more able to get the most out of them, presumably to the advantage of all through their prospective greater contribution. Or the increment could be used to improve the competitive position of the less able. There is no "equally good education" for all; rather there is an allocation of a scarce resource among alternative purposes. If one chooses for moral progress, toward "perfectibility," in the sense of movement toward a "society of greatest equal talent," then it would seem that one should improve the prospects of the less able. And this decision would make against the value of freely competitive association, the mutual attraction of able scholars and students. On the other hand, if the security of the society is in peril, or if economic rationality is to be served and utility maximized here and now, then the prescription is to invest in the best.

I do not see how this issue could be demonstratively resolved, even if considerations of welfare in the most general sense were introduced. Still an exercise of judgment is called for, even if this turns out to be a Berlinian "blend," in which one balances the competing claims and needs of differentiated human beings in the light of some assessment of the total situation. That this is our real condition is only obscured by affirming the desirability of an "equally good education." That cannot be provided, for the question is: Good for whom and for what?

In my view, Kant has bequeathed us a dual metaethic, one seeking precision in the standards of rationality and impartiality, the other more flexible, grounded in our persisting moral attributes, tensions among which are reflected in the complexity of evaluative language. Both ways of thinking have in view a moral

---

[60] Rawls, "Distributive Justice," in Laslett and Runciman (Eds.), *Philosophy, Politics and Society*, p. 71.

equilibrium, and both agree on the direction in which that equilibrium lies from our present situation, and so offer, if not a unique foundation, then both rational and empirical foundations of political obligation.

"THIS DISTINCTIVE AND ALMOST UNLIMITED FACULTY"

Political obligation is a kind of moral obigation, positive and complex, heavily situationally conditioned, and yet universal and compelling in its concern with the direction of human development. It is the obligation to bring about a society appropriate to human nature, a satisfactory institutional articulation of our moral psychology. Of course Berlin is right that political obligation is the central problem of political theory. It is not a question that can be refused an answer, or dismissed as dangerous, or defined out of sight. For it has to do with the kinds of life that are humanly worth living, the supreme question for intrinsically normative beings. To neglect or to default on political obligation is to invite crisis and revolution; to mistake or to misconceive its nature means gigantic death and disaster. A theory of political obligation offers men a sense of purpose that even a common conception of justice cannot provide. Without it institutions begin to feel morally coercive and pointless, as both Rousseau and Marx would testify. Today a functional conception of obligation cannot but assume the shape of ideology, and moral individualism seems to many to be corrupt and fraudulent, a mask for privilege, and not the basis of a good society. The signs are many, as we noticed at the outset, that humanity is in a state of moral and political disarray.

Western political thinking now recognizes a fundamental unity of human nature,[61] and has arrived in both its liberal and Marxist forms, at a conception of human development, which we have used Rousseau's perception of "perfectibility" to describe. Both these political theories also have a conviction of the plurality of values, if we may so interpret Marx's opposition to the

---

[61] See Frederick M. Watkins, "Natural Law and the Problem of Value-Judgment," in Oliver Garceau (Ed.), *Political Research and Political Theory* (Cambridge, Mass.: Harvard University Press, 1968), pp. 58–74.

division of labor and occupational specialization, and both may also have confidence in human rationality.[62] These are large and important areas of common understanding. But where the theories differ fundamentally and decisively is on questions of moral psychology, and hence on how to institutionalize for personal and social integration. Although Marxism in practice has worked out quite differently, Marx does envisage a form of life in which a singular pattern of aesthetic reciprocity informs all human activities; for him this is the key to creativity and "perfectibility." Liberal thinkers, on the other hand, think in terms of moral equilibria and psychological equipoise, and continue to explore their Kantian inheritance.

If we look to all the aspects of our history—moral and political, psychological and linguistic—perhaps a philosophy of life may be discovered in their correspondence and congruence. Moral individualism, in the shape of the doctrine of natural rights, displaced the monistic ways of thinking that I have called moral functionalism; moral individualism is a recognition of value pluralism, and would appear to be firmly empirically grounded in our persisting attributes. Historically there appears to be a moral logic to the development of liberal thought, which today takes the form of a belief in the possibility of a moral equilibrium. This finds expression in Berlin's conception of "blend" and in Rawls' goal of the "most efficient just society." In both conceptions of a moral equilibrium there is present the balancing or integrating force of rationality.

The liberal moral outlook has a parallel in the polarity of psychological processes. The concepts of moral equilibrium and psychological equipoise together constitute a coherent and empirically persuasive moral psychology, one which can explain its historical deflection. Human individuation both requires and promotes the psychological process Zevedei Barbu calls rationalization; that is to say, it carries with it a capacity for rationally

---

[62] "Every social division of labor is an enemy of human freedom, for Marx, insofar as it enforces occupational specialization as a way of life," Robert C. Tucker, *The Marxian Revolutionary Idea* (New York: W. W. Norton, 1969), p. 19. According to Eugene Kamenka, for Marx: "Man, in becoming truly human, is able to exercise untrammeled rationality. Given the common human purposes that Marx assumes, reason can and does provide the basis for complete agreement on all questions, from the allocation of resources to the priority of tasks," *Marxism and Ethics*, p. 29.

articulated forms of social integration. But this developmental process may be reversed in a period of strain. Moreover, Western political history has a rhythmic quality to it, the outcome, I have suggested, of a permanent tension between individual and collective rationality, between individual advantage and collective good.[63] These defining characteristics of human experience—moral equilibrium, psychological ambivalence, and rhythmic politics—do reveal a complexity to our nature, inappropriate to which is the concept of "essence." The more pluralistic concepts such as "need" and "attribute" certainly seem more directly correspondent with historical regularities. Indeed, to the extent that we are unified beings, that unity is best conceived of as dialectical. The structural timbers, both moral and psychological, of human nature are, as Kant alleged, crooked, and what saves is that distinctive and almost unlimited faculty of "perfectibility."

The historical congruence between our moral constitution and our psychological and political dynamics renders it misleading to regard natural rights, and justice, and rationality as deformations of a "communist essence," aesthetically and emotionally conceived. If the ends of life are diverse, and if our mental architecture is a matter of dynamic balance, then a political society articulated according to a variety of principles is that which is best suited to human nature. And where else but in our nature may we hope to find the moral foundations of political obligation?

Moral and political history show that our moral constitution is both purposive and pluralistic. Our pluralistic nature implies that life should be organized according to a plurality of principles and calls for recognition of obligations to support such a form of society. That we are purposive and rational drives us to seek to give these principles appropriate weight and importance. Hence the possibility of political miscalculation and oppression is as inherent in human nature as is the vision of "perfectibility," of a stable and satisfactory moral equilibrium. The precise nature of such an equilibrium continues to elude us. Its definition is at the heart of the problem of political obligation, and to attain it is apparently an ineradicable impulse of human nature.

[63] See my "Voluntary Association and the Political Theory of Pluralism," in Pennock and Chapman (Eds.), *Voluntary Associations, Nomos XI* (New York: Atherton Press, 1969), the closing pages.

OBLIGATION AND THE CONDITIONS OF OBEDIENCE

8

CONSTITUTIONAL OBLIGATION

GRAY L. DORSEY

Discussion of constitutional obligation might proceed from the viewpoint of what the constitution requires of persons in various positions and situations. An instance would be what the federal constitution requires of the judge, legislator, or private person with respect to school desegregation in the light of United States Supreme Court opinions.[1] Obligation in this sense is in the document and results from the formal relations between propositions. The study of formal obligation is important in clarifying and perfecting the structure of constituted

The author thanks his colleague, Jules B. Gerard, for advice concerning the last section of this paper.

[1] *Griffin* v. *County School Board of Prince Edward County,* 377 U.S. 218 (1964); *Goss* v. *Board of Education,* 373 U.S. 683 (1963); *Cooper* v. *Aaron,* 358 U.S. 1 (1958); *Bolling* v. *Sharpe* 347 U.S. 497 (1954); *Brown* v. *Board of Education,* 347 U.S. 483 (1954).

authority within established societies in periods of stability. It is less relevant to periods of rapid change and to the process of distributing authority in newly independent societies. In these situations we want to know whether obligation written into a document will find its way into the persons concerned; whether they will feel obligated. Therefore, I venture to discuss felt obligation, rather than formal obligation.

If felt obligation is present in those who enforce and those who obey, in those who seek to eliminate old injustices, and in those who seek solutions to new problems, all other problems will respond to competence and energy. Without felt obligation no problem will respond to technical processes. Learned Hand makes the point with respect to the root principle of the United States constitution: "Liberty lies in the hearts of men and women; when it dies there, no constitution, no law, no court can save it; no constitution, no law, no court can even do much to help it."[2]

My approach to felt obligation depends on a hypothesis drawn from both natural law and sociological jurisprudence. There is evidence that men constitute structures of authority in accordance with their view of the nature of man and the world. There is also evidence that men constitute structures of authority in accordance with experienced social consequences and desired social results. My hypothesis is that men adhere to, support, obey, and defend constitutional principles in part at least because they believe them to be right (i.e., in accordance with the nature of things) and socially useful. I will not limit the discussion to written limitations on government, but will consider principles that are constitutive of social and governmental organization and action. I will discuss some aspects of general support for a government, obligation within a ruling party, constitutional principle and foreseeability, and interpretation of constitutional principles.

GENERAL SUPPORT FOR A GOVERNMENT

Ideas about the nature of things sometimes take on affective coating, become belief, and so pervade the general con-

[2] Learned Hand, *The Spirit of Liberty* (New York: Knopf, 1960), p. 188.

sciousness as to control thought and action. "Beliefs, to be sure, begin as ideas," says Ortega y Gasset, "But in the process of slowly pervading the minds of the multitude they lose the character of ideas and establish themselves as 'unquestionable realities.' " Ortega gives as one example the medieval European belief in God by whose grace kings ruled. "[They lived] in the ceaseless presence of an absolute entity—God—with which they had to reckon. This indeed is belief: to reckon with an inescapable presence. And this is reality: that which must be reckoned with, whether we like it or not."[3] Writing of the medieval background to modern science, Whitehead speaks of the "inexpugnable belief" in a rational God, which was not merely "the explicit beliefs of a few individuals," but an "impress on the European mind."[4]

Such a general and controlling belief can generate adherence and support for a form of government consistent with its implications. Ortega cites the medieval belief in a ruling God and the even more striking instance of the perfect paralyzing device, the veto, being in the hands of the plebeian Tribunes of Republican Rome for over three hundred years, without being used as an instrument of class warfare because the plebs shared with the patricians "a living faith in the same picture of the universe and of life," according to which only patricians, who had access to the gods, were proficient to rule.[5]

Beliefs die and new ones are born. The Greek natural philosophers destroyed the world in which events were controlled by the gods and created a new belief—and in Ortega's sense, a new reality of natural cause and effect in a rationally ordered world. Roman Stoic philosophers and jurists built a new society and a whole new structure of law on the implications of the new belief.[6] The medieval belief in God as the source of all civil

[3] José Ortega y Gasset, *Concord and Liberty* (New York: Norton, 1946), p. 20.

[4] Alfred North Whitehead, *Science and the Modern World* (New York: Mentor, 1925), p. 13.

[5] Ortega y Gasset, *Concord and Liberty*, pp. 42–43.

[6] Gray L. Dorsey, "The Influence of Philosophy on Law and Politics in Western Civilization," in *Philosophy and Culture—East and West*, Charles A. Moore, ed. (Honolulu: University of Hawaii Press, 1962), p. 533; "The Nature of Our Democratic Civil Order," in *Constitutional Freedom and the Law*, Gray L. Dorsey and John E. Dunsford, eds. (New York: McGraw-Hill, 1965), p. 1.

authority also was destroyed. But generally held beliefs are not relinquished in a day. A belief that has constituted unquestionable reality may sink to the level of being open to question, but it will still hold those who reexamine and reaffirm and those who never consciously adopt or reject but grow, live, and die by prevailing beliefs unless accident or immediate interests attach them to a revolutionary movement. Even when the core idea of the old belief is quite generally rejected at the rational level its accumulated layers of emotions and vested interests will hold many to it, especially with respect to profession, if not always in action.

The real dilemma in allegiance to constitutional principle comes when revolutionists prevail by force at a time when the old belief still has power. Must the new constitutional order of government compromise the purpose of the revolution or else require instant and complete conversion, with the consequent risk of renewing and invigorating the opposition of those who by reason, emotion, or interest are tied to the old belief and the old order?

British constitutional history suggests a way to avoid the dilemma in part, if a distinction made by Walter Bagehot is kept in mind. He said:

> There are two great objects which every constitution must attain to be successful, which every old and celebrated one must have wonderfully achieved: every constitution must first *gain* authority, and then *use* authority; it must first win the loyalty and confidence of mankind, and then employ that homage in the work of government.[7]

Accordingly, Bagehot pointed out that every constitution has *"dignified"* parts, which "excite and preserve the reverence of the population," and *"efficient"* parts, by which "it, in fact, works and rules."[8]

In seventeenth-century England, the medieval God was dead but in landholding, education, religion, and public service, established traditions retained an instinct for hierarchy. Monarchy resonated to this instinct. However, powerful forces in opposition

---

[7] Walter Bagehot, *The English Constitution* (New York: Appleton, 1911), p. 72.

[8] *Ibid.*, p. 72.

to monarchy prevailed. Democracy was espoused by the successful revolutionaries, but the Commonwealth of 1649 was intolerable. On the other hand, so was the Restoration of Charles II. In 1688 England retained monarchy as the symbol to gather the power of the people—their willingness to adhere, support, obey, and defend. But a clear beginning was made toward shifting the exercise of power to democratic institutions of government.

Unfortunately, because of the prestige of democracy or because of the influence of powerful Western states that happen to be democracies, there is a strong tendency among states seeking to modernize to take democracy as the symbol, and to adopt traditional or ad hoc organization of the use of power. An early instance, in which the disastrous result can be clearly seen, is the nationalist revolution in China.

In 1912, under pressure from Sun Yat-sen's revolutionary forces, the imperial dynasty abdicated. Sun promulgated a constitution and proclaimed a republic.[9] It is clear that ideas of equality and individualism had not replaced ideas of hierarchy and social harmony in China. Since the shock of losing the Opium War to Western forces in 1842, China had reacted spasmodically to increasing evidence that its millenia of unquestioned superiority were drawing to a close. First, China thought to repulse the West by acquiring its gunboats and other weapons. The tools of modern national power were not enough. Western physical and economic encroachment increased. China turned its attention to improving national institutions in order to increase national power. The forced granting of extensive leaseholds and spheres of influence to Western nations in 1898 threatened the complete dismemberment and subjugation of China. K'ang Yu-wei and others persuaded the young Emperor to institute governmental reforms based on Western experience. These were quickly nullified by forces around the throne, headed by the Empress Dowager. The reaction grew into the furious and bloody Boxer Rebellion against Western influence. Western troops were brought in to put down the rebellion, and their governments exacted heavy indemnities and took steps to collect them, such as operating Chinese customs offices. The independence of China was further endangered.[10]

[9] Kenneth S. Latourette, *A History of Modern China* (Baltimore: Penguin, 1954), p. 115.
[10] *Ibid.*, p. 92.

The next stage of Chinese reaction to the West was to turn from institutions to reconsideration of underlying ideas. But this stage began about 1916, growing into the May Fourth Movement of 1919. Before that time individual scholars were giving thought to the matter but there was no widespread movement of political and social significance.[11] Sun Yat-sen's Nationalist Revolution of 1911–12 was a part of the effort to improve the effectiveness of institutions in order to save China. Sun chose representative government because it was the political form of the Western nations and hopefully would give China comparable national power. Further it would help to convince the West that China was following the modern trend in governmental organization and was capable of independent self-government. Sun had one other reason for choosing representative government instead of imperial reforms. In his view the antiforeign Taiping Rebellion (1851–64) succeeded until its leaders began to vie for the throne and turned their armies against each other. Sun chose democracy to avoid the rivalry by removing the prize. These two pragmatic reasons are explicit in Sun's San Min Chu I (*The Three Principles of the People*), the bible of the Nationalist Revolution. He said: "So we in our revolution have chosen democracy, first, that we may be following the world current, and second, that we may reduce the period of civil war."[12]

[11] John K. Fairbank, *The United States and China* (New York: Viking Press, 1948); Joseph R. Levenson, *Modern China and Its Confucian Past* (New York: Doubleday, 1964); Franz Schurmann and Orville Schell, *Imperial China* (New York: Vintage Books, 1967); Franz Schurmann and Orville Schell, *Republican China* (New York: Vintage Books, 1967).

[12] Sun Yat-sen, *San Min Chu I* (Frank W. Price, trans.) (Taipei, Taiwan: China Cultural Service, 1953), p. 51. These lectures were given in 1924, years after the start of the revolution. Sun Yat-sen was very busy and mortally ill. The lectures were hurriedly prepared and not thoroughly checked by him before publication. Ch'ien Tuan-sheng has asserted that Sun Yat-sen understood democracy and until 1919 or 1920 worked to establish democratic institutions in China. See Ch'ien Tuan-sheng, "The Kuomintang: Its Doctrine, Organization, and Leadership," in *Modern China,* Albert Feuerwerker, ed. (Englewood Cliffs, N.J.: Prentice-Hall, 1964), p. 70. A reading of Paul M. A. Linebarger, *The Political Doctrines of Sun Yat-sen* (Baltimore: Johns Hopkins Press, 1937), shows that Linebarger's interpretation of Sun's thought, based on all the exegetical material his excellent sources in China could produce, supports, rather than contradicts or qualifies the textual statement of a pragmatic basis for the choice of representative government in modern China. The three principles are nationalism, democracy (People's Sovereignty), and People's Livelihood. Aspects of each principle are discussed

Sun Yat-sen makes it clear that he had not turned from the Confucian idea of collective social harmony to the Western idea of individualism. He rejects the proposition that all men are created equal. He wants to preserve the Confucian ethic, with its hierarchical status system and its requirement of greater responsibility on those in higher positions.[13] The people are to have the appearance of controlling the government, but the able few are to govern, as under the Confucian system of civil-service examinations.[14] Reconstruction is not to be based on the individual and his freedom. Under Confucian culturalism with its minimal level of government control, every individual had so much freedom that China was like loose sand. Under nationalism, unity was to be temporarily preserved by strengthening governmental control in order to preserve and protect the freedom of the Chinese nation. Individual rights were to be subordinated to family, clan, and nation. The old ethics and morality were to be the guides to life, but national pride, power, unity, and prosperity must be brought about by organizational and technological borrowing from the West.[15]

It seems clear that in the Chinese Nationalist Revolution the republican form of government was not intended to organize the use of power. It was adopted as the symbol of modern national power and to eliminate rivalry for the throne. China reversed the 1688 English solution. The use of power was to remain with the Confucian elite, but the symbol of authority was changed from monarchy to republic.

The new symbol attracted no appreciable support. On December 3, 1911, a constitution for the provisional government was promulgated. It provided for presidential dominance. Sun Yat-sen was elected president by the delegates chosen in accordance with that constitution. Another provisional constitution promulgated on March 11, 1912, weakened the presidency and gave

---

in several lectures. The 1942 Calcutta edition of the Frank Price translation, published by the Chinese Ministry of Information, is more satisfactory than the 1953 abridged edition published in Taiwan. Subsequent references are by roman numeral to Principle and by arabic numeral to Lecture.

[13] Sun Yat-sen, *San Min Chu I* (Taipei, Taiwan: China Cultural Service, 1953), pp. 66–91 (II, 2,3).

[14] *Ibid.*, pp. 109–50 (II, 5,6).

[15] *Ibid.*, pp. 28–50 (I, 5,6).

dominance to a State Council. The change was made by revolutionary leaders because Yuan Shih-kai, the most powerful warlord in the country and a former agent of the Manchus, was taking office as president. The 1912 constitution provided that the first parliament, elected under State Council rules, should draw up and promulgate a permanent constitution. On October 31, 1913, the parliament adopted the "Temple of Heaven" draft constitution, which restricted the powers of the president and made the cabinet dominant. President Yuan Shih-kai outlawed the nationalist Kuomintang party, thus depriving parliament of a quorum. He then summoned a constitutional convention which drafted a constitution providing for a powerful president and a weak parliament, which was promulgated on May 1, 1914. Yuan Shih-kai tried to make himself emperor in 1915-16. He failed and died shortly thereafter. The vice-president succeeded him, and summoned the dissolved parliament, which readopted the Temple of Heaven draft constitution.[16]

At this point constitution drafting ceased for more than ten years. The country fell under control of regional warlords, and the central government became virtually powerless and a pawn of the militarists. Sun Yat-sen was reduced to seeking the support of one or another warlord for his program of national reconstruction.[17]

The constitutional experience of the English Revolution of 1688 and the Chinese Nationalist Revolution of 1911-12 suggests that:

A. A distinction can be made between constitutional principles adopted for the symbolic purpose of attracting general allegiance and constitutional principles intended to organize the work of governing.

B. Beliefs once generally held in the society may serve as the basis for symbolic constitutional principles, even though the core idea has been rationally rejected and working constitutional principles are differently based.

C. Constitutional principles cannot serve the symbolic purpose of attracting allegiance if they are based on an idea that has

---

[16] Fairbank, *The United States and China*, pp. 159-61; Latourette, *Modern China*, p. 124; W. Y. Tsao, *The Constitutional Structure of Modern China* (Melbourne: Melbourne University Press, 1947), pp. 1-5.

[17] Fairbank, *The United States and China*, p. 165; Tsao, *Constitutional Structure*, pp. 5-8.

never become a generally held belief in a particular society, regardless of its influence in other societies.

OBLIGATION WITHIN A RULING PARTY

Leninism offers an active and calculated method of securing mass obedience and support that bypasses the problem of direct popular allegiance.[18] The people are controlled by cadres who live among them and vigorously and visibly work for their benefit. The cadres are centrally controlled through the democratic-centralist organization of a ruling party.

When cadres stand proxy for the wider public the question of general allegiance may become moot, but the question of obligation within the party becomes critical. From one viewpoint the directives and decrees of the central committee of the party are too arbitrary to be considered constitutional. But they are constitutive of the only social and governmental organization and action that is taking place in the country at the time. And they raise great problems of felt obligation. In this sense, consideration of obligation within a ruling party is appropriate in a discussion of constitutional obligation. The consideration certainly is relevant in many parts of the world to actual events in the formative process of modern social and governmental organization and action. Again, Nationalist China is an early, instructive instance.

The success of the Communist Revolution in Russia led the Chinese nationalists to adopt the organization and techniques of the Russian Communist party. Beginning in 1924 the Kuomintang party was reorganized with Russian advice. Whampoa Military Academy was formed to train the leaders who would defeat the warlords and bring all China under control of the central government, and Chiang Kai-shek, after a stay in Russia, became Whampoa's president. Chou En-lai, who had become a communist in the early twenties, was head of Whampoa's political department. When Chiang began the northern expedition of 1926–27, he had Russian advice and assistance.[19]

---

[18] Vladimir I. Lenin, *State and Revolution* (New York: International Publishers, 1932).

[19] Fairbank, *The United States and China*, pp. 171–77; Latourette, *Modern China*, pp. 144–45; Schurmann and Schell, *Republican China*, pp. 99–104.

With the reorganization of the Kuomintang and the success of the northern expedition, the nationalists were in control. Now their effectiveness as a ruling party would be tested.

Western encroachment and the course of Chinese reaction to it had created great pressure for social change. Sun Yat-sen proposed to improve the efficiency of Chinese institutions, but he wanted no basic change in the institutions themselves. He wanted the old China, but with enough power and wealth to throw out the West. With respect to nationalism, and People's Livelihood, as with respect to democracy, Sun pragmatically borrowed from the West at the level of organization, hoping to get, along with formal structure, the efficiency of the original.[20]

We have seen evidence to indicate that a pragmatic basis of constitutional principle is not sufficient to enable that principle to be effective as a symbol to attract general allegiance. When constitutional principle is to function not as symbol to attract power, but as guide for the exercise of power, is a pragmatic basis sufficient, even in a country under the control of a ruling party?

United States society and government have often been cited as proof that pragmatism is a sufficient basis for the effective exercise of power. Europeans came to a continent free from the old structures for controlling wealth, education, social influence, and political power. They responded to the frontier conditions of abundant land, abundant necessity to accept and exercise social and governmental leadership, abundant opportunity to acquire the skills needed to build communities in the wilderness.[21] Despite the zeal of revolutionary pamphleteers, based on the common ideas of natural rights and contractual society, and crying the royal threat to individual freedom,[22] the possession or nonpossession of status, wealth, and security seemed to determine whether a colonial American was Tory or revolutionary.[23] Support for various provisions in the United States Constitution

[20] Linebarger, *Political Doctrines*, pp. 122–56; Sun Yat-sen, *San Min Chu I*, pp. 1–50, 151–213.

[21] Frederick Jackson Turner, *The Frontier in American History* (New York: Holt, 1920).

[22] Bernard Bailyn, *Pamphlets of the American Revolution* (Cambridge: Belknap Press of Harvard University Press, 1965), pp. 20–85.

[23] J. Franklin Jameson, *The American Revolution Considered as a Social Movement* (Boston: Beacon Press, 1926), pp. 34–36.

came from those groups whose interests would be served.[24] Yet a strong case can be made for the proposition that in the United States pragmatism was ordinarily effective precisely because of a deep, unanimous, and long-present attachment to the Lockian idea of natural equality and its liberal implications.[25]

The American experience in fact supports the hypothesis of interaction between social conditions and ideas about the nature of things. Before the revolution Franklin was pointing out that in America the individual by his own efforts could attain the status, wealth, and influence that in Europe could be had only by birth or preferment. "He that hath a Trade hath an Estate; and he that hath a Calling, hath an Office of Profit and Honour; but then the Trade must be worked at, and the Calling well followed, or neither the Estate nor the Office will enable us to pay our Taxes," said Poor Richard.[26] Diligence, thrift, and self-reliance could raise up the common man; their absence could bring down the nobleman. "A Ploughman on his Legs is higher than a Gentleman on his Knees, as Poor Richard says."[27] The frontier was not responded to automatically; on the other hand, Americans certainly did not gather in Forum or Academy and reason out the implications of natural equality and then go forth to build. They built to advantage. But advantage was seen increasingly through the eyes of natural equality; and, even more important, *natural equality was the genesis of acceptable rules for limiting the means of seeking advantage and of reconciling conflicting claims and demands.* In colonial America there was competition for this role. The hierarchic idea was economically embodied in many great estates, and laws of primogeniture and entail, both in the North and in the South. Workers on these estates were treated as serfs, not as equal, independent entreprencurs.[28] As men sought their own advantage within the

[24] Charles A. Beard, *An Economic Interpretation of the Constitution of the United States* (New York: Macmillan, 1913).

[25] Louis Hartz, *The Liberal Tradition in America* (New York: Harvest Publishing Co., 1955).

[26] Benjamin Franklin, *The Autobiography of Benjamin Franklin and Selections from His Other Writings* (New York: The Modern Library, 1944), p. 218.

[27] *Ibid.*, p. 222.

[28] Jameson, *The American Revolution Considered as a Social Movement*, pp. 36-43.

equality pattern or the hierarchy pattern they attached their
interest-based emotions to the implications of one or the other
idea. How else does idea become a generally held and controlling
belief? The pamphlets of the revolution did not call men to
commit themselves to the idea of natural liberty. They rallied
men who were already expressing their lives in accordance with
its meaning.

The American revolutionaries had more than the power of
common grievances. They had the power of common belief, on
the basis of which common action can be undertaken and conflicting interests can be reconciled. Between revolutionaries and
Tories either the equality or the hierarchy pattern had to prevail. Tory estates were confiscated and feudal forms of landholding were abolished. But conflicting interests among those who
accepted natural equality could be resolved because the "concord," as Ortega calls it, at the basic level provides a common
frame of reference, a common set of standards and values.[29]
Therefore, the different economic interests expressed in various
positions with respect to the Constitution were reconcilable. The
Constitution was written. It has prevailed. Further, the basic
concord produced a consensus about the direction in which the
United States should develop which avoided the enervating
effects of aimlessness or the frustration of conflicting aims.

If there is any validity to this summary analysis of the United
States experience, effective new social and governmental organization and action need to be built on a commonly accepted idea
which grows into a generally held and controlling belief as men
commit their interests and their emotions to its implications. The
Kuomintang party failed to achieve national reconstruction, and
lost power to the communists, in part at least because its efforts
were not so based. On the other hand, the efforts of the Chinese
Communist party to gain power and to modernize and strength-
en China were so based.

In Sun Yat-sen's writings we find nothing comparable to
Marx's fundamental proposition in the *German Ideology*, where
he turns away from earlier views that religion or reason distinguish man from the animals and says that men distinguish

---

[29] Ortega y Gasset, *Concord and Liberty*, pp. 18-21.

themselves from animals, "as they begin to *produce* the means of life. . . ."[30] The *German Ideology* was written in 1845-46, before the *Communist Manifesto.* Having decided that producing man is more important than praying man, or thinking man, Marx gave that focus to his whole system of thought. With selected elements from German philosophy, English political economy, and French revolutionary theory, he built a massive case for the idea of a nonexploitative society. Lenin added the theory of effective organization and utilization of the power of the masses through the revolutionary and ruling party. Mao Tse-tung, for China, added the theory of basing revolution and reconstruction on the peasants rather than the workers. The idea of the nonexploitative society was capable of generating implications for new relations of land control and use, control of capital, and in fact of all relations of society and government. It could produce a sense of social direction. Commitment to it could give meaning and purpose to individual lives and unity to common efforts. It could provide a basic concord to limit and reconcile the pursuit of individual advantage.

When control of a country is sought to be exercised through a ruling party, the absence or presence of the belief-formation process will be felt primarily in the weakness or power of the party, in terms of generation of programs, discipline within the party, morale and honesty of party members; and secondarily in popular support. In all these respects the Communist party ranked high and the Nationalist party ranked low at the time of the communist takeover of mainland China. General Wedemeyer, in reporting to President Truman on a fact-finding trip to China in 1947, spoke of the "Kuomintang, whose reactionary leadership, repression and corruption have caused a loss of popular faith in the Government."[31] It was bitterly resented by the Nationalists at the time, but it was true. Chiang Kai-shek himself later admitted it. In 1950 he said that the loss of the mainland was not due to the Communists' greater military

---

[30] Karl Marx, *Capital, The Communist Manifesto, and Other Writings* (New York: The Modern Library, 1932), pp. 8,9; Dorsey, "Post-Stalin Soviet Jurisprudence," *The International Lawyer* 1 (1967), 378.
[31] Department of State, *United States Relations with China* (Washington, D.C.: Department of State Publication, 1949), p. 769.

strength, but was "due to the organizational collapse, loose discipline, and low spirit of the [Kuomintang] Party."[32]

Why did the Kuomintang fail to base its program of national reconstruction on a vivifying belief, either established or in process? If the Western aspects of the San Min Chu I were based solely on pragmatism, why could the Kuomintang not turn to the Confucian aspects and use them to direct the exercise of power? The Kuomintang did, in fact, turn back to Confucianism, but not as belief. The nationalist break with the communists in 1927 left the Kuomintang in need of a social and economic program for national reconstruction. The Kuomintang kept the Leninist organization of a ruling party, which fit neatly with Sun's theory that a period of tutelage would be necessary before the people could govern themselves. The nationalists were unwilling to accept the expropriations that would result from the communist class analysis of society, and so rejected the communist program for social and economic reconstruction. In its place the Kuomintang put traditionalism. Here was a return to Confucianism, but as a social device. The Nationalists did not propose to live Confucianism, and did not. They adopted it as a social tool to manipulate the people.[33] The substantive part of the old belief was supposed to guide the exercise of power, but the pragmatic basis of its adoption vitiated any effect it might have had as belief.

Doctrines adopted by the Kuomintang party to manipulate the people could have no limiting effect upon pursuit of personal advantage by party members. What party members could take them seriously as something which one should feel obligated to obey and support? What party member could believe that such doctrines should be vigorously applied in the countryside in order to make China prosperous and strong? With such a basis for the Kuomintang reconstruction program, it is no wonder that social and economic reforms were indefinitely postponed; faction after faction developed within the party; too many Kuomintang officials were dedicated to nothing higher than their own pocketbooks and used positions of trust to prey upon the people.[34]

[32] China Handbook Editorial Board, *China Handbook 1952-53* (Taipei, Taiwan: China Publishing Co., 1952), p. 341.

[33] Joseph R. Levenson, "The Intellectual Revolution in China," in *Modern China*, Albert Feuerwerker, ed. (Englewood Cliffs: Prentice-Hall, 1964), pp. 154-68.

[34] Department of State, *United States Relations with China*, pp. 758-75.

There was one more possibility. Why did the nationalist, noncommunist Chinese intellectuals fail to develop an idea-basis for initiation of the belief-formation process? The answer again is pragmatism. In the discussion above it has appeared that looking to social facts and choosing actions on the basis of social results desired is not an effective way to guide social and governmental organization and action in the absence of a set of generally accepted values based on commitment to implications of a view of the nature of man. Unfortunately this fact could not have been discovered by the young Chinese scholars who looked for guidance to the Western democracies instead of communist Russia.

In the late teens and early twenties of this century, empiricism and pragmatism were at the height of their influence in Great Britain and the United States. And rightly so. Britain for nearly a century, and the United States for a lesser time, had been concerned with rewriting the norms of social and governmental organization and action in the light of the social impact of industrialization. At the start of the American Revolution there were only five towns in America with more than 8,000 population.[35] As long as our economy consisted almost entirely of the small capitalism of artisans and family farms, natural equality's implications of private property and freedom of contract could mean a prohibition of governmental interference in the contract made by buyer and seller. The free market would operate to allocate rewards roughly in proportion to the capital, management, or labor contributed. But, as Veblen showed, when the machines of industrialism came to be controlled through corporate devices, the few who controlled stock and money could arrogate to themselves much of the economic value of the capital, management, and labor of others.[36] I am not referring to the problem of monopoly, which is the domination of an industry by one company, but to the fact that within the corporation the distribution of total corporate reward could be controlled by the few to the detriment of the many. In the light of these changed social conditions the constitutional principles of private property and freedom of contract had to be reconsidered. However, natural equality and democracy were not being questioned.

[35] Jameson, *The American Revolution*, p. 28.
[36] Thorstein Veblen, *The Theory of Business Enterprise* (New York: Mentor Books, 1904), pp. 128-76.

Therefore the task was instrumental in nature—how to carry out the meaning of common belief under changed conditions.

To this task empiricism and pragmatism were superbly responsive. What are the facts about the effect of concentrated capital upon the health, morality, and level of culture of factory workers? What principles need to be reinterpreted and what rules changed to improve their conditions of life and work? The Brandeis brief is the legal technique that brought empiricism and pragmatism to bear upon reinterpretation of constitutional principle. Bertrand Russell in Britain and John Dewey in the United States were deservedly held in the highest regard. In these countries empiricism and pragmatism were the correct philosophies for social problems. General and controlling belief was unimpaired and could be assumed.

But in China the situation was different. Since 1842 the Chinese had reacted against Western intrusion first by acquiring Western weapons, then by reforming institutions. In the cultural aspect of the national revolution, which burst into full fervor in 1919, the Chinese turned to reconsideration of basic beliefs that had supported social organization and action for tens of centuries.[37]

Peking University was the center of the new cultural movement, and the whole course of the intellectual revolution in China can be glimpsed in the choices of a few scholars at that institution. All scholars in the new cultural movement were united in their opposition to everything in the old Chinese tradition. But in their approach to the new they were divided, principally by whether they looked to Russia or to the Western democracies. Hu Shih, professor of philosophy and literature, studied at Columbia University and was strongly influenced by John Dewey. Dewey and Bertrand Russell were visiting professors at Peking University in 1919 and 1920, and Dewey particularly made a deep impression. Hu Shih, as leader of the movement to put all Chinese literature in *pai hua,* the speech of the people, was extremely influential in the nationalist intellectual movement. Hu committed himself to democracy and pragmatism. Ch'en Tu-hsiu, Dean of the College of Literature, became

[37] Ssu-yu Teng and Fairbank, *China's Response to the West* (Cambridge: Harvard University Press, 1954).

convinced that democracy as Dewey presented it, and as seen in
the United States and England, was too slow to solve China's
problems. He adopted communism and dialectical materialism.
Li Ta-chao, librarian of the University, came to communism by
way of social Darwinism.[38]

Ch'en Tu-hsiu and Li Ta-chao carried many students with
them into communism. One of these had worked in the library.
He first came under the influence of K'ang Yu-wei and Liang
Ch'i-ch'ao, who advocated gradual change, and whose work was
done primarily in the period of reforming institutions. Later, at
Peking University, he came under the influence of Hu Shih and
Ch'en Tu-hsiu. Needless to say, Mao Tse-tung also broke with
Hu Shih and, with Ch'en, followed Ma-k'o-ssu (Marx) who by
1922 was "almost competing for the seat of honor with Confu-
cius," as Liang Ch'i-ch'ao put it.[39]

Part of the appeal of Marxism-Leninism was that it came to
China not as philosophy but as the modern, scientific way to
solve all social problems. The prestige of science was tremendous
in China at the time because of the tremendous scientific progress of the West. Those scholars who looked to the democracies
also thought in terms of the scientific method for handling social
problems, rather than this or that philosophy. For Hu Shih
scientific method originated with Bacon and reached its highest
development with Dewey. This method supposedly was capable
of solving every problem.

Tragically, empiricist-pragmatic scientific method was utterly
incapable of solving the problem of what should replace rejected
Confucian constitutive principles. In fact, it immunized noncommunist scholars from any awareness of the problem. They joined
in the general cry of "Down with the Confucian shops;" helping
to destroy the old beliefs and to destroy support for constitutive
principles based upon them, such as the old forms of landholding
and of government. But apparently it never occurred to them
that someone needed to provide the basis for new constitutive
principles. Hu Shih, perhaps the most prestigious of all modern

[38] Chiang Monlin, *Tides from the West* (London: Oxford University
Press, 1947), pp. 124–26; Latourette, *A History of Modern China*, pp. 139–44;
Schurmann and Schell, *Republican China*, pp. 98–104.

[39] Latourette, *A History of Modern China*, pp. 143–46; Schurmann and
Schell, *Imperial China*, pp. 300–05.

noncommunist scholars, never came to grips with the problem. In 1953, after the nationalists had failed on the mainland, Hu Shih lectured on scientific method to the students at National Taiwan University. He presented empiricism and pragmatism from Bacon to Dewey as scientific method. I shall never forget the profound shock with which I heard him give an example of his use of scientific method. During those years in which China under the Kuomintang drifted toward moral vacuum, corruption and paralysis, and eventual collapse, the use of scientific method that Hu considered significant enough to cite as an example was his careful, scientific investigation of all the evidence in order to determine whether a person reputed to be the author of a famous thirteenth-century Chinese novel was in fact the author.[40]

The Chinese nationalist experience between 1924 and 1949 and American experience concerning pragmatism, suggest that:

A. A ruling party, even one that is stringently organized for central control, cannot remain effective over an extended period in the absence of unifying, directing, and limiting constitutive principles generated and supported by generally held common beliefs.

B. Effective constitutional principles cannot be evolved solely out of pragmatic response to social conditions.

C. Destruction of the old order involves destruction of old beliefs and principles as well as institutional structures, and construction of a new order requires general acceptance of new beliefs and principles.

CONSTITUTIONAL PRINCIPLE AND FORESEEABILITY

Who is not reluctant to accept an obligation undefined in nature and extent? Constitutional principles serve to define the nature and extent of obligation, and thus to facilitate the formation of society or government. We tend to think of constitutional principles as organic, capable of growing and changing. So they

---

[40] I had to rely upon a running translation for the content of this speech. But the translator was excellent, and I believe this does not misrepresent what Hu Shih said.

are from the viewpoint of interpretation under changed conditions within an established society. But from the viewpoint of establishing a legal or social community, constitutional principles permit a reasonable degree of foreseeability about the detriments and benefits of entering into the community. Satisfactory provisions in the United States constitution brought the several colonies, and the groups with various economic and other interests, into the new community of the United States of America.[41]

Natural law jurisprudence tends to overlook the limiting, specifying function of constitutional principle. The importance of this function can perhaps be seen most clearly in the international legal community, where the obligation of states has remained fragile. Two cases, in United States courts but applying international law, illustrate such limitation and specification. As I indicated in the introductory paragraphs, I am speaking of constitutive principles, not just written principles limiting government. Since the international community has remained rudimentary, its constitutive principles are of a legal community but not of government. To avoid confusion I shall speak of constitutive principles rather than constitutional principles.

In 1822, Justice Story, on circuit in Massachusetts, decided *United States* v. *La Jeune Eugenie*, 2 Mason 409, 26 Fed. Cas. 832 (No. 15,551). The ship was found not to have violated United States law because it was not owned or operated by Americans. The French owners, demanding restoration, were met with the contention that if they had not violated United States law they had violated international law and therefore were not entitled to restoration. France and the United States had prohibited the slave trade for their own nationals, but no treaty or general custom of nations prohibited the trade.[42] Nevertheless, Story concluded that international law prohibited the slave trade, and he refused to return the *Jeune Eugenie* to its French owners. Instead he turned the vessel over to the French government, on the assumption that it would wish to enforce its own law against slaving.

Three years later, in 1825, in the case of *The Antelope*, 10 Wheat. 66, Marshall, writing for the Supreme Court, reached the

[41] Beard, *Economic Interpretation of the Constitution*.
[42] The court went on the assumption that France had abolished the slave trade, although this was not entirely clear.

conclusion that international law did not prohibit the slave trade. The *Antelope,* a Spanish vessel, was loading slaves on the west coast of Africa when it was captured by privateers. Under command of the privateers it was subsequently hovering off the coast of the United States when it was seized by a revenue cutter and brought into Savannah for adjudication. Slaves from several ships plundered by the privateers were on board. The Spanish consul, for the Spanish owners, claimed the slaves originally on board the *Antelope.* The United States, as next friend, asserted the slaves' right to freedom. The slave trade was not prohibited by Spanish law nor by law or custom in Africa at the place where the *Antelope* was loading.

Story and Marshall were agreed that trading in slaves was contrary to natural law. Relying on the facts disclosed in a congressional report of 1821, Story had concluded that the slave trade "is repugnant to the great principles of Christian duty, the dictates of natural religion, the obligations of good faith and morality, and the eternal maxims of social justice." 26 Fed. Cas. 832, 845-46. Marshall said that the slave trade was contrary to the "generally admitted" principle that "every man has a natural right to the fruits of his own labor," and the necessary inference that no other person can "rightfully deprive him of those fruits, and appropriate them against his will." 10 Wheat. 66, 120. Marshall concluded that it "will scarcely be denied" that the slave trade "is contrary to the law of nature."

Story and Marshall differed on how a rule of natural law becomes a binding rule of a legally constituted human community. Story took the position that every doctrine that can be deduced from natural law principles exists as law in the human community, and where the natural law principles are applied to the relations between nations the deduced rules exist as international law. Universal custom to the contrary, as in the case of the slave trade, can suspend the application of the rule, but cannot wipe it out as law. As soon as any two nations recede from the custom, as France and the United States had by making the slave trade illegal, the rule of international law, in existence all the time, again becomes enforceable between them. On this reasoning Story found the French owners of the *Jeune Eugenie* in violation of international law and refused to restore the vessel to them. 26 Fed. Cas. 832, 846.

Marshall took the position that a rule of international law can be created only by general consent of states, as shown by custom or treaty. He pointed out that both Europe and America engaged in the slave trade, and "for nearly two centuries, it was carried on without opposition, and without censure." Therefore the rule of international law was that the trade is legal. If international law were to be changed to make the slave trade illegal, this would have to be done by general consent. This follows from the equality of sovereign states. Marshall said:

> No principle of general law is more universally acknowledged, than the perfect equality of nations. Russia and Geneva have equal rights. It results from this equality, that no one can rightfully impose a rule on another. Each legislates for itself, but its legislation can operate on itself alone. A right, then, which is vested in all by the consent of all, can be devested [sic] only by consent; and this trade, in which all have participated, must remain lawful to those who cannot be induced to relinquish it. As no nation can prescribe a rule for others, none can make a law of nations; and this traffic remains lawful to those whose governments have not forbidden it. 10 Wheat. 66, 121.

Thus Marshall clearly rejects the Story position that a rule of international law can be created by deduction from principles of natural law. International law is created only by the consent of states. But, and this is the significant thing for our purposes, Marshall does not point to general consent, as shown either in custom or treaty, as the source of the rule he is applying, namely, that international law can be created only by consent. On the contrary, he deduces it from "the perfect equality of nations," of which he says that no "principle of general law is more universally acknowledged." Furthermore, the principle of equality of nations, while everywhere "acknowledged," was not created by consent of states in custom or treaty. It was in turn deduced from the principle of territorial sovereignty, which was created by the consent of states in the treaties of Westphalia in 1648, ending the Thirty Years' War.

The principle of territorial sovereignty was constitutive of the community of modern nation-states. Europe had been in chaos for over a hundred years in part at least because of the Reformation's definitive rupture of medieval Christian unity. In the Christian form in which the Roman idea of universal polity had been preserved, the ruler derived his civil authority from God. Catholic princes and Protestant princes each felt that the other's religious errors destroyed divine warrant to rule and each had been trying to make Europe all Catholic again, or all Protestant. By the middle of the seventeenth century this zeal had given way before the resulting slaughter and devastation. Princes were willing to live and let live provided they could find an acceptable principle by which to distribute among themselves the authority to rule. Territorial sovereignty proved to be that principle.[43]

Territorial sovereignty was acceptable to the statesmen of Europe in 1648 partly because its basis was not the idea of the divine origin of civil authority—which had become divisive—but the secular idea of rational man in a rational world. This idea was in the cultural heritage of both Catholic and Protestant because it was developed in the Stoic philosophy and embodied in Roman law. Grotius, the father of modern international law, was also the father of modern natural-law philosophy. It was part of man's nature, said Grotius, that he had reason and that he needed to join with other men in society so that by division of labor men, the weakest and most helpless of creatures individually, could dominate the earth. Each state, resulting from the voluntary association of rational men, had full sovereignty within its territory and was obligated to respect the full sovereignty of every other state within their respective territories.[44]

The statesmen of midseventeenth-century Europe held in common the natural law ideas of man's rationality and his need for society. But they did not accept as binding in the legal community of nations any implication that might be deduced from those ideas. They accepted the principle of territorial sovereignty. I have shown elsewhere that, of the possible implications of human rationality, territorial sovereignty conceptualized the actual distribution of power that had emerged in the late middle ages, as royal institutions developed tax systems, standing armies, paid civil servants, and better protected life and property

[43] "The Wars of Religion," in *The Cambridge Modern History* (London: Macmillan, 1909), Vol. III.
[44] Hugo Grotius, *Prolegomena to the Law of War and Peace* (New York: Bobbs-Merrill, 1957).

than either feudal or ecclesiastical institutions. Territorial sovereignty could be accepted as useful as well as right, because it distributed authority in accordance with the distribution of power.[45]

Story's position might result in a good solution to a particular case, but it would have been destructive of that measure of felt obligation which has enabled international law to have some modest effect on the behavior of states, especially before the radical changes in conditions and expectations of the past five decades. Because enforcement of international law by international institutions has never been successfully organized, compliance of states has continued to rest to a high degree upon the calculation, under discussion here, of detriments and benefits. The international community has always tended to oscillate between coming together and flying apart, and is for that reason a good source of guidance in some respects to new states experiencing the same instability.

Staying within the implications of the constitutive principle of territorial sovereignty severely limits the possibilities for international agreement or action, as clearly appeared in the 1967 Security Council debates on the Arab-Israeli war. On the other hand, pressing for international action against the implications of the constitutive principle of territorial sovereignty instantly threatens the destruction of such international community as we have achieved. This clearly appeared in the United States backdown from enforcing the Article 19 penalty of loss of vote in the General Assembly against France and the Soviet Union, who had refused to pay assessments for peacekeeping forces established on the authority of the General Assembly instead of the Security Council, where the veto right of those two states could have been exercised.

General principles of humanity and justice appear in the United Nations Charter, but as purposes (Art. 1). But the first organizing principle of the United Nations is "the sovereign equality of all its Members" (Art. 2, Par. 1). The implications of the idea of human equality, political, economic, or other, can be implemented by the voluntary actions of states in the special

[45] Dorsey, "Law and the Formative Process of Social Order," in *Validation of New Forms of Social Organization*, Dorsey and Samuel I. Schuman, eds. (Wiesbaden, Germany: Franz Steiner Verlag, 1968), p. 1.

agencies of the United Nations. But compulsory action running against the constitutive principle of sovereign equality, as in South Africa and Rhodesia, is likely to raise false expectations and result in disillusionment.

The experience of the international community suggests that:

A. Among persons with disparate interests, constitutive principles can make the obligations of community more acceptable by making detriments and benefits foreseeable.

B. Felt obligation is attached to constitutive principles, not to basic purposes, and can be weakened or destroyed by attempts to accomplish purposes for which the constitutive principle is inadequate.

INTERPRETATION OF CONSTITUTIONAL PRINCIPLES

From among the alternative implications of prevailing beliefs and the alternative forms of organization through which response might be made to social conditions, constitutive principles specify the implication and form that will order a society and its government. Constitutive principle performs a limiting and specifying function. But once constitutive principle has been adopted, its meaning is understood partly in terms of the matrix of beliefs and social conditions. This matrix forms a penumbra of morality and utility around the words of the principle, providing the basis for interpretation in accordance with the purposes of the society and social realities.

Dean Pound has pointed out a number of examples of American courts using an ideal picture of American society as the standard for interpretation of constitutive principles.[46] By constitution or statute the various states adopted the common law of England as of 1789, so far as it was not repugnant to or inconsistent with the federal Constitution or the constitutions or laws of the states.[47] A Missouri statute abolished a feudal device for keeping land within a specified line of descendants. The statute provided that when a will purported to entail land the first taker

---

[46] Roscoe Pound, *Jurisprudence*, Vol. II (St. Paul: West, 1959), p. 117.

[47] Max Radin, *Anglo-American Legal History* (St. Paul: West, 1936), p. 341.

held a life estate, and then the land passed in fee simple to the devisee in tail "according to the course of the common law." In *Gillilan* v. *Gillilan,* 278 Mo. 99, 212 S.W. 348, the eldest son of the first taker argued that he should not have to divide the land with his brothers and sisters because primogeniture had been the rule of the English common law. The Missouri Supreme Court held primogeniture to be "radically opposed" to the spirit, if not the letter, of both federal and state constitutions. It said:

> The idea that any such preference in the descent of real property could coexist in the laws of any of the states with the axioms of the federal Constitution guaranteeing equal protection of the laws to all persons and a republican form of government for each state, or with the social and political life modeled on these fundamental principles, is an unthinkable absurdity.[48]

Drawing upon the ideas clustering around the generally-held belief in natural equality and the conditions of abundant opportunity for individual initiative in an economy of agrarian and small-artisan capitalism, the Supreme Court interpreted the Fourteenth Amendment clause "nor shall any State deprive any person of life, liberty, or property, without due process of law" as creating a right of "freedom of contract" which could not be abridged by state statutes requiring minimum wages or making collective bargaining more effective.

At the time the Constitution was adopted, 1789, there was abundant opportunity for individual initiative. The European institutions of privilege and preferment had not firmly established themselves in colonial America and were thoroughly extirpated during and immediately following the Revolution, as the discussion above (section entitled "Obligation Within a Ruling Party") shows. At the start of the Revolution there was every opportunity for the small artisan entrepreneur in the towns and hamlets and only the most self-sufficient could survive and build communities in the limitless frontier. Ben Franklin's Poor Richard was the voice of simple truth. Every man could achieve a position of respect and substance with diligence, thrift, and self-reliance. It was not necessary to join the church to get an

---

[48] *Gillilan* v. *Gillilan,* 212 S.W. 348, 350.

education or to be born of noble family to have substance and respect. Under these conditions a man could expect to receive rewards roughly proportional to the value of the capital he risked, or the quality of his management or labor, provided government did not interfere in the free exchange market. In such a community to require that a workman be paid a minimum wage would be to treat him as having a fixed status in the community which it was the obligation of his betters to protect, rather than having the opportunity to establish for himself any position that his will, effort, and intelligence could achieve through freely contracting with others.

In the period before the Civil War the view was generally accepted that contractual obligation and property ownership were beyond the authority of the state to grant or to take away, in accordance with prevailing natural-law theory. But, according to Edward S. Corwin, the natural-law view of vested property rights was not clearly fixed in judicial interpretation of any constitutional clause prior to the acceptance of the Fourteenth Amendment.[49] Shortly thereafter an effort was made to put the right to engage in a particular business beyond the power of the states to take away. Butchers in New Orleans challenged a statute of Louisiana which for the purpose of regulating the slaughter of animals gave one corporation the exclusive privilege of butchering cattle in that city. Among other grounds the ousted butchers argued that the statute was in violation of the Fourteenth Amendment clause that "No State shall make or enforce any law which shall abridge the privileges and immunities of citizens of the United States." Slaughter-House Cases, 16 Wall. 36 (1873). The Supreme Court rejected the privileges and immunities ground, and also considered and rejected the argument that Louisiana's action violated the due process clause.[50] However, Justice Bradley in a dissent, joined by Justice Field, said:

> Rights to life, liberty, and the pursuit of happiness are equivalent to the rights of life, liberty, and property. These are the fundamental rights which can only be taken away

[49] *The Constitution of the United States of America*, E. S. Corwin, ed. (Washington, D.C.: Government Printing Office, 1964), p. 17.
[50] *Slaughter-House Cases*, 16 Wall. 36, 80–81.

by due process of law . . . [Unless the citizen is free to choose his calling] he cannot be a freeman. This right to choose one's calling is an essential part of that liberty which it is the object of government to protect; and a calling, when chosen, is a man's property and right. . . . a law which prohibits a large class of citizens from adopting a lawful employment, or from following a lawful employment previously adopted, does deprive them of liberty as well as property, without due process of law.[51]

In 1877 the Supreme Court rejected the argument that Illinois violated the due process clause of the Fourteenth Amendment when it regulated the rates to be charged for transportation and storage of grain. *Munn* v. *Illinois,* 94 U.S. 113 (1877). In the next twenty years, however, the Court edged toward the Bradley position.[52] In 1897 the Supreme Court read into the clause "nor shall any State deprive any person of life, liberty, or property, without due process of law" a liberty or freedom of contract that was an almost absolute restriction on the power of the states. The case again concerned a statute of Louisiana. This time the statute prohibited placing marine insurance on any property within the state with an insurance company which had not complied with all the requirements for doing business in the state. The Supreme Court struck down the statute and said in a unanimous opinion:

The liberty mentioned in [the Fourteenth Amendment] means not only the right of the citizen to be free from the mere physical restraint of his person, as by incarceration, but the term is deemed to embrace the right of the citizen to be free in the enjoyment of all his faculties; to be free to use them in all lawful ways; to live and work where he will; to earn his livelihood by any lawful calling; to pursue any livelihood or avocation, and for that purpose to enter into all contracts which may be proper, necessary and essential to his carrying out to a successful conclusion the purposes above mentioned. *Allgeyer* v. *Louisiana,* 165 U.S. 578, 589.

[51] *Ibid.,* pp. 116, 122.
[52] Corwin, *The Constitution.*

The quotation from the Allgeyer opinion is a definitive statement of the free economic man in a free society. Unfortunately, it was no longer true in the United States in 1897, as it had been in 1789 and for some time thereafter, that a man could expect to receive rewards roughly proportional to the value of the capital he risked or the quality of his management or labor. The free market of an earlier small-artisan and agrarian capitalism no longer existed. The United States had moved toward industrialization and urbanization. It is of the essence of industrialization that machines increasingly do the work of producing. Efficiency often requires a substantial concentration of machines. Concentrations of machinery require concentrations of capital for acquisition and concentrations of workers for operation.

The concentration of capital was accomplished primarily through the corporation. The corporation is a legal creation that facilitates the aggregation of capital from large numbers of investors by limiting the risk they take. If the enterprise fails, the stockholder, in most cases, loses only what he paid for the stock. By contrast the natural person engaged in economic enterprise is answerable for all debts out of any property he may have, except for any exemption established by state law, such as the family home. This difference between full and limited liability would seem to have significant bearing on the question of whether the property of corporations, as well as the property of natural individuals, should be included in the "person" who, under the Fifth and Fourteenth Amendments, is not to be deprived of his property without due process of law. However, without any real consideration of the point, the Supreme Court held that corporations, as well as natural persons, are protected by the due process clauses of the Fifth and Fourteenth Amendments. *Sinking Fund Cases,* 99 U.S. 700 (1879); *Smyth* v. *Ames,* 169 U.S. 466 (1898).

The value of the goods and services produced by a corporation is the result of the total contribution of capital, management, and labor of all the persons associated in the corporate enterprise. Assuming a free market economy, the corporate enterprise as a whole receives rewards roughly proportional to the value it contributes to the economy, because its goods and services are offered in open competition and customers choose the best quality for the lowest price. But, with the aggregation of capital, management, and labor into the corporation, the free market no longer determines the reward each person receives for his contribution of capital, management, or labor. This is determined by those in control of the corporation, and by corporation law and economic fact corporate control lies in dominant stock membership and top management. By pyramiding corporations, each of which holds dominant stock ownership in corporations at the next lower level, a few persons with relatively little personal investment could control the distribution of the economic value of the capital, management, and labor contributed by thousands of investors and workers.[53]

The disparity of incomes at the turn of this century indicates that corporation heads used their control to greatly favor themselves at the expense of the workers. In 1900 Andrew Carnegie's income was $23 million, with no income tax to pay. The average annual wage of all American workers was $400 to $500, with no social security, no workmen's compensation, and no unemployment insurance.[54] Congress sought to break the economic power of the holding companies and the money trusts with the Sherman Antitrust Act, passed in 1890. (Act of July 2, 1890, c. 647, 26 Stat. 209.) It recognized the relative ineffectiveness of the Sherman Act when it passed the Clayton Act and the Federal Trade Commission Act in 1914, by which it sought to prohibit acts and practices which if allowed to continue might lead to further concentration. (Act of Oct. 15, 1914, c. 323, 38 Stat. 730; Act of Sept. 26, 1914, c. 311, 38 Stat. 717.)

The Sherman and Clayton Acts proscribed actions by corporations which eliminated competitors and achieved monopoly, but they had no effect whatever on the control of the few over intracorporation distribution of rewards for services rendered. The economic power of even a relatively small corporation is overwhelmingly greater than that of a single workman. When workmen sought to join their power in labor unions and to bargain collectively, the employer corporations used various devices to prevent workers from joining a union or to prevent unions from using certain kinds of effective economic pressure.[55] One of the most effective antiunion devices was the

[53] Thorstein Veblen, *Business Enterprise*, pp. 128–76.

[54] Frederick L. Allen, *The Big Change* (New York: Harper, 1952), p. 24.

[55] Charles O. Gregory, *Labor and the Law* (New York: Norton, 1946), pp. 83–289.

yellow-dog contract, which required workers, as a condition of employment, to withdraw from or refrain from joining a union. Congress and a number of state legislatures passed statutes outlawing yellow-dog contracts. The Supreme Court, under its Ben Franklin interpretation of the due process clause in Andrew Carnegie times, held these statutes unconstitutional under the Fifth and Fourteenth Amendments. *Adair* v. *United States,* 208 U.S. 161 (1908); *Coppage* v. *Kansas,* 236 U.S. 1 (1915). The Court was made aware of the inequality of bargaining power between worker and corporate employer, but it said there will always be "inequalities of fortune; and thus it naturally happens that parties negotiating about a contract are not equally unhampered by circumstances." 236 U.S. 1, 16. Despite the inequality of economic power, the employer and the worker were held to have "equality of right, and any legislation that disturbs that equality is an arbitrary interference with the liberty of contract which no government can legally justify in a free land." 208 U.S. 161, 175.

When it became obvious from numerous reports of state bureaus of labor and industrial statistics, social survey committees, factory investigation commissions, state health commissioners, and the United States Public Health Service that industrial workers often received wages insufficient to buy enough food, clothing, and shelter to restore the energy expended on the job, that they lived in squalid and degrading surroundings and were vulnerable to diseases for which they could not afford treatment, states passed statutes requiring a limitation on hours of employment and the payment of minimum wages. When the facts just mentioned were brought to the attention of the Supreme Court by Brandeis, the Oregon ten-hour law for women was held constitutional. *Muller* v. *Oregon,* 208 U.S. 412 (1908). But no general interpretation was forthcoming that would permit legislatures to come to the aid of workers pinched by the corporate concentration of economic power. The Muller case was decided in the same term as the Adair case which nullified antiyellow-dog contract laws. In 1923 the Court had a case in which a woman elevator operator sued to enjoin enforcement of a minimum-wage law. The Court protected her freedom to work for less than a living wage if she wanted to do so. *Adkins* v. *Children's Hospital,* and *Adkins* v. *Lyons,* 261 U.S. 525 (1923). As late as

1936 the Supreme Court held unconstitutional a New York minimum-wage law for women. *Morehead* v. *Tipaldo,* 298 U.S. 587 (1936).

The Supreme Court's protection of the worker from the degrading assistance of government through its interpretation of the Fifth and Fourteenth Amendments was called "substantive due process." This impress of laissez faire on the constitution was strengthened and supplemented by interpretation of other clauses, such as the holding that the interstate commerce power of Congress did not extend to preventing the movement in interstate commerce of goods produced by child labor. *Hammer* v. *Dagenhart,* 247 U.S. 251 (1918).

When Franklin Roosevelt assumed the presidency in 1933 he proposed to use the full power of the federal government to restore the foundering economy. Congress accepted the President's lead and measures were passed to give farm debtors relief from mortgage foreclosures, to restore the soundness of money, to eliminate the chaotic effects of overproduction of oil products, to establish wage, hour, and working conditions for labor, and to eliminate destructive and predatory competitive practices. In 1935 the Supreme Court narrowly approved the monetary legislation but held unconstitutional farm debtor relief, the oil production code, and the National Industrial Recovery Act, under which comprehensive codes covering labor compensation and competitive practices were promulgated for nearly all industries in the United States.[56] Robert H. Jackson, general counsel of the Bureau of Internal Revenue at the time, later solicitor general and then Justice of the Supreme Court, says the result was that "hell broke loose in the lower courts. Sixteen hundred injunctions restraining officers of the Federal Government from carrying out acts of Congress were granted by federal judges."[57]

The popular unrest and resentment that had resulted in a veterans' march on Washington, sit-down strikes, and farmers' interference with mortgage foreclosure sales were intensified, and Supreme Court decisions became a factor in the 1936 elec-

[56] Robert H. Jackson, *The Struggle for Judicial Supremacy* (New York: Knopf, 1941), pp. 86–114.
[57] *Ibid.,* p. 115.

tions.[58] President Roosevelt's court-packing plan failed, but the Court felt the pressure. According to Jackson the conservatives on the Court realized that they had gone too far in striking down, in the spring of 1936, the New York Minimum Wage Law for Women (*Morehead* v. *Tipaldo,* 298 U.S. 587) and were relieved when Justice Roberts shifted to the liberal side and blockage of New Deal legislation ended.[59]

The change came on Monday, March 29, 1937. Fittingly, the pivotal opinion explaining the shift came in the decision on another minimum-wage law for women; this time from the state of Washington. *West Coast Hotel* v. *Parrish,* 300 U.S. 379 (1937). The Court clearly and unequivocally renounced substantive due process, with its "freedom of contract." The Court said:

> What is this freedom? The Constitution does not speak of freedom of contract. It speaks of liberty and prohibits the deprivation of liberty without due process of law. In prohibiting that deprivation the Constitution does not recognize an absolute and uncontrollable liberty. Liberty in each of its phases has its history and connotation. But the liberty safeguarded is liberty in a social organization which requires the protection of law against the evils which menace the health, safety, morals and welfare of the people. Liberty under the Constitution is thus necessarily subject to the restraints of due process, and regulation which is reasonable in relation to its subject and is adopted in the interests of the community is due process. 300 U.S. 379, 391.

The same day in 1937 the Supreme Court held that the interstate commerce clause gave Congress power to strengthen collective bargaining in the railroad industry, *Virginian Ry.* v. *Federation,* 300 U.S. 515; that the clause granting Congress power to lay and collect taxes authorized Congressional regulation of firearms through registration and taxation, *Sonzinsky* v. *United States,* 300 U.S. 506; and that the revised act granting

[58] Arthur Schlesinger, Jr., *The Age of Roosevelt,* vol. 1 (Boston: Houghton Mifflin, 1957), pp. 224–69.

[59] Jackson, *The Struggle for Judicial Supremacy* (New York: Knopf, 1941), pp. 170-212.

farm debtors relief from mortgage foreclosures did not violate the due process clause, *Wright* v. *Vinton Branch*, 300 U.S. 440.[60] Subsequently, in cases concerning labor relations, federal farm assistance programs, social security, federal power projects, and others the Supreme Court interpreted the Constitution to permit the people of the United States to deal collectively, through representative institutions, with economic and social problems that they could no longer cope with individually.[61] Despite occasional campaign oratory there has never been a serious attempt to end the active role of government in economic and social matters. Supreme Court interpretations that denied government that active role created a serious crisis of constitutional obligation in the 1930s. The Court's change of position ended that crisis.

With respect to social and economic problems arising out of industrialization, legislatures took the initiative. When the Supreme Court reinterpreted the constitution to authorize the active role of government, it had merely to cease obstructing legislative activity. This led to characterization of the new position as "judicial self-restraint."[62] In the 1950s and 1960s the Supreme Court took the initiative with respect to racial justice, equal opportunity, personal liberty and privacy, and the affirmative duty of government to remove inequalities and provide opportunities for all.[63] The Supreme Court has nullified legislative and executive acts upholding segregation, overturned its own prior decisions, required legislatures to reapportion legislative districts, and extended the previously established Bill of Rights restrictions on the federal government to state governments through the Fourteenth Amendment.[64] These opinions have met with some protest. The social unrest of the 1950s and 1960s suggests that a real crisis of constitutional obligation would have been more likely without these opinions than with them, but it is too early for a definitive assessment.

The United States experience with constitutional interpretation discussed above suggests the following:

[60] *Ibid.*, pp. 207–13.
[61] *Ibid.*, pp. 214–85.
[62] A. Cox, *The Warren Court* (Cambridge: Harvard University Press: 1968), pp. 3–5.
[63] *Ibid.*, pp. 5–9.
[64] *Ibid.*, pp. 24–134.

A. Interpretation of the words of a constitution in accordance with the surrounding matrix of beliefs and social conditions enables the purposes of the society to be implemented realistically.

B. The meaning of constitutional provisions should not be fixed for all time by the intent of the framers or by beliefs and social conditions prevailing at the time the constitution was adopted.

C. A crisis in constitutional obligation will develop unless judges interpret constitutional provisions in accordance with a generally prevailing view of the current matrix of beliefs and social conditions.

CONCLUSION

The study of obligation has been presented as a discussion of the factors bearing on the practical effectiveness of constitutional propositions. It was assumed that the principles for constituting the working- and living-together relations of a society will be effective if they are felt by most persons to be right and advantageous. Generally held and controlling beliefs are the ultimate basis of a general feeling that a constitutional principle is right. Social conditions are the ultimate basis of a general feeling that constitutional principles are advantageous. However, there is interaction between the intellectual process of deriving ideal relations from general belief and the social process of seeking individual and group advantage through effective response to new conditions.

A constitutional principle that is expected to stimulate and sustain the flow of power from people to government must have its apparent foundation in generally held belief, as shown by the failure of the "democratic" Chinese revolution of 1911-12. Where the emotional attachment to a long-held belief is still strong, it may continue as the effective foundation for a constitution's symbolic principles even after the implications of that belief for the exercise of governmental power have been rejected. This is shown by the 1688 English revolution.

In countries controlled by a single ruling party, the critical issue of allegiance to constituting principles shifts its locus from the general populace to the party membership. The need is not less, however, for unifying, directing, and limiting constitutional principles and effective constitutional principles cannot be based solely upon pragmatic response to social conditions. They must be supported also by vivifying general belief, as the events in China from 1927 to 1949 demonstrate.

Persons and groups with many conflicting interests can judge the desirability of entering a community of mutual obligations by the constituting principles which limit and specify the obligations to be assumed. Especially when the community remains rudimentary and vulnerable to disintegrative influences, as is the case in the international community and some new states, purposes that cannot be achieved by actions in accordance with the agreed constitutional principle cannot be pursued without destroying the mutual obligation that enables the community to act effectively even with respect to limited goals. An instance is the attempt to end racist practices within South Africa by actions of the United Nations, whose first constitutive principle is "the sovereign equality of all its Members."

Interpretation, and reinterpretation, of the words of constitutional provisions in accordance with the contemporary matrix of beliefs and social conditions assures continued general acceptance of constitutional obligations, and therefore a peaceful and effective society. If interpretation of constitutional provisions does not keep pace with social changes responding to new conditions, the general willingness to honor constitutional obligations will be threatened, as happened in the United States in the first three decades of this century.

9

ON FEELING OBLIGATED TO DO WHAT A CONSTITUTION REQUIRES

GERALD C. MacCALLUM, JR.

Professor Dorsey discusses *feeling* obligated to do what a constitution requires, not *being* obligated. In doing so, he does not clearly distinguish between (a) societies in which persons generally feel obligated to do what the constitution requires, (b) societies in which persons generally adhere or conform to constitutional principles, and (c) societies in which the ruling parties are able effectively to carry out programs consistent with the principles of the constitution. Though he has interesting things to say about each of these, the title of his essay, as well as the appearance of the essay in the present volume, underwrite the importance of the first, and this brief commentary will focus on it.

In assessing the importance of whether persons generally feel obligated to do what a constitution requires, and in searching history for insight into how this feeling is created or supported and how it is subverted or destroyed, much depends on how one thinks people feeling this way will behave. Concerning the importance of the feeling, for example, Professor Dorsey says that if persons generally have it, "all other problems will respond to competence and energy," and if they do not have it, "no problem will respond." The persuasiveness of these claims stands or falls in part on how one supposes people behave who feel obligated and on how one supposes people behave who do not. But, what *are* the behavioral correlates of feeling or not feeling this way?

Among the various kinds of behavior and social conditions Professor Dorsey cites in connection with the presence of the feeling are adherence and obedience to, support and defense of, the principles of the constitution; the generating of programs by the ruling party; the effective carrying out of these programs with high morale and in a disciplined and honest way. Such a collection as this provides his basis both for claims about the importance of feeling obligated and for claims about whether people in certain situations feel or felt obligated.

Suppose we wish to assess his claims about these matters. How would we do so? It would be important, at least, for us to try to distinguish claims that are clearly empirically based and testable— for example, claims about the more or less likely causes or results of the widespread presence of the feeling—from claims that are not, but that somehow have to get settled before there can be any question of empirical investigation of the causes or results of the feeling, namely, claims about how to tell whether the feeling is in fact present or not, widespread or not. Our assessment of the latter sort of claim is less a matter of testing or confirming anything than a matter of trying to get clear what we are talking about when we talk about feeling obligated to do what a constitution requires.

How, then, do we tell whether, in a given society, people generally do or do not feel so obligated? Here, everything depends on how sophisticated a moral and political life the people in that society are living. This is so because everything depends on how specific a thing their feeling so obligated is, and thus depends on the variety of other things from which it must be distinguished. Consider, for example, the following questions:

A. Do persons in the given society generally distinguish (and, if so, how clearly do they distinguish) between doing something because they feel obligated to do it and doing it because they believe that doing so would be wise, prudent, desirable, beneficial, or admirable, and so on? If these or similar distinctions are generally made in the society, and if we are genuinely interested in the specific importance in that society of feeling obligated to do what the constitution requires, and interested in what leads members of the society generally to feel or not feel this way, we would need to develop ways of "reading" situations so as to distinguish these cases.

B. Do the people in the society generally distinguish between legal and moral, and, perhaps, other sorts of obligation? If so, how do they do so, and do they suppose, for example, that there can be cases where the first is present and the second not, or vice versa? Depending on our answers here, we may also see a need to make our inquiry more specific. Are we asking for the conditions under which persons generally feel morally obligated to do what a constitution requires of them or for the conditions under which they feel legally obligated, or both, or neither, and so on?[1] We may see that the behavioral manifestations of feeling obligated in the one way do not have the same pattern as those of feeling obligated in another way; for example, we may see that the kinds of explanations sufficing when persons correctly said to feel morally obligated to do something fail to do it will differ from

---

[1] Persons don't generally talk about feeling legally obligated. This is because, unlike the situation with moral obligations, (a) the extent of legal obligations is sufficiently decidable by clear procedures so that people don't have much occasion or inclination to rely on anything so indefinite as "feelings," (which, in this case, might be something like hunches or intuitions), and (b) none of the deference to the views and sensitivities of others suggested by "*I* feel" seems called for in one's statement of his own legal obligations. To note these points, however, is to expose another range of problems of some complexity. Suppose, for example, that we find ourselves shifting to "belief" talk, so that instead of asking whether people generally *feel* morally or legally obligated, and so on, we find ourselves asking whether people generally *believe* themselves to be so obligated. Are we still talking about the same thing? Is a person who believes himself to be obligated thereby a person who feels obligated? Perhaps not. Vice versa? Perhaps not.

those needed when persons correctly said to believe themselves legally obligated to do something fail to do it.[2]

The relevance of these points to Professor Dorsey's paper is twofold. First, when he suggests the conditions under which the feeling of obligation is present, he cites relationships existing between various categories of constitutional principles, on the one hand, and the society's traditional or prevailing views on the nature of man and the world, on the other hand—views in turn influencing popular beliefs about what is right and what is wrong, what is moral and what is useful. But if the members of the society distinguish between the useful and the moral, the desirable and the obligatory, and so forth, then we must do a finer-scale study of the conditions Professor Dorsey mentions if we are to discover which of them plays a role specifically in supporting a feeling of obligatoriness or obligation relative to action in accordance with constitutional principles. Some of the conditions may, after all, merely support feelings or beliefs that such action is or would be beneficial, wise, admirable, or whatever, and citation of them would thus be off the point.[3]

Secondly, when the members of a society generally make such distinctions as the above (even though somewhat dimly, perhaps) we would need to look more carefully at claims about the social dynamics and results of widespread feelings of obligation to do what the constitution requires. Consider, for example, Professor Dorsey's claim that felt obligation to a constitutional principle can be weakened or destroyed by attempts to accomplish purposes for which the principle is inadequate. Surely, such attempts may weaken adherence or conformity to the principles. But did we read that adherence and conformity rightly when we saw them as manifestations or results of felt obligation? Might they not have been merely the results of widespread feelings or beliefs that doing what the constitution requires was beneficial or desirable, and so on? Could we tell about this without looking again and more closely? Are we quite clear on it?

[2] Though the matter is of course controversial, consider the possible role of references to the availability of sanctions in each of these cases.

[3] One might feel obligated to do something *because* he thought that doing it would be wise, beneficial, or whatever. But even so, we would have to establish whether he felt obligated independently of establishing what his beliefs about these other matters were.

One quick way of cutting through these problems is to claim that the distinctions just noted remain unmade by populations generally, and that, in consequence, feeling obligated is not so specific as the discussion has suggested. Another way is to suggest that even where such distinctions are made they are not of sufficient importance to warrant such a fuss.

One should surely be willing to agree that there have been and probably will be societies in which some of the above distinctions generally have not been made, and perhaps even societies in which none of them has been made. But this is not so obviously and generally so as to permit us to escape entirely the interest and challenge attached to making them in connection with Professor Dorsey's topic. For we ourselves live in one of a cluster of societies in which such distinctions are made and in which great importance is attached to making them. The title of this volume attests to that, and anyone who takes seriously the inclusion of Professor Dorsey's essay in this volume must give the distinctions careful consideration.

10

CAUSES AND EFFECTS OF CONSTITUTIONAL COMPLIANCE

STUART S. NAGEL

SETTING OF THESE COMMENTS

The problem of legal or constitutional obligation may be approached in any of three ways. One approach is to seek a precise definition of the concept of obligation as John Ladd has done.[1] Another approach is concerned with when should the law be obeyed, which James Luther Adams has followed.[2] The third approach is concerned with what conditions are conducive to

This chapter is based on Nagel's comments regarding Gray Dorsey's chapter made at the 1967 annual meeting of the American Society for Political and Legal Philosophy.

[1] John Ladd, "Legal and Moral Obligation," ch. 1, this volume.

[2] James Luther Adams, "Civil Disobedience: Its Occasions and Limits," ch. 13, this volume.

legal compliance. This is the viewpoint that is emphasized in Gray Dorsey's paper.[3]

Professor Dorsey finds four conditions to be particularly relevant to encouraging a felt or empirical constitutional law obligation, as contrasted to a mere formal or legalistic obligation. First the law should contain symbols that evoke a positive response based on generally held beliefs, such as the symbol of monarchy in England in 1688, but not the symbol of republicanism in China in 1912. Second, the law should be administered by a ruling party that advocates widely shared values, such as the value of natural equality as advocated by the American revolutionaries in the late 1700s, but not the value of mere pragmatism as advocated by the Chinese revolutionaries in 1912. Third, the law should contain constitutional principles whose detriments and benefits are foreseeable, such as the principle of territorial sovereignty in international law in the mid-1900s. Fourth, constitutional and other legal interpretations should conform to the social and economic conditions of the time, such as an interpretation of the American Constitution that allows minimum wage laws in the 1900s rather than prohibits such laws as interferences with freedom of contract.

Professor Dorsey's analysis is quite insightful and empirically valid so far as it goes. There seem, however, to be many more factors determining constitutional compliance than those which he has described. The general factors can possibly be grouped into five basic categories. These categories relate to (1) the nature of the specific laws involved, (2) the law makers, (3) the law appliers, (4) the law recipients, and (5) certain facilitating and inhibiting environmental factors.[4] Professor Dorsey possibly has also neglected to make use of relevant behavioral science data dealing with the empirical correlates of constitutional compliance.[5] Perhaps it might be useful to attempt to spell out the

[3] Gray L. Dorsey, "Constitutional Obligation," ch. 8, this volume.

[4] For further detail on the use of these categories to generate empirical hypotheses, see Stuart Nagel, "A Conceptual Scheme of the Legal Process," *American Behavioral Scientist*, VII (1963), 7–10; and Stuart Nagel, *The Legal Process from a Behavioral Perspective* (Homewood, Ill.: Dorsey Press, 1969).

[5] Some of this recent literature is brought together in Theodore Becker, ed., *The Impact of Supreme Court Decisions: Empirical Studies* (New York: Oxford University Press, 1969). Many of the compliance factors are discussed in Samuel Krislov, "The Perimeters of Power: Patterns of Compliance and Opposition to Supreme Court Decisions," paper presented at the 1963 meeting of the American Political Science Association.

subcategories to which these general concepts refer and to tie them to relevant behavioral science data. First, however, the relation should be clarified between Dorsey's concept of felt obligation and the concept of compliance.

RELATIONS BETWEEN COMPLIANCE
AND FELT OBLIGATION

One might say that just because Southern school administrators increased their compliance with *Brown* v. *Board of Education* does not mean they increased their felt obligation. The truth of such a statement depends partly on definitions and partly on empirical fact.

By definition, "compliance" means behaving in conformity with the law. "Obligation in the positive law sense" means having a legal duty as a citizen to behave in conformity with properly passed laws. "Obligation in the natural law sense" means having a moral duty as a human being to behave in conformity with what is considered inherently right. "Felt obligation" means feeling that one should behave in conformity with the law or principle involved.

One can have a positive law obligation or a natural law obligation and still not have a felt obligation if one is unaware of or in disagreement with the law or principle involved. But what about the relation between compliance and felt obligation? It is theoretically possible (situation 1) that a Southern school administrator could have a felt obligation toward Southern custom which is greater than his felt obligation toward the Supreme Court, and yet still comply with law by desegregating his school district because of the financial inducements of federal aid to education. It is also theoretically possible (situation 2) that a Southern school administrator could have a felt obligation toward *Brown* v. *Board of Education,* and yet still not comply by refusing to desegregate his school district because of adverse local customs and pressures.

Definitionally speaking, there is no conflict between compliance and felt obligation in either of the above two examples where the administrator thinks he should not comply but does, or where he thinks he should comply but does not. There is no conflict because the concept of felt obligation is broad enough to

say that if an administrator feels he should comply because of
financial benefits to the school for which he is responsible (situation 1), then that is just as much a felt obligation as where he
feels he should comply because of respect for or agreement with
the law. Likewise the concept of felt obligation is broad enough
to say that if an administrator feels he should not comply because
of local custom and pressures (situation 2), then it is appropriate to say he does not really have a felt obligation to comply and
that his predominant feelings are not in conflict with his behavior, although he apparently has mixed feelings.

Empirically speaking, it is generally contrary to empirical fact
(as studies of cognitive dissonance have shown) [6] for most people's attitudes and behaviors to remain in conflict for very long.
In order to live with themselves, they generally change their
attitudes to conform with their behavior or they change their
behavior to conform with their attitudes. Thus external behavior
is generally a good indicator of attitudes. Indeed if actions speak
louder than words, then actions surely speak louder than conscious and subconscious thoughts.

One important aspect of the behavioral movement in social
science is to emphasize the observable. One can observe compliance, but one cannot directly observe a felt obligation. However,
one can observe responses to attitudinal questions that may
reveal the presence or absence of a felt obligation. It is hoped
that future studies of man's obligations will make more use of
observation to determine what causes both external and internal
compliance and what consequences flow from such compliance.

CAUSES OF COMPLIANCE

With regard to the *types of laws* that are most likely to
produce a felt obligation to comply, the key element seems to be
the extent to which the law deviates from custom or habit.[7] For

---

[6] Leon Festinger, *A Theory of Cognitive Dissonance* (New York: Harper &
Row, 1957); Jack Brehan and Arthur Cohen, *Explorations in Cognitive
Dissonance* (New York: Wiley, 1962); and Robert Abelson, "Modes of
Resolution of Belief Dilemmas," *Journal of Conflict Resolution,* III (1959),
343.

[7] Robert MacIver, *The Web of Government* (New York: Macmillan, 1951),
73-81; Arnold Rose, "Sociological Factors in the Effectiveness of Projected
Legislative Remedies," *Journal of Legal Education,* XI (1959), 470-81.

example, attitudinal and behavioral surveys show that there is a greater propensity on the part of school authorities to comply with Supreme Court decisions outlawing compulsory racial segregation in the public schools than there is to comply with decisions outlawing compulsory prayer and Bible reading in the public schools.[8] These differences in compliance rates are largely attributable to the fact that school segregation before the Supreme Court's ruling was customary only in the South, whereas religious activities in the public schools were more widespread throughout the country.[9] Likewise the University of Chicago jury studies show that juries are much less likely to comply with the letter of the law where the law deviates from customary values, as in the liquor laws or gambling laws as contrasted to laws against kidnapping and arson.[10]

A second key element built into the law itself is the clarity of the standards to be applied in determining whether the law has been violated. Thus when the standard of school segregation was "with all deliberate speed,"[11] there was very little speed. When, however, the Office of Education published its more precise Educational Guidelines,[12] this was a partial factor in accelerating desegregation. Likewise the American Bar Foundation studies of

---

[8] In a survey of 7,000 junior high school principals, 79 percent of the 4,500 respondents indicated agreement with the Supreme Court's racial segregation decisions, but only 45 percent indicated agreement with the Supreme Court's prayer and Bible-reading decisions. Donald Rock and John Hemphill, *Report of the Junior High School Principalship* (National Association of Secondary School Principals, 1966). There is a high correlation between agreement with the Supreme Court and having a feeling of obligation to the Court's decisions, as is shown in Richard Johnson, "Compliance and Supreme Court Decision-Making," *Wisconsin Law Review* (1967), 170–85.

[9] School segregation figures before and after *Brown* v. *Board of Education* are given in the publication of the Southern Education Reporting Service and the Civil Rights Commission. Analogous figures on disestablishment of prayers and Bible-reading in the public schools are reported in Donald Reich, "The Impact of Judicial Decision-Making: The School Prayer Cases," paper presented at the 1967 meeting of the Midwest Political Science Association; and Ellis Katz, "Patterns of Compliance with the Schempp Decisions," *Journal of Public Law*, XIV (1966), 396–408.

[10] Harry Kalven and Hans Zeisel, *The American Jury* (Boston: Little, Brown, 1966), 286–97.

[11] *Brown et al.* v. *Board of Education of Topeka*, 349 U.S. 294 (1954).

[12] Office of Education, "General Statement of Policies under Title VI of the Civil Rights Act of 1964 Respecting Desegregation of Elementary and Secondary Schools," March 1966.

police behavior show that nonenforcement of the law is often due to ambiguity in defining crimes.[13]

With regard to who the *lawmakers* are, recent public opinion polls show that actions taken by Congress are more likely to produce favorable attitudes and compliance than actions taken by the President or the Supreme Court.[14] Likewise there is some polling evidence showing greater respect for federal policy-makers than for state and local policy-makers although this respect probably varies from region to region.[15] Disagreement among the lawmakers is also an empirical factor promoting resistance to their policies.[16]

With regard to the policy *administrators*, one key distinction seems to be whether the law is administered by the courts through injunctions and damage suits (as voting registration discrimination originally was) or, in the alternative, whether the law is administered by executive officials (like the federal registrars provided for by the Voting Rights Act of 1965). Clearly this change in administrative personnel and procedures made a big difference in the percentage of Negroes registered to vote in the Southern states.[17] Executive officials have more time and expertise than judges do, and they can also take the initiative in sanctioning violators.

Another key element at the policy administration stage is the nature of the sanctions available to the administrators. Thus the

[13] Wayne LaFave, "The Police and Non-Enforcement of the Law," *Wisconsin Law Review* (1962), 104, 188–91.

[14] Kenneth Dolbeare, "The Public Views the Supreme Court," in Herbert Jacob, *Law, Politics, and the Federal Courts* (Boston: Little, Brown, 1967), p. 197.

[15] Even in Texas, attorneys are more favorable in their attitudes toward most federal judges below the United States Supreme Court level than they are toward most state judges below the state supreme court level. Bancroft Henderson and T. C. Sinclair, "The Impact of the Selection Process upon the Role of the Judge: An Exploratory Case Study," paper presented at the 1962 meeting of the Midwest Political Science Association.

[16] Stuart Nagel, "Political Parties and Judicial Review in American History," *Journal of Public Law*, XI (1962), 328–40, shows laws passed by a sharply divided Congress are more likely to be declared unconstitutional. Stuart Nagel, "Court Curbing Periods in American History," *Vanderbilt Law Review*, XVIII (1965), 925–44, shows Supreme Court decisions with a high percentage of dissents are more likely to generate court-curbing activities.

[17] This increase in compliance was anticipated in Charles Hamilton, "The Impact of the Civil Rights Acts on Southern Federal Judges," *Wisconsin Law Review* (1965), 72-102.

felt obligation to conform was low when the only sanction against segregation in the public schools was the rare possibility of being held in contempt of court. But when the sanction became loss of important federal aid to education funds, the felt obligation became much higher.[18] Increased compliance here was a result of a change both in the severity and in the certainty of the sanctions involved.

In the context of constitutional obligation, *law recipients* or obligees (to use John Ladd's term) can vary on such relevant characteristics as region, occupation, and political party. As for region, one would expect more resistance to freedom of speech in the more conservative Southern states than in the North, as was shown in Berelson's civil liberties survey.[19] Likewise Arnold Rose finds more resistance to freedom of assembly among countries with a Latin background than among those with an Anglo-Saxon background due to a conservative fear of revolutionary associations combined with a liberal fear of business and church groups.[20] As for occupations, clearly a desegregation law directed toward members of the armed forces is easier to enforce than one directed toward real estate operators.[21] With regard to party affiliation, recent nationwide surveys show significant differences between Democrats and Republicans with regard to their respective support for the constitutional interpretations of the Supreme Court.[22]

The fifth general compliance determinant refers to the facili-

[18] Jim Leeson, "Faster Pace, Scarcer Records," *Southern Education Report* (January 1966), 28–32.

[19] Samuel Stouffer, *Communism, Conformity, and Civil Liberties* (Garden City, N.Y.: Doubleday, 1955).

[20] Arnold Rose, "On Individualism and Social Responsibility," *Archives of European Sociology*, II (1961), 163–69.

[21] Contrast ch. 11, "The Armed Forces" with ch. 8, "Housing and Real Property," in Jack Greenberg, *Race Relations and American Law* (New York: Columbia University Press, 1960). For a national survey on how different occupations react to the Supreme Court in general as contrasted to specific Supreme Court decisions, see William Daniels, "Public Attitudes toward the Supreme Court," paper presented at the 1967 meeting of the Midwest Political Science Association.

[22] Walter Murphy and Joseph Tanenhaus, "Public Opinion and the United States Supreme Court: A Preliminary Mapping of Some Prerequisites for Court Legitimation of Regime Changes," paper presented at the 1967 University of Iowa Shambaugh Conference, and Stuart Nagel, "Editorial Reaction to the Church and State Cases," *Public Opinion Quarterly*, XXX (1966), 647–55.

tating and inhibiting *environmental conditions*. The communications media and educational facilities are particularly important, since the degree of felt obligation may depend substantially on how the law is presented to those who are expected to comply with it. Thus Richard Schwartz in a recent systematic controlled experiment showed that appeals to conscience and to a sense of civic responsibility can produce greater compliance with the income tax laws than can threats of punishment.[23] Likewise a recent questionnaire study of numerous communities shows a high correlation between increased police education programs and increased police adherence to legality in the field of search and seizure.[24] Favorable or unfavorable economic, political, or other social conditions may also be quite important in producing compliance, which explains why periods of economic depression or unpopular war sometimes lead to constitutional upheavals.[25]

In tying this material together, the key question does not seem to be, "Why do people feel an obligation to obey the law?" Rather it is a series of five questions. First, why do people feel an obligation to obey some types of laws more than others? Second, why do people feel a greater obligation toward some lawmakers than others? Third, why are some law appliers more effective than others even when the content of the law is held constant? Fourth, why do some people feel a greater obligation to obey the law than others do? Fifth why under certain social conditions is there more legal compliance than in the absence of those conditions?

EFFECTS OF COMPLIANCE

Moreover, instead of asking the question, "Should people obey the law?" it seems more meaningful to ask three analogous

[23] Richard Schwartz and Sonya Orleans, "On Legal Sanctions," *University of Chicago Law Review*, XXXIV (1967), 274–300.

[24] Stuart Nagel, "Testing the Effects of Excluding Illegally Seized Evidence," *Wisconsin Law Review* (1965), 283–310.

[25] For a quantitative study of compliance to the school desegregation decision that places emphasis on environmental variables as well as the nature of the law administrators and the law recipients, see Sheldon Stoff, *The Two-Way Street: Guideposts to Peaceful School Desegregation* (Indianapolis, Ind.: David-Stewart Co., 1967).

questions that relate to the specific laws, law recipients, and environmental conditions involved. First, what are the effects of noncompliance to certain specific laws like the selective service law as contrasted to laws against highway speeding? Resistance to the selective service law may save lives by encouraging the government to make a greater effort to seek peace, whereas resistance to speeding may jeopardize lives, not save them. Second, what are the effects of noncompliance by certain specific persons like an idealistic law student as contrasted to a Students for a Democratic Society activist who has been repeatedly convicted of various violations? The idealistic law student may by his noncompliance destroy his chances of passing the bar's character and fitness committee, thereby sacrificing the opportunity to become a social reform lawyer, whereas the SDS activist may advance his political career by his noncompliance. Third, what are the effects of noncompliance under certain specific conditions such as the presence of a foreign policy based on the destruction of fascism, as in World War II, versus a foreign policy based on the protection of fascism, as some say is involved in the Vietnam War? Clearly, one cannot say that the conditions under which a war is fought are irrelevant to the degree to which one should obey the selective service laws. In general, just as the likelihood of noncompliance varies with the nature of the law, the personnel, and the conditions, so also do the effects of noncompliance vary.

The effects of noncompliance have not been as much studied by social scientists as the causes of noncompliance. Nevertheless Joel Grossman of the University of Wisconsin's Law and Sociology program is conducting a study of the impact of civil rights civil disobedience activities,[26] and various social scientists are in the process of studying the effects of the race riots which constitute an extreme form of noncompliance with basic legal principles.[27] A few political scientists have touched on the effects upon certain segments of the public of compliance and noncompliance

[26] Joel Grossman, "A Model for Judicial Policy Analysis: The Supreme Court's Response to the Sit-In Cases," paper presented at the 1967 University of Iowa Shambaugh Conference.

[27] Some preliminary discussion of the consequences of the 1967 race riots are given in the symposium issue of *Transaction* (September 1967).

by various law administrators.[28] There are also studies of the
effects of specific laws or judicial pronouncements rather than
the effects of compliance and noncompliance in general.[29] The
increased concern for impact studies in law and political science
may yield numerous findings and theories in the future with
regard to both the effects and causes of compliance.[30]

In closing I want to emphasize that constitutional compliance
or obligation can be viewed as either a dependent or an independent variable. When viewed as a dependent variable or an effect,
the problem is to determine what the independent variables or
causes of compliance are. When viewed as an independent variable or cause, the problem then is to determine what are the
dependent variables or effects of compliance or noncompliance.
In addition to determining these cause and effect relations, it is
important to define operationally the concept of compliance or
manifested obligation so that it can be quantitatively correlated
with other variables. What is especially encouraging is the fact
that the tentative cause and effect answers offered by social
theorists and philosophers are being increasingly tested by behavioral scientists. Thus the field of legal compliance and obligation is another area where philosophy and behavioral science
are constructively working together.

[28] Richard Johnson, *The Dynamics of Compliance: Supreme Court
Decision-Making from a New Perspective* (Evanston, Ill.: Northwestern
University Press, 1967); Jack Peltason, *Fifty-Eight Lonely Men: Southern
Federal Judges and School Desegregation* (New York: Harcourt, Brace, 1961).
[29] Theodore Becker, see note 2.
[30] Arthur Miller, "On the Need for Impact Analysis of Supreme Court
Decisions," *Georgetown Law Journal*, 53 (1965), 365-401; Ernest Jones,
"Impact Research and Sociology of Law: Some Tentative Proposals," *Wiscon-
sin Law Review* (1966), 331-39.

11

ROME: *FIDES* AND *OBSEQUIUM,* RISE AND FALL

DAVID C. RAPOPORT

Rome was originally, when poor and small, a unique example of austere virtue; then it corrupted, it rotted, it slowly absorbed vices; so little by little we have been brought into the present condition where we are neither able to endure the evils from which we suffer nor face the remedies needed to cure them. . . . Wealth has made us greedy . . . in love with death both individual and collective.

A portion of this essay appeared in "The Corrupt State: The Case of Rome Reconsidered," *Political Studies,* XVI (October 1968), 411-32. I wish to thank the editor for his permission to republish, the SSRC and the Chancellors Committee on International and Comparative Studies, UCLA, for helping to subsidize the original and subsequent research, and William Loiterman and Herman Loew for their assistance.

The purpose of this essay is to describe Roman concepts of fidelity as they are expressed in different institutions, particularly military, governmental, and educational arrangements. I shall divide Roman history into three periods; the *Republic,* for our purposes, ends when the Gracchi brothers are assassinated, the *Transformation* culminates in Augustus' attempt to modernize Rome, and the *Imperial* or *Corrupt Age* carries us to the disintegration of the state in the West.—Livy

THE REPUBLIC

The goddess of faith [*Fides*] . . . was worshipped not only in her temples but in the lives of the Romans; and if that nation was deficient in the more amiable qualities of benevolence and generosity, they astonished the Greeks by their sincere and simple performance of the most burdensome engagements.—Gibbon

Man is a social creature, a group animal, we often say. Still his social capacities never have been fully realized. Simply living together is difficult, acting together is often impossible. Even when the requisite purposes and personal qualities are present, the desired actions may not occur. Something else is necessary.

Four brave men who do not know each other will not care to attack a lion. Four less brave, but knowing each other well, sure of their reliability and consequently of mutual aid, will attack resolutely.[1]

When risks are shared unequally, men must have confidence in each other's intentions and capacities before they will cooperate. The larger the field of action, the more critical the role of confidence or credit looms; *everyone* becomes dependent upon individuals and information he cannot actually know or truly assess.

Some cooperative enterprises are most efficient when different roles and responsibilities are fixed—when an organization is

---

[1] Col. Ardant du Picq, *Battle Studies* (Harrisburg: 1946), p. 110.

created. Organization can prevent delay and confusion. Through organization, competence can be assessed, responsibility attributed, and past experiences retained. Because the life of organizations can be immense, they have a potential for storing a supply of credit far greater than the resources of individuals and immensely useful to them.

Success creates credit. Failure can spur leaders and organizations to attack problems in a resolute, intelligent manner, eliminating the incompetent and redistributing the rewards and obligations that all reforms imply. But since the common benefits aspired to can only be realized in the future, failure is only a valuable stimulus when credit *already* exists.

Credit must be used because action never ceases and no matter how great the original store, unless replenished by fresh success, failures will ultimately exhaust it. In the life of every organization there is a flashpoint where failure suddenly discredits all appeals—where criticism is viewed as recrimination, the call to sacrifice is understood as a desire to retain privilege, and a common failing is interpreted as a failing of individuals. In this context everyone begins to take from the organization more than he is willing to give, having become convinced that everyone else is doing the same thing.

Of all the ancient peoples the Romans understood the importance of credit in cooperative ventures most clearly, as their worship of *Fides,* the goddess of credibility, indicates. *Fides* was the first virtue to be deified, and the seminal source for all others. She literally created *moral* obligation since no Roman believed himself bound until he had given his pledge, and through her, ties were forged between men, between communities, and between men and the gods. *Fides,* moreover, was peculiar to Rome; at least the Greeks had no corresponding deity or concept.[2]

Fides was a goddess and a quality (*fides*) residing in men,

---

2 E. Fraenkel, "Zur Geschichte des Wortes *fides,*" *Rhein. Mus.,* 71 (1916), 187-99; R. Heinze, "Fides," *Hermes,* 64 (1929), 144–66. Heinze argues (p. 165) that Epictetus incorporates *fides* into Stoic thought, the first and only time a Greek philosopher borrows a concept from Rome. Bertrand de Jouvenel, more than any contemporary, emphasizes the significance of credit in cooperative activity and appropriately underscores the Roman worship of *Fides.* See *Sovereignty* (Chicago: 1957), esp. pp. 119-20.

institutions, and gods which one could solicit for protection and help.[3] To have *fides* was to have the power to stimulate confidence, for *fides* fundamentally signified dependability and truth. The noble man demonstrated, preserved, and enhanced his *fides* by accomplishing deeds which gave evidence of capacities to master difficult, changing circumstances.[4] The inevitable result was to attract others to seek his counsel and protection, the measure of his *fides* being the number and quality of those who placed their confidence in him.

By the nature of the case, a reputation for having *fides* was gained slowly as one showed his merits in a variety of undertakings, but even a great reputation could be quickly and irretrievably lost by a single reckless act. Hence *fides* presumed capacities for self-control and prudent judgment.

A man who wishes to dispose of his future (by making promises) must first have learned to separate necessary from accidental acts; to think causally; to see distant things

[3] For a discussion of Roman religion, see H. J. Rose, *Religion in Ancient Greece and Rome* (New York: 1959); F. Altheim, *A History of Roman Religion* (London: 1938); J. B. Carter, *The Religion of Numa* (London: 1906); W. W. Fowler, *The Religion Experience of the Roman People* (London: 1911); and H. Wagenvoort, *Roman Dynamism* (London: 1947). In ordinary Latin a plea for the protection of someone's *fides* is simply a cry for help.

[4] The Roman's religion seems preeminently designed to make one appreciate the importance of acting in time—a cardinal virtue of great statesmen and generals.

The singularity of one special day, particularly of a day of decisive historical or political importance—and the Fortuna assigned to it, means something definitely Roman . . . Everything is concentrated on single decisive acts; the special quality of different moments of history is persistently felt. . . . For all Roman temples, the year and day, not only of dedication but also of vowing, lives on in memory. This is in complete contrast to the procedure in Greece where such historical relationships even where they exist usually remain unimportant . . . The Roman gave to [the] historical moment and in fact to history as a whole, a peculiar importance . . . Whereas to the Greek the single manifestation in time has no more than accessory value, whereas even in the divine world everything is revealed as a being beyond time, [to the Roman] the single manifestation can rise to a point at which it can overshadow, even replace, being. The Roman conception of deity is eminently historical and reveals itself in time, confronts the supra and extratemporal nature of the Greek gods as an independent and intelligible world of its own. Being and time, ontology and history, can always be confronted as independent spiritual realms, each resting on its own base. (Altheim, pp. 190–92.)

as though they were near at hand; to distinguish means from ends. In short, he must have become not only calculating, but himself calculable, even regular to his own perception, if he is to stand pledge for his own future as a guarantor does.[5]

Fides connoted strength; it husbanded, concentrated, and created energy.

If you lend a talent to a Greek and bind him by ten promises, ten sureties, and as many witnesses, it is impossible for him to keep his word. But among the Romans, whether in accounting for public or private funds, people are trustworthy because of the oath they have taken.[6]

He who is able to depend upon the *fides* of his fellow citizens is thereby enabled to use his strength freely elsewhere. He need not deploy it to defend against distrust and isolation.[7]

Fides signified fidelity, but it was always the special quality of those strong enough to trust their own judgments. The fidelity of lesser men was *obsequium*—the quality of the client who could not stand alone, and owed his patron unquestioning homage because he had asked to be placed under the protection of his patron's *fides;* and the quality of the soldier who selected a commander whose judgment he could rely upon. Unlike *fides,* *obsequium* always implied the possibility of a legal sanction, and hence was not wholly a moral relationship.[8] A man who be-

[5] Nietzsche, *Genealogy,* II, 1.
[6] Polybius, VI, 6. *Cf.* Cicero, *Pro Flacco* IV, 9. So disturbed at the prospect of a violated oath were the Romans, that Jupiter's priest was forbidden to swear one lest he loose a disaster upon the entire city. Plutarch, *Roman Questions* 44. *Cf.* Cicero *De Off.* I, 39, 40 and III, 99–113.
[7] Heinze, "Fides," p. 164.
[8] It is important in the nature of an ethical commitment that no governmental order guarantees adherence to it. That piece of the ethical personality lost by a breach of *fides* cannot be regained by the fact that the guilty party is forced by legal means to pay a certain sum of money. Thus the patron cannot be held legally responsible, Heinze, p. 159.
The patron-client relation and friendship, both wholly governed by *fides* (and hence, outside the law), were the two fundamental ties of Roman group

lieved he possessed *fides* could pledge *obsequium* for limited purposes. By demonstrating *obsequium* he could become chosen for a magistracy, whereupon the Senate, noting that the People had acknowledged his *dignitas,* suggested that he "act as it seemed good to him in accordance with the national interest and his own *fides.*"[9]

Political and military action always involved risks, and the prudent Roman welcomed powerful allies. He pledged *obsequium* to solicit the *fides* of institutions and gods. His concern for formal proprieties astonished the ancient world, but he was convinced that procedures which had worked in the past would do so in the future. *Obsequium,* spawned by *fides,* had given birth to *pietas.*[10]

Fides, obsequium, and *pietas* express the Roman understanding of formal organization. Some make decisions; others carry them out. The strength of the cooperation depends upon the belief that the decisions made are most suitable for the action contemplated. Ultimately confidence rests upon success achieved or anticipated, and in the long run success requires that leaders are chosen in a rational manner and are willing to adhere to rules found useful in the past. However, since no set of rules can comprehend all situations, a sphere must be reserved for personal judgment, for those most likely to know all the relevant circumstances to act as their consciences dictate.

To achieve its end an organization must distribute privileges unequally, but members may begin regarding those privileges as ends in themselves, undermining the requirements for organiza-

---

politics. Note also the *fidei-commissium,* a bequest made by a person begging his heir to transfer something to a third person, was not enforceable by law until the corrupt age when *obsequium* governed most relationships.

The Roman made international settlements by offering a pledge of *fides;* unlike a modern treaty the act precludes the possibility of legal adjudication. See E. Badian, *Foreign Clientelae* (Oxford: 1958), chs. 1 & *ff.* The medieval pledge—troth—leads to a contract with specific obligations, and hence stands in contrast to *fides,* which presumes unlimited confidence. Social contract theorists have troth in mind except for Hobbes, who may visualize a patron-client relationship. See F. S. Lear, *Treason in Roman and Germanic Law* (Austin: 1966), XII *ff.*

[9] F. E. Adcock, *Roman Political Ideas and Practice* (Ann Arbor: 1964), p. 13.

[10] *Pietas* entails scrupulous observance of all the traditional rites. Roman religion combined a very vague theology with very precise rituals.

tional success. For the Roman the critical matter was keeping alive the desire to excel; men must be assessed by their *deeds,* and every potential competitor must be given frequent opportunities to demonstrate worth. These simple aims led the Roman to devise institutions so cumbersome that they appear unworkable. Yet they produced such remarkable results for centuries that the fund of credit and level of talent established seemed well-nigh inexhaustible. The military arrangements are a case in point.

Every year her armics were freshly organized. In fact, there literally was no Roman army. Normally served by two wholly independent forces, occasionally by more, Rome established no formal links between them, no chain of command, no general staff. Commanding officers, elected in military assemblies, recruited and organized their own forces. Since the recruit pledged *obsequium* to his commander, not to the state, it was difficult to detach men from one command to reinforce another. Moreover, the *dignitas* of the Roman commander provided him with an immunity unequaled in the ancient world; the Greeks and Carthaginians thought it more sensible to scrutinize all battlefield decisions, and make officers liable to criminal prosecution for defeats.[11]

In refusing to question a commander's decisions after deeming him suitable for responsibility, the Romans occasionally left an army in incompetent hands for a year, but the long run advantages soon became clear.

> For they judged it was of the greatest importance for those who commanded their armies to have their minds entirely free and unembarrassed by any anxiety other than how to perform best their duty, and therefore they did not wish to add fresh difficulties and dangers in an undertaking itself so difficult and perilous, being convinced that if this were done, it would prevent any general from operating vigorously.[12]

[11] A dictator was elected to deal with unusually dangerous situations. But as the Romans were almost always at war, it is striking how rarely thcy used the office.

[12] Machiavelli, *Discourses,* I, 31. Col. T. A. Dodge commends the practice for different reasons. "The government never investigated misfortunes lest the legions be alarmed at the gravity of the situation and the reputation of the commanders be weakened." *Hannibal* (New York: 1891), p. 43.

By insisting that no command be held for two *consecutive* years, they deprived themselves of the services their best generals could provide; but they reaped other, perhaps more important, benefits. "The [commanders] annually elected brought to the helm ... a fresh vigor of mind and continual supplies of renewed ambition."[13] The passion to excel stimulated the impulse to innovate, and decentralization made military experiment less costly and results easier to compare.

> The main reason for the Romans becoming the master of the world was that, having fought successively against all peoples, they always gave up their own practices as soon as they found better ones. . . . The cutting swords of the Gauls and the elephants of Pyrrhus surprised them only once. They made up for the weakness of their cavalry . . . by providing for [lightly armed infantry]. . . . The love of glory, the contempt for death, and the stubborn will to conquer were the same in [the Romans and the Gauls]. But their arms were different. The buckler of the Gauls was small, and their sword poor. . . . And the surprising thing is that these peoples, whom the Romans met in almost all places, and almost all times, permitted themselves to be destroyed one after another without ever knowing, seeking, or forestalling the cause of their misfortunes.[14]

The notoriously small size of the individual armies made it easier to relate rank to merit, and the insistence upon annual reorganization, constantly establishing new opportunities, gave Rome an enormous reservoir of experience, talent, and enthusiasms that a more restricted system of specialists with vested interests could never provide. It is not fanciful to treat the arrangement as analogous to an economic system which stimulates productivity through competition, with perpetual war serving as a market mechanism.

Despite some great disasters, Rome rarely lacked eager recruits; and their high quality enabled her to devise tactical units hither-

[13] Adam Ferguson, *The Progress and Termination of the Roman Republic* (Edinburgh: 1791), I, pp. 66–67.

[14] Montesquieu, *Considerations.* . . .   Chs. 1, 2, 4. Although the connection seems obvious, no one, to my knowledge, has related the Roman innovating impulse to his decentralized practices.

to unparalleled in the scope allowed the individual soldier to use his initiative.[15] Personal as well as patriotic incentives made military service attractive. The commander sought a triumph, which was the supreme state honor—a ritual peculiar to Rome, signifying that one's *fides* for one day had been equal to Jupiter's.[16] Potential leaders used war as a political stepping stone; all major offices had corresponding military responsibilities, and candidates for even the lowest elected position had to serve in a minimum of ten campaigns. Every soldier, moreover, knew that war *could* yield him booty.[17]

The law did not regulate rewards of discharged soldiers—a condition which could promote invidious comparisons and feelings of injustice. Still, the Romans were convinced that when the aim was to stimulate the desire to excel, laws often become impediments because the standards set could never be high

---

[15] Compared to the legion, the Greek phalanx, Col. Dodge notes, was a mass formation militating against specialization and initiative (p. 43).

[16] Lest a triumph intoxicate a commander, during the procession a slave kept whispering in his ear, "Remember you are only a man." The Romans reserved their great honors for heroic acts which contributed to organizational success. Joseph Georges, in private correspondence, notes that the Israelis alone among contemporaries have a similar notion, awarding the highest medals to those whose heroism contributes directly to battlefield success. For a comparison of Israeli and Roman military ethics with that of Western states, see my "A Comparative Theory of Military and Political Types," *Changing Patterns of Military Politics*, ed. S. P. Huntington (Glencoe: 1962), pp. 71–101.

[17] The Roman made money in war, but had that been his principal object Roman armies, like mercenary ones, would have disintegrated when plunder was available. Discipline obviously maximized opportunities for material gain; but it was not the desire for gain which led to restraint but the capacity for restraint which made gain possible. Max Weber makes the point in a different context. The capitalist ethic should be understood as a check on the spirit of gain, a restraint which paradocically makes acquisition on a grand scale possible.

The impulse to acquisition, pursuit of gain, of money, of the greatest possible amount of money, has in itself nothing to do with capitalism. This impulse . . . has been common to all sorts and conditions of men at all times and in all countries of the earth wherever the objective possibility of it is or has been given. It should be taught in the kindergarten of cultural history that this naive idea of capitalism, must be given up once and for all. Unlimited greed for gain is not in the least identical with capitalism, and is still less its spirit. Capitalism *may* even be identical with the restraint, or at least the rational tempering of this irrational impulse. But capitalism is identical with the pursuit of profit and forever *renewed* profit by means of continuous, rational capitalistic enterprise. *The Protestant Ethic and the Spirit of Capitalism* (London: 1930), p. 17.

enough. Better to treat each case separately. Hence soldiers looked to the *fides* of the Senate and the People (the popular assemblies), bodies composed of qualified judges with military experience. The credibility of the process was protected by the limited effect of each decision; every soldier had an independent means of subsistence and ample opportunities to compete for recognition again and again.

The Roman constitutional experience is extraordinary too. The original government of the Republic contained so many checks and balances, so many independent offices held on non-renewable annual tenure, and so many obstacles to new laws that it is hard to imagine an instrument better contrived to inspire disrespect by encouraging incompetence and delaying action, until men in desperation are driven to go outside the law to achieve their ends. One might expect that as Rome expanded from a tiny peasant community to a large heterogeneous empire, the constitutional form would have been progressively sim-plified; instead the Romans complicated it further by designing new autonomous offices for special needs. They acted as though they were convinced that among men with *fides,* a complicated constitution protects and expands the area of mutual confi-dence.[18]

A simple constitution makes it easier to concert policy, but by the same token, when failure occurs the source of authority and hence the whole system becomes more vulnerable to discredit. In a complicated constitution the failure of a particular power has more circumscribed effect; the resources the system can muster for repair have not also been damaged. By reducing the number of independent offices and by assuring occupants long tenure, we prepare the way for expertise. But simultaneously, restricted participation reduces opportunities for fresh approaches, frus-trates the development of political capacity elsewhere in the civic body, and increases the possibility that important decisions will be misunderstood by those on whose behalf they were conceived.

If a law is difficult to make because men want to persuade each

[18] Jose Ortega y Gasset, *Concord and Liberty* (New York: 1946), pp. 39 *ff.* Ortega is the most recent of a long line of political theorists since Polybius who have believed that Roman constitutional history demonstrates that "complicated" or "mixed" forms can produce the most extraordinary cohesion.

other of its value first, they are likely to find that enforcing the law afterwards will be relatively simple and will nourish few resentments. In Rome the laws literally seemed to execute them- selves; at least no state has ever used less physical coercion. No armed man was permitted inside the city's gates, and for nearly seven centuries she did not need a police force. The immunities of an accused person still astonish us; there are simply no parallels in our world.

> A citizen, while accused of any crime, continued at liberty until sentence was given against him, and might withdraw from his prosecutors at any stage of the trial. . . . A voluntary banishment from the Forum, from the meetings of the Senate and the assemblies of the people, was the highest punishment which any citizen, unless he remained to expose himself to the effects of a formal sentence, was obliged to undergo.[19]

In the last century of the Republic, the Romans went even further, and forbade magistrates to arrest a *convicted* citizen without giving him a chance to escape![20]

The political community is created to last indefinitely, and to preserve their inheritance and accomplishments, men must in- duce appropriate temperaments in their children. Greek writers invariably argued that a sound state had to assume direct respon- sibility for civic education. Even Polybius, whose admiration for everything Roman seemed unlimited, found her wanting here; for she lacked schools and laws to regulate education.[21] Yet the irony remained; the enormous Greek passion and energy to systematize education did not yield many generations of good citizens—its chief object—while the Romans succeeded without making the aim a collective responsibility.

The Romans, typically, achieved success in a way which will always seem absurd to those who assume that a collective end cannot be achieved by individual means. They refused to

[19] Ferguson, *Roman Republic,* I, p. 91.
[20] H. F. Jolowicz, *Historical Introduction to the Study of Roman Law* (Cambridge: 1952), p. 330.
[21] Polybius' criticism has been lost; but Cicero refers to it, *Rep.* IV, 3.

prescribe educational standards, feeling that only those who knew the child best, cared for him most, and whose interests were directly involved with his success—namely his parents—could be entrusted to develop his potentialities.[22] Every father had the right to reject and even to expose a newborn infant but in signifying his willingness to receive the child, the relationship was secured by *fides.* The child, or more precisely the charge he represented, was treated as an "object of almost religious veneration."[23]

Roman education aimed at teaching a child a tradition by direct observation and early participation. When he reached the age of seven he accompanied his father everywhere. (If the father was dead the family would choose an illustrious citizen to serve in his place.) At home the son worked beside him on the farm. On festival days he was an acolyte assisting in religious ceremonies. The son was always present when the father gave and received hospitality. He attended all meetings in the Forum; and if his father was a Senator, the son sat on the Senate floor too. The consummation of the boy's education occurred at the age of sixteen or seventeen when he became for a year the companion of the most distinguished available friend of the family still active in public life.[24]

The entire educational process seemed peculiarly designed to affect *both* teacher and pupil, thereby heightening the sense of personal responsibility throughout the actual and the potential civic body. Conscious of the child's presence, anxious to gain his admiration, aware of the potential discrepancy between words

22 "But Cato thought it not fit, as he himself said, to have his son reprimanded by a slave; . . . nor would he have him owe to a servant the obligation of so great a thing as his learning." Plutarch, "Life of Cato," 20. The essay contains the best description of the Roman educational ideal. The ancient (i.e., pre-Exilic) Jewish and early Christian tradition approached education in a similar spirit regarding the child as closer to God and his parents as best qualified to educate him.

23 A. Gwynn, *Roman Education from Cicero to Quintilian* (Oxford: 1926), p. 77. The symbols of the boy's holiness were his purple striped toga, purple being the color reserved for magistrates and sacrificing priests, and the *bulla,* a locket originally a sign of patrician origin, of men who first displayed *fides.*

24 "[Young men] must attach themselves to men who are wise and renowned, men who are famous for their patriotism, if possible men of consular rank, men who played and are playing their part in public affairs." Cicero, *De Off.* II, 4.

and deeds, the father had to be aware of the effect his example produced.[25] And since the child would be constantly seeking the reason for certain public procedures, the father was never allowed to forget their meaning himself.[26]

Education prepares one for the future, but the Romans, convinced that to master future uncertainties one had to have firm links with the past, allowed no child to forget his predecessors. Every clan had its own real and legendary heroes, whose *imagines* were objects of religious worship, reminding the child of the quality of his lineage and the way in which his own deeds might one day receive the devotion of his progeny.[27] History was a collection of models "calling to our minds illustrious and courageous men and their deeds not for any gain but for the honor that lies in praising their nobility itself."[28] Each generation entered "a competition with its ancestors,"[29] vying to do great deeds on behalf of Rome (*virtus*). *Ignavia* and *inertia*, laziness and lack of energy, were terms applied to those who refused to compete for public honors.

> To a purely private cultivation of personal virtue the Roman tradition was always hostile. . . . The proper service of the state demanded private goodness but such goodness without public achievement was of no account. . . . Outside the service of the Republic there existed no public office, . . . no *gloria*, no *nobilitas*, no *auctoritas*, no *virtus*.[30]

[25] "[The Romans] took their children out to dinner not so much to control the child but to make the fathers behave with modesty and temperance because children were present." Plutarch, *Roman Questions*, 33.

[26] The Jew anticipated the problem too. "The parent must be ready to give an answer when thy son asketh thee in time to come saying what means the testimonies and statutes and the judgments which the Lord our God has commanded you." *Deut.* XI, 19.

[27] Polybius, VI, 53. Polybius' emphasis on the effect of the *imagines* on the young child gives one reason to suspect that he has more respect for Roman education than Cicero acknowledges.

[28] Cicero, *De Fin* I, 10, 36.

[29] Tacitus, *Ann.* III, 55 and *Hist* I, 3.

[30] Donald Earl, *The Moral and Political Tradition of Rome* (London: 1967), pp. 23, 35. Note the complaint of young Scipio Aemilianus. "I am told that everyone thinks me idle and lazy and far removed from the true Roman character and energy because I do not choose to plead in the law-courts. They say that the family I come from needs a champion. . . ." quoted by Earl, p. 26.

The Roman hero . . . by his courage and wisdom . . . saved his country. . . . A very different type . . . from the rather wild and imaginative Homeric hero, a deserter like Achilles . . . who brought the Achaean army to the verge of destruction simply through sulking and returned to the fight only to avenge a friend.[31]

THE TRANSFORMATION

Augustus . . . [established] a form of government which justified itself on the ground of efficiency and sought to substitute the expert for the amateur.
—G. H. Stevenson, *Roman Provincial Administration*

Fides fundamentally was a religious concept, and in time Greek philosophers made sophisticated Romans aware of the intellectual shortcomings of their religion. But most Romans still believed in the old religion, and the Greeks could not supply a doctrine to inspire mass enthusiasms. When Polybius suggests that Roman officials were using religious forms for the public's benefit,[32] it is evident that a decision of revolutionary importance had been taken. Although no one could detect changes in behavior, the principle of religious justification had been changed.

Following a practice because it is right is one thing; manipulating one believed to be useful is another. By the logic of the second case men must eliminate inconvenient elements, and the cumulative effects will be vast although it may be some time before they are clearly seen. A century after Polybius, the priests could no longer conceal that they had taken extraordinary liberties with religious forms.

The calendar became terribly disordered and this again had its reaction on religion for the calendar month occasionally fell so out of gear with the natural seasons that it

[31] Henri Marrou, *A History of Education in Antiquity* (New York: 1959), p. 235.
[32] *History*, VI, 6.

was impossible to celebrate some of the old Roman festivals which had a distinct bearing on some of the seasons of their year.[33]

As Roman religion lost credibility, the educational process was transformed. The great expansion dispersed the governing class, putting enormous strains on the capacity to sustain the intimate personal contact and access to the center of activity which a traditional education presupposed. Divorces became commonplace, and since in Roman law the child remained under the father's jurisdiction, the mother lost her incentive to meet her special responsibility to provide the child with his earliest education.

Perhaps the deep sense of personal responsibility which *fides* evoked in the educational process had to be sacrificed.[34] But a good school system would have reduced the loss; in nineteenth-century Britain the strains of a greatly expanded imperial administration upon child-rearing were partially resolved by the rapid growth of boarding schools which aimed quite explicitly at developing "character." The Roman difficulties, however, were much more deeply rooted. Few free-born citizens were willing to become educators, being firmly convinced that working for wages was a sign of inferior status.[35] The Romans, therefore,

[33] Carter, *The Religion of Numa,* p. 132.

[34] Who knows how much more the Romans could have done to compensate for the consequences of expansion? When the polis required less from its governing class, the Greek father excused himself from educating his son because he had "too much business" to attend to. See Plato, *Laches.*

[35] Cicero ranks teaching, medicine, and architecture as equally honorable professions *"for those whose social position they become." De Off.* I, 42. (My emphasis.) The Romans were hostile to any activity carried on solely for material gain except agriculture, especially if one was put in a dependent position thereby. Once slave teachers became common, the invidious aspects of the profession were firmly established.

[T]he ancient[s] . . . could never find a sufficient number of men willing to work for wages . . . [and] were always forced back on slaves . . . [The Roman had] little liking for work and still less for subordination. He [would] work a little as an artisan or trader if he [was] not subjected to control; and he [would] resign himself to dependence on others as a retainer or armbearer . . . if he [was] thereby saved from working; but he [would] never voluntarily submit to work and to be in dependence. He would rather beg or steal. G. Ferrero, *The Greatness and Decline of Rome* (London: 1907), p. 25.

adopted the Greek practice of using pedagogues, slaves or former slaves, to replace the father before the child reached school age, and in addition they were satisfied to let slaves give most of the instruction in the schools themselves. The consequences could have been predicted.

> The Roman boy was in the anomalous position of having to submit to chastisement from men whom as men he despised. Assuredly, we should not like our public school-boys to be taught or punished by men of low station or of an inferior standard of morals. It is men not methods that really tell in education; the Roman schoolboy needed someone to believe in, someone to whom to be wholly loyal; the same overpowering need which was so obvious in the political world of Rome in the last century BC. . . . The schools taught morality. . . . But we know the fate of our copy-book maxims; . . . it is not through them that our children become good men and women but by the unsystemized precepts of parents and teachers.[36]

Roman education could no longer be an explanation of a tradition by men who understood and loved it. Its ideals, no longer experienced in concrete contexts, where nuances and subtleties were significant and where the conditions and consequences of action were apparent, inevitably became slogans useful for recrimination but for little else. The pronounced Roman inclination for practical concerns found an outlet in the study of "techniques," divorced from the political contexts which gave them life. A debased form of Aristotle's *Rhetoric* became the most popular subject, consisting of "rules for swaying masses"— scarcely a substitute for understanding the forces which made men loyal to one another.

Success slowly transformed military, economic, and political

---

[36] W. Warde Fowler, *Social Life in the Age of Cicero*, pp. 184–85. Although the early Roman, Jew, and Christian all approached education in a similar spirit, only Jews and Christians maintained that spirit in their schools. Thus, the Talmud says, "A teacher should be venerated almost as much as God himself," and after schools were established among the Christians in the fourth century, those who later became bishops were often great schoolmasters first.

institutions too. After the defeat of Carthage the Romans encountered richer and fatter peoples further and further away from home. War became lucrative but also very expensive. The plutocrats, now necessary to finance military expeditions, were in the best positions to exploit the vast quantities of booty and slaves procured. Unable to compete, many citizens sold their land, and hence their military capital, to gravitate to the swollen metropolis, leading a hand-to-mouth existence, bartering their votes in the mass assemblies. Being bought is never the same as being convinced, and it was not surprising that stupid policies and incompetent magistrates were chosen, that Rome began to experience serious defeats at the hands of primitive foes. To repair disasters able soldiers were given extraordinary *ad hoc* renewable commissions.

The development of logistic capacities made it possible to fight at great distances for long periods of time. Man lacking property to require their attention periodically were increasingly welcomed. Both commander and soldier thus had new coinciding interests; each was directly dependent upon the caprices of government, the former because he could now renew his tenure and the latter, now without an independent means of subsistence, because he wanted state lands to retire upon.

Great strains were placed upon the *fides* of the Senate and People to reward soldiers fairly: the scope and consequence of individual decisions grew and fewer members of those bodies had military experience, the military requirements for citizenship and public office having been increasingly waived.

Some aimed to reduce uncertainties by providing soldiers with legal guarantees. But most constitutional officials displayed cynical carelessness about public affairs. Often the Senate could not get a quorum. When it met it displayed a striking tendency to put off important questions, to be concerned with trivial matters. The potential difficulties of a complicated constitution became apparent: no one could compel the negligent by legal means to recognize their responsibilities. The results were:

> anarchy in the government, an incapable and discredited Senate, Comitia reduced to a travesty, impotent and invariably divided magistracies . . . law courts ruled by corruption

and intimidation, finances in utter disorder, . . . anarchy in
the streets, which armed gangs turned into daily bat-
tlefields.[37]

It was only a matter of time before the most dedicated soldier felt
justified in pressing his claims through *direct action* as everyone
else seemed to be doing. Three massive bloodbaths in as many
generations could not dissolve the Republic's imperfections.
Augustus aimed to solve Rome's predicament by simplifying
government and providing opportunities for men of talent and
devotion. Fundamentally, "modernization" was conceived in administrative terms. The most critical jurisdictions were reorganized in hierarchical forms, logically ordered in functional schemes,
and isolated from the political maelstrom. The approach
was most manifest in the military sphere. All soldiers pledged
obsequium to a commander-in-chief, *imperator,* or emperor.
(Weber characterizes the arrangement as "democratic," because
the emperor was "a free trustee of the masses . . . unfettered by
officers and officials whom he selects freely and personally."[38])
The army became a voluntary professional standing force, and a
uniform system of promotion based on merit and seniority was
established. The emperor alone was responsible for military
finances to preclude possibilities that the profits of war could
spawn a new plutocracy and that pay would become the subject
of competing political factions.

Although Augustus did control Rome's first police force, which
cleared the streets to provide an orderly atmosphere for public
deliberation, and he guaranteed all citizens a minimum standard
of living, a policy later generations labeled "bread and circuses,"
his constitutional powers extended primarily to the provinces
where his army resided. Elsewhere traditional forms prevailed;
the Senate retained supremacy over unarmed provinces, the
Popular Assemblies survived, and magistrates were still elected.
Cities remained self-governing, and everywhere men were encouraged to establish new municipalities. The plan was mag-

---

[37] Leon Homo, *Roman Political Institutions* (London: 1962), p. 3.
[38] "Bureaucracy," *From Max Weber,* eds. Gerth and Mills (New York:
1946), p. 202.

nificent—a vast federation of city-states with Rome at its head and the emperor responsible mainly for matters directly impinging on military matters. For forty years Augustus gave Rome the peace and prosperity she craved. With deadlocks broken and manifest corruption eliminated, government regained its credit. The imperial system was secured, or at least no future generation wanted to restore the Republic or to imagine a new order.

But something was drastically wrong. Augustus had stopped the bleeding but the wound still festered. For at least two centuries no massive hemorrhage occurred; nonetheless, the patient's strength dwindled and his activity was restricted accordingly. As the metabolic efficiency of a diseased man diminishes, more energy is consumed in the simple effort of trying to stay alive; similarly the task of routine administrative maintenance increasingly absorbed Romans. Diocletian had more helpers but less help than Marcus Aurelius, the latter in turn envied Augustus, and Augustus understood Livy's astonishment at the endless vitality Rome displayed during the Punic Wars. In various ways for more than four centuries every writer expressed the collective anguish and impotence.

> Our fathers were worse than our grandsires;
> We have deteriorated from our fathers;
> And our sons will cause us to be lamented. . . .

THE CORRUPT OR
IMPERIAL AGE

"Through you we hold our honours, our property, and everything!" both repeated twenty-eight times, . . . "to prevent the constitutions being interpolated, let all codes be written in longhand" repeated twenty-five times.

"Debate" preceding the adoption of the Theodosian Code

In an unsystematic, confused manner, Roman poets and historians reassessed national experiences. They held the competition for personal recognition—*gloria* and *dignitas*—to be inherently destructive because it elevated the individual at the expense of the community, and they attributed the Republic's successes to self-abnegation or complete dedication to Rome, a sentiment largely dissipated during *The Transformation*.[39]

Tacitus, especially in his *Life of Agricola,* attempts to show how altruism might be translated into a specific ideal for contemporary men—*obsequium.* To Tacitus, *obsequium* signifies being faithful to the state, or more precisely to the emperor's commands, relying on his *fides* because in no other way could *otium,* peace and amenities, be enjoyed. *Gloria* and *dignitas* belong to the emperor who bestowed and withdrew them as he saw fit.

To the Republic, *obsequium* had been a lesser virtue. All organized activity required it; still, unless associated with a standard which sets the individual apart, *obsequium* frustrates initiative and creativity, equally relevant to an organization's efficiency and survival. Quite obviously *obsequium* is an ideal most appropriate to administration, and the emperor's civil and military bureaucracies explicitly embraced it. But its limited viability even in this sphere ultimately depends upon the political world from which the critical directing impulses come. It is striking, therefore, that Roman writers do not distinguish politics and administration, or specify ideals and conditions appropriate to each sphere. It is almost as though they believed that *obsequium* should take root everywhere!

Did the early emperors expect something else from politics? In cultivating Republican manners and institutions, and in treating Senators and magistrates as persons with *gloria* and *dignitas* in their own right, they might have wished to regain some of the Republic's vitality. But a republican spirit did not emerge; men used political offices to secure the administrative careers they

---

[39] Earl, ch. IV. In refusing to admit that the traditional ethic did have value, the real questions were bypassed, namely, what conditions undermined the ethos, what possibilities were there of maintaining its more valuable elements, and what were the problems in introducing and sustaining a new ethic.

Plato's discussion is far more impressive. Honor is the only motive for public service the polis knew, and the honorable man needs material possessions to secure his independence and offices to display merit. But honor implies a love of self, and under certain conditions the timocrat discovers that he can accumulate rewards without having his worth truly assessed; consequently, the concern for honor weakens and mistrust envelops the whole community. The solution is a wholly different and higher motive, altruism, and Plato subsequently defines an appropriate political environment. Not until St. Augustine do we have an impressive discussion of the Roman problem.

treasured more, and the emperor became too powerful to be secure. For those who could not appreciate the significance of these two conditions, the downfall of Sejanus provided an unforgettable lesson.

Alarmed at his lieutenant's popularity but too weak to confront him openly, Tiberius, Augustus' successor, by a series of masterful secret stratagems, tested Sejanus' intentions and the determination of his supporters. The unsuspecting hero was then dispatched to the Senate to hear Tiberius' letter.

At first, before it was read, they had been lauding Sejanus, thinking that he was about to receive the tribunician power, and had kept cheering him, anticipating the honours for which they hoped and making it clear to him that they would concur in bestowing them. When, however, nothing of the sort appeared, but they heard again and again just the reverse of what they had expected, they were at first perplexed, and then thrown into deep dejection. Some of those sitting near him actually rose up and left him; for they now no longer cared to share the same seat with the man whom previously they had prized having as their friend. When finally the reading of the letter was finished all with one voice denounced and threatened him, some because they had been wronged, others through fear, some to conceal their friendship from him, and still others out of joy at his downfall. . . . Thereupon one might have witnessed such a surpassing proof of human frailty as to prevent one's ever again being puffed up with conceit. For the man whom at dawn they had escorted to the senate-hall as a superior being, they were now dragging to prison as if no better than the worst; . . . him whom they were wont to protect as a master, they now regarded as a runaway slave . . . him whom they had adorned with the purple-bordered toga, they struck in the face; and him whom they were wont to adore and worship with sacrifices as a god, they were now leading to execution. The populace also assailed him, shouting many reproaches at him for the lives he had taken and many jeers for the hopes he had cherished. They hurled down . . . all his images, as though they were thereby treating the man himself with contumely, and he thus became the spectator of what he was desined to suffer. . . . [T]he Senate . . . voted to have a statue of Liberty erected

in the Forum; also a festival was to be held under the
auspices of all the magistrates and priests, a thing which
had never before happened; and the day on which Sejanus
had died was to be celebrated by annual horse-races and
wild-beast-hunts . . . another thing which had never before
been done.[40]

The politics of the Republic involved perpetual competition
between durable rival groupings whose individual members were
bound through *fides* in client and friendship (*amicitia*) relations. The struggle between groups strengthened the sense of
commitment within groups until at times the conflict threatened
to paralyze the state. But when the crises were resolved, the
particular agreement achieved had extraordinary durability. A
leader could represent his followers to the public, and conversely his own prestige made an explanation of the public's needs
credible to them. Politics brought men together through competition. In the Empire a leader often arrived on the public
scene suddenly, having cultivated the favor of important officials,
and because appearances suggested he would enjoy continued
success, he would attract followers. But when the future seemed
less certain, they might turn on him. Commitments could not be
taken at face value; everyone lived in apprehension of the slight
change of circumstances which transformed friends into enemies.
No one could represent anyone, even himself, and in the constant shuffling and reshuffling men were driven further and
further away from each other and from themselves.

When historians who are themselves Roman examine the
public debates of the Republic, they take them to represent the
true state of public opinion. Men meant what they said, and as a
consequence the state gained in strength because officials could
choose between alternative courses whose consequences were
defined, and for reasons which the public could understand and
accept. The competition for place and group gains, in other
words, resulted in production as well as redistribution—wiser
policies were chosen, better officials selected, public cohesion and
determination made more firm, and above all, since men were

---

[40] Dio, VII, 68, 10 *ff.* Compare with the joy ostensibly enthusiastic
supporters of Nkrumah expressed upon his downfall. *The Times* [London]
February 24, 1967.

secure in thinking that the honors attained would survive public retirement, they were encouraged to give their best energies to the state.

The same historians approach the debates of the Empire in a different spirit. Public argument obscured issues, consequences, and alternatives; men felt *compelled* to say what they did not really believe, and who could blame them if they did not feel obliged to obey laws they themselves had made? If, occasionally, wiser policies were chosen, better officials selected, and public cohesion made more resolute, those events occurred in spite of, rather than because of, the practices which governed politics.

The continual debasement of the political process functioned as a Gresham's law, driving the better men out of politics generation after generation. Once the Roman had regarded politics as the only place to demonstrate merit, looking upon abstention as a mark of moral unfitness; now, increasingly, he hailed withdrawal as the only way to protect his virtue.[41]

The imperial constitution was a *paper constitution*. The Popular Assemblies and the candidates for office rarely used institutional processes for criticism. Yet in every reign the masses rioted, and magistrates attempted the assassin's knife themselves or encouraged others, especially the emperor's domestics and confidents, to try their hands. In the early reigns the Senate, the emperor's principal counselor, demonstrated independence, but as time passed senators disguised their true feelings. Most emperors themselves had been senators and understood that body's anxiety. Each upon accession promised to restrain himself; although many intended to keep their promises, few could do so. Restraint encouraged ambitious conspirators to believe the emperor was weak, while an imprudent or suspicious imperial move revived painful memories and fresh conspiracies on other grounds. Security that hung on the will of one man could not inspire confidence. No one forgot that Tiberius and Caligula began by asking the Senate to assume more responsibilities and later initiated reigns of terror. But those two could argue that conspiracies forced their hands, and point to Domitian's complaint that "no one believed them when they discovered a

---

[41] Lucan, *Pharsalia*, VIII, 49, and Seneca, *Epistles*, XXVIII, 8. The change suggests an entirely different view of human nature and prepares Romans for Christian arguments.

conspiracy until they were murdered."[42] Senators might well have rejoined that they were often forced to condemn colleagues falsely so that the emperor might confiscate estates to defray military expenses. Only extraordinary emperors could cut through the fog of mutual distrust, which conditioned men to interpret events in their worst possible light.[43]

The Senate's failure to maintain, let alone increase its credit was partly due to the willingness of members to betray each other out of fear, personal gain, or sheer envy. Once a place in the Senate had been an end in itself, a reward for a service already rendered; now it was a springboard for future imperial patronage. When not busy slandering colleagues, Senators were consumed with the desire to flatter the emperor and to anticipate his wishes. Caligula might taunt them for their servility, Vespasian might admonish them for their unwillingness to separate private from public considerations, but a unanimous Senate did not register their true views, and a publicly divided one was only concerned with trivial matters. In either case contempt for the Senate grew—a vexing problem for emperors who understood that an impotent opposition is a violent one, and that a body without strength to resist them publicly was also one too negligible or untrustworthy to support them.

When public debate lacks credibility, the significance of rumor grows. Rumors developed naturally from a desire for details when the proper authority was unwilling to tell the truth or when his testimony could not be trusted.[44] Rumors were circulated to excite mobs and to undermine the mutual faith of the

---

[42] Suetonius, "Domitian," 21.

[43] The propensity is familiar enough to students of Roman history, but few have appreciated the relevant political circumstances. Note, for example, T. S. Jerome's fascinating *Aspects of the Study of Roman History* (New York: 1962). At a loss for a sensible reason to explain the "lack of objectivity" in the senators' attitude towards the emperors, he first suggests "habit," then "psychological disorders," and finally "jealousy and hatred." They "obviously" had no reason to be afraid because so few were executed. If future historians related the fear and distrust McCarthyism induced to the number who lost their jobs, they too would be mystified.

[44] Dio, 7, LIII, 19, and Tacitus, *Annals*, III.

Discussing a recent threat to shoot looters, D. Bruckner writes:

The mayor is a man of immense and sincere responsibility, and he was enraged that, once the riot started, welfare workers were sent home, offices closed early, and worst of all many schools closed . . . and youths roamed the streets. The mayor suggested that there was a conspiracy of irresponsibility among officials and the existence of an organized rumor mill . . . he simply

emperor and his closest supporters. *Columare audactor, semper aliquid haered* (always slander, something sticks) became the standard preparatory move for a *coup d'état*, and simultaneously a device emperors could employ to break the mutual trust of suspected conspirators. Everyone became absorbed in developing his own sources of information, to unravel the personal implications of each event and attempt the impossible task of keeping each foot in separate boats, so that no matter which sank he would stay afloat.

Tiberius remarked that governing Rome was like holding a "wolf by the ears," and so it must have seemed. In the first two centuries from Augustus to Commodus the average reign was approximately thirteen and a half years and nearly one-half of the emperors were murdered; in the last two centuries, when the wolf seemed to have one ear free, the average reign lasted four years and almost two-thirds of the emperors died by foul means. When we bear in mind that the average British and French reign prior to the French Revolution was twenty-one and twenty-three years respectively and that only a few monarchs were executed, the significance of Roman insecurity is highlighted. The paranoid tendency among emperors had a solid existential basis; all experienced conspiracies by trusted subordinates, and Sejanus' fate reminded the latter that once the emperor's suspicions and fear were aroused, no one could depend upon a fair hearing.[45] Uneasy officers struck down emperors whom they

---

did not understand the temper of his own city in these times. It is filled with rumors which become general panic with little instigation. A public rumor-helding service run by the city handled 40 routine calls the day before Dr. King was murdered. By the following Monday, with troops all over the streets, it was handling more than 10,000 calls a day. This is no conspiracy; it is panic. . . . Last week he broke for a time under the strain and talked like a frightened bully. He sounded like the rest of us then, and unquestionably his outburst has made the city less safe for all of us. For a brief moment, he talked with the incoherent illogic of the mob. *Los Angeles Times,* April 21, 1968.

Contemporaries have never treated the political significance of rumor systematically.

[45] See Jehu Baker's edition of Montesquieu, *Considerations* . . . (New York: 1901), pp. 346 *ff.* I have omitted Julius Caesar from the list. The "Decadents" and the French psychopathologists commonly attributed the inclination of Roman Emperors toward insanity to physiological degeneracy. A. E. Carter, *The Idea of Decadence in French Literature: 1830-1900* (Toronto: 1958), pp. 62 *ff.* But Plato, in linking insanity among rulers directly to the political tensions some systems produce, makes much more

imagined *might* suspect them. All were locked together in an Hobbesian embrace, where action and reaction kept intensifying mutual fears making the one common desire for self-preservation daily more chimerical.

The most trivial incidents—unexpected arrests, unintended insults, rumors, ambiguous information, disturbances at gladiator shows—might provide opportunities for an upheaval. When men will not give each other the benefit of doubt, ordinary occurrences can breed consequences no one forsees, as recent riots in American cities demonstrate. It is easy to understand why the emperors thought it more important to boast of their clemency than of their justice and why they kept statues of *Fortuna* in their bedrooms.[46]

Hoping to revive the Republic's tradition of teaching moral obligation by personal example, the early emperors educated their sons personally. But most citizens continued to regard education as the transmission of skills, and schools staffed by slaves spread everywhere, intensifying hostility toward all forms of authority. "They undermined instead of strengthening the children's morals . . . and if they furnished their minds with a certain amount of information, they were not calculated to perform any loftier or nobler task."[47] The students fought the system in their own way to defeat its very limited purposes.

In the fourth century Vegetius could not take it for granted that new recruits for the army would be literate enough to keep the books. Instead of . . . intellectual curiosity vital to

---

sense. When one learns that the late President Kassim of Iraq frustrated forty-four assassination attempts in as many months we can believe that his judgment became perverted as many claimed. See two splendid, ignored pieces, B. Constant, "De l'Esprit de l'Usurpation" and G. Ferrero, *The Principles of Power* (New York: 1942). *Cf.* my "Coup d'Etat: The View of the Men Firing Pistols," *Revolution*, ed. C. J. Friedrich (New York: 1966), pp. 53–74.

[46] Julius Caesar first speaks of clemency as a public virtue, and as the Empire takes root, coins reveal that men praise clemency more than justice—the aim of Republican government. See M. P. Coatsworth, "The Virtues of a Roman Emperor," *Proc. Brit. Acad.*, XXIII (1937), 113 *ff.* Cicero sees justice as the difference between a king and tyrant, while Seneca argues for clemency.

[47] J. Carcopino, *Daily Life in Ancient Rome* (New Haven: 1940), pp. 106–07.

later life, school children carried away the gloomy recollection of years wasted in senseless, stumbling repetitions, punctuated by savage punishments. Popular education . . . was a failure.[48]

Higher education was no better. A perverted Aristotlelian rhetoric was the major subject, a study in which the original aim, a discussion of public issues, gave way to elaborating flamboyant techniques for praising men and deeds.

The number of men able to cooperate with others as equals or to act independently decreased; the loss, as one might expect, was most apparent in the sphere of collegial and elected governments which kept failing everywhere, impelling emperors, frequently against their will, to extend their administrative services, to place more faith in *obsequium.* A century after Augustus the extraordinary misgovernment of cities led to restrictions on municipal autonomy. So badly ruled did the population of the Senate's provinces feel themselves to be, that they beseeched emperors to govern them. Roman political imagination seemed to wither; there was one solution for every problem—more bureaucracy under the Emperor's supervision.

The original bureaucracy was small and notoriously efficient; as it expanded the evidence of malfeasance grew. Simultaneously with the collapse of local government, a secret corps of spies was organized to oversee the bureaucracy which filled the vacuum. The great military troubles of the next century snowballed the movement. More officials were required, more money needed, more men hired to collect it, more spies employed to check government agents, and more spies to investigate the spies. A disastrous inflation developed, and bureaucratic salaries tumbled to one seventh of those paid by Augustus, stimulating further administrative abuses.[49]

The excessive demand upon taxpayers strengthened the determination to evade. Rich men literally buried their capital in the

[48] *Ibid.,* p. 115.
[49] A. H. M. Jones, *The Later Roman Empire* (Oxford: 1964), Vol. 1, p. 51. Roman bureaucracy increased thirty-fold in four centuries, and still it seemed less able to perform original functions. A similar development is occurring in Indonesia where the bureaucracy has grown nearly thirty-fold in two decades. Guy Pauker, "Indonesia, The Age of Reason," *Asian Survey,* VIII: 2 (February 1968), 168.

hope of better days. Fields were abandoned, crafts given up, and economic associations dissolved. Everyone seemed to be running away from the tax-collector—into swollen cities where anonymity and circuses provided relief, into the bureaucracy which supplied protection, or into marauding bands preying on those who elected to "stick it out."

To meet the manpower shortage, to guarantee essential supplies, Diocletian instituted a limited caste-state socialism, which ultimately only increased administrative problems. The emperor Gratian reckoned that two thirds of the government's revenue went into private purses. The historian Lactantius felt that the number collecting taxes exceeded the number paying them, and Popes Innocent II and Siricius ruled that a holder of a public post was forever ineligible to join a holy order!

Power was redistributed and concentrated because of *weakness*—this was the imperial story. Each major redistribution acted like a drug stimulating new bursts of energy, only to leave the taker more exhausted than ever when the first effects wore off, and less able to resist the suggestion of a new dose even though fully aware of the ultimate consequences.

> The machine tended always to work more slowly and to become more expensive to run. Moreover more and more routine work was piled on the central ministers and above all on the emperor himself. . . . [H]e was thus placed at the mercy of his ministers and clerks who . . . unscrupulously exploited their opportunities. . . . Emperors were not infrequently obliged to announce in their laws that rescripts contrary to their provisions, even if they bore their own signature, were invalid.[50]

The fearful threats of the Theodosian Code manifested imperial impotence and how far Rome had come from the Republic's unwillingness to use coercion against the most humble citizen. "Back! rapacious hands of public officials, back! I say, if after being warned once, they do not draw back, let them be cut off."

Even Parkinson would find difficulty imagining the scope of conventional administrative abuses.

---

[50] Jones, *Later Roman Empire*, Vol. II, p. 410.

Numbers always tended to swell, despite periodic purges, especially in the grander and most lucrative offices. . . . Absenteeism was rife. In 378 Gratian laid down a scale of penalties for . . . (officials) who exceeded their leave. Six months absence cost five places in seniority, a year's ten, four years' forty; only if he stayed away more than four years without leave was a clerk cashiered![51]

In the palatine ministries numbers tended to be so swollen and promotion so slow that prudent parents enrolled their sons as infants. . . . [A] clerk . . . remained in [office] for life, and rose by strict seniority. . . . [He] might be cashiered for gross misconduct, or lose seniority . . . by persistent absenteeism over several years, but he could not accelerate his promotion by special diligence—though he might do so by graft. . . . The senior officials were often, as the laws admit, past active work, and the junior clerks had to pass long years of frustrating inactivity.[52]

The deterioration of the army followed a similar pattern. The first imperial armies were probably better than those the Republic had produced, but something was wrong, as Augustus' lament for the three legions Varus lost in Germany suggests. While the Republic seemed to have an endless supply of trained eager reserves, the early emperors found the task of replacing losses difficult: few volunteered, training costs were great, and men could not be spared from the economy.

The emperors restricted the army to defensive roles, arguing that Rome could no longer absorb conquered lands. Their critics believed they really feared able generals. Whatever the reason, by drastically reducing the military sphere in Roman life, the capabilities which can only come from enthusiastically engaged activity were restricted to fewer persons, and if it seemed that Rome was husbanding her resources by not using them, this was because no one thought of a calculus which would relate activity to the generation or deterioration of potentialities. Without the stimulus of competitive Republican practices, Roman eagerness for tactical and technological improvements began to disappear.

[51] *Ibid.,* p. 604.
[52] *Ibid.,* pp. 600–02.

The changes in the third and fourth centuries were determined simply by the desire to save money, or by the necessity to employ poorly motivated recruits.

Augustus' small establishment was designed for war and massed in large frontier garrisons. A century later the emperors reluctantly yielded to provincial demands and detached units to aid the police. Rioting and brigandage grew more extensive, and in the third century most troops were dispersed in small police formations, largely unaccustomed to grouping in large numbers for a military campaign. Simultaneously, soldiers accepted and usurped positions within the civil administration, and by the fourth century the term *militia* referred equally to all public agents.[53]

In a striking parallel to his counterpart in contemporary underdeveloped states, the soldier also became a producer in the economy. Earlier the army undertook the Emperor's vast construction projects and it also supplied contract labor and tools for enterprises by other public and private bodies. Later dispersion made military technical supplies more available and more difficult to supervise. When "full-time" soldiers illegally accepted employment, providing government materials in the process, civilian technicians could not compete. As the supply of the latter diminished, the Empire as a whole was further impoverished, and the local dependence on the uneconomic military monopolies crippled government's ability to concentrate soldiers in response to military necessity. One reason the third-century civil wars extended for decades was that soldiers would not leave local areas to give one candidate decisive striking forces. Too many were busy making profit and, as the careless, ill-conceived constructions of the third and fourth centuries suggest, they were not giving value for money.[54]

[53] R. MacMullan, *Soldier and Civilian in the Later Roman Empire* (Cambridge, Mass.: 1963), pp. 75, 158. M. Rostovtzeff offers the classic discussions of the military aggrandizement, *The Social and Economic History of the Roman Empire* (Oxford: 1941), 2 vols.

[54] Made of coarse materials in mortar, rather than of fine stones deftly prepared, they were erected too fast. The buildings of Constantine's reign bear the same hasty character of improvisation as the social reforms of that emperor. . . . It has been said, not without some justification, that "After the great architects of the Antonines, there are only masons!" Ferdinand Lot, *The End of the Ancient World and the Beginnings of the Middle Ages* (New York: 1961), pp. 136–37.

To save money, to get more recruits and more amenable ones, the third century emperors introduced conscription. Like all imperial reforms, in time it became more costly and more inefficient than preceding arrangements. The early imperial army was one third as large as its fourth-century successor, but it always put twice as many on the battlefield! No one knew how many names on the late military payrolls represented fictitious persons, or men too old, too young, or too deeply involved in commerce to perform military duties. Everyone knew that whereas every soldier of Augustus and Trajan had been superbly trained and equipped, the Roman now often reported for duty undrilled and sometimes after having sold his equipment to civilians or even to the enemy. As distaste for military service grew, self-mutilation to avoid induction became commonplace. In despair the last emperors raised a "cheap" volunteer army—barbarian troops led by their own chiefs "who had neither the luxury of Roman soldiers, nor the same spirit, nor the same pretensions"![55]

The Romans felt that the pursuit of "luxury," an appetite first stimulated during the Transformation,[56] destroyed their economy. Since the nineteenth century this argument has become increasingly unacceptable, for we have "learned" that a popular desire for amenities spurs economic development; what the Romans called corruption we are likely to deem progress! Yet surely no single relationship between consumption and production exists.

The Roman genius for rationality, for relating reward to contribution, never found an outlet in economic life. If the Republic did not encounter economic difficulties it was because public expenses were largely subsidised from the private purses of officeholders and military volunteers and, therefore, carefully restrained by those who had to pay for them. But during the Transformation many citizens withdrew from productive activity, and the burden of supporting them fell on persons who lacked the civic rights necessary to resist openly. Industry became a more important element in the economy, but the Roman, who had always been a farmer, deemed commerce worthy of lesser

[55] Montesquieu, *Considerations.* . . . Ch. 18.
[56] See G. Ferrero, "Corruption in Ancient Rome and its Counterpart in Modern History," in his *Character and Events of Roman History* (Chautauqua: 1917), pp. 3–35.

men and remained unappreciative of their needs and potential creative energies.[57] The agony of the Roman *dolce vita* story makes sense only in the context of constantly rising public expenditures and corresponding diminishing incentives to produce.

The "free bread and circuses," the senseless conspicuous consumption, the vast useless monuments which the Emperor Julian said were necessary because imperial politics deprived men of the Republican certainty that they would be *remembered:* all these things and many more took their toll. The most determined autocrat was helpless before this ancient "revolution of rising expectations." Take the indulgence of the urban masses as one case in point: during the late Republic the capital enjoyed the privilege of sixty-five annual holiday festivals. Two centuries later in Marcus Aurelius' reign, the privilege had been extended to include most large cities and one hundred and seventy-five holidays! Even when Rome lacked money for defense, no one could induce metropolitan masses to curtail their demands.

The first emperors battled against the tide, building a dike to restrict wants rather than a channel to employ them. They vigorously sponsored sumptuary legislation and religious revivals, and they issued constant admonitions to live in the frugal manner of the early Republic. But the citizen felt traditional norms to be obsolete or irrelevant to his new circumstances. The enemy was distant and impotent, a professional army did all the fighting, and the Roman kept seeking luxury in the fruitless effort to end his boredom. As the Empire grew older, consumption demands pressed harder and harder against economic capacities, and the capital of previous generations was consumed.

[57] All gains made by hired laborers are dishonorable and base, for what we buy of them is their labor not their artistic skill; with them the very gain itself does but increase the slavishness of the work. All retail dealing too may be put in the same category, for the dealer will gain nothing except by profuse lying and nothing is more disgraceful than untruthful huckstering. Again the work of all artisans is sordid: there can be nothing honorable in a workshop.—Cicero, *De Off.* I, 42, 150.

The Romans had always been too occupied in ruling other nations to become proficient in trade and industry; . . . [T]he stigma attaching to the productive labor of freemen . . . was the blind alley from which the Roman world had no way out; slavery was economically impossible, the labor of freemen was morally ostracized.—F. Engels, *The Origin of the Family, Private Property, and the State* (New York: 1942), pp. 135-37.

In the fourth century Rome could neither feed her citizens, provide for the upkeep of her administration, nor pay her troops; every year her people were becoming more impoverished and her burdens heavier, while at the same time her forces were less.[58]

CONCLUSION

Politics, we often hear, is simply a problem of distributing goods, an "authoritative allocation of values," the most relevant question being: "Who gets what, when, and how?" But the Roman experience teaches us to regard the political community more fundamentally as a producer and destroyer of goods and to study distribution as it contributes to either possibility. Rome's rise illustrates one dynamic. Rome outstripped all rivals because she understood best how to make competition and personal independence liberate latent capacities and energies. Her fall illustrates the contrary movement. Men can devise institutional shackles which forever depress the level of energy and talent available. In the end "the Romans were so weak that there was no people so small it could not do them harm."[59]

Trust nourished the Republic but trust depends upon fashioning standards corresponding to man's nature. *Fides* was a political creative energy few possessed but all could depend upon. Organized cooperation presumes inequality, and inequality is welcomed only when accompanied by deeds manifesting excellence.

The Republic was destroyed because the property and offices a man with *fides* needs as means, in order to cultivate independence and demonstrate worth, always attract men who seek them as ends in themselves. But the administrative altruism imperial writers proposed as an alternative was built on a distrust of capacities and hence was not in conformity with nature. *Obsequium* was an egalitarian ethic, and made fewer demands on men because they could set limit to their efforts by referring to specific rules. But *obsequium* was an impossible ethic, destroying the creative energies of the few and demanding that all take satisfaction in rewards and punishments which have no obvious

---

[58] Albert de Broglie, *L'Eglise et l'Empire Romain au IV Siècle* (Paris: 1856–66), Vol. II, p. 229.

[59] Montesquieu, *Considerations. . . .* Ch. 19.

relation to truth and merit. No one can deny the evidence of his senses, and if men despair of the possibility that their system can conform to truth, each considers himself released of all obligations and fights it alone by taking more than he gives.

12

POLITICAL OBLIGATION AND COLLECTIVE GOODS

NANNERL O. HENRY

The problem of political obligation has often been called the most fundamental question in politics, and it has exercised a great many thinkers in the history of political discourse. It is a complex problem no matter how one attacks it. But some of the tangles in the matter can be straightened out by avoiding confusion of the various questions involved. For example, "Why ought men to obey their governments?" and "Ought I to obey law X?"

I wish to acknowledge gratefully the valuable comments on an earlier draft of this paper made by Professors Robert Keohane, J. Roland Pennock, and Raymond Hopkins of Swarthmore College, and Robert Lyke of Princeton University. One version of the paper was read in a Swarthmore College political science department colloquium, and I have profited from that discussion by my colleagues Professors David G. Smith, Richard Mansbach, Paul Lutzker, and Frederick Hargadon.

are clearly related questions, but they are not the same question. They involve two different perspectives: the first takes the viewpoint of the student of polities as wholes, the second, the viewpoint of the individual moral decision-maker.[1]

Some political philosophers have concluded that the first question is a pseudoquestion and that only the second is worth asking. According to these writers, there is no generally valid theory of political obligation.[2] These philosophers do well to remind us that there is no simple answer to our first question, but they are too hasty in assuming that it is unanswerable. It is quite true that most answers that have been given to the general question about political obligation hold only in certain circumstances, or on the basis of special assumptions not universally accepted as valid or relevant to the problem of political obligation. And it may well also be true that our obligation to obey certain kinds of governments is greater than our obligation to obey other kinds. Even if both these statements are true, however, it does not follow that our first question is meaningless. It is still worthwhile to sort out the answers that have been given to the question and to attempt to see whether any theories of political obligation manage to establish the obligation to obey government as an important moral datum in its own right, to be taken into account by an individual who is weighing various obligations and goods in a particular decision to obey or disobey a law or command.

In this chapter, we will look briefly at a number of theories of obligation and then explore more thoroughly one type of theory that has received less attention than it deserves. We shall first examine the theory in its most familiar form, as presented by Hobbes and Hume, and then see how this theory of obligation can be expanded by taking some insights from Aristotle and Rousseau.

[1] Joseph Tussman, in *Obligation and the Body Politic* (New York: Oxford, 1960), p. 12, draws this distinction between the perspective of the individual decision-maker and the "descriptive-predictive" perspective of the external observer.

[2] This argument is made by Miss Margaret Macdonald in her essay "The Language of Political Theory," *Logic and Language*, first series, ed. Antony Flew (Oxford: Blackwell, 1952), pp. 167–86, and by J. C. Rees in "The Limitations of Political Theory," *Political Studies*, II (1954), 245–53.

I

Most of the answers that have been given to the general question about political obligation are variations on a few basic themes and they fall into two different categories. Some theories of political obligation require special prior assumptions—religious, historical, or metaphysical. Other theories focus on certain acts of the subject that are held to create obligation.

The first category includes theories of divine right, the argument from tradition, and the Hegelian idea that we are obliged to obey our governments because the individual is but a moment in the full realization of human life and development embodied in the state. Divine right theory begins with the Pauline injunction that "the powers that be are ordained of God," and then justifies a particular dynasty or regime on the grounds of special divine sanction. Under such a theory, in order to acknowledge our political obligation, we must first believe that there is a God who commands us to do certain things that we are obliged to obey, and believe further that he has ordained governments and commanded us to obey them. The argument from prescription or tradition holds that since a particular regime has historically governed my state, I am obliged to continue the obedience rendered by my forefathers. This argument requires that the citizen accept a Burkean reverence for, and feeling of responsibility to the history of his own country, and then connect this reverence with a present duty to maintain the ancestral constitution. The Hegelian view rests upon special metaphysical assumptions about the relationship between the state and the individual, and the abolition of any dichotomy between them.[3]

The second group of theories focuses on certain acts of the subject, and includes theories of consent and authorization. In the first place, I can be held to be obliged to obey my government because I have consented to do so. This is the view of those who use the language of contract to argue that my obligation to obey my government depends upon my having, in some determi-

[3] These familiar theories are discussed at greater length in other typologies of answers that have been given to the question of political obligation; see especially Anthony Quinton's introduction to his volume *Political Philosophy* (Oxford: 1967), 9–12, and S. I. Benn and R. S. Peters, *Principles of Political Thought* (New York: The Free Press, 1959), ch. XIV.

nate sense, agreed to do so. Some theorists argue that I am obliged to obey my government not because I have consented, but because I have authorized its actions. As a result, they are in some sense my own actions, and I cannot without absurdity refuse to acknowledge my own acts. I am obliged to obey government because I have given it the right and power to act in my name.[4]

Now there are two different ways in which this sort of theory can be interpreted. In a strict interpretation of consent or authorization theory, the giving of consent or the act of authorization creates the obligation to obey; and such a theory can apply only where some definite, solemn act of commitment, having the status of a vow or a promise, has taken place. Since such an act of solemn commitment is not a common political phenomenon, this theory explains political obligation only in rather special circumstances. However, consent theory has usually been interpreted more broadly than this. It is held that only governments that enjoy the continuing consent of their citizens in some looser and less solemn sense have a valid claim on their subjects' obedience. Interpreted in this way, the focus of the theory shifts from an act performed by the subject to the characteristics of the polity itself. What kind of polity qualifies as a consensual polity? Traditional consent theory has not been very helpful in answering this question, for at the crucial point the theory relies on an artificial device—a contract, or signs of formal consent—rather than discussing the kinds of political organization, goals, or leadership that elicit and involve exceptional popular support.

A third category of theories of obligation, less often discussed but potentially more fruitful than the other two, includes theories basing political obligation directly on the performance of

---

[4] John Locke's is, of course, the clearest example of consent theory; see the *Second Treatise of Government* (New York: Liberal Arts, 1952), ch. VIII. On the general problems with consent theory, John Plamenatz gives valuable clarification in his *Consent, Freedom and Political Obligation;* see especially the appendix to chapter VII, and the "Postscript" to the second edition (Oxford: 1968). The "authorization" device is used by theorists such as Hobbes and Rousseau who are specifically concerned to deny that there can be a contract of government, as distinct from a social contract. See *Leviathan,* chs. XVI and XVII (Oxford: Blackwell, 1957), esp. p. 112, and the *Social Contract* (New York: Dutton Everyman, 1950), 13–14. For Rousseau, it is clear that my obligation to obey the general will arises in part because it is my will.

certain tasks or functions by the government. Two kinds of theories come under this heading: aristocratic and utilitarian theories.

An aristocratic theory of political obligation makes reference to the qualifications, knowledge, or foresight of those who govern. It assumes that some men are endowed with superior political qualifications of some kind, whether skill, monopoly of political resources, or knowledge about the purposes and goals of social life. If the subjects of such rulers see their relationship to their rulers correctly, they will recognize that they owe obedience to their political superiors, just as they think it proper for those with skill in any area of life to guide those who lack such skill. According to this theory, then, we are obliged to obey our rulers if and because they have the skill and knowledge to perform political tasks more competently than the average citizen.[5]

The major trouble with aristocratic theories, of course, is that it is difficult to obtain generally acceptable criteria for judging political excellence in leadership. The aristocratic argument provides a basis for obligation only in a society where the governors claim to be the persons best qualified to govern according to criteria generally believed to be relevant, and the governed accept the truth of that claim and recognize that it entails obligation.

Utilitarian theory holds that we are obliged to obey governments if and because they promote the greatest happiness or general good. This theory has usually been dismissed by critics as either too narrow or too vague.[6] If general happiness is defined sufficiently precisely that it can be measured, so that we can

[5] Plato, who is not commonly thought of in connection with political obligation, gives us throughout his political writing a straighforward case for obligation based upon political excellence; see particularly the *Republic*, ed. Cornford (Oxford: 1945), 125, 194-97, 210. There is an analogous argument in the Leninist theory of the dictatorship of the proletariat, in which the claim of the vanguard to guide the rest is based upon their superior foresight about the goals to be worked for; see Benn and Peters, *Principles*, p. 360. In a looser form, the same argument appears in any justification for a government by an aristocracy; see, for example, Aristotle, *Politics*, 1284a-b, ed. E. Barker (Oxford: 1948), 159-60.

[6] Macdonald, "The Language of Political Theory," pp. 181-83, and Hanna Pitkin, "Obligation and Consent, I," *American Political Science Review*, LIX:4 (1965), 992-93. Both Miss Macdonald and Mrs. Pitkin point out that there are several different versions of the utilitarian theory and that none is finally acceptable.

determine whether or not obedience is justified, then the theory
is too restrictive; for any available measure—the GNP or population growth rate or health statistics—fails to take into account
more than a fraction of the purposes of government and hardly
provides a convincing justification for general obligation in
terms of social effect. On the other hand, if the general good is
defined more broadly, then it is held that the theory is tautologi-
cal and therefore useless. I should like to argue, however, that
the theory can be stated in such a way that it has both wide
validity and explanatory power.

II

Hobbes gives us the utilitarian theory in its bluntest form,
although he does not rely upon it entirely. Students of Hobbes
have been able to discover a number of theories of obligation in
his work. He was concerned to establish obligation on the strongest possible grounds, and it is not surprising that he supports it
in several different ways. But the most basic theory of obligation
to be found in *Leviathan* is that which concerns us here.

In Hobbes' view, human beings, in spite of their radically
antisocial traits, cannot avoid human contact, and are in fact
driven to seek each other's society because human psychology is
such that our enjoyments all require recognition by other human
beings. But society is impossible without a political superior to
maintain order and establish rules. In order to escape perpetual
conflict, individuals come together and institute "a common
power to keep them in awe and direct their actions to the
common benefit." According to Hobbes, the only way in which
the association can work is for all to obey this common power in
all things necessary to their peace and defense. And it is the
prerogative of the sovereign to decide what things are so necessary. In chapter XXI, Hobbes makes the basis of that obligation
quite clear.

> For in the act of our submission [he argues], consisteth both
> our *obligation* and our *liberty*: which must therefore be
> inferred by arguments taken from thence; there being no
> obligation on any man, which ariseth not from some act of

his own; for all men equally, are by nature free. And because such arguments, must either be drawn from the express words, *I authorize all his actions*, or from the intention of him that submitteth himself to his power, which intention is to be understood by the end for which he so submitteth; the obligation, and liberty of the subject, is to be derived, either from those words, or other equivalent; or else from the end of the institution of sovereignty, namely the peace of the subjects within themselves, and their defence against a common enemy.[7]

Authorization, then, is not the only basis for political obligation; a man's obligation to obey can be derived from the goals of political society and the fact of his living therein. A person's intention, as a member of a polity, to enjoy the benefits of that polity sufficiently obliges him to obey the authority that makes those benefits possible. His obligation continues just as long as the sovereign is able to deliver the political goods, and no longer.[8]

This argument in Hobbes is the most basic form of what I propose to call the argument to obligation from the performance of political tasks, or the provision of certain essential goods and services. According to this argument, government performs a set of functions that we necessarily desire and need as human beings in society. Since obedience by subjects is essential to the performance of these functions, we ought to obey government.

Such a statement of the argument raises at least two questions that need clarification: (1) What is the content or meaning of the functions or tasks that government performs; what goods and services does government provide? and (2) What is the status of the "ought" in this argument; how does the provision of goods

---

[7] Hobbes, *Leviathan*, p. 141.

[8] Hobbes, *Leviathan*, pp. 143–44. So far as I know, this interpretation of Hobbes' theory of obligation emphasizes an aspect of his thought that would be recognized by most students as part of what Hobbes "meant," but has not generally been seen as part of his strict theory of obligation. Contributions to the ongoing debate about Hobbesian obligation include Warrender's *The Political Philosophy of Hobbes* (Oxford: 1957); John Plamenatz, "Mr. Warrender's Hobbes," A. G. Wernham, "Liberty and Obligation in Hobbes," both in *Hobbes Studies*, ed. K. C. Brown (Oxford: Blackwell, 1965); and Brian Barry, "Warrender and his Critics," *Philosophy*, XLIII (April 1968), 113–37.

and services create an obligation for the recipients of those goods? Most of the rest of this chapter will discuss the first question; the second can be more quickly dealt with.

The use of ought here is intended to establish a moral obligation with the same status as other moral obligations, and it is analogous to two different moral obligations generally recognized as valid: the obligations to pay our debts, and to keep our promises. We ought to obey government (a) in return for, and (b) in order to make possible, the political benefits received. Our obligation (a) is similar to our obligation to pay any other kind of debt for goods received; and the reason obedience is the coin in which this particular debt must be paid is that political services cannot be provided unless subjects obey their governments. Therefore, we are obliged to obey in order to make those benefits possible—obligation (b). This second kind of obligation is similar to our obligation to keep our promises: as Hume pointed out, they have exactly the same status, and both derive their moral sanction from their essential contribution to human social relationships.[9] Prolonged and fruitful interaction among human beings is not possible without, or at least is greatly facilitated by being able to count upon other people's keeping promises; therefore, we ought to keep promises. It is the same with our obligation to obey our governments.

I am arguing that social life is instinctive and necessary to human beings, and that some political order is essential to society. Obviously men can live without social life; but human beings do not normally have this option. Aristotle was surely correct in holding that there is something inhuman and incomplete about such a life. My assertion, then, is that the fact that social life and political order are constitutive of our life as human beings can make a particular form of behavior— obedience behavior—obligatory for us as moral beings.[10]

⁹ David Hume, *Treatise of Human Nature*, III:ii;8 ed. A. D. Lindsay (New York: Dutton, 1911); Everyman edition, vol. II, p. 243. The same point is developed skilfully by Hanna Pitkin in the second part of her essay "Obligation and Consent," *American Political Science Review*, LX:1 (1966), 45-9.

¹⁰ If we look at this problem from the viewpoint of the individual decision-maker, it is clear that his personal obedience is not essential to making political benefits possible; it does not necessarily follow from the fact that I desire to obtain the benefits of political association that I must,

It does not follow from this argument that political obligation is absolute, that any citizen is bound to obey in any situation. Just as our obligation to keep promises can be nullified or overridden by other obligations, so can our political obligation. But it is obedience that should be the norm and disobedience that must be justified. The traditional way of stating the question about political obligation is misleading. Instead of beginning with the individual human being and asking "Why should he obey his government?" we should recognize a basic presumption that obedience is obligatory. The obligation is suspended in two different kinds of cases: (1) where obedience comes into conflict with other things that are also strongly obligatory; and (2) where it can be shown that the government in question does not, in fact, provide the services that governments are supposed to provide, upon which the obligation is based.

---

individually, pay taxes and obey laws. If most other members of my polity did so, for whatever reasons, it is probable that I could obtain benefits without paying the cost. This is a point often made by economists in discussing the concept of "public goods," which we shall take up later in this paper. Since it would be rational for me, as a self-interested "economic man," to avoid paying costs for public goods if I could do so while continuing to enjoy the benefits, such payments have to be made compulsory. On this issue, Mancur Olson's discussion in the first chapter of *The Logic of Collective Action* (Cambridge: Harvard University Press, 1965), is especially useful.

Even though it would not be in my self-interest, narrowly defined, to pay for public goods in the absence of compulsion to do so, this does not exclude the possibility that I have a moral obligation to do so. This obligation can either be seen as analogous to my obligation to pay my debts or else can be based on some statement such as "I ought to obey government because if this rule were not followed by members of my society generally I would be worse off, and it is only fair that I should do what I ask others to do." However, in this chapter we are not concerned with the individual, but with society as a whole; and we are making a statement about a case in which a fundamental need or interest shared by all members of a group can obligate members to perform certain behavior to make possible the attainment of that interest. The argument from needing or wanting to obligation is discussed in an illuminating article by A. C. MacIntyre, "Hume on 'Is' and 'Ought,' " *Philosophical Review,* LXVIII (1959), 463.

An assumption of a similar kind is made and developed in an interesting argument by Christian Bay in "Needs, Wants and Political Legitimacy," *Canadian Journal of Political Science,* I (September 1968), 241. Bay writes: "For the purposes of this discussion the only acceptable justification of government, which also determines the limits to its legitimate authority, is its task of serving human needs—serving them better than would be done without any government." Bay's article includes a useful set of definitions of the vague notions of "wants" and "needs."

Hobbes, of course, presented our political obligation as absolute; he denied that we could ever be released from that obligation, either by the greater claims of any other obligation or by any alleged shortcomings in the government in power over us. According to Hobbes, a government, simply by existing, provides essential services, and therefore we are obliged to obey it. We are released from our obligation only in the case of complete breakdown of the government's sovereign control; in such a case, we are again at liberty to submit ourselves to a new government. A corollary of this assertion is that Hobbes' argument, unlike many theories of obligation, is intended to establish political obligation in general, and to rule out of court the assertion that some polities have a more valid claim upon our obedience than others. For Hobbes, any civil order is preferable to anarchy or civil war; any political condition, even the most oppressive and miserable, is better than any feasible alternative.

In this inexorable rigidity, Hobbes' theory is virtually unique. Most political philosophers have argued that some governments are less good than others and that some governments are so perverted that they have no valid claim on their citizens' obedience, and ought to be overthrown. Most political thinkers justify resistance to tyranny and maintain some connection between political evaluation and the discussion of obligation. One difficulty with such arguments, however, is that in contrast with the uncomfortable clarity of Hobbes' theory, most theorists who justify resistance are quite vague about specifying the conditions under which government becomes so perverted that citizens are no longer obliged to obey it.

Hume, for example, gives us another, more explicit, version of Hobbes' argument to obligation from the provision of political goods and services, and yet wishes to argue that our political obligation is not absolute. In the same passage where he argues that political obligation and the obligation to keep promises have an original status and are derived from the same kinds of social benefits, Hume goes on to say that the interest or advantage that forms the basis of our obligation to obey government is "the security and protection which we enjoy in political society, and which we can never attain when perfectly free and independent." Since the interest forms "the immediate sanction of government," our obligation lasts just as far as the provision of the protection, "and whenever the civil magistrate carries his oppression so far as to render his authority perfectly intolerable, we are no longer bound to submit to it. The cause ceases; the effect must cease also."[11] Hume's language suggests that only when citizens are goaded beyond human endurance, so that their situation is "intolerable" and they cannot help but revolt, are they justified in rebelling. If this is what he means, justification becomes rather redundant when the inevitable reaction to unbearable oppression takes place. If this is not what he means, his theory is too vague to be of any use to citizens trying to decide whether or not their government is sufficiently oppressive to deserve to be overthrown. But however one interprets him, it is clear that Hume wishes to make our political obligation sufficiently strong that rebellion is rarely justified. He agrees with Hobbes that resistance to civil authority is a rare and serious matter and that "in the ordinary course of human affairs, nothing could be more pernicious and criminal."[12]

Hobbes and Hume, therefore, give us an answer to the question "Why ought men to obey their governments?" that is coherent, cogent, and universal in its applicability. They do not, however, allow us to argue that our obligation to obey "good" governments is greater than our obligation to obey government as such. This is true of Hume because he fails to specify ways in which we could make such judgments, and of Hobbes because he intentionally rejects such arguments altogether. Is there any way we can make such arguments, while not losing sight of the "performance perspective" of Hobbes and Hume? In order to do so, we are first required to specify more concretely the goods and services that it is the task of governments to provide, and then to show why it is that some governments perform well and others, badly.

---

[11] Hume, *Treatise*, II, 243, 250.

[12] Hume, *Treatise*, II, 253. Hume continues: "As numerous and civilized societies cannot subsist without government, so government is entirely useless without an exact obedience. . . . The common rule requires submission, and it is only in cases of grievous tyranny and oppression, that the exception can take place." *Cf. Leviathan*, p. 120, on the "horrible calamities" that befall "masterless men."

III

Both Hobbes and Hume describe the basic task of government as the provision of political order in the most minimal sense: security and protection—defense of citizens against external attack, and settlement of internal conflict. Even if the task of government be defined so narrowly, it can be argued that some governments, by using their power to oppress and harry their citizens rather than provide them with security, do not perform their function. This is what Hume means to argue, and Hobbes' refusal to admit this as a possibility gives his argument an air of unreality. However, neither Hobbes nor Hume writes consistently as if this minimal function were the sole work of government. They describe the sociopolitical order as one in which human life is less brutish and more civilized, not solely because of the increased security, but also because of the more commodious life which such security makes possible. Material comforts, economic exchange, arts and sciences—all these goods for human life are made possible by government: they are a part of the civil order supported by political order in the narrower sense. Neither Hobbes nor Hume argues that it is the task of government directly to provide all these things; but by assuming that they will flow naturally from the establishment of political order, the two writers do raise considerably the value of what we gain by government, and they let this weigh into the consideration of our grounds for obligation to obey.

Furthermore, Hobbes particularly is quite clear that government provides a number of important moral goods in addition to simple physical security. The establishment of the Leviathan makes possible moral discourse or communication, that is, the sharing of known rules governing human social behavior, and a common language for assessing and teaching such behavior.[13] Government also makes possible the enjoyment of justice, which is merely latent in the state of nature. All these important goods, according to Hobbes, are provided by government in making and enforcing rules about right and wrong, in settling conflicts.

Such considerations allow us to expand our notion of the "political order" that it is the task of government to provide. In

[13] The best treatment of this aspect of Hobbes' thought is by Sheldon Wolin in *Politics and Vision* (Boston: Little, Brown, 1960), ch. VIII.

addition to physical security against external attack and the prevention of internal war, governments also provide other public or collective goods for their citizens.[14] Economists have used the notion of public goods to denote goods that benefit members of a group in such a way that if the benefits are available to any members, they cannot feasibly be denied to other members of that group. Charles Lindblom, in his discussion of the concept of the public interest in *The Intelligence of Democracy,* uses a term analogous to that of public goods, "collective values." According to Lindblom, "a value is collective to the degree that a benefit from it cannot accrue to one member of the citizenry without accruing in some significant amount to many others, and cannot be withheld from one member without being in some significant amount withheld from others."[15]

It is generally recognized that the major task or purpose or function of government, the reason for its existence, is to provide goods of this kind, goods that are collectively valuable, but which cannot or will not be provided without common organization and coordinated direction of effort. Examples of such collective

[14] Cf. Adam Smith's catalogue of the "duties of the sovereign" in *Wealth of Nations,* Book V, ch. I, parts 1–3; (1) "protecting the society from the violence and invasion of other independent societies"; (2) "protecting, as far as possible, every member of the society from the injustice or oppression of every other member of it"; and (3) "erecting and maintaining those public institutions and those public works, which though they may be in the highest degree advantageous to a great society, are, however, of such a nature, that the profit could never repay the expense to any individual or small number of individuals, and which therefore it cannot be expected that any individual or small number of individuals should erect or maintain. The performance of this duty requires too very different degrees of expense in the different periods of society."

[15] *The Intelligence of Democracy* (New York: The Free Press, 1965), p. 279. On "public goods," see the discussion in Olson, especially pp. 13–16. Olson refers to a number of articles that define the concept in different ways. For a political scientist, the most interesting of these articles are by Paul Samuelson in the *Review of Economics and Statistics,* XXXVI (November 1954), 387–90; XXXVII (November 1955), 350–56; and XL (November 1958), 332–38. In these articles, Samuelson speaks of the provision of public goods as "functions of government."

Olson uses the term "collective good" interchangeably with "public good." Since "public good" is a specialized term in economic theory with several definitions current, I have used the less familiar term "collective goods" to refer to the various goods provided by government for members of society, some of which do and some of which do not fall into the category "public good" in the different senses proposed by Samuelson and others.

goods are aids to economic production and exchange, the establishment of courts of justice and the application of laws in the settlement of disputes, the protection of certain rights claimed by members of the polity, and contributions to the welfare of citizens in matters such as health and education.

Given such a concept of collective goods as part of the order provided by government, it is clear that some governments do a better job at providing such goods than others and it is therefore possible to argue that our obligation to obey such governments is greater than our obligation to obey less successful governments. It does not necessarily follow that our obligation increases with the amount or number of collective goods provided; we are not forced to conclude that our obligation is greatest to obey a government that virtually annihilates private areas in life. Just as political theorists differ about what things are properly in the public realm and what things are not, so each polity has a different concept of the proper mix between public and private goods, and that concept changes within a given society as well.

However, we can say, first of all, that there are certain broad values commonly recognized as important for the satisfaction of human needs, and that our obligation is greater to obey a state that does a better job than most in providing for these needs. Roland Pennock has developed the concept of "political goods," which he defines as goods that "satisfy human needs whose fulfillment makes the polity valuable to man, and gives it its justification."[16] As examples of such goods, he has named security, welfare, justice, and liberty, and he has given us some interesting suggestions on measuring the provision of these goods and comparing this from polity to polity. Pennock's concept is broader than the economist's notion of public goods, but there are clearly connections between the provision of collective goods in the narrower sense and the satisfaction of basic human needs in Pennock's sense. Particular collective goods contribute to the attainment of Pennock's political goods: water purification and education, for example, are two kinds of public goods that increase the levels of welfare within a society.

Second, we can also say that since societies differ, the most

[16] J. Roland Pennock, "Political Development, Political Systems, and Political Goods," *World Politics*, XVIII:3 (April 1966), 415-34.

appropriate and efficient ways of satisfying basic human needs will differ from society to society. Therefore, our obligation to obey a government is greater to the extent that it provides the range and kinds of collective goods that meet the needs of members of that polity. The problems then become: How are the needs of the members of a polity to be determined? And how can it be determined whether the collective goods provided by government satisfy those needs appropriately and efficiently? Political theorists propose two different ways of dealing with such problems: the aristocratic answer and the democratic answer. According to aristocratic theory, the needs of a society and the most appropriate methods for their satisfaction can best be determined by an enlightened elite. According to democratic theory, no elite can determine the needs of the members of a society and the best means for satisfying them as well as the people themselves; and therefore the citizens should be given a chance to participate significantly in the making of political decisions.

In the next two sections, we will turn to the work of Aristotle and Rousseau for help in assessing the merits of these two different theories. Aristotle and Rousseau are certainly not utilitarians by any definition of that rather slippery word. Yet they do use an argument that is similar to our argument to obligation from the provision of collective goods. And they see a connection, that Hobbes and Hume do not recognize, between the satisfaction of basic human needs—the provision of "political goods" in Pennock's sense—and a particular kind of government: one in which the citizens themselves play a large part in the making of decisions about collective goods.

IV

It may seem strange to bring Aristotle's name into a discussion of political obligation, since he never addresses himself to the question in the sense familiar to us. He never assumes that the individual has the option of membership in the polis; a formal theory of obligation positing an isolated individual would strike him as absurd. However, the highly individualistic theories of obligation offered in the seventeenth and eighteenth centuries do not provide the only way to talk about obedience as an obligation. Aristotle also uses an argument that relates obedience to political performance and gives us a useful antidote to the extreme individualism of Hobbes.

At the opening of the *Politics,* Aristotle argues that the polis is one of the species association, and that this implies several things about the political system. In the first place, in Aristotle's teleological universe, all associations have an end. Therefore, political associations also have an end or peculiar good. The end of the political association, the most inclusive of all, is the most inclusive of goods, the good human life. For Aristotle, this means that a polity provides the same kinds of goods that Hobbes discussed— security, a common agreement about values, and a common concept of justice. But Aristotle also believed, unlike Hobbes, that a polity should have a more general political good as its aim, the provision of the "good life" in a wider sense than Hobbes would have endorsed. For Hobbes, the task of government was to provide a framework of rules and common values within which individuals could pursue a more commodious life. Aristotle also believed that in a healthy polity, each individual would be able to pursue the good life as that individual conceived it. But Aristotle wished the polity to take a more active part in shaping that concept of the "good life," and also assumed that more collective goods were essential to the good life than Hobbes would have thought proper.[17]

Aristotle argues, secondly, that the polis is one of that class of associations which exists by nature. Political life is natural to man; man is by nature a *politikon zoon.* Finally, Aristotle argues that any compound is composed of a ruling element and a ruled, and that the same two factors are to be found in a political association.[18]

From these three fundamental Aristotelian assertions, we can derive our argument to obligation from the provision of political goods or the satisfaction of human needs. Political association is natural to man; its particular end is the good life, and it is necessary to his achieving the good life. It includes an element whose function it is to rule and one whose function it is to obey.

[17] Aristotle, *Politics,* 1280b–1281a, pp. 138–39; 1252a, p. 1; 1278b, p. 128; and 1323a–1324b, pp. 326–33.
[18] *Politics,* 1252a–1253a, pp. 1–8.

In order for the political association to be maintained, each element must behave in the appropriate manner. Those charged with ruling must make the decisions, and those who are ruled must accept the decisions and carry them out.

Since Aristotle did not look at this matter from the viewpoint of the individual decision-maker, it would be distorting his argument to say that this adds up to a theory of obligation in the sense of the individual duty to obey. But it is surely a theory of political obligation in the sense that concerns us here: it describes a pattern of association fundamentally characterized by authority and obedience. The association works properly only if both functions are exercised. Obedience is the obverse of authority, the necessary and proper response to authority, what is *owing* to authority to make the association work.[19]

Thus far Aristotle is in agreement with Hobbes and Hume, but from this point the arguments are very different. Hobbes and Hume posit the individual duty to obey and the sovereign's right to govern, and rigidly maintain the polarity between ruler and ruled. Aristotle, in contrast to Hobbes and with greater precision than Hume, argues that not all associations that look like political associations really deserve the name. The properly functioning polity has two distinguishing marks, according to Aristotle.

First, a true political association is composed of equals, rather than a naturally superior and naturally inferior class. One of the distinguishing factors about a political compound, as opposed to other authority relationships, is that the ruling and ruled elements are offices or roles, not permanent natural categories. A citizen is one who participates in political life, who shares political power, not simply one who acquiesces in its use or enjoys its benefits. Therefore, in a healthy polity, all members regularly go through the transition from ruler to ruled.

Second, Aristotle argues that only constitutions directed toward the common interest—that is, the good life for all citizens—are right ones. Those that consider only the personal interest of

19 In the *De Regimine Principum* of St. Thomas, which is in many instances simply a gloss upon Aristotle, the similarities between the Aristotelian argument and our theory deriving obligation from function become even more explicit. See *Aquinas: Selected Political Writings*, ed, d'Entrèves (Oxford: Blackwell, 1954), pp. 5-7; and the passages in the *Summa Theologica* concerning obedience and its limits, pp. 177-79.

the rulers are perverted or faulty. This means that only those political systems constructed so that the rulers direct their efforts toward providing collective goods and toward enriching the citizens' way of life, instead of concentrating on the rulers' own narrow interests, really deserve to be called political associations. And since each polity is characterized by a different conception of the good life, this requirement means that the rulers must devote their attention to providing the collective goods necessary for the attainment of the good life *as it is understood by* the members of that polity—not some abstract, universalized conception of the good life.

After establishing these two basic principles, much of the rest of Aristotle's *Politics* is devoted to discussing ways in which various forms of government approach or deviate from this second standard. His argument for the particular form of mixed state that he calls the polity is precisely that it most easily approximates the standard. This is because, in his theory, the notion of the common interest is intricately connected with the notion of justice.[20] Any particular economic class or group of power-claimants in a state can have only a partial conception of justice—i.e., only a partial, group interest—not a grasp of the interest of the whole. Each of the power-claimants also brings particular contributions to the business of governing—the judgment of the many, the wisdom of the few. Allowing all groups to take part in the making of decisions, then, is the surest way to ensure that the common interest will be regarded, that a complete rather than a partial perspective on justice will be obtained.[21]

It is clear that Aristotle's two basic axioms about the marks of a true political association are closely related. In order for the common interest to be attained, it is not absolutely necessary that all citizens have a hand in governing. It is conceivable that one good man or a few good men could attain a complete perspective and perform the business of governing just as well. But it is much more likely that the common interest will be realized if all

[20] *Politics*, 1282b, p. 150: "The good in the sphere of politics is justice; and justice consists in what tends to promote the common interest."
[21] *Politics*, 1280a, pp. 135–6; see also 1281 a-b on the advantages of involving the many in the process of deliberation.

voices are heard. The regular exchange between ruling and being ruled is not only the natural condition for equals and desirable because political participation is itself part of the best kind of life; such an arrangement is also instrumental in securing the good life for all.

There are several reasons why such participation is instrumental. The first is the one we have just discussed: only if all partial interests are heard will the full requirements of the common interest emerge. Second, unless large numbers of citizens actually concern themselves with politics, it is very difficult to ensure that the magistrates, the few who are left to govern, will not look to their private advantage instead of concentrating upon working for the common good. And third, if citizens are excluded from political participation and feel themselves disfranchised and disregarded, they may withhold loyalty from the regime, and the existence of the polity will be endangered.[22] Aristotle believed that the most fruitful participation that citizens in general could engage in was as members of the deliberative body designed to deal with the common affairs of the polity and to appoint and oversee the magistrates. In this way, the talents of the ordinary man en masse could best be utilized and every man could regularly go through the transition from ruling to being ruled: as a member of the assembly, he was in office; as subject to its deliberations and decrees, he was in obedience.

In sum, Aristotle's theory tells us that only the polity that has constitutional arrangements ensuring that it looks to the good life for all will perform its function, providing political goods, correctly. This is not the same as saying that only democracies provide good governments, or that I am obliged to obey only a government to which I have consented. But it restates in a different way what is true and useful about such arguments. According to Aristotle, the general good can normally be obtained only when the voices of all members of a polity are heard in the making of its rules and policies. Allowing all citizens to participate in, or substantially influence at some point the decision-making process is the best way to ensure that the views and needs of all will be taken into account.

[22] *Politics*, 1308b, pp. 267–268; and 1281b, p. 145.

V

Rousseau writes as though he had Aristotle in mind when he constructs a strikingly parallel argument in the *Contrat social.* Like Aristotle, Rousseau argues that the political situation is essential to the good life, because participation in political society brings into being justice and moral activity and creates an order of values, a better, more human life for man. In political society, Rousseau goes on to say,

> [man's] faculties are so stimulated and developed, his ideas are so extended, his feelings so ennobled, and his whole soul so uplifted, that, did not the abuses of this new condition often degrade him below that which he left, he would be bound to bless continually the happy moment which took him from it for ever, and, instead of a stupid and unimaginative animal, made him an intelligent being and a man.[23]

Now it is important to note that in this passage Rousseau introduces a possibility absent in Aristotle: that the political situation, if it does not work properly, degrades man instead of ennobling him. Rousseau, then, stands with Hume against Hobbes in arguing that the "new condition" does not automatically work toward the good life; the political situation can brutalize man as well as endow him with true humanity. Therefore, Rousseau's search in the *Contrat social* is for an explanation of what makes the social order legitimate, which for him means: what kinds of social arrangements ennoble rather than brutalize? And in this search, Rousseau seems to have been guided by Aristotle's distinction between a true and perverted political association.

At the very outset, Rousseau affirms that force cannot create obligation; we are obliged to obey only legitimate powers. He then argues that a legitimate political association is one in which the general will is sovereign, formed of the mutually committed wills of the individuals who compose the social order. After

---

23 Rousseau, *Social Contract*, I:viii, 18. The entire transition from the state of nature to the sociopolitical state is discussed at greater length in the first version of the *Contrat social*, I:ii.

describing the formation of the sovereign general will, Rousseau writes:

> In order then that the social compact may not be an empty formula, it tacitly includes the undertaking, which alone can give force to the rest, that whoever refuses to obey the general will shall be compelled to do so by the whole body. This means nothing less than that he will be forced to be free; for this is the condition which, by giving each citizen to his country, secures him against all personal dependence. In this lies the key to the working of the political machine; this alone legitimizes civil undertakings, which, without it, would be absurd, tyrannical, and liable to the most frightful abuses.[24]

In this passage, Rousseau is using contract-language to argue that we are obliged to obey the sovereign general will, because otherwise the whole political association would collapse. In other words, we have here another variant of the argument to obligation from the provision of political goods: the political situation is fundamental to the good life for man; in order to make the political machine work, we must obey the sovereign; if we are remiss and fail to obey, then we can logically, by the terms of the association, be forced to do so. But Rousseau is quite clear that we cannot *rightfully* be forced to obey just any government: we are obliged to obey only a government endowed with authority by the general will, and responsible to that sovereign will. Only the fact that it is the general will that coerces us legitimates this coercion; otherwise it would be absurd and tyrannical. As Rousseau says explicitly at a later point in his argument, if a government once usurps the sovereignty from the general will, its subjects may then be forced, but are no longer obliged, to obey.[25]

---

[24] *Social Contract*, I:vii, 18. To say that government X is legitimate, and to say that I am obliged to obey government X, is to make two statements which have overlapping meanings, but do not, for most political theorists, mean precisely the same thing. The connection between legitimacy and obligation is a complex one, and therefore I have avoided this particular tangential problem by not using the term *legitimacy* except in this discussion of Rousseau, since his basic point is that the two terms are synonymous.

[25] *Social Contract*, III, ix, 86: the French reads "forcés mais non pas obligés d'obéir."

Rousseau is arguing, just as Hume does, that we are obliged to obey government because it makes possible a better life for all, and therefore are obliged to obey only if it makes possible that better life. But Rousseau goes beyond Hume to say that only a government based upon the general will can perform its task, making possible a better life; and therefore we are obliged to obey only a government based upon the general will.

According to Rousseau there are two reasons why only a government resting on the general will is legitimate. These are exactly the same two points Aristotle makes about the characteristics of a true political association. First, Rousseau believes it to be essential to the good life for man that the individual remain free, in the sense of free from subjection to the will of another human being. The only way to maintain this freedom in political society, he argues, is to set up the particular form of association that creates the general will, in which each "may still obey himself alone, and remain as free as before." In such an association, "each man, in giving himself to all, gives himself to nobody."[26] In this argument, Rousseau simply gives a new connotation to Aristotle's point about political life involving ruling and being ruled in turn, as opposed to any form of unnatural permanent subjection. For Rousseau, this becomes the following: "The essence of the body politic lies in the reconciliation of obedience and liberty, and the words subject and Sovereign are identical correlatives the idea of which meets in the single word 'citizen.' "[27]

Second, only a government based upon the general will creates the obligation to obey because

> the general will alone can direct the State according to the object for which it was instituted, i.e., the common good: for if the clashing of particular interests made the establishment of societies necessary, the agreement of these very interests made it possible. The common element in these different interests is what forms the social tie; and were there no point of agreement between them all, no society

26 *Ibid.*, I, vi, 14.
27 *Ibid.*, III, xiii, 91; *cf.* Hobbes: "in the act of our submission consisteth both our *obligation* and our *liberty*."

> could exist. It is solely on the basis of this common interest
> that every society should be governed.[28]

In other words, the general will is, among other things, a piece of
political machinery for the consideration of collective goods. It is
the intersection or common denominator of particular perspectives on the common good; the will for the general good in the
particular wills taken together.

In order to appreciate what Rousseau does with this theme of
interest and why it is important to his theory of obligation, let us
go back for a moment and see how Hobbes and Hume use the
concept of interest. Hobbes tells us that among most political
creatures the common good is realized by the simple expedient of
each individual's pursuing his private benefit.[29] But because of
man's particular desires and needs, this simple equation does not
hold good in human society. A common power must be set up
among men to "direct their actions to the common benefit,"
which means that the natural harmony obtaining in other societies must be approximated in human society by artificial means.
Since this is the major task of the sovereign power, it follows that
the best government is that in which "the public and private
interest are most closely united." He or they who govern will
have private interests of their own; and since these private
interests will inevitably be their primary concern, the public
interest is best advanced where it is most nearly identical with
the private interest of the ruler. According to Hobbes, this is the
great advantage of monarchy as a form of government, for upon
his conception of a monarchy, it appeared evident that in monarchy "the private interest is the same with the public. The
riches, power, and honor of a monarch arise only from the
riches, strength, and reputation of his subjects."[30]

Hume also argues that good government depends upon the
identity of the private and the public interest, but he puts the

[28] *Social Contract*, II, i, 23.

[29] *Leviathan*, 111–12; see *De Cive* V;5 for a further discussion of this same
theme.

[30] *Leviathan*, 122–23; *cf.* Rousseau's reflections on this matter at the
beginning of Book III of the *Social Contract*, and particularly his acerbic
criticism of the Hobbesian assumption, p. 70.

matter in rather a different way. According to Hume, the institution of government is ingenious precisely because it makes it in the private interest of a few people to work for and protect the public interest shared by all. Those who are set up in positions of authority are motivated by the most direct and powerful passions of immediate self-interest to uphold justice, arbitrate conflicts, and promote projects for the common good. By taking office they identify with the perspective of the public and have a far stronger interest in doing their job well than in taking the viewpoint of any particular interest that comes into conflict with the requirements of the common interest.[31]

According to Rousseau, this is too risky an assumption upon which to build a political association. It is not enough to rely upon the optimistic assertion that our governors will recognize the identity of their private interests and the common interest, or even to expect that they will be led by their private interest to provide collective goods. Rousseau believed that there is only one sure method for realizing the common good. First, the views of all must be taken into account in major decisions concerning the provision of collective goods. And second, just as the citizen who ignores his obligation to obey must be forced to be free, so the governors who do not recognize their responsibility to follow the dictates of the general will must be brought to account. For both these tasks, Rousseau, like Aristotle, believed that the best institution was the sovereign, deliberative body of all the members of the political association. This body should be charged with making laws, which in Rousseau's theory meant giving concrete expression to the general will; and the same assembly should also appoint and examine the work of the government or civil ministers.[32] The sovereignty of law and the responsibility of the government to the governed will provide a double guarantee that the government works for the common good.

VI

We have argued that Hobbes and Hume provide an answer to the question about general political obligation that

---

[31] *Treatise*, II, 238.
[32] *Social Contract*, II, vi, 35; III, xvii–xviii, 98–101.

holds for all governments: we ought to obey government because of, and in order to make possible, the benefits it brings us, benefits we desire and need as human beings in society. These benefits we have called collective goods, and we have argued that members of society share a common interest in the provision of these goods.

On the basis of theories developed by Aristotle and Rousseau, we have then argued that governments that involve a large measure of popular participation in the making of decisions about collective goods are more likely to do a good job at satisfying the needs of a society than those that do not. It is not impossible that an aristocratic government, without significant popular participation, could provide collective goods which satisfied the needs of its people and do so efficiently and fairly. But Aristotle and Rousseau demonstrate that government by an elite is less likely to be successful in this than a government which relies upon popular participation, for several reasons.

First, popular participation provides a unique guarantee that leaders actually do work to provide collective goods, instead of concentrating on their own private interests. No other method of control in this matter has ever been devised that is nearly as effective as the responsibility of the governors to the governed and broad popular participation in the supervision of the work of government.

Second, according to Aristotle and Rousseau, political participation is itself a good for a human being. If one accepts this as a basic human value, then one must agree that the range of political goods, in Pennock's sense, cannot be complete unless there is some opportunity for the citizens to play a role in the making of decisions governing their lives.

Finally, popular participation in the determination of the kinds of collective goods to be provided in a society is the simplest and surest way to determine what a people actually needs and how these needs can most appropriately be satisfied. It would be misleading to say simply that the democratic theory is right, and the aristocratic theory wrong. There are several senses in which the elitists are right in saying that a people's leaders "know better than the people themselves what is good for them." The kinds and range of collective goods that people will support will probably be strongly affected by their shortsighted unwillingness to pay the costs for those goods. A people's wants may be uncertain and inchoate until they are offered meaningful choices about collective goods by their leaders. But these are arguments for the necessity of there being a government, in order that collective goods be provided in a society, not arguments which prove that that government must be an elite uncontrolled by the people themselves. All four of our theorists, and many others, have pointed out that in order for the common interests of a society to be served, there must be a particular body charged with attending to those interests. Collective goods cannot and will not be provided without such a body to give an authoritative coordination of effort and to allocate costs for public goods and enforce payment, since there is no direct connection between enjoying benefits and paying costs in the case of such goods.

Yet it is still important that members of a society who are to benefit from collective goods have a major say in what those goods are to be. This is true even if one rejects the extreme utilitarian argument equating what is good with what is desired. For the decisions of any elite will reflect the values given special weight by the particular segment of society from which the elite is drawn—the rich, the wellborn, the talented, the enlightened, the virtuous, or the possessors of revealed truth, religious or ideological. And even if an elite could somehow be selected that was representative of a society in every sense except one—that the members of that elite possessed the skills requisite for decision-making in a specially high degree—there are good arguments that the complexities of political decisions in modern society are such that all the alternatives cannot be encompassed by one or a few decision-makers, and that more efficient results will be obtained if decisions involve a large amount of participation by members of a society.

It was one of Aristotle's major contributions to political thought that he stressed the importance of both the wisdom of the few and the views of the many in the determination of the common interest. In this, he saw further than many who came after him. Hobbes relied too heavily upon the rulers' awareness of the identity between their private interests and the public interest, and Hume put too much faith in the "role perspective" of the magistrates once in office. Rousseau, though he developed some of Aristotle's ideas more fully and related them specifically to the problem of obligation, was too suspicious of the interaction between leaders and followers, individuals and groups; and he put unwarranted emphasis on the isolated individual's understanding of the common good. Aristotle, more than any of these, had a sense of the importance of the *process* of determining the common interest, a process necessarily involving all members of a polity working together. He was aware of the importance of leadership in decision-making; but he was equally aware that no elite can have as vivid or complete a sense of the common interest as leaders and people taken together, each offering a different perspective on that interest. And thus he, of all our theorists, most clearly indicated the kind of government likely to perform its functions well, and therefore to deserve our allegiance and have a valid claim upon our obedience.

CIVIL DISOBEDIENCE

13

CIVIL DISOBEDIENCE:
ITS OCCASIONS AND LIMITS

JAMES LUTHER ADAMS

In a day when an increasing number of people, especially students and blacks, are speaking of the present "transition from dissent to resistance" as the advent of the second American Revolution, there could scarcely be a more timely subject for discussion than civil disobedience. As a sanction for this dissent and resistance an appeal is made to the first American Revolution, to Jefferson and Locke, and also to Thoreau and Gandhi.

To a theologian, civil disobedience suggests the names of figures from an earlier period, for example, John Knox, John Lilburne, or George Fox. Even these names, however, come from a late period in the history of Christianity. From its very beginning Christianity was an outlaw religion committed to disobedience to the "world." The slogan "Christianity is illegal" may be traced back to the second-century figure Tertullian, a lawyer by training. By the time of the second century something like civil disobedience was already an old story, for the Christian group had long been considered an "illicit" religious association in the Roman empire; its transcendental and transpolitical orientation had brought the Christians into radical conflict with civic religion. Early Christian martyrdom was occasioned in the main by this rejection of civic religion. A sanction for this disobedience was found in the familiar axioms of the New Testament, "Render unto Caesar that which is Caesar's and unto God that which is God's" and "Man must obey God rather than men." Similar disobedience appears in the prophetic tradition of the Old Testament and is symbolized by the narrative in the Book of Daniel about Shadrach, Meshach, and Abednego, who were cast into the fiery furnace by Nebuchadnezzar. In Judaism and Christianity much of the history of the theory of disobedience to civic authorities could be documented by examining in succession through the centuries the sermons and commentaries on the Book of Daniel. On the other hand, there has been a much more influential and opposing tradition of obedience stemming from Jewish respect for law and from the Pauline admonition of Romans 13, "Let every person be subject to the governing authorities. For there is no authority except from God, and those that exist have been instituted by God."

It must be recognized, moreover, that insofar as disobedience was sanctioned or practiced by Christians in the New Testament period and in early Christianity it was scarcely in accord with modern conceptions of civil disobedience. We can confirm this judgment only if we have in mind a clear definition of the modern phenomenon.

A synoptic view of modern civil disobedience yields some such definition as the following. Civil disobedience is (1) a nonviolent, (2) public violation (3) of a specific law or set of laws, or of a policy of government having the effect of law, (4) which expresses a sense of justice in a civil society of cooperation among equals and (5) which is generally undertaken in the name of a presumed higher authority than the law in question (6) as a last resort (7) for the purpose of changing the law and (8) with the intention of accepting the penalty which the prevailing law imposes. Here we have a conception of disobedience considerably broader in range and purpose than that found in early Christianity.[1]

Certain features that are implicit in this definition should be mentioned at the outset. Civil disobedience is occasioned by a major grievance that calls for immediate protest in the name of justice. In a democratic society it reflects the indisposition to wait upon the slow processes of the ballot box and other political procedures that bring about change in the law; at the same time the civil disobedient is willing to be subject to legal police action and he respects just court procedures. In general, then, civil disobedience presupposes a general acceptance of legal authority, due process, and the legitimacy of the legal system as a whole. That is, it aims to function within the framework of a legal system. Yet, it expresses a sense of moral obligation to disobey a specific law for the sake of conscience and of improving the law and thus of serving the public good. In this sense it is conscientious disobedience. The law against which it protests may or may not be deemed constitutional. In many instances civil disobedience aims to test the constitutionality of the constitutional assumptions of a law or policy. In this respect it belongs to a large class of litigation and thus approaches the character of normal procedure.

There is, however, another type of civil disobedience, that which obtains when an individual or group violates a valid law with which it has no quarrel but does so in order to call attention to and to protest against some other law or policy which may or may not be related to the law which is being violated. In a loose way this kind of disobedience is sometimes called indirect civil disobedience. A major purpose of this indirect disobedience is to gain effective publicity for the protest. This motive usually attaches also to direct, civil disobedience. In this respect there is

---

[1] According to the definition given here, the disobedience of the early Christians was civil disobedience only in a narrow sense. Although they did refuse to pay religious homage with incense and wine to Caesar's image, the purpose of their disobedience was not to improve the law; they thought the end of the age was at hand. Nor did they attempt to promote the freedom of other religious associations. Yet, they did express a nonviolent protest against a demonic state and against a civic religion. At the same time the means were not available to them to undertake to change the law. Only in restricted ways, then, can early Christian disobedience be considered civil disobedience as the latter is understood today.

generally a dramatic or melodramatic element in all civil disobedience. If it is to affect public opinion and to change the law it must be able to rivet attention on the evil that is under attack.

Another aspect of civil disobedience deserves to be stressed. Ordinarily, civil disobedience expresses a sense of justice in a civil society of cooperation among equals. Two important presuppositions or implications attach to this view. First, the principle of reversibility: the civil disobedient presupposes that his demand for justice possesses a universal validity and therefore holds that it would be appropriate for other citizens or associations to undertake similar civil disobedience. Second, civil disobedience presupposes the right to protest and the right to participate in the shaping of public policy. In this respect it is an appeal to the principle of the consent of the governed.

On the other hand, we should recognize that a certain religious type of civil disobedient is not primarily concerned with the purpose and motives we have mentioned. He is concerned rather to "bear witness" to a set of values which he holds to be quite incompatible with the ways of the world. He may be willing to undergo severe suffering for the sake of his faith, but he does not expect to improve the law. In his view the world is under the control of the principalities and powers of evil. Accordingly, his disobedience is almost "systemic," but it is not the sort of disobedience that looks toward the creation of a better society. Nor does he appeal to the state to achieve its essential character and purpose or to overcome the inconsistencies between its best and its worst laws. A member of Jehovah's Witnesses, for example, in refusing to salute the flag, has no hope for a better world or for improvement of the state under the present dispensation. He looks for a new dispensation to be inaugurated by the apocalyptic action of God. In general, we may say that this kind of disobedience has been characteristic of groups which Ernst Troeltsch has called "withdrawing sects."

In certain instances, what appears to be civil disobedience in one legal context may be viewed as civil obedience in a different legal context. In the civil-rights movement in the United States disobedience was often undertaken in protest against a municipal ordinance or a state statute. But this ordinance or statute was itself held to be in contradiction to the basic law of the land, that is, to federal legislation or to decisions of the Supreme Court. Therefore this type of disobedience is ambiguous in character, for it claims to be also a form of obedience to law.[2]

Our definition of civil disobedience may be clarified if we further indicate what it is not. It does not resort to force. It is not clandestine evasion of the law, as is ordinary crime. It does not conceal the evidence but offers it to the authorities. Nor does it employ the strategy of evasion which deliberately attempts to postpone the application of the law. Civil disobedience, moreover, is not a "systemic" disobedience, a total rejection of the legal system; nor does it aim to promote general lawlessness; nor is it anarchy or conspiracy (as ordinarily understood). It is not infidelity to law, for it willingly accepts punishment at the hands of the law, and it is not merely an expression of individual frustration, for it aims to change the law and to contribute to the good of the society. Motivated by a sense of justice, it is not undertaken for merely personal advantage or privilege.

It may be useful to "place" civil disobedience as defined here on a spectrum of disobedience. It may be distinguished from resistance (*Widerstand*) which may be in part clandestine; this form of resistance appears in a totalitarian society where no legal or open organizational means for securing change in the law exists. Civil disobedience is ordinarily distinguished from military disobedience (though a change in definition appears to be taking place today in this respect); from insurrection, the use of collective violence for a specific end; from rebellion, the forceful attempt to overthrow the social or legal order; from anarchism, a "systemic" rejection of all government as evil; and from dissent, a protest that does not entail disobedience. And in the United States today it is to be distinguished from religious conscientious objection to all war, an objection that was previously a form of civil disobedience but which is now legally defined as permissible. To be sure, the definition is still being contested, toward the end of broadening the concept of the "religious" grounds of conscience.

---

[2]For a discussion of this form of nonobservance and of related issues see Charles L. Black, "The Problem of the Compatibility of Civil Disobedience with American Institutions of Government," 43 *Texas Law Review*, 492–506. It should be pointed out here that although Martin Luther King's civil disobedience in general fits the description in the text, he did disobey also in defiance of a state court injunction.

These distinctions, if sound, are not in widest commonality familiar. Apart from technical legal writings, the pertinence of making them is of fairly recent vintage, though to be sure the distinctions have been recognized in previous periods. It is a striking fact that in one of the most widely used books in Protestant circles, John C. Bennett's *Christians and the State,* published in 1958, civil disobedience is not discussed.[3] Within the next few years, however, the whole question rapidly came to the fore in connection with the civil-rights movement. In 1964 a National Study Conference on Church and State met to formulate "Advice to the National Council of Churches and Its Member Denominations," and in its report it articulated the essential ingredients of civil disobedience in the following statement:

> In a state in which redress for wrong exists, and legal and organizational means for change are normally available, the Christian may nevertheless find certain laws and customs intolerably unjust. When the governmental processes are not realistically adequate to correct them, resistance [or, more precisely, we should say *disobedience*] to civil authority is a valid course for Christians to take. Such action includes the willingness to accept the consequences. While affirming his responsibility to obey civil authority generally, a Christian may well serve justice by disobeying a particular unjust law. Disobedience to civil authority in this context is intended to serve the government, to serve the good it has accomplished, and to move it another step toward becoming a more just institution.

It should be added here that 13 out of 245 delegates to this conference recorded their dissent to the whole section of the report from which the above paragraph is quoted.

An important issue that is not taken into account in this report or in my definition above is the question of whether the law that is disobeyed in civil disobedience is considered to be formally valid or is considered to be invalid because it is unjust. The latter view was held by Thomas Aquinas. For him, the law must be just and in harmony with the common good; otherwise,

---

[3] See, however, Prof. Bennett's article, "The Place of Civil Disobedience," *Christianity and Crisis,* XXVII, No. 22 (December 25, 1967), 299–302.

it is devoid of the nature of law. If the former issue is raised, that is, if the claim is made that the law in question is not formally valid, we encounter civil disobedience of a somewhat different sort. Some of the citizens who today engage in civil disobedience in the face of the administration's policy in Vietnam claim that the policy is not formally valid, in the sense that it is a violation of treaties or that it has not received proper approval by the Senate.[4]

A more fundamental question than that of the legal or moral validity or invalidity of the law must also be taken into account. In some quarters all civil disobedience as such is rejected in principle, as serving no conceivable public good. Here the authority to which civil disobedience makes appeal—for example, a higher law or conscience—is radically called in question. The civil disobedient is contemned even though he declares his willingness to accept punishment at the hands of the law.

A different formulation of the objection to civil disobedience as such is the charge that it is nothing but lawlessness. For example, Judge Charles E. Wyzanski, Jr., in an article discussing civil disobedience to the draft, asserts: "Every time that a law is disobeyed by even a man whose motive is solely ethical, in the sense that it is responsive to deep moral conviction, there are unfortunate consequences. He himself becomes more prone to disobey laws for which he has no profound repugnance. He sets an example for others who may not have his pure motives. He weakens the fabric of society."[5] Here Judge Wyzanski says that he agrees with G. E. Moore, who in *Principia Ethica* concludes that "in most instances civil disobedience is immoral," and he goes on to say that a dramatic precursor of Moore was Socrates, who "swallowed hemlock . . . rather than refuse obedience to the laws of the city-state which had formed and protected him."

These formulations are no doubt intended to stress the obligation to obey the law, but they leave much to be desired insofar as they imply an absolute and unqualified obligation to obey even

---

[4] For a discussion of civil disobedience in protest against a law or policy that is allegedly unconstitutional, for example, the draft law and the war in Vietnam, and also for a discussion pro and con of government policy with respect to this type of disobedience, see Ronald Dworkin, "On Not Prosecuting Civil Disobedience," *New York Review of Books*, June 6, 1968.

[5] Charles E. Wyzanski, Jr., "On Civil Disobedience," *Atlantic*, 221, No. 2 (February 1968), 59.

in the face of tyranny. The formulations raise other questions, too. Why, for example, should one point only to the possibility that civil disobedience may lead to other forms of disobedience which are irresponsible? Why not assume also the likelihood that the high moral seriousness of authentic civil disobedience as a public protest will enhance elements of moral seriousness in the community? The civil disobedient's acceptance of legal punishment by reason of his conscientious disobedience might be expected to enhance rather than to erode moral seriousness in the community. This consequence is by no means a weakening of the "fabric of society." Of course there are no guarantees in these matters, no more than with respect to the use and abuse of a razor.

These considerations lead to other questions about Judge Wyzanski's formulations regarding the weakening of the "fabric of society." A danger not taken into account by his argument is the danger that the fabric of society at a given time may actually be too tightly woven as a consequence of demonic repression or the apathetic routinization of conscience. In this kind of situation the civil disobedient holds that his protest is a public and not a secret protest against *one* law or policy and that by his remaining law-abiding in other regards and by his accepting punishment for his disobedience he shows his respect for law and helps to maintain the fabric, and yet that as a last resort his disobedience aims to improve the law and to rectify the fabric of society. The civil disobedient, and anyone else for that matter, may also rightly claim that what obtains under the rubric of law in the society often turns out to be only camouflage for egregious class or race interest or for jingoistic and destructive patriotism. He may also claim that, far from weakening the fabric of society, authentic civil disobedience is a means of reducing the demand for rebellious and violent protest against the law. Actually, the term "fabric of society" is somewhat misleading insofar as it implies that the complex of law and obligation in any society is a neat, readily identifiable package.[6]

Probably none of these arguments will influence the radical critic of civil disobedience unless he recognizes the bludgeonings

---

[6] On this point see our later extensive quotation from Joseph L. Sax (pp. 318–319).

of conscience in a patently intolerable situation that demonstrates for a protracted period that it cannot be effectively challenged by normal political procedures. It would be instructive for grasping the full force of the critic's argument if one could know whether he holds that John Lilburne or George Fox or Gandhi or Martin Luther King, Jr., should never have practiced civil disobedience—that is, whether these civil disobedients may be properly characterized as only having weakened the "fabric of society."

The claim that civil disobedience constitutes mere lawlessness and the subversion of legitimate authority sometimes takes the form of simply identifying it with crime. For example, United States Senator Sam Ervin, protesting against a statement on civil disobedience by the Methodist General Conference (1964), declared that it was prompted more by "impatience than reason," and then he went on to say: "I make an affirmation which is subject to no exception or modification. The right of clergymen and civil rights agitators to disobey laws they deem unjust is exactly the same as the right of the arsonist, the burglar, the murderer, the rapist and the thief to disobey the laws forbidding arson, burglary, murder, rape and theft." It is sufficient to indicate the indiscriminate character of this declaration if we observe the occasions that have called forth civil disobedience.

The occasions for civil disobedience have been numerous. They include opposition to slavery, to suffrage restricted by race or sex, to prohibition of alcoholic beverages, to compulsory school attendance, to vaccination, to military conscription, to taxation for war purposes, to war and the preparations for nuclear and biological warfare, to laws against collective bargaining, to race discrimination in education, housing, and employment, and to conscription for a particular war. These occasions for civil disobedience are obviously of a quite different character from arson, murder, and rape. For one thing, the latter are not acts of conscience.

A similar variety may be observed if we consider the specific sanctions and the scope of these different occasions for civil disobedience. In some instances the civil disobedient appeals to a sanction of morals beyond (or "higher" than) the law or to "the best elements in the American tradition." In other instances the sanction appealed to is explicitly theological; in yet others it is religious in a broader, humanistic sense. With respect to scope: in some instances the civil disobedient seeks to change a law that directly affects people in all classes; in others he is concerned to correct injustices that obtain for particular groups or classes—in our day especially for deprived groups such as the blacks and other ethnic minorities.

Another kind of classification is worth noting. If we consider the ethical issues that have given rise to the forms of civil disobedience listed above, we find that the specific goals of protest are few in number. It is true that in most of these forms of disobedience the protection of human dignity and the promotion of self-determination are involved, but the social and personal values may be reduced to five, namely, equality, due process, the rejection of certain types of violence authorized by the state, the protection of private morality, and certain eccentric religious sensitivities. In the main, however, the issues at stake have been the values of equality and nonviolence. As against the present war in Vietnam, civil disobedience seeks to restore peace and also the honor of the nation. Civil disobedience in protest against slavery or race discrimination is undertaken in the name of equality and due process, as is civil disobedience for the sake of a broader suffrage or for the sake of collective bargaining. Here the demand for equality is in large measure a demand for power in the sense of capacity to participate in the making of decisions regarding public policy. The protest against the prohibition of alcoholic beverages, however, is motivated by the desire to protect private morality against legal enforcement. Opposition to vaccination and school attendance rests upon unique religious presuppositions. But conscientious objection to military conscription and to participation in a particular war represents a protest against what is considered to be mass violence at the hands of the state.

CIVIL DISOBEDIENCE AND THE DOCTRINE OF THE JUST WAR

The references to violence point to a striking feature of civil disobedience in general, indeed to a somewhat surprising feature that has not been noticed hitherto. If we ask for the tests by which authentic civil disobedience is to be measured, we find that some of the most pertinent tests are similar to those employed in the doctrine of the just war. The tests are pertinent for our purpose despite the fact that in many quarters the doctrine of the just war is emphatically held to be outmoded.

It is not surprising that the similarity has not been noted, for we encounter here a curious paradox. The tests of the just war relate to the norms for the use of violence; at the same time they can serve as the norms of authentic civil disobedience, even though civil disobedience often represents a protest against violence. How is one to explain this paradox? Perhaps the answer is that both war and civil disobedience deviate from the normal procedures that prevail between states or between the individual and the state.

The norms traditionally employed in just-war doctrine have been the following: (1) The cause must be just. (2) War must be the last resort. (3) War must be made by a lawful public authority. (4) There must be a reasonable hope of victory. (5) The intention of the government engaging in war must be free from mere hatred, greed, cruelty, or glee. (6) There must be due proportion between the good probably to be accomplished and the probable evil effects. (7) The war must be rightly conducted through the use of right means.

In the definition of civil disobedience set forth at the beginning of this paper some of these norms have been mentioned. Here we shall consider these and other features insofar as they are analogous to the norms of just war. This consideration will bring to the fore certain aspects of the question regarding proper authority and of the question regarding the circumstances under which or the limits within which civil disobedience is justifiable.

First, the cause must be just. In authentic civil disobedience the citizen appeals in the name of justice (fairness, equality, self-determination, due process). This is true not only in the sense that he attempts to correct an injustice but also in the sense that in some instances he hopes to bring about the redefinition of the content of justice. He does this by claiming to appeal from the less-informed conscience to a better-informed conscience. His appeal is ostensibly an appeal in the name of a universal value. Therefore, the authentic civil disobedient recognizes that others besides himself are in normal circumstances entitled to do what

he himself is doing. Indeed, he hopes that others will lend
support to his challenge to injustice.

It must be admitted that the conscientious objector will often
appear to be arbitrary in his claims. He may even elicit the
charge that he is pathologically conditioned to be a mere public-
ity-seeker. But in these respects the civil disobedient is not
unique. Anyone who turns to normal political procedures to
effect change may have to face similar charges. In the long run
public opinion and due process must be relied upon to determine the issue in an open society.

The second criterion of the just war is the claim that war is the
last resort, other means of securing justice and peace having
failed. In both military policy and civil disobedience the concept
of "last resort" is a weasel concept. The appeal to it is therefore
always subject to vigorous disagreement. Here the difference
between war and civil disobedience is of crucial significance. The
civil disobedient can be brought to book by legal agencies (and
generally the warring state cannot). Indeed, he stands ready to
accept punishment at the hands of these agencies. But this fact
does not clarify the application of the concept.

In support of the claim of "last resort" the civil disobedient
should be able to point to evidence of the fact that the slower
political processes are egregiously ineffective or that immediacy
of decision is necessary. Here the timing of the civil disobedience
becomes important in several ways. The clearest example of the
demand for immediacy of decision is in civil disobedience that
opposes military conscription. In the area of race discrimination
the claim of "last resort" can point to the intolerable delay that
has attended the correction of the evil. Here the civil disobedient
can claim that his disobedience and that of others may help to
accelerate political processes that bring about change in the law
or in the enforcement of the law. Who can deny that the civil
disobedience attending the civil-rights movement has actually
served in many instances to affect legislation regarding civil
rights, or has served to bring about more quickly the enforcement of law that is supposed to protect civil rights? To this
consideration one may add the argument that delay in these
matters could be a stimulus to violence as a last resort. In the
face of this contingency the civil disobedient can claim that in
the long run his disobedience may serve to strengthen confidence

in the legal system by stimulating it to achieve its true ends; in short, he may claim that that it is a nonviolent protest calculated to reduce violence and to increase lawfulness.

One further consideration regarding the claim to "last resort" should be taken into account here. As we have observed, civil disobedience as a last resort presupposes that normal procedures have been tried and have been found to be seriously in default. The civil disobedient is not entitled, however, to make this presupposition if he has not himself participated vigorously in these processes. But even if he has made this effort, he can claim, for example, that the outcome of balloting has been ambiguous and thus has fallen short of presenting a clear mandate. Or he can claim that governmental authorities have refused to obey a mandate or have failed to enforce the law. Or he may be able to assert that normal political processes are not available to him by reason of his not yet being of voting age, yet that the law or policy in question directly affects him. And does not the black likewise the more understandably engage in civil disobedience as a last resort if by law or custom he has not been permitted to participate in the political processes that determine law or policy? And is not the citizen belonging to an ethnic minority to be expected in an open society to turn to civil disobedience as a last resort if majority rule normally ignores or violates his rights? Here the principle of the consent of the governed is at stake.[7] Nothing said here, however, can properly eliminate nonviolence from the criteria of civil disobedience.

The third criterion of the just war is that it must be made by a lawful authority. At first blush this criterion may appear not to be pertinent for testing authentic civil disobedience. Actually, however, it has been the occasion for struggle over a long period of time. Think how horrified the general public was when civil disobedience was first practiced by people claiming the right to

[7] For a somewhat broader interpretation than that which is suggested here see Ralph Conant, "Rioting, Insurrection and Civil Disobedience," *The American Scholar*, XXXVII, No. 3 (Summer 1968). Prof. Conant states that civil disobedience is justified (1) when an oppressed group is deprived of lawful channels for remedying its condition; (2) when government takes or condones actions that are inconsistent with values on which the society and the political system are built; and (3) when a change in law or policy is demanded by social or economic need in the community and the normal procedures of law and politics are inadequate, obstructed, or held captive by antilegal forces.

freedom of religious association or by workers claiming the right to bargain collectively. Civil disobedience in protest against war is still considered in many quarters to be a sign of treason or at least of absence of patriotism, especially when many citizens are risking or giving their lives in war effort. A whole complex of moral and political issues is involved in the examples just cited. But criticism and change in these areas, and also individual responsibility, are impaired if individual conscience must be suppressed. In this context the presupposition that the individual is a legitimate "authority," entitled to demand the consent of the governed, is axiomatic in modern society. Open conflict between perspectives is essential for the maintenance of integrity in the society and in its members. My colleague Professor George Hunston Williams, Hollis Professor of Divinity at Harvard, in an unpublished letter to Pope Paul VI elucidates this view when, in referring to selective rejection of military conscription, he says, "In the present crisis of conscience it is not the Christian Emperor, nor the Christian King, nor even the Christian knight with his consecrated sword but the individual democratic citizen who is ultimately accountable for what constitutes just war." Today, as we shall see, the freedom of association is also at stake. In a democracy the citizen with a conscience is a lawful authority for exercising civil disobedience under the conditions we have been considering. But he must leave it to the legal agencies to determine whether he has misconceived or abused his authority. In doing so he stands ready to be punished.

Reasonable hope for victory, the fourth criterion of the just war, is not easy to apply to either war or civil disobedience. In its initial formulation the criterion intended, among other things, to preclude suicidal war. If we were to apply this aspect of the criterion directly and literally to civil disobedience, the application would not be without pertinence, for suicide has sometimes been resorted to as a desperate measure to register conscientious objection and to draw attention to the evil being protested.

But apart from this application, is the criterion pertinent for assessing civil disobedience? What is the positive meaning of "victory" with respect to civil disobedience? Here we may refer back to the major purpose of civil disobedience. Reasonable hope for victory, then, would mean reasonable hope to change a particular law or policy. If, however, we view the history of civil disobedience in retrospect, we must acknowledge that such a hope must be a long-range hope. In the light of this fact, we should perhaps alter the formulation "reasonable hope for victory" in order to take into account a long process that occurs by stages. The process is one that first requires a change of public opinion. In this process civil disobedience may engender new sensitivities, new prickings of conscience, in the public domain, new sensitivities that move the community in the direction of a more ample sense of justice. Obviously, the translation of a new attitude into new law or new policy generally requires the tedious process of normal political processes. The question, then, regarding reasonable hope for victory, is the question regarding the proper efficacy of civil disobedience. And the answer to the question is that civil disobedience is efficacious when it contributes to the process we have just described.

To be sure, the actual change in the law or the policy may not be precisely what the civil disobedient had hoped for. Yet the change in the climate of opinion which brings about an unpredictable, though relatively desirable, change can properly be assessed as a sign of the efficacy (the victory) of civil disobedience. Presently we shall return to these considerations in another context.

Another important aspect of civil disobedience should be mentioned in connection with this criterion of "reasonable hope for victory." The civil disobedient will often assert that regardless of whether or not his action is to issue in the change of a law or policy, he nevertheless will disobey for conscience' sake. Here we encounter an aspect of the "ethics of conscience" in contrast to the "ethics of consequences." In the present context the civil disobedient motivated by the "ethics of conscience" asserts that loyalty to conscience is an end in itself, and that the possible consequence of change in the law or policy is a "plus" that is not decisive in determining his action. We must acknowledge that this kind of civil disobedience in a measure qualifies the definition we have proposed at the outset. Under the "ethics of conscience" the essential purpose of civil disobedience is not change in the law but maintenance of personal integrity under all circumstances. To be sure, this conception of integrity and of fidelity to conscience can become a form of irresponsibility, particularly if the civil disobedient in the name of conscience asserts that he is in no way concerned with consequences, whatever they may be. This view of conscience is a narrow conception indeed. The truly conscientious man should be willing to consider himself at least in part responsible for reasonably foreseeable, destructive consequences of his action. This sense of responsibility for consequences as well as for purity of motive belongs under the rubric of conscience when the latter is properly understood.

The fifth criterion of just-war doctrine is that the war action should be just in the sense of being free from vindictive hatred, greed, cruelty, or glee. So also authentic civil disobedience is not a search for revenge or an attempt to injure others or to ventilate frustration. Nor is it a free-wheeling activity designed merely to bring about obstruction or annoyance; nor is it teen-age sport indulged in order to see what the authorities will do. In human affairs, whether in war or in civil disobedience, the criterion of freedom from hatred or from desire for revenge is obviously difficult to satisfy. To ask for complete absence of these motives is utopian, especially in connection with racial tensions and even opposition to war.

The sixth criterion is that there must be due proportion between the good probably to be accomplished and the probable evil effects of the war. In many quarters today this criterion is held to be an anachronism. The probable evil effect of all-out war, it is said, could be nuclear and bacteriological genocide on the one side and national suicide on the other. Even apart from this consideration, however, the criterion is still applicable to the situation in Vietnam, and even among people who know little about just-war doctrine as such it figures largely in the continuing criticism of the American military effort there. In any event, the criterion is pertinent for application to civil disobedience.

As in its application to military matters, however, the use of this criterion in assessing civil disobedience is fraught with difficulty. How, for example, does one determine due proportion between the good probably to be accomplished and the probable evil effects? Only in the instance of obvious disproportion between the good and the evil does the criterion seem to yield clear guidance. But even to identify the situation that clearly precludes civil disobedience is sometimes difficult. If, for example, the protest is against the Vietnam war, the civil disobedient quite plausibly says that the very occasion for the protest is the already evident evil in the Vietnam venture, the great loss of life among combatants and noncombatants, the use of napalm, the destruction of villages and crops, the dwindling hope for victory, the support of the Van Thieu regime, the ineffectiveness of the pacification program, and the unlikelihood of successful remedy of this policy.[8] The civil disobedient in resolving to protest asserts that little he can do can remotely approach on the domestic scene the evils perpetrated in Vietnam. Due proportion between the good probably to be accomplished and the probable evil effects, he says, is relatively easy for him to establish. We need not rehearse here the rejoinders given by the supporters of current Vietnam policy. For quite different reasons they hold that the greater good is probably to be accomplished by somehow maintaining the essential policy in Vietnam, and they warn against the probable evil effects of discontinuing it; and they view civil disobedience accordingly. Indeed, they envisage as intolerable any success enjoyed by the civil disobedients in promoting draft resistance and in influencing public opinion. Meanwhile, the government enjoys an immediate advantage over the disobedients by reason of possessing more effective access to public opinion and by reason of its control over the agencies of the law. We shall presently return to this matter when we consider the Spock case.

At the moment we should pause to observe that the fact that quite opposite evaluations are derived from applying the criteria of just-war doctrine (for example, that the war must be just and the means just) demonstrates that the criteria are inadequate. The inadequacy, it is held, issues from the abstract character of the criteria; that is, these criteria do not carry with them an explicit definition of justice. Accordingly, the opposite evaluations presuppose or emphasize different ingredients of a theory of justice, and they also emphasize different aspects and interpretations of the situation.

This observation gives occasion for us to emphasize that, though in our presentation here we have referred again and again to conceptions and ingredients of justice appealed to by civil disobedients, we have defined the efficacy of civil disobedi-

---

[8] For a brief discussion of just-war doctrine in relation to the Vietnam war see Ralph B. Potter, *War and Moral Discourse* (Richmond, Va.: John Knox Press, 1969), ch. 5.

ence as the capacity to raise or reformulate the ethical issues in such a way as to contribute to the process whereby public opinion reexamines them with reference to a particular law or policy. And, as we have already indicated, from the point of view of authentic civil disobedience the outcome of the process hoped for is the change of the law or policy.

This question of efficacy gives special significance to the last of the criteria of just-war doctrine as applied to civil disobedience, namely, that the means must be just. As we have indicated, civil disobedience, viewed in terms of its major purpose, is more a strategy of persuasion than an occasion for merely announcing or registering a concern of conscience. The concern of conscience and its appeal for a more ample conception of justice is the nerve of the strategy of persuasion. Therefore the adoption of unjust means not only calls in question the conscientiousness of the civil disobedient; as a consequence, it also frustrates the efficacy of the strategy of persuasion. Moreover, besides violating the obligation to use just means, it reduces or nullifies the likelihood of due proportion obtaining between the good probably to be accomplished and the probable evil effects.

We have stressed the view that authentic civil disobedience is nonviolent. But one should recognize that violence is not easy to fend off when civil disobedience functions as a group activity. In a tense situation what starts out to be nonviolent can degenerate into producing chaos or near-chaos. We recall that resistance to the draft in 1863, accompanied by cries of "the rich man's money and the poor man's blood," gave rise to serious disturbances in New York City when rioters seized City Hall and invoked a reign of terror which took more than a thousand lives. With respect to draft-resistance the situation appears to have become less volatile today. In World War I there were over 300,000 draft delinquents, but the number of draft-resisters today is relatively small. Nevertheless, radical criticism of the war in Vietnam is widespread, and the situation is sufficiently volatile.

Likewise, in the sphere of race relations the civil disobedient cannot today properly disregard warnings, not when he recalls that ours is the only industrialized democracy in which one has come to expect riots every summer, and that some people are shouting that violence is an old American tradition and that in Vietnam it provides an example for violence at home.

Somewhat in this vein, perversion of civil disobedience appears in the group burning of draft cards, in the slogan "Clog for peace—the streets are yours," and in the plea for "nonviolent, creative disruption" or for "a Christmas mill-in—a merry disruption." Many of the civil disobedients and demonstrators assert that they march "unarmed, with no intention of violence." Others assert, however, that "it is irresponsible to say that all we can use against this terrible evil are the traditional forms of protest—picketing and marching." Accordingly, they go on to say, "We don't think there will be any change in the Government's policy unless we can raise the cost of war in terms of political harassment, social disruption and real money costs."[9] Generally, these kinds of harassment get out of control, whether according to plan or not. None of these tactics, however, justifies police harassment or brutality, or inordinate detention or sentence. Perversion does not justify perversion, even though it elicits it. On the other hand, just means do not exclude the deliberate use of dramatic group confrontation, though the civil disobedients might be expected, precisely for the sake of efficacy, to select time and place with prudence.

This consideration suggests that group tactics should be related to a general strategy calculated to avoid violence and to respond to it with nonviolence. Not that there is any violence-proof strategy. Gandhi, it will be recalled, despite all his admonitions against violence, was not able to prevent his supporters from resorting to it (whereupon he would undertake a fast in protest and penitence). Actually, the more a strictly nonviolent strategy is successful in eliciting public sympathy, the more likely it is to encounter lunatic-fringe violence. Once can say here that the ethical demands ideally should guide the civil disobedient into the mean between feckless timidity and reckless courage.

One could go on devising formulations of this sort with the intention of refining them so as to take care of every contingency. As with most ethical formulations dealing with complex and volatile situations, however, they are nets to catch the wind. The sum of them would probably embrace and fill in all the crannies of Pascal's axiom, practice opposite virtues and occupy all the distance in between.

---

[9] *New York Times*, November 22 and December 24, 1967.

DELAYED CIVIL DISOBEDIENCE

In the light of the hazards of civil disobedience for the commonweal and with a very restricted conception of it, Judge Wyzanski counsels what he calls "delayed civil disobedience." He advises the civil disobedient "to await at the very least an induction order before resisting. Indeed, since, when inducted, one does not know if he will be sent to Vietnam or if sent, will be called upon directly to do what he regards as an immoral act, it may well be that resistance at the moment of induction is premature."[10] Earlier in this article he says that "no one can tell whether, as the resisters hope, they . . . by provoking the responsive passions of the belligerent, would set the stage for a revival of virulent McCarthyism, an administrative system of impressment into the armed forces, and the establishment of a despotic tyranny bent on impairing traditional civil liberties and civic rights."[11] Group action, then, runs the special danger of arousing a virulent backlash.

Judge Wyzanski acknowledges that during the winter of 1860–61 Oliver Wendell Holmes, Jr., the future Justice, "joined the small group of Abolitionists who made themselves responsible for securing the physical safety of Wendell Phillips against the threats of Boston mobs, a protection which the Boston police seemed unlikely to provide,"[12] and he adds that "if it was morally right to break the laws supporting slavery even when it cost the nation its unity and helped to precipitate what, despite W. H. Seward may not have been an 'irrepressible conflict,' one cannot be so certain that it is morally wrong to resist the war in Vietnam if one deeply believes its purposes or methods are wicked." Yet, he holds that "each of us may bide his time until he personally is faced with an order requiring him as an individual to do a wrongful act." In support of this view he cites the

---

[10] *Op. cit.*, p. 60. It should be noted here that not all of those who turn in their draft cards are directly resisting military service. Some have turned in their cards in order to protest alleged injustices in the selective-service system; others seek confrontation on the constitutionality of the law requiring the physical possession of a draft card. As a consequence of civil disobedience for these purposes some of the theological students have been punished by their draft boards: they have been reclassified 1–A, and have been called for induction.

[11] *Ibid.*, p. 59.

[12] *Ibid.*, p. 59.

example of Sir Thomas More, who did not rush to protest the Act of Henry VIII's Parliament. "Only when attempt was made to force him to subscribe to [the Oath of Supremacy] did he resist." Judge Wyzanski concludes the article with a note of caution: "Those who look upon Sir Thomas More as one of the noblest exemplars of the human spirit reflecting the impact of the love of God may find a delayed civil disobedience the response most likely to give peace of mind and to evidence moral courage."[13]

Before proceeding to consider further the concept of delayed civil disobedience we should note in passing two related issues posed by Judge Wyzanski in this connection. "There are situations," he says, "when it seems plainly moral for a man to disobey an evil law promulgated by a government which is entirely lacking in ethical character. If a man has lost confidence in the integrity of his society . . . then there is much justification for his disobedience." This statement is not intended by the judge to qualify his preference for delayed civil disobedience. But we should observe something else here. He refers to civil disobedience, but strictly speaking the statement has little to do with civil disobedience properly defined. In authentic civil disobedience, as we have already observed, the civil disobedient has not "lost confidence in the integrity of his society"; nor does he hold the government to be "entirely lacking in ethical character." For this reason he aims to disobey within a legal framework, in order to improve a specific law or policy. With confidence in the integrity of his society and its government he invites legal agencies to deal with him, even to punish him, and he expects them to deal with him fairly. Complete loss of confidence in the society, as described by the judge, would seem to call for "systemic" disobedience from morally conscientious men; that is, it would call for rebellion and not for civil disobedience.

In order to fortify the definition of civil disobedience set forth in this paper I would like to raise a second question about Judge Wyzanski's conception. As we have noted, he says in recommending delayed civil disobedience, "Each of us may bide his time until he personally is faced with an order requiring him as an individual to do a wrongful act." Here again the nature and

---

[13] *Ibid.*, p. 60.

purpose of civil disobedience are overlooked. The authentic civil disobedient is not motivated merely by the desire to escape personal complicity in the performing of wrongful acts. He is concerned to make a public protest and to bring about the change of a law or policy. He is not acting merely for the sake of keeping his conscience clean; he intends to act as a citizen, fulfilling the responsibilities of conscientious citizenship.

In the light of this purpose of civil disobedience I am inclined to say that Judge Wyzanski's conception of delayed civil disobedience, restricted as it is to isolated, individual, and delayed action, would seem in practice to have the effect of reducing to a minimum the social efficacy of the disobedience. It reduces almost to a vanishing point the publicity that might move public opinion. Is it not asking a great deal of civilly disobedient draft-resisters to go one after the other silently and meekly to jail to join the thousand other resisters already there and thus to be unnoticed or forgotten by the general public? Indeed, is it not asking them to nullify a basic purpose of their disobedience? These considerations are pertinent not only for assessing protest against war; they obtain also for civil disobedience in other areas, as for example in the sphere of the civil-rights movement.

One should emphasize, however, that Judge Wyzanski's cautions deserve heeding. Civil disobedience, especially in dramatic, group form, can bring into play a social law of action and reaction; that is, it can give rise to irrational and violent response. Having said this, we should add that the dangers latent in a tense situation are aggravated the more when backlash reaction is allowed free rein as a consequence of the massive inertia of comfortable and indifferent "citizens." Plenty of evidence exists of the "law" of action and reaction in stormy bursts of the winds of doctrine. Judge Wyzanski speaks of the danger of a "revival of virulent McCarthyism." The present rash of proposed legislation in various states which combines the worst features of the old Smith Act and the McCarran Act confirms this warning.

It is clear that civil disobedience should not be entered into lightly or unadvisedly but discreetly and soberly. Nevertheless, risks must be taken. It would be futile, and also immoral, at the present time to ask civil disobedients to desist for the sake of the public safety. Only a clear and present danger to the stability of the social and legal order could justify such counsel.

THE RESPONSIBILITIES OF THE GOVERNMENT

We have considered at length the responsibilities and dangers attaching to civil disobedience, but we have by no means completed the reckoning. The heavier weight of responsibility and of possible danger appears on the other side of the scale. Therefore, we must now consider the hazards encountered by the civil disobedient in his attempt to vindicate his action in the face of and within the legal system. Here the crucial responsibility belongs to the agencies of government and to the general public. Indeed, the agencies of government can seriously fall·short of their responsibility to the citizen who in the name of justice and conscience challenges a law or policy. This means that in their performance here they can also fall short of their responsibility to society in general and to the constitution in particular. Judge Wyzanski, speaking of the intemperatre response of the government and the public to civil disobedience, warns against the possibility of the "establishment of a despotic tyranny bent on impairing traditional civil liberties and civic rights." We have mentioned already the current attempts of certain legislators to revitalize the Smith Act and the McCarran Act. More familiar is intemperate and brutal police action. The civil disobedient in an immediate way provides the occasion for the appearance of these forms of restriction, but he is not primarily responsible for them. The primary and direct responsibility rests more squarely upon the general public and upon the government. Again and again in the history of the United States the agencies of government have permitted or promoted the violation of civil liberties—freedom of speech and of association. They have done this through the perversion of due process and through other repressive policies. It is striking and scandalous that only recently (August 1969) has a court ordered the trial of a suit to test the constitutionality of the House Internal Security Committee. It is to the credit of the U.S. Court of Appeals (Seventh Circuit) that it has ordered this trial. Professor Arthur Kinoy of the Rutgers Law School, one of the seven lawyers for the plaintiffs, on hearing of the Circuit

Court's ordering of the trial, said, "What that means is that we will finally have the right to prove in a court of law that the committee has conducted a 30-year witch hunt in violation of the Constitution and the rights of citizens."[14] The examples of the failure of government to protect the First-Amendment rights of citizens, including civil disobedients, are legion and may be traced far back in American (and European) history.

In the face of civil disobedience the agencies of the state are immediately and inescapably brought into action, either to enforce the law or to maintain and protect the government policy under challenge. In a government of separation of powers, the functioning of the state to deal with civil disobedience entails a division of labor. Thus the police and the legislative and judicial functions involve different agencies. If the rights of civil disobedients are to be protected adequately, the integrity and efficacy of public opinion and nongovernmental agencies of the community are extremely important. If these agencies are not alert and critical, the agencies of the state are the more likely to overreach themselves. A large number of these nongovernmental agencies function in any vital democracy, agencies representing the general welfare and also special interests. In the sphere of civil disobedience today one of the most significant nongovernmental agencies is the American Civil Liberties Union. We should also mention here the Legal Defense Fund of the National Association for the Advancement of Colored People. Both these agencies have been active in attempting to keep the public properly informed regarding both fact and law and in bringing or supporting court action.

This kind of function performed by nongovernmental agencies is succinctly formulated in the "Statement on Civil Disobedience" (February 1, 1969) of the American Civil Liberties Union. Here the ACLU defines its purpose as that of attempting to promote equal protection of the laws and also due process of law in the community's or the state's treatment of civil disobedients, particularly in terms of the First and the Fourteenth Amendments of the Constitution. In pursuing these purposes the ACLU

---

[14] *New York Times*, August 10, 1969.

of course does not attempt to protect the civil disobedient from all punishment as a consequence of his disobedience. In this connection, the Statement asserts: "The right to counsel must be provided, the trial held in an atmosphere that is not prejudicial to the rights of the accused, and the sentence imposed not more severe than would be imposed on another person who violated the same law." It is not difficult to cite cases in which atmosphere prejudicial to the rights of the accused has prevailed. Moreover, state courts have sometimes employed excessive bail determination not only to detain and punish but also to prejudice the fairness of trial of individuals or groups that hold allegedly antisocial beliefs or are too poor to pay for their release. Thus the "bail system" can serve to violate the equal-protection guaranteed by the Fourteenth Amendment. Sometimes the government prejudices fairness of trial in the definition of the "crime," and with the same effect as a prejudicial determination of bail. These devices can influence the jury and the public to assess the "crime" of civil disobedience as fearful and horrendous. Fortunately, these devices can win reversal from a higher court.

In the judgment of many the U.S. government in its concern during recent years to maintain and enforce its war policy and the military-draft law has come close to perverting due process and to impairing both freedom of speech and freedom of association. This tendency has been detected in the government's handling of the Spock case, particularly in its decision to indict for conspiracy and in the misguidance of the jury. This case has won such wide publicity that we do well to give attention here to aspects of it which exemplify fundamental problems to be encountered by civil disobedients in face of the government and the community.

THE SPOCK CASE

The issues involved in the Spock case are complex, and this complexity has been compounded by reason of the decision of the First District Court of Appeals (Nos. 7205-08, July 11, 1969) to acquit two of the four defendants, Dr. Benjamin Spock and Michael Ferber, and to order a new trial for the Rev. William S.

Coffin, Jr., and Mitchell Goodman. At the time of this writing
the government has not yet decided what action to take with
respect to the new trial.

In the context of the present essay three aspects of the Spock
case deserve our notice. First we should observe an aspect of
every legal system. Often we hear it said that ours is a government of laws and not of men. But this cliché conceals the fact
that important areas of discretion obtain within the legal system.
These areas of discretion are pertinent for any discussion of cases
dealing with civil disobedience. An important preliminary decision must be made by the law-enforcement agency of the government. The government may exercise discretion, indeed it
cannot avoid exercising it, in the decision *whether* and *when*
to indict. Moreover, if indictment is to be sought, the prosecutor
has the freedom or discretion to formulate the terms of the
indictment. And then the grand jury and the court in turn
exercise judgment in the decision to accept or reject the definition provided by the prosecutor. And, finally, the trial jury is in
principle free to accept or reject the definition.

Professor Joseph L. Sax of the University of Michigan has
made very cogent comment on the discretion belonging to the
prosecutor. His comment deserves extensive quotation here:

> Through the miracle of prosecutorial discretion—a device
> central to the operation of the legal system, but widely
> ignored in discussions of civil disobedience—criminality can
> be, and is, produced or ignored virtually at will by law-
> enforcement officials. Businessmen know that if the build-
> ing and fire laws were fully implemented they could be in
> court virtually every day.
>
> Justice Jackson once said that "a prosecutor has more
> control over our life, liberty, and reputation than any other
> person in America . . . he can choose his defendant . . . a
> prosecutor stands a fair chance of finding at least a techni-
> cal violation of some act on the part of almost anyone.
>
> The law is so vast in its technical coverage and so
> open-ended in its possible interpretation by police officers,
> prosecutors, and judges that it becomes almost meaningless
> to talk about civil disobedience as if there were conduct
> which "the law"—as some external force—declared illegal.
>
> In fact, no society could operate if it did not tolerate a
> great deal of technically or arguably illegal conduct on the

ground that certain laws were absolute and others unwise
as written or as applied to particular situations.[15]

These observations have considerable bearing upon our previous
discussion of the "fabric of society" in its legal aspects. This
fabric is a good deal more ambiguous and flexible than Judge
Wyzanski's argument (cited earlier in this paper) suggests when
he asks for delayed civil disobedience.

The comments of Professor Sax have equal bearing upon the
"prosecutorial discretion" exercised in the Spock case. The crucial discretion exercised by the government in this case is manifest
in the Attorney General's and the prosecutor's decision to define
the "crime" not merely as counseling, aiding, and abetting refusal and evasion of the draft (section 12 of the Military Selective
Service Act of 1967) but also as conspiracy to counsel and aid
(here the Court appealed not to legislation but rather to alleged
precedents).

It is difficult enough to define precisely the meaning of the
charge of counseling and aiding the commission of a crime. In
this case the defendants had proclaimed far and wide their view
that the war in Vietnam is immoral and illegal. Is it possible
to do this without in effect counseling and abetting refusal of t'·e
draft? If not, does the legislation abridge free speech? But it ıs
even more difficult to define authoritatively the crime of conspiracy.

In making the charge of conspiracy the government imported
a vague and amorphous concept, indeed one that has served
again and again in history to repress freedom of speech and of
association, not to speak of violating due process. It was employed a century and a half ago to indict trade unions as
criminal conspiracies, and also more recently in the Joseph
McCarthy era in extrajudicial efforts to subvert the protections
of the First and Fourteenth Amendments.

Despite the protest of Mr. Justice Harlan in the Grunewald
case (353 US 91) that "every conspiracy is by its nature secret,"
the decision of the Court of Appeals asserts that the element of
secrecy is not essential. Thus conspiracy in this case, according to
the Court decision, consisted of an "agreement" that was legal
insofar as it entailed opposition to the war and the draft (an

[15] Joseph L. Sax, "Civil Disobedience: The Law Is Never Blind," *Saturday
Review*, September 28, 1968, p. 22.

exercise of the right of free speech) but which was illegal in "that the means or intermediate objectives encompassed both legal and illegal activity without any clear indication, initially, as to who intended what." This conspiracy, be it noted, was not secret; it was loudly and publicly proclaimed. Moreover, the illegal action of others—refusal of the draft on the part of young men—occurred later.

In noting the gap between the counseling and the acts of disobedience of the young men Judge Frank M. Coffin in his dissenting opinion calls the Court's view "a delayed fuse approach." Arguing also that the use of the conspiracy charge represents a dubious extension of precedents, he raises the question whether "reason and authority" compel the application of the charge of conspiracy "to a wholly open, amorphous and shifting association, having a broad focus of interest in changing public policy, and encompassing a wide spectrum of purposes, legal and illegal." In his dissent from the order for a new trial for the Rev. Mr. Coffin and Mitchell Goodman, Judge Coffin says that "such diverse groups as Clergy Concerned, a consumers' boycott of California grapes, a parents' group for so-called 'freedom of choice' plans within a Southern school district might find themselves facing a conspiracy indictment." He therefore asks whether "the nation's well-being and security cannot be as well served in less repressive ways," and he suggests that the broad interpretation placed by the court upon conspiracy will have a "chilling effect" on the exercise of freedom of speech and association. "Even if the Court's safeguards were rigorously applied," he says, "the ranks of individuals enlisted in a controversial public cause would visibly shrink if they knew that the jury could find them to be members of a conspiracy." In the main, then, Judge Coffin's dissent is based on the view that applying the doctrine of conspiracy in these cases is "not consistent with the First Amendment." And in this connection he adds, "It would be small comfort to be told that one could still be vindicated via the appellate process after an expenditure of time and money in substantial amounts."

Judge Coffin concludes this remarkable dissenting opinion with words of salutary warning:

> This is a landmark case and no one, I take it, supposes that this will be the last attempt by the government to use the

conspiracy weapon. The government has cast a wide net and caught only two fish. My objection is not that more were not caught but that the government can try again on another day in another court and the court's rationale provides no meaningful basis for predicting who will find themselves within the net. Finally, there is the greater danger that the casting of the net has scared away many whom the government had no right to catch.

Judge Coffin's objections to the court's acceptance of the indictment for conspiracy reminds one of the statement of Mr. Justice Jackson in which he called conspiracy "that elastic, sprawling and pervasive offense . . . so vague that it almost defies definition . . . the looseness and pliability of the doctrine present inherent dangers which should be in the background of judicial thought wherever it is sought to extend the doctrine to meet the exigencies of a particular case" (concurring opinion, *Krulewitch* v. *United States*, 336 US 446, 449). This citation is given in the *amicus curiae* brief of the Unitarian Universalist Association.

This brief submitted by the Unitarian Universalist Association analyzes in considerable detail the incompatibility between the government's charge of conspiracy and its obligation to protect the right of the citizen to criticize government policy and to enter into association with others for the purpose.

This brings us to the third consideration which is of special significance in the Spock case, the relation between civil disobedience and freedom of association. Citing precedents, the brief emphasizes the idea that "persons acting in association do not lose their first-amendment rights even if on other occasions or on the same occasion they engage in separate, illegal conduct." But how did the government attempt to proceed in the Spock case? The brief asserts that "as the case was submitted, the jury may well have believed that *any group* criticism of the government alone permitted an inference of an illegal conspiracy."[16]

We need not discuss here the reasons for the Court's acquittal of Dr. Spock and Michael Ferber or the reasons for the ordering

[16] For a lively, sharp treatment of earlier phases and consequences of the litigation and also for an analysis of the strikingly inadequate reporting and interpretation of the case by the press (including James Reston of the *New York Times*), see Jessica Mitford, "Guilty as Charged by the Judge," *Atlantic*, August 1969.

of a new trial. It suffices to say that the two defendants were
cleared of the conspiracy charge and that the retrial of the
remaining two defendants was ordered on account of the misconduct of the previous trial.

We have given extensive attention to the Spock case and the
related cases because they provide examples not only of the large
role of discretion belonging to the government in civil disobedience cases but also of the ways in which the government may
undertake to impair the freedom of speech and the freedom of
association. The relevance and legal status of the conspiracy
charge in these cases has not yet been settled. It is significant that
there is no evidence that members of the jury considered this
question.[17] And for that matter, if the Coffin and Goodman cases
are finally appealed to the U.S. Supreme Court, it is possible that
the Court will not give a ruling on the conspiracy charge. It may
not be necessary for it to do so (though it has done so in the
past), for already in the District Court's decision one can see that
the crucial issue may turn out to be a distinction between
freedom of *expression* and affirmative aiding and abetting of
violations of the draft statutes. Moreover, in a previous case
before the Supreme Court, when the conspiracy charge had been
made against Communists, the Court ruled only against the
suppression of free speech and did not rule on the conspiracy
charge.

In any event, the government in the Spock-case indictment, far
from protecting the rights of speech and of association, used its
discretion to bring an indictment for conspiracy. As a consequence it has administered what Judge Coffin has called a
"chilling effect" to many citizens who might have been disposed
to criticize, or to enter into association to criticize, government
policy in Vietnam. The "chilling effect" was probably intended
also for any young men who might have been considering undertaking civil disobedience in protest against this policy or against
the draft statutes. It matters not that Dr. Spock and Michael
Ferber have been acquitted "via the appellate process after the
expenditure of time and money in substantial amounts" (again

<hr>

[17] Prof. Sax, writing about Judge Francis Ford, who presided over the first
conviction of the defendants, says that "another judge could have found a
dozen cogent reasons, all supported by precedent and good legal logic, to have
dismissed the indictment before the trial ever began" (*op. cit.*, p. 24).

the words of the dissenting opinion). It matters not that in the remaining cases the conspiracy charge may drop out of sight. The "chilling effect" may already have served one of the purposes of the government, regardless of the final disposition to be made of the cases by the courts, indeed regardless of whether or not the government ever expected the conspiracy charge to be vindicated.

We have been discussing the Spock case as an illustration of civil disobedience and of government discretion in the face of civil disobedience. According to our definition of civil disobedience, however, the defendants should have been expected to plead guilty and to accept the penalty. But in actuality they decided to challenge the indictment. The reason for their doing this was made quite clear by the Rev. Mr. Coffin soon after the announcement of the indictment for conspiracy. "I was persuaded," he said, "that fighting this indictment would be the best support we could offer to those who are resisting the draft." He elaborated this statement by saying, "Unchallenged, the precedent it would set might make it much too easy for the Government to indict anybody for conspiracy, and this would diminish the possibilities of dissent and the exercise of the rights of conscience."[18] What was at stake, then, was the maintenance of the rights of freedom of speech and of association, and also the right of conscience to criticize government policy or to undertake civil disobedience without incurring the charge of conspiracy.[19]

[18] Fred C. Shapiro, "God and That Man at Yale," *New York Times Magazine*, March 3, 1968, p. 62.

[19] Before leaving this section of the paper on the responsibilities of government in civil disobedience matters I would like to call attention to a highly instructive and suggestive discussion of the topic by Ronald Dworkin in the article referred to earlier here, *New York Review of Books*, June 8, 1968. In this article the author considers, among other things, the responsibility of government to recognize the contributions of civil disobedients to the clarification of public issues and of the meaning of civil rights in a changing social and legal situation. For example, the civil disobedient challenges laws and policies which are of dubious moral and legal character, stimulating the public and the courts to scrutinize anew these laws and policies; he may expose violations of due process and of the right to equal protection of the law; he may also bring to the attention of the public and Congress the need for the amendment of laws that are unclear or repressive.

Specifically, civil disobedience in our day has brought to sharper focus many questions regarding the compromised rights of ethnic minorities, regarding the validity of the military draft laws, and regarding immoral and

CIVIL DISOBEDIENCE AND
FREEDOM OF ASSOCIATION

In the previous section we have seen that the Spock litigation illustrates the large role of "prosecutorial discretion" in civil disobedience cases. In the previous paragraph we have observed another important aspect of our subject: generally, civil disobedience is not merely the act of a single individual alone; it usually turns out to be the exercise of freedom of association.

In the "Advice to the National Council of Churches," cited above, appears the statement that even when the civil disobedient "is alone in his disobedience, he acts as one who is a member of a fellowship committed to obedience to God." A sense of fellowship or of common commitment among civil disobedients is strikingly evident in the history of democracy—in social reform movements that have employed civil disobedience,[20] and before that in the left-wing, aggressive Protestant sects. Initially democracy itself was conceived in civil disobedience and first became incarnate in freedom of association, that is, in voluntary associations formal and informal. Indeed, the voluntary association has become a characteristic and indispensable organ of the democratic polity, a principal medium of group commitment and fellowship. Indeed, it has been voluntary organizations which

---

illegal aspects of the Vietnam war, and this at a time when government policy is being increasingly questioned by the public. In this connection the author asserts that society can tolerate some disobedience (especially in the light of the considerations just mentioned) and that the prosecutor, in the face of certain types of disobedience, may and should, as in other types of cases, decide not to press charges. Society suffers a special loss, he says, if it punishes a group that includes its most thoughtful and loyal citizens. In this whole complex of law and circumstance the government has a special responsibility to recognize the social value of the development and testing of law and policy through experimentation by citizens and through the adversary process. All in all, one can infer from these views that the government and the public have the responsibility to recognize the subtle and even illegal ways in which enlivened conscience can give new meaning to both the law and the spirit of the law. One is reminded here of the famous statement of Judge Learned Hand in which he urged that justices 'be aware of the changing social tensions in every society which make it an organism [and] which will disrupt it, if rigidly confined.'

[20] After the present writing was completed the author's attention was drawn to the essay on the sense of mutual obligation that develops among civil disobedients, by Michael Walzer, "The Obligation to Disobey," in David Spitz (ed.), *Political Theory and Social Change* (New York: Atherton Press, 1967), pp. 185–202.

have impressed upon the community and the state the demands for democratic rights. One sees this most clearly in the activities of the Puritans in dissent and in civil disobedience. The history of civil disobedience is thus closely bound up with the history of political democracy, with the interplay between voluntary associations and the state, an involuntary association in its distinctive features.[21]

The voluntary association is an old institution. It was given new thrust in early modern history by civil disobedients who protested against the monolithic principles of the involuntary political and ecclesiastical Establishment. At the beginning of the struggle, civil disobedience and the idea of freedom of association were viewed by the Establishment as a radical threat to the stability of society. Thomas Hobbes, in opposing these free associations, asserted that they were completely incompatible with the sovereignty of the ruler. Voluntary associations, he said, "are worms in the entrails of the natural man." And in his view they of course should be wormed.

These associations included not only the independent churches and social reform associations but also scientific and professional societies like the one that has brought us together here today. Along with universities, labor unions, and pressure groups they have come to represent the organizational ingredients of modern pluralistic society.

It was partly from associations such as these that the principle of loyal opposition entered into modern democratic theory and practice. The late A. D. Lindsay of Balliol College, Oxford, has pointed out that this principle came into the modern state especially from the independent churches of the seventeenth century which insisted not only upon their rights as minorities but also upon the protection of the minorities within their own churches. Only through this sort of organization, they held, could the Spirit blow where it listeth.[22]

---

[21] A wide range of these phenomena is dealt with in D. B. Robertson (ed.), *Voluntary Associations* (Richmond, Va.: John Knox Press, 1966); and in J. Roland Pennock and John W. Chapman (eds.), *Voluntary Associations, Nomos XI* (New York: Atherton Press, 1969).

[22] For a well-documented account of "The Origins of the Idea of Loyal Opposition," see the chapter by George H. Williams in D. B. Robertson, *op. cit.*

In the democratic state's adoption of the idea of loyal opposition a principle of nongovernmental associations was taken over into the government. The birth of political parties was related to this development. If we observe that this development followed upon the appearance of the claim for freedom of religious association, we may say that pluralism (or nonconformity) in religion was followed by pluralism within the state itself. (Compare the theory of checks and balances.)

An analogous prototypical development in earlier Western civilization came in part from the doctrine that the Christian must render unto Caesar that which is Caesar's and unto God that which is God's. Speaking of this New Testament axiom, Alfred North Whitehead was wont to say that there appeared here a new principle of social organization.[23] The state was not only placed within limits and under criticism, but this criticism was to be supported by an association independent of the state. This independent religious association in no way considered itself the creature of the state. Quite the contrary. That would have made the church merely a function of the state, that is, of civic religion. It is striking to observe, however, how short a time this pluralistic conception was able to maintain itself and survive. By the fifth century Christianity had almost acquired the status of a civic religion.

In the modern period the idea of freedom of association gave rise to a pluralistic conception of the relation between the community and the state. Here the state is viewed not as the creator but as an organ of the community, and it is only one of these organs. The state as an involuntary association has its particular, changing functions, but properly understood it operates in cybernetic interplay with other associations in the community. Both the state and the voluntary associations are expressions of and within the embracing, open community. To be sure, many of these cells represent "special interests" rather than universal concern for the general welfare. On the other hand, the church claims a transcendent reference beyond the community and even beyond itself. Indeed, individual conscious may make an analogous claim.

[23] Alfred North Whitehead, *Adventures of Ideas* (New York: Macmillan Co., 1933), p. 69.

These voluntary associations serve as mediators of sensitivity, of expanding conceptions of justice and mercy, of new prickings of conscience, which are transmitted from minority groups to the community at large. Already by the end of the first quarter of the eighteenth century the Friends, veterans of civil disobedience, had devised the major technique of the modern pressure group, as an extension of their strategy of persuasion, in the transition from dissent to politics.[24]

The mediating institutions, however, are not confined to nongovernmental instruments. The jury, for example, can serve as a mediating instrumentality between the community and the state, transmitting to the legal process new sensitivities (or old prejudices), so much so that it has often been remarked that in effect the jury offers modification of the law. Accordingly, Sir Edward Coke asserted that "the jurors are chancellors."[25] The prerequisite of the jury as a mediating instrument is of course the ethically sensitive juror. In civil disobedience cases the advocate for the defendant looks for the juror who can respond to burgeoning moral demands.[26] The prosecutor on the other hand tends to look for the juror who seems to be a "right-thinking" citizen who believes in "law and order" as defined by a government bent on enforcing (that is, forcing) its policy. All too often a jury does not represent a full cross-section of the community; it represents instead the "microcosm of the system and the central prejudices of the community." It is not easy to find jurors of the sort that will be patient of civil disobedience. Nor for that matter is it easy to find a judge who will carefully and completely instruct the jury regarding its prerogatives. The consequence oftentimes is that the jurors suppress or even pervert their own function as a mediating agency.

The voluntary associations that develop in connection with

[24] Norman Hunt, *Two Early Political Associations* (New York: Oxford University Press, 1965).

[25] Cf. Charles E. Wyzanski, Jr., *Whereas—A Judge's Premises* (Boston: Atlantic-Little Brown, 1965), p. 12; also Patrick Devlin, *The Enforcement of Morals* (New York: Oxford University Press, 1965), chaps. 1 and V.

[26] Philip J. Hirschkop, Washington civil-rights trial lawyer, gives a striking, colloquial description of the juror sought for in civil-rights cases. "We look," he says, "for guys who are in conflict with themselves. The only chance we stand, in many instances, is to get a man who will delve into his own conscience. . . . Forget about the straight-shooter—the guy who is very sure of himself." *Washington Post*, Potomac section, January 28, 1968.

civil disobedience are likewise mediating agencies between the
community and the state. Of course, the enterprise is not always
efficacious; it may even turn out to be an expression of egregiously distorted conscience. When properly effective, however, it
expresses a burgeoning modification of consensus within the
community. As such it stirs the apathy of the citizen from its
dead center, reminding him that his routine conscience may have
missed something. It brings about new alignments and new
creative tensions.[27] In this way civil disobedience expresses and
impinges upon the consciousness of the whole community and
ultimately upon the processes of government. It does this within
the framework of a legal system, modifying precedents out of the
past and making new precedents for the future. Without this
disturbance the legal system and the social order can become a
stagnant haven of injustice, a harbinger of violence or of revolutionary action. When other checks and balances in the society
and the government do not function adequately, civil disobedience can step into the breach and promote the fundamental
values of a just democratic society. That it has done this in the
current situation at least in some measure is to be observed in
recent court decisions expanding the legal freedom of citizens to
use certain public facilities for sit-in demonstrations and for the
distribution of literature of protest; and accomplishments besides
these have been indicated elsewhere in the present paper.

Why, one may ask, cannot this disturbance be engendered and
channeled through normal political processes? And does not the
disturbance through civil disobedience weaken "the basic fabric
of society"? The answer is that:

> those who think resisters are tearing the fabric of the

[27] This process is indicated in a genial way by Yale's Dean E. F. Thompson
in his comment on the influence of the indictment (for conspiracy) of the
Rev. William S. Coffin, Jr., Chaplain of Yale University: "I'm very fond of
Bill; I argue with him all along. But now I have to look at my own position
and see if there isn't something basically wrong with our society if an
intelligent man who has given a lot of thought to it finds himself forced to
disobey the law." Quoted by Fred C. Shapiro, op. cit., p. 56. Compare the
comment of Yale President Kingman Brewster: after stating that he is
constrained to "disagree with the chaplain's position on draft resistance, and
in this instance deplore his style," he says that "thanks in large part to his
personal verve and social action . . . the rebellious instinct, which elsewhere
expresses itself in sour withdrawal, cynical nihilism and disruption, is here [at
Yale] more often than not both affirmative and constructive, thanks in
considerable measure to the chaplain's influence" (Ibid., p. 56) .

society might wish to consider the possibility that a society is best able to survive if it permits a means for taking an issue back to the public over the heads of public official-dom; when it recognizes that a government may have so implicated itself in a wretched policy that it needs to be extricated by popular repudiation in a forum more immediately available—and less politically compromised—than the ballot box.[28]

This consideration becomes the more pertinent in a time when (especially in the area of race relations) society is being reordered, but when an increasing number of blacks are questioning the ability of the established political system to meet their desire in the name of consent of the governed to share the benefits of the most productive society on earth, and when a Walter Lippmann can question the ability of Congress to deal in proper time with the maladjustments.

In a time like this the process of disturbance does not become efficacious through the action of individuals alone. It requires the crystallizing of sentiment, the establishment of morale among the dissidents, and a certain mobilization for action. These goals are possible of achievement only through association. This is the reason freedom of speech tends to stand or fall with freedom of association. Darnell Rucker is correct when he says that "civil disobedience is the last bastion of the individual against his society,"[29] but it would be more accurate to say that the last bastion is freedom of association, for without this freedom civil disobedience is not likely to be efficacious. Here again we see the significance of the Spock case and the threat to democratic principles in the government's charge of conspiracy in that case.

By reason of the character of disturbance at the hands of the civil disobedients the demands upon the community and the legal system are of paradoxical order. If the process is to promote an open and viable legal order, courage will be required of the trustees of the law as well as of the civil disobedients, of the Creons as well as of the Antigones.[30]

---

[28] Joseph L. Sax, "Conscience and Anarchy: The Prosecution of War Resisters," *Yale Review*, LVII, No. 4 (June 1968), 494.

[29] Darnell Rucker, "The Moral Grounds of Civil Disobedience," *Ethics*, LXXVI, No. 2 (January 1966), 142.

[30] Harry W. Jones, "Civil Disobedience," *Proceedings of the American Philosophical Society*, 111, No. 4 (August 1967), 198.

In a concluding word, how shall we assess the significance of authentic civil disobedience? We have tried to indicate something of its character, its hazards, its dangers, its accomplishments, its possibilities, its limits. But at the end here we must recognize its built-in limitation, a limitation of which many a civil disobedient is aware.

Civil disobedience, obviously, is not adequate to cope with the basic problems of positive construction required in a mass, technological society. It offers essentially a criticism and a correction from the margin. Because of this character and limitation there are many civil disobedients today who undertake their disobedience out of despair and not in reasonable hope of victory. They do this by reason of the feeble results of their efforts. Some of them engage in civil disobedience really as an act of withdrawal. They sometimes suspect that civil disobedience is a strategy that enables a society to evade the fundamental problems of social transformation: it enables evasion precisely because it does not compel widespread fundamental rethinking and positive action. As for war and poverty and discrimination in employment and education, many a civil disobedient recognizes that progress has been intolerably slow and ambiguous in these spheres. The black leader LeRoi Jones, in despair by reason of the inefficacy of nonviolence and civil disobedience, even argues that nonviolence is a device that by default serves primarily to leave the status quo undisturbed. "Nonviolence in the American context," he says, "means, at its most honest evocation, a proposed immersion into the mainstream of a bankrupt American culture, and that's all. . . . Even the proposition is, finally, a fake. No such immersion is even possible. It is much too late."[31]

It is the limitation of civil disobedience that it cannot make broad, frontal constructive attack on these problems. In short, it cannot replace normal political procedures. Indeed, this should never be its intention. But normal political procedures will not make frontal attack in any moment short of crisis. At its best, then, civil disobedience makes its contribution only in a long-range timespan that covers decades. In the immediate situation its principal contribution is to offer the challenge of quickened

[31] *Home: Social Essays* (New York: William Morrow & Co., 1966), p. 149.

conscience and, along with other forces, to elicit that sense of crisis which from time to time bestirs a people into concerted action. The alternative to these slow processes is revoltuion. Civil disobedience by its strategy repeatedly reminds the nation of the wisdom articulated by Walter Bagehot: "Strong beliefs win strong men and make them stronger."

14

A CONTEXTUAL APPROACH
TO DISOBEDIENCE

KENT GREENAWALT

Lawyers, especially prominent ones, have a propensity to consider themselves experts on civil disobedience. Most of them are against it, though some do acknowledge that it may be justified in special circumstances.[1] Edmund Burke once said that

[1] See, e.g., A. Cox, "Direct Action, Civil Disobedience, and the Constitution," in A. Cox, M. DeW. Howe, J. R. Wiggins, *Civil Rights, the Constitution, and the Courts* (Cambridge: Harvard University Press, 1967); A. Fortas, *Concerning Dissent and Civil Disobedience* (New York: Signet, 1968); E. N. Griswold, George Abel Dreyfous Lecture on Civil Liberties, at Tulane University School of Law, April 16, 1968; E. F. Morris, "American Society and the Rebirth of Civil Obedience," 54, *Amer. Bar Assoc. Jour.* 653 (1968); E. V. Rostow, "The Consent of the Governed," Address at Monticello, reprinted in 114 Cong. Rec. No. 123, 90th Cong., 2d. Sess, July 17, 1968. And see "A Declaration of Confidence in Columbia's Future," statement of members of the Columbia Law School Faculty, May 16, 1968. Since the arguments discussed in this

the rebelliousness of colonial América was largely a consequence of the size and prominence of the legal profession, under whose influence the people "snuff the approach of tyranny in every tainted breeze."[2] Why it is that lawyers are now much more likely to snuff the approach of rebellion and anarchy is beyond the scope of this chapter. One of the points I do wish to make, however, is that in judging the morality of disobedient acts, the lawyer's perspective is limited.

Disputes over whether an illegal action is morally justified in a particular instance can be reduced to one or more of four kinds of disagreement. 1. Is the goal pursued desirable and sufficiently important? One might condemn an illegal act to promote racial segregation on the ground that no efforts toward that end are morally defensible. Massive dislocation to improve food in the college cafeteria might be rejected because the goal, though desirable, is not very important. 2. What are the probable effects of disobedience? This is theoretically a factual inquiry, though the relevant "facts" may be unascertainable and highly complex. It encompasses both the likelihood that the actor's goal will be achieved and any other possible effects of the act. 3. Are the probable effects desirable? If particular consequences are predictable, one may think them good or bad. This evaluation will be particularly difficult if one value, say equality, is promoted at the expense of another, say security. And if among many consequences some are good and others bad, their respective importance must be weighed. 4. Is obedience to law a moral claim on individuals that overrides other moral claims? As the discussion below indicates, my own conclusion is that the answer to the last question depends on the answers given to questions 2 and 3, but others may believe it an independent inquiry. Indeed, one possible position is that this is the only necessary inquiry; if one is always morally obligated to obey the law, goals and probable effects are irrelevant. Few, I think, would take this position upon serious reflection.[3]

---

chapter are generally familiar, I do not, for the most part, cite the persons who have made them.

[2] E. Burke, "Speech on Conciliation with the Colonies," *Speeches and Letters on American Affairs* (New York: Dutton, Everyman ed., 1908), p. 95.

[3] It is most effectively rebutted in R. A. Wasserstrom, "The Obligation to Obey the Law," 10, *UCLA L. Rev.* 780 (1963). My debt to his analysis in the development of other positions taken in this essay is considerable.

Of these four kinds of questions, the second is the one with which the social scientist is best equipped to deal. The other three are most closely within the domain of the social and moral philosopher. Certainly no discipline has a monopoly on relevant truth or understanding in these areas. The questions involving values are ones to which human reason can provide no final answers, and the "factual" inquiries are too complex for social science to give confident responses. It is also true that though these inquiries are not central to his professional training, a lawyer is used to weighing values and making judgments about complex social facts. But that is hardly enough to justify the sublime confidence with which some members of the bar pontificate on the subject. We lawyers would do well to recognize that when we do discuss this topic, we are stepping beyond the narrow area of our particular professional competence. We should also be aware of the possibility that our own vocational commitment to the law is double-edged. At the same time it enriches our comprehension of conflict management and the worth of orderly process, it may lead us to a partial view of the relative importance of observance of legal norms and other social values.

In this chapter, I first suggest an unoriginal criterion for determining when disobedience of law is morally justified, one that refers to the probable consequences of the disobedient act. This leads me to reject the conclusion advanced by some commentators that certain conditions, such as nonviolence and a willingness to be punished, are always essential if illegal behavior is to be justified. I do try to demonstrate, however, why factors such as these are highly relevant to questions of justification. The criterion and its application do not produce a simple answer to the question whether disobedience is morally justified in a particular situation. But simplicity of application, whatever may be its importance for legal norms, is not, in my view, a necessary hallmark of a principle of moral judgment.

As the generality of my language has already indicated, the discussion is not limited to illegal acts falling within the category of civil disobedience. This is partly a result of the difficulty of definition. But more importantly, I believe the reasons thought to justify civil disobedience overlap with those advanced to defend other kinds of illegal behavior. These matters are dealt with in more detail below.

My focus is on the arguments one would put for and against a particular disobedient act before it is done, and the criteria for deciding if it was correctly undertaken. Since I am interested in judging the act rather than the actor, I am not concerned with the actor's motives. I by no means want to deny the significance of evaluating the actor in light of his act or even to imply that passing a moral judgment on the act is more important than passing a moral judgment on the actor. We are continually engaged in making both sorts of judgments. Here, however, I discuss only the reasons one would put for and against someone's engaging in certain acts, rather than the circumstances in which an actor should be considered personally blameworthy for what he has done. For my purposes, a well-intentioned but predictably disastrous action would not be justified, and an act might be morally justified though undertaken hatefully. Thus, helping a slave to escape might be morally justified even if the actor was moved solely by a wish to harm the owner whom he dislikes. By "morally justified" I mean an act that would be done by someone who is well-intentioned and well-informed, and can judge objectively.

It seems wise at the outset to put aside explicitly two issues rightly given attention by lawyers, with which I do not deal. The first is when an act of apparent disobedience is not really disobedient because the law violated may be unconstitutional. Few analysts doubt that a citizen properly refuses to comply with a statute that clearly contravenes the Constitution. The problem is more difficult when, as is commonly true, a statute's constitutional status is not evident. When may such a statute justifiably be disobeyed because of its possibile invalidity? When the citizen believes it likely to be held unconstitutional? When he is doubtful of success but wishes a test of constitutionality? When he is nearly certain on the basis of past decisions that the courts will sustain the law but thinks it should be held unconstitutional? Only when he has made an attempt to get the law changed through other means? These issues are not explored here, though the more general discussion that follows has implications for how they might be treated. The analysis proceeds here on the assumption that the law to be obeyed or disobeyed is plainly valid within the system of positive law, that is, is legally valid in the sense that any law passed by the Parliament in Great Britain is valid.[4] I recognize that in the United States the contention that a statute is immoral can on many, probably most, occasions be the basis for a plausible argument that it violates the Constitution in some respect, but the core issues of disobedience are most clearly seen when an apparently illegal act can not be defended as consistent with underlying positive law.

The second subject not considered is the appropriate attitude of those who enforce the law toward persons who claim that moral justification supports their illegal acts. Most lawyers believe that such persons should be punished. They would rest this judgment on the notion that the law should be applied with an even hand. Though many lawyers would admit that belief in moral justification may be a ground for mitigation of punishment, some would argue that such claims show disrespect for law and encourage emulation, and may occasionally necessitate punishment even harsher than ordinary. One writer has argued that those moved by moral concerns to commit illegal acts should sometimes not be prosecuted at all.[5] I am not concerned here with whether, or when, a prosecutor should exercise his discretion to decline to prosecute or to seek a mitigation of punishment because he believes either that an act is in fact morally justified or that an actor's motives are praiseworthy. Nor do I discuss whether a jury or judge should be affected by such considerations in determining guilt or imposing sentence. I shall, however, assert that the actor's evident willingness to accept punishment may bear on the possibility of justifying the act morally.

MORAL JUSTIFICATION DEPENDS ON PROBABLE CONTRIBUTION TO THE SOCIAL GOOD

My basic criterion for judging acts of disobedience can be

---

[4] I mean to avoid the controversy over whether some laws are so immoral they are not properly called laws at all. In this chapter the term *law* does not include any implicit notion of moral acceptability.

[5] R. Dworkin, "On Not Prosecuting Civil Disobedience," *New York Review of Books,* June 6, 1968, p. 14. Cf. Note, "Sentencing In Cases of Civil Disobedience," 68, *Colum. L. Rev.* 1508 (1968).

stated simply. An act with social consequences is morally justified if it will probably contribute to the social good. Before considering the application of this vague utilitarian formulation, I must enter some disclaimers and clarifications and consider some possible qualifications. It is not my purpose to develop a systematic theory of what it means to say that an act is moral or immoral, a task that, in any event, I am not equipped to undertake. Such a course might be necessary if I believed that disagreements on this point were responsible for most disputes over the morality of illegal acts. On the contrary, I think that frequently those with sharply divergent views accept, explicitly or implicitly, some premise approaching the one suggested above. At any rate, that premise, subject to the possible qualifications discussed below, does reflect my own view. Even for those who reject it, the main body of this essay will have relevance so long as they think social consequences are of some weight in making an evaluation of disobedience from a moral perspective.

Definitional Clarifications

The criterion "will probably contribute to the social good" requires some elaboration. I do not intend any mystical concept, such as the "common good" or "general will" are sometimes thought to be; social good for these purposes is synonymous with "desirable social consequences." Nor is the phrase "social good" meant to exclude any relevant favorable or unfavorable consequences. I do not mean to decide difficult questions by definition. The moral acceptability of abortion turns largely on whether a fetus should be considered as having interests that should be protected. I would not dispose of that problem by saying that a fetus is not a part of society and so possible claims on his behalf have no bearing on the social good. Any relevant favorable or unfavorable consequences should be weighed, even if some of them might best be considered nonsocial, either because the entity on whose behalf claims are rightly made is not a member of society or because the claim, though made by a member of society, is a nonsocial one, such as the avoidance of eternal damnation. Social good is simply a shorthand for the kinds of values that are commonly involved when social acts are performed.

No attempt is made here to decide what is socially good. Those who disagree most strongly about disobedience are often in general agreement over the human values a society should protect and enhance. And when critics of disobedience do reject the notions of social good of disobedient actors, they commonly wish to make arguments against the illegal acts that would be valid even if those notions were accepted. If a disagreement over disobedience can be reduced to a conflict over what social ends are desirable or the comparative priorities of admittedly desirable social ends, the discussion should then be about those broader questions, rather than the appropriateness of disobedience to law as a means.[6] Although I do not engage in any extensive analysis of what is socially good, I do in the remainder of the chapter assume the desirability of social values I believe widely shared by thoughtful persons in contemporary society.

The formulation I have chosen not only begs the question of what social good, but also that of whose social good. It is obviously true that most people act as if their own interests and those of their in-group are more important than the interests of outsiders. This is perhaps most sharply evident in the realm of foreign affairs, where each country pays comparatively little attention to the interests of other countries except in so far as they coalesce with its own advantage. It is possible to defend at least some forms of special attention to in-group interest as consistent with ultimate acceptance of a principle that interests should be weighed equally. When a wage-earner turns money over to his family rather than to strangers who may actually need it more, he might argue that given societal institutions, he has special responsibilities for his own family that others will not fulfill; if he fails to support them reasonably well the family unit is likely to be destroyed, to the long-run detriment of its members and of society. Pressing the claim of a particular group in the social process to the exclusion of the interests of other groups could commonly be defended on the ground that, given the general selfishness that pervades society, any one group would

---

[6] The matter is more complicated than the text suggests. When either of two competing social ends could be embodied in law, racial segregation or racial integration, private property or public ownership, discussion about the desirability of these ends can be separated from discussion about the appropriateness of disobedience as a tactic. When, however, one of the ends may be inconsistent with disobedience, say the security of fulfilling expectations created by law, the two discussions are not equally divisible.

receive less than its due if it did not assert more than its due. Thus, barring widespread reform of human nature, ultimate fairness is served by a group's weighting its own claims very heavily. This defense of attention to in-group interest is particularly persuasive if the group has been consistently disadvantaged by society at large. In some circumstances apparent emphasis on the interests of a particular group may actually reflect emphasis on the overriding importance of particular social values. If one considered freedom from discrimination to be by far the most important social value, he might in this society press the claims of blacks with little attention to those of whites, not because black interests count for more than white interests but because blacks are the ones who now suffer deprivation in regard to this, hypothetically, most basic interest.

Though special attention to in-group interest can sometimes be persuasively reconciled with a principle of equal weighing, this is often not the case. Even when it is not true, actors may assert that the interest of their own group is consistent with those of the other members of society. Such assertions are common in this society where the assumption that humans' interests should be treated as roughly equal is widely accepted, if not observed. These assertions are sometimes hypocrisy, but frequently they are honest rationalization. Other actors may bluntly acknowledge that they are concerned with the welfare of a particular social group and have little or no regard for the welfare of others.

Plainly two persons who agree on what kinds of social consequences are good may still disagree about the desirability of a social action if they weigh the interests of affected groups differently. Let us suppose that the Vietnam war is moderately good for the United States but very bad for South Vietnam. The person who believes policy should be premised on the assumption that the interests of one American are equal to the interests of one-hundred Vietnamese may come to a conclusion about the war contrary to that of the person who thinks the interests of one American and the interests of one Vietnamese should be treated equally. Some arguments over disobedient acts can, no doubt, be reduced to this kind of disagreement. Since hypocrisy and rationalization do often obscure such divergences,[7] spadework will

[7] Discussion about the war is a good example. Supporters invariably contend that it is good for both the United States and South Vietnam and opponents invariably contend that it is bad for both.

often be required to expose the ultimate point at issue, but once it is exposed it should be the focus of discussion. I do not try to resolve this complicated ethical problem.[8] I do assume in what follows that the interests of all those who live in a society count. My own view is that each person should count equally. If there are those who unyieldingly think that only the interests of their own group count, the only relevant arguments against an act for them will be ones that demonstrate probable harm to that group.

The standard "contribute to the social good" would, of course, include situations in which all one can do is minimize impairment of the social good. Reducing losses is as much a contribution as increasing gains. There are some acts with no consequences of moral importance, and, theoretically at least, there may be some in which good and bad consequences are evenly balanced. Since performing such acts is not immoral, I shall speak of them as being morally justified though nonperformance would be equally justified.

The concept of "probably contribute" requires more lengthy elucidation. I am looking for a criterion that will include all the facts and arguments that could be presented to an actor before he acts. Consequences that are fortuitous, given the limits of human knowledge, are not relevant, nor are consequences predictable only on the basis of what I shall describe as private knowledge. A recent tragic example will demonstrate the distinctions. Students barricaded a university official in his office for some hours. That night he suffered a heart attack. Let us assume, plausibly, a causal relationship. If the official had never had heart trouble before, neither the students nor anyone else could have predicted that he would be affected in the way that he was, though they should have weighed the general risk that persons subject to emotional strain may have serious adverse physical effects. If the official's doctor had privately diagnosed heart trouble, again the particular consequence was not foreseeable for the students. If, on the other hand, the official was publicly known to have a weak heart, the students should have estimated a particularly high risk of an attack following their acts.

[8] A related problem is how the interests of future generations should be weighed in comparison with those of present members of society. See M.P. Golding, "Ethical Issues in Biological Engineering," 15, *UCLA L. Rev.* 443, 451–63 (1968).

I have earlier indicated why for my purposes actual motive is irrelevant. A more thorny problem is the state of the actor's knowledge. Here we may distinguish facts of which he was aware, facts of which he was not aware but of which he should have been aware, and facts of which he was not aware but which might have been known by him or by someone of greater intelligence standing in his shoes. If the primary purpose was to pass a moral judgment on the actor, one would condemn him when ignorance leads to an undesirable act, only if he could reasonably be held responsible for not ascertaining the facts correctly. My concern is not with what knowledge a particular actor should be held responsible for, but rather with how a reflective, intelligent, and well-informed observer would recommend that he act. When I speak of an act as morally justified I mean that given any knowledge available before the act and judged at the point of time of the act, the act appears to be desirable, that is, will probably contribute to the social good.

Some Possible Alternatives and Qualifications

Although this chapter contains no systematic defense of a standard for judging disobedience that focuses on probable social consequences, it seems wise to discuss three commonly asserted complete or partial alternatives.

Citizens are bound by consent to obey. One position is that citizens have an overriding moral obligation to obey the law because they have consented to be bound by it. This, of course, is the heart of social contract theories of political obligation. For Locke and others, the consent of the governed is the source of the duty to obey laws. The obligation to obey is analogous to the obligation of a person who has made a promise, that is, who has agreed voluntarily to perform a certain act. Let us grant for a moment that there is an obligation to obey the law in the same sense as there is an obligation to keep a promise. Does it follow the law should always be obeyed? Certainly not, since virtually everyone would acknowledge that it is sometimes good to break a promise.[9] A more difficult question is whether the obligation to

---

[9] Some theologians have argued that acts like lying or breaking promises are always evil, though they may be in some circumstances lesser evils than alternative courses of action. I mean by good or justified any preferable course of action judged from a moral point of view.

keep a promise does constitute an independent source of moral duty. To put the question a different way, can the duty to keep promises be subsumed totally under a duty to perform socially beneficial acts (usually it is useful to keep promises)? The classic example posing this issue is whether one should keep a promise to a dead man if more desirable social consequences will ensue from breaking it. No attempt is made here to resolve this dilemma. But if promises do constitute an independent source of moral duty, that is, if the obligation to keep them can not be subsumed under some broader duty, then the obligation to keep a promise must be weighed against a conflicting moral duty when the two collide. Thus, even if the "consent" of the governed is like a promise, the most that follows is that there is an independent duty to obey the law, which will sometimes, but not necessarily always, override considerations of social consequence if those would lead to breaking a law.

There are, however, strong reasons, discussed in some detail in this volume by John Ladd,[10] for not treating the average citizen's responsibility toward the law like his responsibility to keep promises. Locke's core notion is explicit voluntary consent; in leaving the state of nature, people agree to live together in society and accept the decisions of those placed in positions of authority. But faced with the problem that most people in most societies never give such voluntary consent, Locke retreats to a concept of tacit consent:

> I say that every man that hath any possession or enjoyment of any part of the dominions of any government doth thereby give his tacit consent, and is as far forth obliged to obedience to the laws of that government during such enjoyment as any one under it; whether this his possession be of land to him and his heirs forever, or a lodging only for a week; or whether it be barely traveling freely on the highway; and in effect it reaches as far as the very being of any one within the territories of that government."[11]

In these broad terms any one enjoying the benefits of a society has consented to its government, however tyrannical, and laws.

---

[10] J. Ladd, "Legal and Moral Obligation," ch. 1, this volume.
[11] J. Locke, *Of Civil Government, Second Treatise*, ch. VIII, § 119.

Now it makes some sense to say that acceptance of social benefits implies correlative social duties, but this acceptance is quite different from explicitly and voluntarily undertaking to obey the society's governors. Every human lives in some society, so acceptance of social benefits, including the protection of a legal system, is unavoidable. Since the prospect of living alone on a desert island is rarely a viable alternative, it is not very helpful to say one chooses to live in society. Even the possibility of moving to a different society is hardly a live one for most people, and such a change inevitably involves serious disabilities. The choice to remain in one's native country is not a choice in the normal sense, and genuine choice is central to the notion of consent. Finally, it seems strange to say that because one accepts the benefits of society, including its legal system, one is under a duty to obey the law even if the social welfare of the other members of society will be promoted by disobedience. In short, an acceptance of social benefits may be useful in explaining why a citizen should obey the law if obedience conflicts with his self-interest or perhaps the interests of those outside his society, but it does not afford a basis for arguing that the law should be obeyed when an illegal act would contribute to the good of his own society.

A more defensible theory is that in a representative democracy, citizens by participating in the process of government consent to its laws. As J. P. Plamenatz puts it in a new postscript to his earlier book *Consent, Freedom and Political Obligation*:

> Where there is an established process of election to an office, then, provided the *election is free,* anyone who takes part in the process consents to the authority of whoever is elected to the office. This, I think, is not to ascribe a new meaning to the word *consent* but is only to define a very ordinary and important political use of it. The citizen who votes at an election is presumed to understand the significance of what he is doing, and if the election is free, he has voluntarily taken part in a process which confers authority on someone who otherwise would not have it. . . .
>
> By consenting to someone's authority, you put yourself under an obligation to do what the possessor of it requires of you. . . .[12]

[12] J. P. Plamenatz, *Consent, Freedom and Political Obligation*, (Oxford, 2d. ed., 1968), pp. 170, 171.

This contention is relatively persuasive if one imagines a small meeting at which everyone understands that a majority vote will decide a specific question and at which it is implicitly understood that the act of voting implies consent to the result. If, for example, at a faculty meeting a participant announced that he had no intention of abiding by the result if his side lost, his right to vote on that issue, and perhaps even his continued participation in the community, might be questioned by others. In such circumstances, the act of voting, at least absent a disclaimer, may be considered an implied promise to accept the result. This analysis is less convincing when applied to the role of a citizen in a complex society. In the first place, in most liberal democracies the avowed revolutionary is permitted to vote. Thus someone would be allowed to vote even if he explicitly stated: "I believe in the violent overthrow of this corrupt society. I am willing to use any means to change it, but since the situation is not yet ripe for revolution I will do my best to alter it by the ballot." It is hard to see how his vote represents consent to the authority of the winner of the election. But even in the case of a citizen generally satisfied with the political system, voting in a public election is very different from participating in and voting at a meeting. He votes for someone who will then decide on a broad range of particular issues, many unforeseen at the time of election. His choices even in regard to individuals are severely limited by a preliminary political process. He has no real chance to present his own views directly to the body voting on the laws.[13] In short, though it may be correct to say that in some sense the person who accepts the system has consented to the authority of the person elected, it is much more difficult to argue than with regard to the small meeting that he has impliedly promised to accept the result of every deliberation of the body in which the person elected sits. One may contrast here the public official, such as a judge, who voluntarily swears to uphold the law; how much stronger his obligation of fidelity to the law seems to be.[14]

[13] I do not wish to denigrate such forms of political action as testimony before legislative committees and letters to representatives. These opportunities, however, are still far removed from direct participation in the deliberations of a legislative body, and relatively few citizens have the time and information to use them effectively.

[14] This may suggest one relevant distinction between the disobedient citizen and the governor who blocks a student's entrance to the state university after a contrary court order.

In summary, accepting the benefits of society and voting in public elections are not related to obeying the law in the way that making a promise is related to keeping the promise. Even if we grant that a promise is an independent source of moral duty, participating by voting in an industrial democracy may not be. That is to say that such an act imposes no obligation that must be weighed against desirable social consequences, even if such a weighing must be undertaken when desirable social consequences conflict with a promise.

Some readers may remain unconvinced by this differentiation. They may believe that voting is enough like a promise to constitute an independent source of duty, though the duty may be weaker than in the case of an explicit promise. Such a premise would require modification of, but would not destroy, what follows. I assume that the relevant criterion for judging disobedience is whether it will probably make a contribution to the social good. This could be modified to whether it will probably make a contribution to the social good large enough to outweigh the independent moral duty to obey the law. This modification would envision some situations in which desirable social consequences would be sacrificed to another moral claim. The reader who believes that there is a "promise-like" obligation to obey the law can make the appropriate modification in the subsequent material. (Even if such a modification is not thought needed for ordinary laws, perhaps it is appropriate for considering someone's disobedience of rules he has participated in formulating or to which he has given explicit consent, as by joining a club.) Let me add at this point that I will later argue that the form of government is highly relevant to whether disobedience is justified, but on bases that are not independent of social consequences.

The law should be obeyed because individual judgment is unreliable. It can be argued that social consequences are so difficult to predict and an individual's judgment so subjective and biased that opposing one's own judgment to that of society as reflected in its laws is never justified. This argument may appear to be inconsistent with a social-consequences criterion but in some forms at least it is really an application of that criterion rather than an alternative. If positive laws invariably do a better job of formulating rules of action than the judgments of even the most intelligent and dispassionate individuals, then we could conclude that disobedience of law will never "probably contribute to the social good." This is not to say that an illegal act will never do more good than harm, but only that it can never be predicted that an illegal act will do more good than harm. Thus, the social consequences criterion would not be inconsistent with a conclusion that individual judgment is so unreliable laws should always be followed. A second, more limited version of the unreliable judgment argument is that although individuals can sometimes correctly judge that positive laws are harmful, disobedience will be even more harmful, both because of its immediate ill effects and because its example will cause disobedience in other situations in which the law is good. If this were true, disobedience again would never probably contribute to the social good. A third form of the argument is more difficult to deal with. It is that although on some occasions some individuals can correctly conclude that the social good will be promoted by disobedience (even after taking into account the likely effects of the example), on most occasions most people exercise woefully inadequate judgment; therefore the use of such a flexible criterion will be socially harmful because it will be more often misused than well used. The argument has some force that people do better with clear moral standards that usually produce good results than they do with complicated standards that are theoretically more accurate but easier to misapply. If people come to believe, for example, that adultery is sometimes justified, they may commit it more often when it is not justified than when it is justified. Even if this argument were fully compelling I should be inclined to say that an act is justified when the more complicated, much abused standard is correctly applied. When one speaks of a moral act he means, I think, what a completely objective and reasonably intelligent person would do. If humans are so far removed in character from this model that the best society can do is to inculcate simple norms which, if followed, usually produce the right result, it still makes sense to speak of an act as morally justified if it conforms to the more difficult standard with which society could trust objective and intelligent actors. At any rate, my own view (which I hope is persuasively advanced by the end of this chapter) is that the fallibility of individual human judgment is highly relevant in determining the proper occasions for disobedience, but that it should not rule out disobedience in all circumstances. *Unjust laws should be disobeyed.* Unlike the last two possible objections to a social-consequences criterion for judging disobedience, this one is raised by those claiming moral justification for disobedience. Illegal acts have often been defended on the ground that the law requires something that is absolutely forbidden from a moral or religious point of view. When early Christians refused to worship pagan gods, it was not because they feared such worship would have adverse social consequences.[15] Antigone did not refer to the social good when she defied Creon's edict. If someone were told by a tyrant to choose five out of six innocent people to be killed, he might well decline even if certain that in the absence of his choosing all six would be killed. There may, in short, be some acts that are immoral whatever the social consequences. In my view, such acts are rare. It is difficult to imagine more appalling acts than those required of Jewish prisoners at the camps where their fellow Jews were put to death. Refusal by one person to cooperate in the execution of mass murder would simply have resulted in another death, serving no constructive purpose. The book *Treblinka,*[16] reconstructing the lives of these prisoners at one death camp, makes a persuasive argument for their staying alive, in the hope one day of revolting and reporting to the world outside what had gone on. South Africa's apartheid laws are surely among the world's most iniquitous, yet I would argue that a responsible opponent of those laws should act in a way likely (if any way is likely) to achieve their demise; he should not just disobey them all. If the example of disobedience is, in fact, the method most likely to lead to change, then disobedience should take a form that will create an example strongly and widely felt.

Although the Jewish death camp and the law of race relations in the Union of South Africa are exceptional in degree, no social institution is entirely free from evil. Participation in any existing society involves compromise with what would be ideal. There is

---

[15] Some of them may have been moved by a different kind of consequence, the prospect of a desirable life after death, but fervent religious behavior is rarely so calculating.

[16] J. F. Steiner, *Treblinka* (New York: Simon and Schuster, 1967).

room for argument, of course, when, if ever, compromise becomes so intolerable the morally responsible act is withdrawal of
one's participation regardless of consequence. One influential
modern writer on Christian ethics, as well, of course, as the
classic Utilitarians, can conceive of no such situation. For Joseph
Fletcher, "one's 'duty' is to seek the goal of the most love possible
in every situation,"[17] and this means for him always being guided
by the likely consequences of one's acts. One need not accept the
proposition that probable consequences are always determinative
of the morality of an act to believe that at least across most of the
spectrum of social behavior the rightness or wrongness of an act
depends on its consequences.

In addition to the narrow class of circumstances in which I
would find the claim at all persuasive that a law is so evil
obedience is morally wrong regardless of consequence, there is
another reason why I shall not discuss these claims further. Such
absolute moral assertions may invite disagreement, but not analysis. Those who do believe that there are a significant number
of circumstances in which disobedience is absolutely enjoined
whatever the consequences can consider what follows as relevant
to circumstances that do not fit within that category.

Before leaving this subject, I should note what strikes me as a
paradoxical element. It may well be that a defense of disobedience, or for that matter any social act, will have a greater impact
on others if couched in absolutist moral terms than if phrased in
more qualified language. (Compare "This war is so evil any aid
to it is absolutely immoral," with "This war is evil and nonparticipation seems to be the best way to end it.") It is, therefore,
quite possible, assuming a situation in which disobedience is
justified, that it may be socially useful for those who disobey to
advance an absolutist ethic. It is also possible, of course, that in
situations where the law should be obeyed, absolute moral injunctions, such as "A citizen should never violate the law," may
be more effective in winning obedience than some weaker less
sweeping moral principle. We might conclude that, on some
occasions at least, an ethic that disregards social consequences is
actually valuable to society because it helps promote the social
good.

---

[17] J. Fletcher, *Situation Ethics* (Westminster, 1966), p. 96.

APPLICATION TO DISOBEDIENT ACTS
OF THE CRITERION OF PROBABLE
CONTRIBUTION TO THE SOCIAL GOOD

In this section, I suggest the relevance for questions of justification of some varying characteristics of illegal acts. As the earlier discussion indicates, I do not, as most writers do, start with a definition of civil disobedience. The breadth of the definition often seems to depend on the writer's approval or disapproval of particular kinds of violations of law, the unspoken implication being that illegal acts that can not be defined as "civil" disobedience are impossible, or at least more difficult, to justify. In his essay, J. L. Adams adopts a definition that is rather narrow and fairly common in its essentials. For an illegal act to be civil disobedience, the purpose must be to change laws and better society, the act must be nonviolent and public, and the actor must intend to accept punishment.[18] Howard Zinn, on the other hand, is much more expansive; civil disobedience is defined as "the deliberate violation of law for a vital social purpose."[19] No one, I think, would dispute that acts meeting Professor Adams' criteria are acts of civil disobedience. What are generally thought of as typical acts of civil disobedience, those of the civil rights movement in this country and those led by Gandhi in India, do conform to it. One could, of course, try to decide which of the elements of those acts are essential for the acts to qualify as civil disobedience and which are inessential. My concern, however, is with whether disobedient acts are morally justified, and I do not think the line between morally justified and morally unjustified illegal acts is coincident with the line between acts that are civil disobedience, however defined, and those that are not. Thus, I do not attempt a definition of my own. I wish to indicate the wide spectrum of kinds of distinctions among illegal acts, many of which are also central to various definitions of civil disobedience, and to discuss why some of these distinctions bear on the issue of moral justification.

Before proceeding to this task, I should here make explicit an

[18] J. L. Adams, "Civil Disobedience: Its Occasions and Limits," ch. 13, this volume.

[19] H. Zinn, *Disobedience and Democracy: Nine Fallacies on Law and Order* (New York: Vintage, 1968), p. 39.

obvious corollary of the standard of "probable contribution to the social good." In deciding whether a particular social act is morally justified, tactical judgments are of the utmost importance. When one is trying to accomplish a desirable end it is morally preferable to use productive rather than futile tactics, assuming similar indirect consequences. Of two tactics equally likely to produce the desired end, it is immoral to use the one that will have more harmful consequences. And when the only tactics available to achieve a particular end are likely to cause more harm than the good obtained from the end accomplished, the moral course is to bear the existing evil. In the extreme case this is obvious. No one would advocate a mass slaughter of university officials to improve the food in the cafeteria, even if that were the only means likely to succeed. And few would suggest killing nine-tenths of the country's white population if that were the only way of reaching genuine racial equality. In short when it is sometimes said, "In those circumstances any tactic is justified," the speaker is guilty either of inaccuracy or hyperbole. As Professor Adams indicates in his suggestive analogy to the doctrine of just wars,[20] notions of proportionality are central in judging acts of disobedience.

The major kinds of distinctions drawn among illegal acts by those who discuss disobedience can be broken into four broad inquiries: what damage is done to the interests of others; what is the purpose of disobedience; do the actors willingly accept punishment; under what form of government does the disobedience occur. In the remainder of the chapter, I shall develop some of the distinctions within these major categories and their relevance to moral justification.

Damage to the Interests of Others

Illegal acts may or may not seriously interfere with the legitimate interests of other individuals. I have used the term "interest" rather than "right" because of its broader connotations; the citizen has an interest in having the roads open after a snowstorm but he may have no such right, at least not a legally enforceable one. The qualifier "legitimate" is employed to

---

[20] J. L. Adams, ch. 13, this volume.

allow the possibility of excluding asserted interests that deserve no recognition. For example, the strong desire of a sadistic parent to beat his child may not be worthy of any consideration.

Some acts violative of the law involve no direct interference with the interests of others. A law may be designed to protect those interests but not do so in particular circumstances. A good example is very low speed limit, twenty miles per hour, set to protect pedestrians in a crowded area. For the sake of convenience the law does not vary at different times of day, but at five o'clock on a Sunday morning the law serves no genuine protective purpose. Other laws are designed to protect the person against whom they are directed. Laws against jaywalking are meant to protect pedestrians against their own bad judgment. People are required to take cover during civil defense drills as a part of training for their own protection. Laws against drug use and consenting deviant sexual behavior are similarly not designed mainly to protect the interests of others. (In regard to deviant acts it can be argued that knowledge of their performance offends the sensibilities of other members of society. Whether that is a legitimate interest is a point much debated; it is enough to say here that it is an interest much less direct than those now to be discussed.)

Some illegal acts cause inconvenience to others. A loudspeaker that exceeds permissible limits of noise will disturb persons engaged in other activities. The person who double-parks is likely to slow down traffic. So also are demonstrators who block a bridge and subway employees who go on strike. Students who take over buildings interfere with the educational process, as do teachers who go on strike. By calling these interferences "inconveniences," I by no means intend to minimize them. They may be slight or very serious. For the person paid by the hour losses of time can be translated into losses of money, and though the calculation for others may be less precise, time wasted is time lost for valuable activity.

These situations may, however, be distinguished from those in which something that is "owned" is taken or destroyed, that is when property rights are impaired. The line between inconvenience and loss of property is not a clear one; it depends largely on what interests the legal system raises to the status of legal rights,[21] though a strong sense of owning something is not always based on legal right. Members of a family, for example, may consider objects as theirs that are legally owned by someone else in the family. Some forms of illegality involve aspects of both inconvenience and impairment of property. When striking teachers or demonstrating students take over a building, they interfere temporarily with the exercise of rights of property by the institution that owns the property. So also does a person who takes a one-day joy ride and then returns the car to outside the owner's house.

A different kind of damage is physical injury to persons. Even when no physical injury occurs, inconvenience or impairment of property may be accompanied by a threat of personal injury. The robber pulls a gun expecting not to use it; students in a building say no one will be allowed to come in, not really expecting to have to repel entrants by force. On other occasions, even when the actor does not directly injure someone physically, such injury may be a predictable consequence of what he does. When fuel oil drivers strike in midwinter during a flu epidemic, it is a near certainty that some people will die who otherwise would have lived.

Some violations of law involve only a possibility rather than a certainty or a probability of injury to the interests of others. In the vast majority of traffic violations, for example, no one suffers, though the violations do increase the risk of property loss and physical injury.

It is obvious that the degree of injury to others is relevant to whether disobedience of law is justified. The more serious the injury,[22] the greater must be the good accomplished by the act. If there is no such injury or risk of it, little or no countervailing good is required. One should be hesitant to conclude, however, that even in circumstances involving no direct injury others will not be harmed by illegal acts. First, there is no clear line between self-regarding and other regarding acts. The person who commits suicide may leave a family emotionally and financially bereft. So

[21] In this sense, "property" might include legal rights, such as contractual ones, that would not strictly be called property rights within the legal system.
[22] If people have a moral responsibility to protect themselves, as well as others, from injury, then possible harm to the actor must also be considered.

also, the incompetent jaywalker may injure the car that runs over him, delay traffic, and cause monetary and emotional hardship. Pacifists who refuse to take shelter during a civil defense drill may, if jailed, leave families temporarily without support. When it is plain that the law has been violated, either because the illegal act is open or because there is other evidence that the law has been broken, society expends resources to determine guilt and to impose appropriate punishment; that social cost is often very considerable.

Two other kinds of possible harm are less apparent. One is the need of humans to discipline themselves. Men are creatures of habit as much as reason. The driver who does not observe speed limits when it is safe not to do so is more likely, one would guess, than the driver who observes them scrupulously, to become sloppy or make an error of judgment and speed when it is not safe. The other problem is that of example. Examples are rarely, if ever, perceived by others precisely as the actor intends, and the limits of an example of disobedience may be missed. The teenage son who sees his father speeding may not understand that speed limits can be disobeyed only in special circumstances. The nimble-footed jaywalker encourages less artful traffic dodgers. The actor who wishes to do something itself socially harmless must take into account the possible unintended encouragement of harmful acts.

Most illegal acts cause some more direct injury to others. There is no need to argue that inconvenience, loss of property, and personal injury are social harms. Death and physical pain, and the fear of them, are everywhere considered bad; so also is the loss of the power to enjoy or enrich life, to which time and property contribute. But the matter is much more complicated than that. Human beings come to expect that certain of their interests will be protected by society. When this protection fails, the reaction is not only one of loss, but also of frustration and insecurity. The sense of insecurity, at least, also extends to others who fear that at some future date they may be subjected to similar harm. Most persons probably suffer inconveniences more readily then equally costly losses of property. The sense of loss is usually stronger when what is taken is something that one actually "owns"; the deprivation of social expectations is felt more immediately and sharply.[23] Thus destruction of a given amount of property is a more serious social harm than traffic delays causing the same amount of financial damage. Perhaps this aspect of the analysis should be qualified when damage is to institutional property, e.g., a government building, about which no individuals have a sense of ownership. A sense of insecurity is likely to be most intense when it involves fear of one's physical well-being.

Frustration and insecurity are bad not only because they are unpleasant emotional feelings, but also because they are destructive of fruitful social intercourse. Human contact, particularly with the group from which one fears injury, is made more difficult. If a sense of insecurity is pervasive enough, members of society lose confidence in themselves and their social institutions to solve problems, and either personal withdrawal (insofar as possible) or the acceptance of extreme measures to remedy the situation is likely to result. Foremost among the possibilities is strong suppression of those who are thought to cause the insecurity.

It is conceivable, however, that the emotional disturbance caused by loss will lead to good results. The person injured may be shaken to question his complacent assumptions and come to recognize the injustice of the law or policy against which the persons who directly damaged him were protesting. So, radicals may believe, keeping students forcibly away from class may contribute to their long-term radicalization, a desirable consequence in their view. Certainly this theory has little general plausibility when the injury to interest is a loss of property or physical harm. Even when what is involved is only inconvenience, perhaps accompanied by a threat to use force if necessary, one doubts whether that is more likely to achieve the result of radicalization than other tactics that will gain attention and polarize the uncommitted, but not directly interfere with their interests.

Another possible counterweight to the social harm of injuries to others is the chance that the infliction of them will benefit the

[23] This conclusion, like other empirical observations in this chapter, is based on introspection, conversation, and general reading rather than specific scientific evidence. It, like the other observations, is, of course, subject to any qualifications revealed by more precise evidence.

actors. Speaking of violence directed at colonial oppressors, Frantz Fanon states:

> But it so happens that for the colonized people this violence, because it constitutes their only work, invests their characters with positive and creative qualities. The practice of violence binds them together as a whole. . . .
> At the level of individuals, violence is a cleansing force. It frees the native from his inferiority complex and from his despair and inaction; it makes him fearless and restores his self-respect.[24]

Fanon seems to be saying that a violent overthrowing of colonial rule is preferable to peaceful tactics, even if the latter are equally likely to win. To this unprofessional reader, there is a disturbing discrepancy between this kind of rhetoric in the front of Fanon's book and his description in the back of mental disorders arising out of colonial war. Even if his argument has validity in the colonial context, the situation is very different when the oppressed must continue to live with the oppressors after their fight is won. Nevertheless, if it is in fact true that some acts of disobedience promote the psychological health of those engaging in them, that is a relevant consideration.

Also of relevance is the possibility that acts that do some injury are the only substitute for acts that do more injury. A leader who convinces a mob set on murder to block traffic instead has performed in a highly desirable way if he correctly judges that the mob could not be persuaded to forego all antisocial acts.

With regard to many instances of disobedience that cause harm to others, there is an important difference between expected harmful consequences and hoped-for beneficial ones. The former are virtually certain. If a bridge is blocked, traffic will be slowed; if students occupy buildings, classes can not be held; if an assassination succeeds, the victim will die. What good will be accomplished by acts like these is usually problematic. The greater the uncertainty that any good will be achieved, the greater that good would have to be to outweigh a certain or

[24] F. Fanon, *The Wretched of the Earth* (New York: Grove, 1968), pp. 93, 94.

highly probable amount of harm. Here is a point at which the fallibility of human judgment is important. The responsible actor should recognize how complex and little understood are the reactions of social organisms, and how uncertain any judgments of nonimmediate social consequences are. He must also consider the tendency of virtually all humans to overestimate not only the weight of their own claims for satisfaction in comparison with those of others but also the potential significance of their acts in achieving desirable change. He should, therefore, be slow to conclude that contemplated long-term goods will outweigh certain and immediate harms.

Both because of obvious immediate harmful consequences and highly probable, indirect, harmful consequences, any disobedient act that interferes in a significant way with the interests of others can be justified only by strong countervailing reasons, and the greater the interference the stronger the reasons must be. It does not follow, however, that even the worst kinds of interference are never justified. Most observers would commend rather than condemn the conspirators who planned to kill Hitler, even though the bomb planted was also likely to kill others more innocent than he was. Few Americans consider the Revolutionary War immoral, though extensive loss of life was a certain consequence. I shall consider below the assertions sometimes advanced that violent disobedient acts are never justified in a democracy and that revolution is something entirely apart from other acts of disobedience. It is enough to conclude this section with the observation that the kind and degree of injury done to others bear heavily on whether a disobedient act is justified.

The Reason for Disobedience

Most illegal acts are committed by persons pursuing their own interests at the expense of others; these actors would not usually advance a moral justification for what they do. But many illegalities are thought by the actors not to be morally wrong. Often they believe they do not do real harm. The person who drives at 30 m.p.h. in a 20 m.p.h. zone at five o'clock on Sunday morning would defend his nonobservance of the letter of the law on the ground that he proceeded in a way to protect all social interests sheltered by the law. On other occasions an actor might acknowledge a slight increase in the risks the law was designed to minimize, but assert that these were outweighed by a more pressing claim, say the need to get his wife in labor to the hospital as quickly as possible. A starving man who stole some bread might make a similar claim. These persons need have no objection to the law they violate or any other law, yet they would claim a moral justification for their disobedience.[25]

When people believe a law is unjust, they may violate it simply to avoid its impact or in order to get it changed. Those who take drugs do not use them, at least primarily, in order to get the law changed. Nor did those who violated the fugitive slave laws do so to obtain repeal as much as to ameliorate the unjust consequence of an unjust law. On the other hand, in what we think of as the typical instance of civil disobedience, the object is to get some law or policy changed. Sometimes the law violated is the one to which the actors object. On other occasions a law to which the actors do not object is violated in order to get a different law changed, a policy altered, or a new course of government action undertaken. When demonstrators unlawfully block traffic to protest racial segregation they have no objection to the traffic laws. Sometimes illegal acts may be aspects of a revolutionary course of behavior designed to overturn the existing government or entire social system and substitute a new one.

This categorization makes it clear, I think, that purposes other than the open protest normally associated with civil disobedience may underlie a valid claim that disobedience is morally justified. Sometimes a law is so wicked that the actor rightly tries to circumvent it. The person who contrary to the law assisted Jews to escape Nazi Germany acted morally. It is also clear that disobedience is sometimes justified, as when the husband speeds his wife to the hospital, although the law violated is acknowledged to be a just one. When the violation is designed not to ameliorate an unjust law or evade a just one in special circumstances, but to draw attention to some injustice and get the government or other authority to change its laws or policies, does it matter whether the law disobeyed is the one thought to be

---

[25] In some criminal codes, failure to observe the letter of the law in circumstances such as these may not be criminal. See, e.g., *Model Penal Code* § 3.02 (Proposed Official Draft 1962); *NY. Penal Law* § 35.05 (McKinney, 1967).

unjust? Abe Fortas thinks so, for he says: "In my judgment civil disobedience—the deliberate violation of law—is never justified in our nation where the law being violated is not itself the focus or target of the protest."[26] One problem with this position is the elusiveness of its application. If someone who violates the draft law thinks the Vietnam war is immoral but accepts the need for a peacetime draft, is the draft law the focus or target of the protest? If Negroes sit-in at a voluntarily segregated restaurant, do they violate the general trespass law (to which they do not object) or the existence of legal principles that allow segregation?[27] The difficulty of applying this test points up the more serious concern over whether the distinction drawn is relevant. It might be argued that if the law violated is the focus of concern, the interests impaired are not ones deserving of protection. But this is not necessarily so. The violation of a state law requiring segregation in stores (assuming, incorrectly, for the moment, the constitutionality of such laws) will hurt the interests of the store owners subject to the sit-ins, but not the interests of other store owners. The inequality with which adverse consequences will fall and the fact that they may fall on persons individually innocent are socially undesirable results even though the law itself may be completely unjust. It may well be that the interests of those owners are outweighed by other considerations, but they are not negligible. One consequence of a refusal to submit to the draft is that another young man who would otherwise have escaped the draft will be called up. If the draft is unjust, or unjust at a particular time because of a given war, the call-up of an innocent young man willing to be drafted violates an interest deserving protection.

A stronger argument for the Fortas distinction is that if disobedience of just laws is countenanced, the danger to society is much greater and the interference with legitimate interests much more extensive. He seems to have in mind massive disruptive activities like a general strike. It is certainly true that such actions are likely to do more substantial harm than disobedience to one unjust law, both because of their contemplated impact and because of the greater danger that violence will erupt. They

[26] A. Fortas, *supra* note 1, p. 63.
[27] This sentence assumes, wrongly given existing federal legislation, that those who sit-in have no statuory right to service.

would therefore require much stronger justifying reasons, but that cannot be said of every illegal act not directed at the law violated. A peaceable but trespassory sit-in on government property may cause less harm than would actual violation of a law protested against. Howard Zinn gives the following example of disobedience designed to elicit positive government action: After a child has been killed by an automobile, mothers block traffic on their street to pressure the government into installing a traffic light.[28] In neither of these two instances would the harmful consequences of disobedience be widespread.

The breadth of the example provided to others who believe laws are unjust or would like to change policies is also relevant for the Fortas contention. If action is directed only at the unjust law itself, the example has a self-limiting scope. The principle extends only to acts of disobedience directed at other laws believed by the actors to be unjust. (For reasons suggested earlier, the limiting principles in the mind of the actor are unlikely to be fully perceived by others, and disobedience directed to an unjust law may give others some encouragement to engage in broader forms of disobedience not directed at the law to which the actors object.) The only limiting principles for disobedience of laws not the focus of complaint are highly flexible weighings of probable social harm against probable social good. The misapplication of these principles by others is quite likely. Therefore, it may be that an act of disobedience will create a more dangerous percedent if not directed at an unjust law. If this is so, it would take even stronger grounds to justify such an act than one directed at an unjust law itself, but that hardly leads to the absolute principle laid down by Fortas. If, contrary to the assumption of the immediately preceding analysis, one accepts Professor Zinn's view that people are too eager to obey the law,[29] then the fact that a particular kind of disobedience would serve as a broad example might be counted in its favor.

Writers often seem to regard the question of a right to revolution as entirely separate from other issues of disobedience to law. Once it is admitted, however, that revolution—that is, armed

[28] Zinn, *supra* note 19, pp. 21, 32.
[29] *Ibid.*, pp. 16–18.

overthrow of the government—is sometimes justified, it follows that other violence short of revolution might also be justified. If the evils of a social order are great enough to justify the suffering inevitable during revolutionary violence, they are great enough to justify lesser forms of violence, if the latter are likely to accomplish as much good. In answer to this proposition, it might be argued that only a revolution can assure a breadth of change great enough to outweigh the harm of violence, and only when a revolution occurs can a society put past violence behind it. The second assertion is highly doubtful; revolutions seem as likely to lead to subsequent violence as other violent illegal acts. With regard to the first assertion, revolutions frequently lead to smaller changes than are envisioned and sometimes very substantial changes are accomplished without an overthrow of government. While it may possibly be true that violent acts short of revolution are rarely likely to achieve enough good to justify them, it cannot be laid down as an absolute rule that this is always so. A different point about revolution is also worth making briefly. When one undertakes a revolutionary course of action, he still should obey laws, except when disobedience will contribute to the revolution or some other positive goal. Being a revolutionary is not, as is sometimes implied, a wholesale warrant for disobedience of all legal norms.

Is Punishment Willingly Accepted?

The typical criminal seeks to avoid punishment, but those who have violated laws as a form of protest have often willingly accepted punishment. There are two separable elements in the ordinary willingness to accept punishment. One is that the actor behaves in a manner that allows the authorities to impose punishment if they wish. The second is that the actor acknowledges the appropriateness of punishment if it is determined that the law has been violated. Raising possible legal defenses is not, of course, inconsistent with either of these elements. Sometimes the first element will be present without the second, that is an actor will submit without resistance to penalties but deny society's right to punish him.

At first glance the distinction between avoiding and accepting punishment may appear to coincide with that between surreptitions and open violation of the law. But the perpetrator of a carefully planned surreptitious murder may, as soon as he is successful, give himself up and willingly subject himself to legal penalties. Conversely open violations are not always accompanied by even the first element of this willingness. A rioter may count on not being apprehended; those engaging in unlawful strikes may rely on the pressure they can bring to bear to avoid penalties; students who take over a building may attempt to gain amnesty as a condition of settlement.

A willingness to accept punishment is not always a condition of a morally justified act of disobedience. If someone was illegally engaged in helping Jews escape from Nazi Germany, to have given himself up would have made it impossible for him to continue in that aid. It would have been perfectly moral for him to try to avoid punishment. But it does not follow that acceptance of punishment is never essential to moral justifiability. The effect of an illegal action is likely to be significantly different if the violators submit to punishment. First, the frustration, resentment, and insecurity caused to those whose interests may be injured will be substantially reduced if they realize that those who have caused them harm are themselves willing to pay a costly price. Second, submission to punishment serves as a test for the actor of the strength of his conviction. When he puts to himself the hard question of whether he is willing to be penalized, he will be, more likely, careful to consider his course of action and its value; thus submission to punishment imposes some check on irresponsible judgment. Third, submission to punishment demonstrates to others the depth of the actor's conviction. People are understandably skeptical when others merely assert a strong sense of injustice about particular laws or policies; common use of language includes a great deal of hypocritical rhetoric, rationalization of self-interest, and simple overstatement. Illegal action to change a law is, of course, further evidence that feelings are strong, but it is not nearly as convincing as a willingness to suffer serious penalties. Thus, insofar as actors wish to convince others of the magnitude of the injustice against which they protest, they are likely to be much more persuasive if they submit to punishment.

Submission to punishment also sets an important limit on the example of disobedience. If an effort is made to avoid punish-

ment the actors seem to be saying to others: If you believe a law
or policy is very unjust, you can think yourself justified in
disobedience to try to alter it. Now "very" is a vague term; future
actors may underestimate the strength of feeling that supported
actors before them, and they may overestimate their own feelings. There is, on the other hand, a substantial and less amorphous restriction on when disobedience can be thought justified
if the example seems to say: If you believe a law or policy is so
unjust you are willing to suffer serious penalties to alter it, then
you can think yourself justified in disobedience.

(A word of explanation is required here about the phrase
"think yourself justified." As I have used the term, justification
exists only when an action will probably promote the social
good, not when the actor thinks that is the case because he
misconceives what is good. In this sense, the person who violates
the law in order to promote integration may argue that his acts
provide no example at all for segregationists, since, whatever
their tactics, their aims are harmful, and therefore any acts to
achieve those aims are unjustified. But this response is too facile.
The action of the integrationists is in part their implicit statement of when disobedience is an appropriate tactic, and that
part of the example may well affect others with different ideas
about what is socially good. The only response of the original
actors if that part of the example is followed by those pursuing
segregationist ends is "You have picked the wrong goal." If that
response fails, they have no other argument against disobedience. I use "can think yourself justified" to include situations in
which the only doubt about justification relates to the good
sought rather than the tactic of disobedience.

The reasons so far advanced for willing submission to punishment would be largely satisfied simply by a course of action that
allows the authorities to impose punishment, without an acknowledgment of its moral appropriateness. For the points that
follow, both these elements of willing submission are important.
If punishment is accepted, the actors demonstrate a commitment
to the fundamentals of the existing social order. Though they do
not accept the judgment of society as expressed in the law about
the proper course of behavior, they do ultimately accept that
judgment in the form of punishment for behavior which society
considers wrongful. This may involve an implicit admission that

society may possibly be right after all, and therefore express a certain humility about the actor's moral judgment, but it need not. Even the most self-righteous and morally certain person might believe that society operates most fruitfully if the judgments expressed in law are accepted as the final criterion of what is wrongful behavior, even when those judgments are plainly misguided. By the possible admission of fallibility of judgment, by adherence in at least one respect to the existing method in society for determining what is wrongful behavior, the actor reaffirms his sense of being a member of the community at the same time he defies its judgment. This is virtually certain to reduce the sense of anxiety and anger that disobedient acts may cause to other members of the community. And the affirmation of community reduces the probability that the actor will be considered an outsider, a heretic who has rejected the basic premises of a social system. It, therefore, reduces the likelihood of massive repression by those who disagree with his positions; successful repression, it must be remembered, may not only undo any good the actor has achieved, but itself may do great social harm.

As the preceding discussion suggests, the argument for submission to punishment is strongest when actors are primarily concerned with the moral force of their example (rather than with trying to put pressure on bad men who are beyond redemption) and when they accept the basic premises, at least, of the social system.

The Form of Government Under Which Disobedience Takes Place

Disobedience may occur in any kind of society. Many commentators on civil disobedience have thought it relevant whether laws are made in a democratic way. Since disobedience may be directed against privately made rules as well as positive laws, the argument that rule-making is undemocratic may be available even in a democratic society. Students have made this claim against university rules. The proper analysis here is plainly complex because this arguably undemocratic rule-making power is conferred by democratically made laws and supported by the sanctions, e.g., for trespass, provided by those laws.

It is sometimes said that violent disobedience, though it may sometimes be justified under other forms of government, is never justified in a democracy. It is usually not clear whether this is thought to follow logically either from the people's power to choose decision-makers or from their power to influence decisions, or represents a rough empirical generalization about the limits of injustices likely to occur in a democracy. Let us return to the attempted assassination of Hitler. If Hitler had been freely elected as an absolute ruler for four years in 1941, would that have made unjustified the attempt on his life? Given the enormity of his crimes and the destruction of German life likely to result from his continuing role as ruler, I should think not. Nor does the fact that a policy is approved, or even made by a majority necessarily lead to the conclusion that a minority should not use violence to overcome it. If a majority of Germans approved genocide, would not a minority be justified in violent resistance, at least if that resistance promised some greater hope of success than alternative courses?

It may be argued, of course, that a genuine democracy would simply not evolve such a wicked policy, and, if it did, more peaceable alternative courses of action would be equally available to change or ameliorate it. Given the sad history of mankind, I lack confidence that a democratic majority would never approve policies wicked enough to justify violent disobedience; after all, a majority in a large part of this country once approved of slavery. It seems wrong to conclude without careful examination of particular instances that peaceable alternatives would always be equally effective in leading to change.

But if absolute limits on disobedience may not be drawn from the fact of representative democracy, more moderate conclusions are warranted. If leaders are popularly elected and citizens can affect policies by open discussion and peaceable petition, it may be more likely that policies and laws will promote the social good. If this is accurate, a citizen in a democracy has an extra reason to question whether his fallible judgment that a law or policy may be unjust is wrong. This is particularly true when the democratic system does fairly represent competing interests, say labor and management; it would be less true for foreign policy decisions. It is equally important that in a democracy there is a greater opportunity to affect what the government does by peaceable means with less harmful social consequences. The occasions, then, when extralegal steps are justified may be more limited.

There are also some more complicated considerations. In a representative democracy, most of the citizens believe the system for reaching decisions is reasonably fair. And they regard the results of that system as a generally equitable balancing of the interests of diverse members of society. To the extent that they do have this attitude they are likely to view disobedient acts as a blow not only at the government but at the majority of the population including themselves. And they may be particularly resentful because that blow comes from others who are themselves allowed to participate in the decision-making process. Thus, the sense of outrage caused by illegal protests against felt injustice is likely to be greater in a democracy than under a more authoritarian government. This in itself may be a social harm of some consequence, but it also enhances the possibility of hostility toward, rather than sympathy for the demonstrators' goals and the eventual likelihood of repression that is popularly supported. If these consequences do occur, disobedience is likely to be counterproductive.

Another reason for not resorting to disobedience in a democracy may be the general desirability of having decisions made by orderly process. Though one thinks a particular policy or law unfortunate, he may believe the process generally reaches good results. If the example of disobedience is followed by others of different persuasions, and the ordinary processes for reaching decisions are circumvented with some frequency, the result may be more often harmful than good. There is, of course, also the possibility that repression will shut off not only extralegal tactics but also reduce the availability of legal methods of change.

These arguments, which if valid make it much more difficult to justify disobedience in a democracy, are weakened insofar as the society and government do not actually reflect the democratic model, particularly if the supposed injustice occurs at a point where the discrepancy between the model and the reality is greatest. Perhaps the clearest kind of case is one in which part of the population is denied a political voice. Athens is the classic example but the United States before the Civil War serves just as well. A majority of the voting population accepted slavery (and if we discount the denial of the franchise to women, which is probably not relevant for this purpose, the great majority of people in the country could vote), but that hardly provided an assuance that the interests of the slaves were fairly reflected in the system. Nor could anyone protest that if slaves declined to follow the law, they had unfairly departed from orderly processes for expressing their views, since they had no access to those processes. If the existence of democracy was not relevant to acts of disobedience contemplated by slaves, what was its relevance to those who wished to support the slaves? On the one hand, it might be argued that their ability to participate in decision-making limited the kind of acts that could be justified. On the other, one might contend that since they had chosen to act on behalf of a nonparticipant group, they could act in any way that would be justified for a member of that group. For me the truth lies somewhere between these two views. Their continuing participation in the democratic process (limited as the process was) was relevant, since illegal acts performed by them would have had some consequences different from illegal acts performed by nonparticipants. But the arguments against disobedience based on the likelihood of wrong judgment and the fairness of the process were as inapplicable to the supporters as to the slaves themselves, since there was little reason to suppose that a process in which a group was totally unrepresented would produce results fair to that group.

It is important to note here that exclusion from the channels of orderly change may be partial rather than total. When women were fighting for equal rights, they could not vote but they could bring considerable influence to bear without departing from lawful channels. The same is true now of young people who cannot vote. Given the vast difference between the owner-slave relationship and the husband-wife relationship, there was also more reason to hope that the interests of women were sympathetically dealt with by the full participants in the process. The same may now be said about the interests of those under twenty-one.

Apart from children, virtually everyone can now participate in the formal political process, but it does not necessarily follow that laws and policies in the United States conform to a model of representative democracy that includes the notion that people's interests are to be given roughly equal consideration. One theoretical possibility is a permanent minority, a group whose numbers are fairly represented but always outvoted. Given the shifting alliances and extensive political compromises in this society, that possibility is probably of less practical significance than the unequal distribution of political power. Money, personal influence, professional position, education, and intelligence all add to one's potential weight in the political process. The possibility that the president of General Motors or the editor of *The New York Times* can affect the course of public decisions can hardly be compared with the prospect of an individual ghetto resident's doing so. If one makes the plausible assumption that the interests of the wealthy and influential in society often conflict with those of the poor and less articulate, one may conclude that laws and policies will be balanced in their favor to a greater degree than their numbers would dictate.

According to social philosophers like Robert Wolff and Herbert Marcuse, the situation is much worse than this simple difference in political weight might suggest.[30] The accepted pattern of interest-group representation and reconciliation tends to exclude those not part of some recognized interest group and to divert attention from problems common to all members of society, such as air pollution. Moreover, the very values and assumptions which underlie the claims of society's members are themselves largely determined by those who control the flow of information, that is, the government and other members of the Establishment. In foreign policy, for example, the government defines the posture of this country on the basis of ideological assumptions and evaluations of interest which pervade its public statements. The unwitting citizen accepts these as substantially accurate, so firmly are they embedded in most discussions of foreign affairs questions, and is not likely to challenge the policies that emanate from them. The government can than be repressive, in the sense of preventing effective dissent from its fundamental directions, at the same time it is tolerant of radical criticism.

[30] See, e.g., H. Marcuse, *One-Dimensional Man* (Boston: Beacon, 1964); H. Marcuse, "Repressive Tolerance," and R.P. Wolff, "Beyond Tolerance," in H. Marcuse, B. Moore, Jr., and R.P. Wolff, *A Critique of Pure Tolerance* (Boston: Beacon, 1965).

I do not wish to engage in extensive analysis of this critique of pluralist democracy. It is enough to point out here that insofar as it is valid, it weakens those arguments against disobedience based on the desirability of following orderly processes in democracies. If the existing channels of political decision-making are rigged, then one who disagrees with laws may have little reason to doubt his own judgment of their unfairness and little confidence that orderly attempts to achieve change will succeed. He may also believe that shock rather than ordinary persuasion is required to jolt people into questioning the society's shared but misguided assumptions. I suspect that many disagreements about the justification of disobedient acts do come down essentially to divergent estimates of the health of the political order.

CONCLUSION: A PERSONAL NOTE

If this chapter seems inconclusive, it is because I do not believe disobedience of law is subject to any simpler judgments from a moral perspective than other kinds of social behavior. The moral appropriateness of an act can be determined only by examining its probable effects in a concrete context. It is impossible, I have argued, to categorize some kinds of illegal acts as always unjustified, and the considerations that bear on whether a particular act is justified or not are many and complex. Too often in arguments about disobedience, they are neither openly identified nor candidly discussed, and debate proceeds with each side engaging in rhetorical reiteration of premises the other side rejects.

The general standard I have suggested for judging issues of justification is highly flexible; its application can lead to conservative or radical conclusions, depending on one's social values and estimation of human potentialities and the processes of change in a highly complicated society. The reader is entitled to some notion of how I would apply it. I am much impressed by the subjectivity and unreliability of human judgment, especially when the interests of the person making the judgment are at issue. Although this society is far from perfect, it is not nearly so bad as the radical critique suggests. Since it is hard for me to conceive of a society in which the political processes are not geared to some extent to favor those who benefit from the status quo, I am skeptical that any new order would be highly preferable. I also believe that this society is relatively responsive to the claims of oppressed groups and that these claims are put before it with reasonable effectiveness through legal means, though not as rapidly or as fully as one would like. I regard substantial inroads on people's sense of security as serious social harms, which may be counterproductive to the goals of those who cause them. That attempts are made to deal with the claims of the oppressed is in part a reflection of genuine idealism which is bound to suffer from a continuing confrontation atmosphere. In social affairs at least, most people are primarily self-interested and great pressure is likely to make them more so rather than more altruistic. And if pressure causes anxiety it may narrow rather than broaden their view of their self-interest. I think a social order and particularly vulnerable fragments such as universities are much more fragile than advocates of extensive disobedience acknowledge, and I lack confidence that a profound crisis would lead to more desirable change than use of orderly processes. Such a crisis might well produce repressive change of the most detrimental sort. In short, I believe that the appropriate occasions for disobedience as a tactic to change laws and policies are very limited in this society, and that even then justification will usually depend on nonviolence and willing submission to punishment, which reduce the destructive potential of disobedience. I would urge sober reconsideration and great restraint on those moved to disobedience as a form of protest. Still, I would refrain from trying to lay down absolute rules and would admit that my own views are based on arguable assumptions about complex social facts.

15

SOME TRUTHS AND UNTRUTHS ABOUT CIVIL DISOBEDIENCE

GERALD C. MacCALLUM, JR.

  Feelings about civil disobedience run high during times of public stress, and high feelings, in turn, lead to crude perceptions of the phenomena one is hastening to defend as acceptable or praiseworthy or hastening to condemn as outrageous and dangerous. One may find parallel deficiencies in the work of scholars and other serious writers who, seeking to be helpful by laying certain issues to rest or by providing a unified perspective of the phenomena, hasten in their own, sometimes indirect, way to various defenses or condemnations.

  Take the matter of what civil disobedients are up to. Though lip service is occasionally paid to significant diversity in the aims, intentions, hopes, and expectations of civil disobedients, and though one sometimes finds at least implied recognition of the occasional multiplicity of these aims, and so on, the prevalence of over-simple and artificially constrictive accounts of them has bedevilled our thinking about the character, limits, effectiveness, and justifiability of civil disobedience. That, at least, is the thesis of this paper.[1]

The thesis will be developed through an examination of each of a small set of claims currently playing important roles in discussions of civil disobedience. The claims are alike in having acquired in extensive quarters, and even in some of the most serious discussions of the topic, the status of unquestioned truths— or at least of truths not seriously questioned. They are also alike, as will be shown, in that each is either flatly false or badly in need of an analysis sorting out what is true and what is false in it. They are alike furthermore, as will also be shown, in that each rests in part upon over-facile assumptions concerning what civil disobedients are up to.

Showing these things is not a purely negative task. It provides a basis also for seeing questions we ought to be asking ourselves about civil disobedience. Some of the questions emerging will not be surprising. They will seem old and familiar. Others will be recognizably fresher, if only in the sharpness of their focus. We should ask them too if we wish to get straight about civil disobedience.

I

Consider the claim:

I. That civil disobedience is nonviolent.

Since the time of Gandhi, claims about the nonviolence of civil disobedience have gained increasing prominence, though

---

[1] The key question here is, What are civil disobedients up to? One can sometimes answer satisfactorily questions about what a person is up to by speaking of the person's aims, sometimes by speaking of his intentions, sometimes by speaking of his hopes, his expectations, or even his attitudes. I have spoken impartially in this variety of ways in this paper—recognizing that there are important differences, for example, between intentions, on the one hand, and hopes, on the other, but being careful always to speak of each only insofar as it focuses answers to the question: What is he up to?

their precise strength and import have not always been clear.[2] Most centrally, these claims have played a role in exhortations (as by Gandhi) concerning the spirit and method of this kind of disobedience. But they have also figured in attempts to reassure publics confused and distraught by the phenomenon, and even in attempts to support radical cynicism concerning the disarmed docility and consequent ineffectiveness of ordinary or traditional civil disobedience.

All this attention to the nonviolence of civil disobedience has encouraged some persons (to judge by debates I have heard) to see nonviolence as the principal if not sole significant limitation on the demeanor of civil disobedients. These persons have, furthermore, found it easy to suppose that demeanor is always either violent or nonviolent and not both. This supposition in turn has put a variety of strains on the credibility of assertions about whether the behavior of purported civil disobedients has or has not been nonviolent. Those persons starting with common notions of violent behavior as behavior likely to produce destruction of property or physical injury to persons see all other behavior as nonviolent and thus of a piece; they thus suppress our perfectly legitimate interests in whether force has been used, whether the behavior has been resistant or nonresistant, considerate or inconsiderate, restrained or unrestrained, polite or impolite, active or passive, and so forth. They even suppress our interests in what are clearly the ramifications or expectable consequences of the behavior in question—e.g., our interests in whether the behavior has been obstructive or nonobstructive, disruptive or nondisruptive of the activities of other persons (or, to cite a special case, of the routine operations of governmental agencies or other institutions).

If, on the other hand, they start from the super-rich but extensionally narrow notions of nonviolence encouraged by Gandhi (who thought of humility, self-restraint, considerateness, politeness, and truth-telling as important features of nonviolent

[2] That is, it has not always been clear whether the nonviolence of the disobedience is being considered a necessary, a 'characteristic,' or (when combined with openness) a sufficient condition, or all three, of civil disobedience or of that civil disobedience deserving of toleration, or of both. The use of the expression "authentic civil disobedience" in many discussions points up one portion of the problem: it so nicely echoes the common equivocation between claims about what civil disobedience is, and claims about when civil disobedience is justifiable or at least deserving of toleration.

behavior), they will see violence where others do not ordinarily see it (e.g., as with Gandhi, they will see it in lying, hatred, insults, economic and social boycotts, fasting against a tyrant, and even in impatience).[3] Clearly, we need to correct this situation either by rejecting the assumption that all behavior is either violent or nonviolent or by allowing the notions of violence and nonviolence to shrink back to plausible size and making open and independent use of a richer stock of contrasts.[4] But, supposing that we do return to a more reasonable understanding of the richness and multiplicity of our interests here, can we also come to an understanding of the temptation to name nonviolence and perhaps other kindred limitations on demeanor as, in some way, defining conditions of civil disobedience?

The rationale most readily offered cites the word "civil" in the expression "civil disobedience."[5] This qualifier is often cited also, of course, in explanation of other alleged features of civil disobedience—e.g., its political, public, or noncriminal character. These matters will be discussed below. But in the present context, the qualifier is seen as operating straightforwardly to delimit a range of eligible demeanors. The suggestion drawn from it is that demeanor must somehow qualify as polite, restrained, mannerly, decent—i.e., 'civil.'

One may ask, however, why such a restriction on what is to count as civil disobedience is reasonable or fitting. Here one treads on shaky ground though this is not often realized. A short reply to the question is to say that disobedients whose demeanor did not fall within these limits simply would not be *civil* disobedients; but, though even Gandhi gave it at times, this reply is hardly better than a pun.[6] It merely leads to

---

[3] See M. K. Gandhi, *Non-Violent Resistance* (New York: Schocken, 1961), pp. 41–42, 73, 77, 79, 145, 148, 161–62, 182.

[4] These matters seem hinted at in Professor Adams' discussion (ch. 13, this volume) of the applicability to civil disobedience of the fifth criterion of just war. That paragraph of his could be used happily as a springboard, at least, for reaching the above points.

[5] In this paper, double-quotes are used around expressions that are mentioned but not used and around expressions quoted from other writers or speakers (actual or hypothetical). Single-quotes are used as scare-quotes around expressions that are being used and to which special attention is being called.

[6] See Gandhi, *op. cit.*, p. 173 and also pp. 4, 60, 172.

the question of why a notion of disobedience so limited should ever become so prominent.

A deeper rationale may be thought provided by pointing out connections between the limitations, on the one hand, and the presumed point or aim of civil disobedience, on the other hand. The argument would be that the limitations are reasonable in the light of the aim. Materials for such an argument could be found in the work of Gandhi and of Martin Luther King.

Both Gandhi and King saw civil disobedience as a form of nonviolent resistance, and they justified their interest in the latter by way of characterizing it as a certain very special kind of effort to change societies. The nonviolence of the resistance, and hence also of that form of it called "civil disobedience," was seen for the most part to follow from the nature of the effort involved.

King, for example, asserted that violence "destroys community and makes brotherhood impossible. It leaves society in monologue rather than dialogue."[7] He thus focused a view of civil disobedience as part of an effort and as itself constituting an effort to achieve social and political change through creation of a dialogue that would awaken in members of the society a sense of community and brotherhood with the victims of injustice in their midst. This view of the aim or point of civil disobedience makes available a seemingly profound rationale for the "civil" of "civil disobedience," viz., that the disobedience in question is "civil" because it embodies an effort to change societies by building, strengthening, and utilizing communal ties between the victims of injustice and other members of the society. In this, the rationale obviously closely parallels those mentioned above pointing to the alleged public, political, or noncriminal character of civil disobedience, but it affords much firmer guidance in the further task of exposing the appropriateness of the "nonviolent" constellation of limitations on the demeanor of civil disobedients. The limitations are more easily and plausibly seen to be reasonable in the light of this expanded understanding of the aim.

Gandhi, whose work had inspired King, had earlier character-

---

[7] M. L. King, *Stride Toward Freedom* (New York: Harper & Row, 1958), p. 213.

ized civil disobedience (and other forms of nonviolent resistance) as resistance to the acts but not the persons of those in power. He did so on an explicit understanding of nonviolent resistance as an effort to achieve change through soul force—i.e., through personal suffering designed to convert through love, "touching the heart and appealing to reason rather than fear."[8] This was the understanding of the aim of civil disobedience that made his disallowance of resistance to the persons rather than merely the acts of those in power seem so reasonable. It was also an understanding that afforded a rationale for stress on the nonviolence of the resistance; the limitation, again, served to rule out behavior that would be counterproductive to achievement of the aim, the aim being to touch the heart of those in power and to appeal to their reason, not their fear.

Such accounts as these of the roots of stress on the nonviolence of civil disobedience, rationalizing the nonviolence by connecting it with the aim, are surely attractive.[9] But their acceptability rests in the end not only on (i) the correctness of various empirical and conceptual claims about how nonviolence is connected with effective achievement of the supposed end or aim of civil disobedience (e.g., *does* violence always leave society in monologue rather than dialogue?) but also on (ii) the correctness of the profered identifications of this end or aim. The discussion in the next section is intended to expose the dubious-

---

[8] Gandhi, *op. cit.*, esp. pp. 17, 32, 64, 87, 169, 172. See also p. 69. For emphasis on the ramifications of the appeal of reason and thus to the importance here of truth, see pp. 6, 29, 34, 40–42.

[9] If one were pressed to sum up their definitional point, perhaps the argument would run as follows: Just as an object may lend itself so little to the uses for which hammers are designed that it cannot reasonably be considered a hammer at all, so certain demeanors are so out of line with or counterproductive to the aim or point of civil disobedience as to disqualify what so happens as an act of civil disobedience.

Such an argument would at best be convincing, however, only in the most gross cases of lack of fit between aim and demeanor. There doubtless are such cases, but attempts to apply the argument to specific instances of disobedience will be plagued by the controversiality of many of the empirical claims needed to underlie the assertion that there is a lack of fit (see text below). This difficulty, furthermore, when combined with the common lack of extremely well-defined aims on the part of persons who violate the law in circumstances roughly approaching these (again, see text below), shows how unsafe it is for us to do here what men commonly do in a wide variety of other circumstances, viz., make imputations about a person's aims on the basis of observations of his demeanor.

ness of the latter. What is shown is that such over-simple accounts of the end or aim of civil disobedience are implausible,
and that there is thus a need to rethink the whole question of the
importance of nonviolence in connection with civil disobedience. If the appropriateness of nonviolence is contingent upon
the end or aim of civil disobedience, then we had better be
careful that we have correctly identified this end or aim. The
argument below, however, is that claims that civil disobedience
per se has any such central aim or point are so far from the truth
that no general account of the importance of nonviolence is
possible. This does not in itself, of course, mean an end to
reasoned stress on the importance of nonviolence. It means
merely that the reasoning will have to be richer (to suit the
multiplicity of aims that may be involved) and will have to vary
to suit the cases (as the aims vary).

II

Consider the claim:
II. That civil disobedience has one central aim or point.

One who looks carefully at the relevant literature will soon
recognize that a wide variety of aims has been imputed to
persons engaged in civil disobedience. Civil disobedience has
variously been seen as an effort to maintain or achieve or "witness
to" moral integrity or a morally sound position on some issue, or
to communicate something to law enforcement officials or to a
government or members of a community, or to change or nullify
or test or produce some law or policy. From this plentiful array,
sometimes one, sometimes another of the imputations occupies
the center or even the whole of the stage. Occasionally the result
amounts only to a difference of emphasis. Sometimes it
amounts to a sharply etched disagreement.

For example, the view of Gandhi and King that civil disobedience is to be understood at least as part of an effort to achieve
social change must surely be questioned by persons who believe
that open and unevasive noncooperation with contemporary
selective service regulations should count as a form of civil
disobedience and have noticed that many such noncooperators
seem interested only in establishing or maintaining a certain

personal style of life, and declare themselves (and appear to be) totally uninterested in the reactions of other people to what they are doing.[10] Again, consider a recent difference of opinion between Judge Wyzanski and Fortas. Wyzanski holds that civil disobedience does not involve an aim of testing the constitutionality of the law or policy being protested; Fortas holds that when it is endorsable it involves precisely that—at least in the United States.[11]

The importance of such disagreements and of the wide spread in the range of aims normally cited goes, of course, far beyond an interest merely in finding a secure rationale for the common stress on the nonviolence of civil disobedience. As has already been suggested, for example, it goes to definitional issues or at least to issues that threaten to be definitional ones. The differences in the aims cited, especially when accompanied by the working (though perhaps not the theoretical or acknowledged) assumption that civil disobedience has a single characteristic aim or point, raise the question of what is going to count as civil disobedience. Insofar as our notion of what a person is up to does count in our determination of whether he is engaged in civil disobedience (as it surely does), disagreements such as the above suggest that various persons purportedly engaged in dialogue about civil disobedience may not be talking about the same thing at all, or, at least, that they see what they are talking about under such different aspects as to make further disagreements among them not only understandable but inevitable.

In coping with this situation, we must justify our eventual inclusion or exclusion of various aims or intentions as eligible ones. Presumably, we will be guided by an interest in preserving distinctions between civil disobedience and certain competing con-

---

[10] The appearance of disagreement on the matter could of course be dissipated if Gandhi and King were understood to have meant only that civil disobedience is an instrument of social change; for that in turn might mean only that civil disobedience can function so as to promote social change regardless of the intentions of the participants. This, however, appears to alter drastically what Gandhi and King intended to say.

[11] Charles Wyzanski, "On Civil Disobedience," *Atlantic Monthly*, February 1968 (see also Joseph Sax, "Conscience and Anarchy," *Yale Review*, 57 (June 1968), 481, 485); Abe Fortas, *Concerning Dissent and Civil Disobedience* (New York: Signet, 1968), esp. pp. 16, 32–34, 63. They do, however, agree that civil disobedience is an act of protest and an effort to communicate protest. This, as we have just seen, is at least equally controversial.

cepts (e.g., lawful dissent?) or contrasting concepts (e.g., nullification?).[12] But it is clear that our arguments will not be knock-down ones. Aside from the likelihood that the role of references to aims and intentions in characterizing the relevant and most clearly viable candidates for competing or contrasting concepts (e.g., lawful dissent, nullification, 'common criminality,' revolution) —a role that must be worked out very carefully—will not in the end be clear, none of these candidates is unarguably a competing rather than merely a contrasting concept to civil disobedience. Thus, knock-down arguments will not be available because such arguments on these matters are at best possible only in the case of clearly competing concepts (e.g., this thing *can't* be a tiger, because it clearly *is* a lion). Concerning, for example, the status even of 'lawful dissent' relative to this issue, there are sound reasons exposed elsewhere in this paper for uncertainty about whether it is a competing rather than merely a contrasting concept.[13]

If, consequently, a permissive attitude toward these definitional issues relative to the aims of civil disobedients seems advisable, the wide spread in the range of aims normally cited has also a considerable further importance. Depending upon the circumstances of actual or contemplated civil disobedience, there may very well be an appreciable lack of congruence in the patterns of reasonable and unreasonable, productive and counterproductive behavior relative to various different but, by hypothesis, equally eligible aims.

For an example that is difficult but centrally located, the behavior required in order truly to 'witness' what one might wish to witness may, under the circumstances, be counterproductive to the success of efforts to communicate to law enforcement officials the grounds for one's witnessing or of one's beliefs about the need for change in law enforcement policies. This divergence is possible, perhaps, only because the 'witnessing' is often to oneself or to God, and not (necessarily) to other persons such as governmental officials. Its possibility has been obscured, however, be-

---

[12] The use of competing and contrasting concepts in arriving at reasoned determinations of whether a given thing 'is an x' is worked out by Thomas R. Kearns in "On Vagueness" (unpublished Ph.D. dissertation, University of Wisconsin, 1968). Kearns offers, among other examples, 'lion' and 'tiger' as competing concepts; 'game' and 'gang-war' as contrasting concepts.

[13] See note 16 and Section IV below; and compare carefully the discussions cited in note 11 above.

cause people have not noticed the importance of the shift from an interest in witnessing to oneself or to God, to an interest in communicating something successfully to, e.g., governmental officials, and because there have been too many facile assumptions about the latter.[14] Given that it exists, we must surely understand which of the two aims is present before we can think clearly about whether the piece of actual or contemplated civil disobedience is (or will be) either effective of justifiable.[15] And if both

[14] What will succeed in efforts to communicate to officials depends on what the officials are like and what the circumstances are. The assumption that nonviolence, considerateness, and so on will always be reasonable or productive, for example, seems grounded either on dubiously generalizable empirical claims or on further restrictions on the 'communicative' efforts in question—e.g., that they be efforts to communicate through Gandhian soul force. But, in the first place, the generalizability of the empirical claims is not certain, the issues being not merely, for example, whether nonviolence might not occasionally be less productive than violence, but also whether it might not on occasion be downright counterproductive. Gandhi of course understood this, and was careful to argue these points in upholding his claim that communication through soul force would always be maximally effective. But many persons find his claims dubiously generalizable, and the claims certainly merit continuing investigation (though part of the dispute here is doubtless due to lack of clarity and agreement on what is going to count as 'communication' or a 'communicative effort'—an important matter, considered in Section III).

Restricting the communicative effort to efforts to communicate through soul force might eliminate the possible noncongruence of productive behavior, and so forth affirmed above. But even if such restricted efforts were always maximally effective, the restriction of civil disobedience on definitional grounds to the use only of such efforts would hardly seem plausible. That is, it would hardly seem clear that efforts to communicate in any other way would reasonable *thereby* be disqualified as acts of civil disobedience. Thus it hardly seems clear that the possibility of noncongruence cited in the text would be eliminated.

Perhaps, nevertheless, one might hold that there are other (somewhat broader) plausible restrictions on eligible communicative efforts—and, indeed, on any or all of the loosely characterized aims mentioned at the beginning of this section—and that, given these restrictions, congruence in the patterns of reasonable and unreasonable, productive and counterproductive behavior for the achievement of each would be guaranteed. But this prospect seems highly speculative, and I do not see how one could establish (so securely as to dissipate concern for the problems discussed here) the necessary presence of one or more of these restricted aims in every case of genuine civil disobedience (cf. note 22 below and the text at that point).

[15] Normally our interest in the effectiveness of what a man is doing is an interest in whether his activities will contribute to the achievement of aims we assume him to have. Thus there should be no question about the claim just made insofar as it concerns effectiveness. But the role of assumptions about a man's aims is equally important to consideration of the justifiability of what he is doing, though this may not seem so clear. The importance is

aims are present, we must understand this also if we are to perceive the depths of the problems into which both civil disobedients themselves and those called upon to respond to them may be plunged.

As a prolegomenon to closer pursuit of these issues, one could consider some such general taxonomy as the following of the intentions/aims/hopes/expectations commonly attributed to law violators:[16]

obvious where the justifiability question is (as it often is) about whether the man is reasonable to do what he is doing, given his aims and beliefs. But even where the question veers more clearly in the direction of concern for the moral acceptability of what he does, we can hardly reach the full range of this concern if we eliminate consideration of his aims, intentions, hopes, and expectations in doing it. Even if one is something of a utilitarian, for example, and assesses the rightness or wrongness of what a man does solely in terms of an estimate of 'its' probable consequences, 'it' is most often not identifiable independently of consideration of the man's aims, intentions, and so forth in behaving as he is behaving (e.g., as in the case of lying), and, even where it is so identifiable (e.g., grabbing food out of someone's hand?), estimates of its consequences could seldom exclude consideration of the consequences of the fact that his aims in doing it were imputed by others to be thus and so, or even that they were thus and so (the former because the influence of his act on other persons may be in part *via* their impression of what he is up to, and the latter because the effects of the act on the development of his character and thus on his future actions may depend importantly on his view of what he is doing).

[16] Putting the matter concerning law violation awkwardly but accurately, civil disobedience is generally conceded to be a kind or manner of violating, or a violating in certain circumstances, of an actually or purportedly valid law or an actually or purportedly lawful and authoritative order or command. These distinctions between what is actual and what is purported do not become of especial importance until Part IV, and are consequently ignored until then though, of course, they bear upon the issue already raised concerning whether 'lawful dissent' is a competing rather than merely a contrasting concept to 'civil disobedience.' The distinction between laws and orders and commands is ignored here entirely because it is not of especial importance to anything discussed here, though it would be important if we were, for example, to discuss the ways in which various persons in a society (e.g., persons who happen to be policemen, prosecutors, judges, jurors, legislators, ordinary citizens) should or might acceptably but diversely respond to civil disobedience. Further, though we commonly speak of orders and commands being disobeyed and of laws being violated, this distinction is also ignored here for the sake of simplifying discourse and because nothing said hangs on it, though something might sometime hang on it because the practice among scholars of speaking also of laws being disobeyed—and thus of civil disobedience in connection with some (purported) violations of these laws—may persist only as a survival of the mistaken view that laws are orders or commands.

1. 'Secretive' violations, where we impute an aim to avoid both detection and arrest, and
   a. a primacy of interest in personal advantage, as in so-called ordinary crime.
   b. a political aim, as in some assassinations of public figures.
   c. an aim of helping others, as in some so-called crimes of compassion (e.g., the beneficent abortionist).
   d. an intention of following the dictates of one's conscience, as in crimes connected with the operation of the Underground Railway in the nineteenth-century United States.[17]
2. Nonsecretive violations, where we impute little or no aim to avoid detection, and
   a. no sober thought of arrest, either because the case involves assignment of criminal liability for the consequences of irresponsible or negligent behavior or because the act is seen as 'insane' or a 'crime of passion.'[18]
   b. an expectation of avoiding arrest
      i. through timely payment and forfeiture of bail, or timely payment of fines, as in cases of deliberate and open traffic offenses by railroad companies whose operations block crossings beyond the legal limits, or through the normal exercise of police discretion in failing to make arrests for certain kinds of 'minor' violations.

[17] Clearly, the borderlines between the above classes are not always crisp, and the classes are not always mutually exclusive (which is to say that sometimes one and the same act may correctly be described in several of the ways listed). This is true also of the items listed under 2 below, and its importance there is considerable.

The listings above may seem superfluous because agreement appears unanimous that civil disobedience is nonsecretive. Nevertheless, both here and elsewhere where the taxonomy may appear excessively extensive, its extensiveness is not idle. The taxonomy exhibits, and its extensiveness suggests, some of the rich variety of law violations with which, as one may find, civil disobedience may usefully be contrasted. Endless confusion in discussions of civil disobedience seems to me to have been produced by failure to see and discriminate sufficiently these contrasting cases.

[18] Including in the latter, of course, such crimes as homicide occurring during the course of a drunken brawl.

ii. through influence of personal prestige or bribery,
     and so on in leading enforcement officers to look
     the other way.

iii. through (possibly coordinated) audacity in commit-
     ting the violation, as in smash-and-grab raids, day-
     light bank robberies, massive looting, or even coups
     d'état.

c. a hope or expectation of contributing to overthrow of
    the administrative apparatus presently giving the con-
    cept of arrest clear application in the society in ques-
    tion, as in the storming of the Bastille, putsches, and
    most guerrilla warfare.

d. a hope or expectation of nullifying the law or order in
    question, at least with respect to its applicability to
    oneself or some class of violators, by violating it in a way
    or under circumstances making arrest of any, or perhaps
    only of most, violators impracticable, as in the behavior
    of some Bostonians in connection with the Fugitive
    Slave Law of 1850.

e. a hope or at least an expectation of being arrested, and
    an intention not to resist arrest. Relevantly distinguish-
    able cases here of what the violators may be up to are
    suggested by the seeming appropriateness or inappropri-
    ateness of imagining the following remarks in their
    mouths:

    i. "Please put me away for my good (or for yours)," as
        with the town drunk who wants a night's shelter, or
        a person who believes that he is dangerous to himself
        or to others.

    ii. "I want to get this into the courts and am using a
        'standard' way of doing so," as with an inductee's
        refusal to step forward for induction when he thinks
        that, under the existing law, he has been wrongly
        classified.[19]

    iii. "I want to confront you with the need to arrest me,
        in order to get you or those on whose authority you
        are acting to reconsider what you or they have done
        (or have failed to do) ";[20] and, further,

---

[19] Cf. *Dickinson v U.S.* 346 US 389 (1965); *Estep v U.S.* 327 US 114 (1946).
[20] The aim here may not be to focus attention on the very law violated or

      "Do you really, now that you are confronted with
the issue, intend to enforce this law—e.g., against
persons such as myself?"

    .. "Shouldn't you, in view of this manifestation of the
strength of my feelings, rethink the whole matter?"

iv. "I cannot, in conscience, accept or conform to the
law, and seek, in my present violation,

  . to avoid an evil worse than the violation itself."

  .. to bear witness to my stand and thus 'be right' with
myself by this positive affirmation of what I believe."

  ... to disassociate myself from complicity in, and thus
answerability (to whom?) for, the law or policy."[21]

v. "I will not obey 'laws' such as these; they have no
legitimate claim to my obedience because

  . they are instruments of my oppression, not my welfare."

  .. they are immoral."

  ... the government administering them lacks legitimacy because:

      it is not a power establishing justice" (cf.
Thoreau).

      its charter is deficient."

      its form is not acceptable—e.g., not democratic,
not rule by a super-race, not theocratic:

        . though it purports to be."

        .. and it doesn't even purport to be."

      no government whatever is legitimate."

This taxonomy is at best suggestive of what might eventually
be needed in order to deal with the issues raised earlier. Its
sketchiness is perhaps indicated most dramatically by the fact
that one cannot, even on the assumption that every question but
the question concerning what the person thinks himself up to
has been settled favorably to an act's being a case of civil

---

even to focus attention on any law at all. It may instead be to focus attention
on the absence of a law (e.g., of an open housing law) or on the way (some)
laws are administered—e.g., as in inequitable issuing of parade permits.
(Whether such variations can count either as genuine or as justifiable civil
disobedience is controversial. Cf. Fortas, *op. cit.*)

[21] The differences between entries iii and iv respectively correspond very
roughly to the differences between Gandhi's 'aggressive civil disobedience' and
his 'defensive civil disobedience.' Cf. Gandhi, *op. cit.*, p. 175.

disobedience, point to any one spot on the format and say noncontroversially, "Here, at least, is a clear case of civil disobedience." One cannot do so because the intentions and so on mentioned are not yet fully enough delineated. Reference back to the discussion of Gandhi and King would show this, as would reference to the views of yet other persons who believe that civil disobedience must embody an effort to achieve or contribute to the achievement of justice, equality, or freedom of association, and so forth.[22] As can readily be seen, even the sections of the taxonomy most congenial to these suggestions do not reach this far.

Nevertheless, the sketch can be used as it stands to pinpoint and sharpen the definitional and other issues raised earlier.

Note that, while certain positions on the format can be excluded noncontroversially from the ambit of civil disobedience (e.g., 1; 2a; 2b, all three subsections; 2e, i), and others might reasonably or justifiably be excluded (e.g., 2c; 2d; and all those under 2e, v)—though not by knock-down arguments—there is clearly no hope of reasonably or justifiably reducing the ambit of civil disobedience to only one or even two or three of the positions. This result, furthermore, is not merely an appearance resulting from peculiarities of the taxonomy offered here. It would emerge even if alternative plausible taxonomies were used—taxonomies whose basic divisions might fall along lines quite different from those used here and involve aims, etc., not even mentioned in the present one (though it is difficult to imagine any less controversial basis for the major divisions than attitudes toward detection and arrest). For, though these alternatives might put immediately to one side some of the positions on the presently offered format (e.g., those listed first in this paragraph), and might considerably narrow the scope of others, none could eventually avoid inclusion of the others, however narrowed or segmented. Thus, unless one is going to argue that all of the remaining entries (e.g., 2e, iii, all subsections; 2e; iv, all subsections), perhaps narrowed or segmented in some way, must apply in every genuine case of civil disobedience (and why should they?), the need for some definitional permissiveness with respect to the aims of civil disobedients will be inescapable.

22 Cf. the essay by Professor Adams, ch. 13, this volume. For another dimension of possible further specification, see note 20 above.

Much of the importance of the multiplicity of the remaining aims to the other issues mentioned earlier, however, would survive even if one were to accept the claim that these (perhaps narrowed) aims must all be present in every genuine case of civil disobedience. It is true of course that the aims—at least those under 2e, iii, and 2e, iv—could all be present simultaneously. Furthermore, situations where some several of them, and others on the format as well, are so present seem more common than not among persons generally thought to be engaging in civil disobedience. Consider, for example, the S.N.C.C. workers sitting-in in the South ten years ago (reference: 2e, iii, both subsections; 2e, iv, at least the second subsection; 2e, v, the first subsection; and [at least marginally?] 2e, ii). And consider the more politically oriented of today's draft resisters (reference: 2e, iii, at least the second subsection; and 2 iv, at least the first and third subsections). Often persons so situated, and others in allied movements, do not seem to have fully marked and discriminated their multiple aims. For example, within the span of three pages of *Stride Toward Freedom,* King offers, as characterizations of the message of the movement he is summing up, several of the variations appearing in our format; but he does not mark the differences between them, nor does he mark his shifts from one to another.[23] If these are to stand also as characterizations of the aims or points of the civil disobedience associated with the movement, then we must ask whether participants contemplating or engaging in civil disobedience and inspired by such words fully recognize the multiplicity and diversity of the aims cited. If they do not, they will not understand that in some circumstances action productive or justifiable relative to some (one of) the aims might be counterproductive or unjustifiable relative to another. They will not even be in a position to think clearly about whether this is so.[24]

If, for example (to echo a case offered earlier), circumstances were such that their attempts to 'be right' with themselves (2e,

[23] King, *op. cit.,* pp. 216-18.

[24] Thus, something would seem amiss even if productive behaviors, and so on, were in the end congruent.

One might say of these people that their definiteness of intention would not be sufficient for these tasks. [The expression "definiteness of intention" is taken from Arne Naess, "Toward a Theory of Interpretation and Preciseness," in Leonard Linsky, *Semantics and the Philosophy of Language* (Urbana: University of Illinois Press, 1952), p. 248. See especially pp. 256-57.]

iv, second subsection) would involve them in behavior more likely to provoke escalation of the evil in question than to encourage reflection on its possible abandonment (2e, iii) —as where tensions were high and those persons securely in power were becoming increasingly vindicative about dissent—these actual or potential civil disobedients would not be fully equipped to recognize and understand this. Nor would they be equipped to explain their situation to others, or guide others to appropriate responses when, as would not be surprising, others were not responding appropriately. They would not fully see or understand that persons responding to them or even (perhaps only temporarily) they themselves might be seeing or emphasizing one of these aims but not the other, and consequently mistakenly assessing the reasonableness (or unreasonableness) of estimates that either or both of the aims might be achieved by the civil disobedience in question, or mistakenly assessing the justifiability of seeking to achieve the aims by such means.

In confronting such difficulties, of course, the actual or potential civil disobedient is in a position no different from that of many men in many situations. What men do very often expresses a multiplicity of aims, hopes, and expectations, sometimes only dimly recognized, and things don't always work out smoothly nor can they always even be planned smoothly without the confrontation of dilemmas. The commonness of this fact, however, is all the more reason why we should stop approaching civil disobedience as though it were all of a piece, internally a smoothly coherent act with a single unifying theme, and so on. Such a view only prevents us from recognizing fully the importance of the possible variations in aims just discussed and keeps us from systematic and orderly investigations of their ramifications. It is not surprising that, insofar as such an over-simple view has expressed our expectations concerning the subject matter, some of us have seen some segments of the truth and others have seen other segments of the truth and we have all been sent off in different intellectual and emotional directions. Nor, of course, is it surprising that, in the face of the actual richness of the phenomena, we should be subject to bouts of doubt about the rational basis of the common emphasis on the nonviolence of civil disobedience.

III

Consider the claims:

III. That civil disobedience is a political act, an act of protest, an act of communication.

The applicability of the remarks made in Section II to these claims is not immediately obvious. To say, for example, that civil disobedience is a political act may be only to say that it is politically significant—either because it has ramifications that are or may be politically relevant or important, or becasue it marks a person's attempt to establish or alter his personal, moral, or even legal relationships to certain political events or circumstances (e.g., by disassociating himself from further responsibility for them—though, of course, questions remain about whether he *can* do this and about what it would mean to do this). The first interpretation makes the claim unobjectionable though it hardly differentiates civil disobedience from any other purportedly illegal act nor from any of an enormous range of purportedly legal acts. The second (because it has to do with what the person is up to) is, at least as a perfectly general claim, readily questionable on grounds exposed in Section II.

More commonly, however, the claim that civil disobedience is a political act amounts to a claim that the act is done for the sake of expected or hoped-for political consequences, that it is (part of) an engagement in or continuation of politics, an exercise of a technique for influencing the political life of the community.

Because this view too is grounded on claims about what the disobedient is up to, it also is readily questionable on the grounds exposed earlier. But its popularity and the popularity of the related views cited at the beginning of this section excuse giving them special attention. Furthermore, further careful thinking in these restricted cases about what civil disobedients are or might be up to will be helpful in exposing roots of further serious confusions about civil disobedience.

Most broadly, of course, the views in question slight the inward-looking concern for one's own moral integrity and identity that occupies the center of attention for some civil disobedients (e.g., the noncooperators with selective service regulations mentioned in Section I), and may on occasion do so even for the more politically oriented disobeyers. The view, for example, that civil disobedience is the exercise of a technique for influencing the political life of a community carries the suggestion that civil disobedience can comfortably be arraigned alongside such activities as electioneering, to be judged and criticized in much the same terms—with only perhaps the special and especially interesting disadvantage that it is illegal. The wrongheadedness of this approach as a perfectly general one is indicated by the occasional but predictable inappropriateness of remarking to a man (e.g., a Jehovah's Witness) who has just been confronted with a need to choose obedience or disobedience *now* and has chosen to disobey, "That is not a legitimate way of trying to get the law changed."25

But even where an outward-looking aspect dominates, and an act of civil disobedience is appropriately seen principally as part of an effort to bring about political or social change, one should not suppose that it can thereby be characterized quite comfortably in any or all of the above ways—viz., as a political act, an act of protest, or an act of communication. The issue hangs on important differences in how the actor sees his law violation as contributing to political or social change.

He may see it as a means (hopefully) of initiating a court test of some law or policy.26 Alternatively, he may see it principally as a means of notifying authorities or the public generally of the presence of his dissent (and perhaps of the dissent of others of whose dissent his is representative). He may think that this latter is all that can reasonably or appropriately be expected of civil

25 One might of course criticize the man for not having tried earlier to get the law changed so that he would not now have been confronted with a need to make the present dreadful decision. But if he had tried and (obviously) failed, we hardly evidence full understanding of his situation if we say only "Be a good loser," or, more solemnly, "Having tried to use the mechanisms of change, you implied acceptance of their use and thus of their outcome, and it is dishonorable for you now not to submit to their outcome." The point is that the man may be trying to save himself—not so much his life (for there might be dishonorable ways of trying to do that) but his integrity, his moral identity or even his soul (what would be dishonorable ways of trying to do these things?) —and his earlier efforts might best be compared to the efforts of a man trying to talk a gangster out of killing him, i.e., not as efforts that somehow bind him to acceptance of defeat if they don't work.

26 Though if he sees it only as this, with none of the further visions detailed below, we would run afoul of Judge Wyzanski's position—though not that of Fortas—in regarding the violation in question as a genuine case of civil disobedience. Cf. note 11 above and the text at that point.

disobedience in contributing to change, and that such notification itself must be depended upon to initiate further processes leading to change or to provide an entering wedge for further activities by himself and others leading to change.[27]

Or he may see his act not only as notificatory but also as persuasive with respect to the merits of his dissent. One of Gandhi's reasons, for example, for thinking of civil disobedience as something for the very few—to be engaged in only by persons of great moral purity—was that he depended upon the capacity of the act to persuade in this way; only if the authorities were confronted with persons of recognizable and steadfast moral purity would they be led to think again about and doubt the merits of a policy that would have to be enforced against such persons.[28]

Lastly (for our present purposes) the civil disobedient may instead see his act as embodying a threat to the authorities and to the public generally, a threat of impending administrative difficulties if they do not accept his position. (Even some of Gandhi's remarks suggest this view.) [29]

In conflations of these last three views, and in confusions about borderlines between them we obviously find a source of much unease about civil disobedience. An effort to notify is not, at least in isolation, comfortably describable as a political act. Neither is an effort to persuade comfortably describable as an act of protest. Nor is a threat comfortably describable as an act of communication. The popularity of reliance on such descriptions, and careless readiness to interchange them, thus quite naturally put a strain on the credibility of assertions about civil disobedience—even in cases where that disobedience is clearly outward-looking and part of an effort to achieve social or political

[27] As, for example, if he were hoping to initiate a court test of a law or policy by 'notifying' the public prosecutor of his willingness to be prosecuted, but fixing his eye past the prosecutor and the court and on the legislature or the public, thinking to utilize the probable negative outcome of the court test as an instrument in further efforts to influence the legislature or the public.

Concerning why he might think such a dramatic means of notification needed in cases where he does not have his eye at all on the outcome of a court test, see below.

[28] Gandhi, *op. cit.*, especially pp. 35, 77, 178.

[29] *Ibid.*, pp. 14, 131. See also Harry Prosch, "The Limits to the Moral Claim in Civil Disobedience," *Ethics*, 75 (1965), 103–04. Thus, as some commentators might say, we approach the border between civil disobedience and nullification or even revolution.

change. The descriptions too often seem awkward and somehow unfitting. The unease thus produced is further compounded by general realization that neither disobedients nor their respondents are always so clear as they might be about when the borderlines between the above three efforts have been crossed.

There are, it seems (to go a bit deeper into the matter), two major sources of this unclarity. The first is a failure to examine carefully enough at the start what can reasonably be expected of civil disobedience as an instrument of social or political change. Much talk about the effectiveness of civil disobedience deals only with whether it succeeds in producing the changes ultimately desired. But, while perhaps fitting into a program designed to bring about change, civil disobedience need not be thought of as the quintessence of such a program any more than a feint by a basketball player need be thought the quintessence of an effort to sink a basket. Just as the feint might be entirely successful (its aim being to pull an opponent off guard) though the basket is not sunk, so the aim or point of civil disobedience might be fully achieved even though the hoped-for change does not occur. There is at least nothing decisive to exclude such a view of the role of civil disobedience in contributing to social change, and there is much to be said in its favor.

Insofar as this is the case, one would be reasonable to ask again whether the aim is to notify or to persuade or to threaten, and to ask precisely what—if the civil disobedience in question is indeed to be seen as only *part* of a series or sequence of efforts to achieve social or political change—precisely what is supposed to come after it, and precisely how it is supposed to prepare the way for what comes after and thus fit into a sustained effort to achieve change. These questions have not been sufficiently considered, and thus we have remained confused about the appropriateness of viewing civil disobedience (even in the outward-looking cases) in the various ways suggested by the cluster of claims collected in III above.[30]

Confusion here has been exacerbated, however, by another

---

[30] This in turn has, among other things, left us unclear about issues that must be dealt with in debates about whether civil disobedience does (or is intended to) put a society on a slippery slope toward anarchy, or, perhaps, toward tyranny. Cf. also the discussion by Stuart M. Brown, Jr. of whether acts of civil disobedience may be implicitly treasonous. Brown, "Civil Disobedience," *Journal of Philosophy*, 58 (1961), 669, 677–78.

peculiarly modern conceptual difficulty, viz., the difficulty in settling on acceptable and, in modern social and political conditions, helpful criteria for determining when one has been successful in notifying others of his dissent.

Under the simplest conditions one may, for example, post a letter to another man, and, for certain purposes, this may count at law as notifying the other man. But surely, unless one is certain of thereby triggering certain legal responses and is counting on these responses as further steps in another 'notifying' process (cf. note 27 above), *this* 'notifying' is not all that is wanted by persons who see civil disobedience as a step in the achievement of social or political change. What is wanted is more like eventually telling a man something to his face.

But even in this latter case the man's attention may have been momentarily distracted; he may not have heard. Or, perhaps though no markable distraction has occurred, what has been said doesn't seem to have sunk in. Has the man heard or hasn't he? Such problems are compounded in mass, and at least somewhat democratically run, societies. In such societies, depending upon the law, policy, or condition from which one is dissenting, the number of people who have to be 'reached' or notified may possibly be very large and their specific identities may not be clear. In such societies, furthermore, something sharp, shocking, or dramatic may be thought needed, especially by those who are not fortunate enough to be generally considered men of light and leading, to penetrate or even to gain opportunity to penetrate (by gaining notice in the mass media) the consciousness of those who must be reached. The spiraling escalation in the forcefulness of tactical devices and ever higher thresholds of public sensitivity to which such considerations have led are already familiar. They have led from techniques of clearly lawful dissent to civil disobedience and beyond, and from isolated to massed as well as massive acts—acts which may serve only to 'notify' members of the larger community consisting of the nation, but which are threatening and coercive-seeming to the smaller communities in which they sometimes occur.

In the midst of such circumstances, perfectly legitimate concerns for when dissent has been heard, supplemented perhaps by firm conviction of the rightness of the cause and faith in the vindication of one's judgment by a public actually made aware of it and of its grounds, have sometimes swelled to such proportions as to be satisfied only by policy changes dramatically in the direction of the dissent. Dissent not markedly agreed with has increasingly been thought in some circles to be dissent not heard. This conviction has led to harder pushes to 'be heard.' And efforts of the most forceful and even coercive nature thus travel under the title of efforts to be heard.

In such circumstances, important distinctions between notification, persuasion, and threat fade away. But the process of escalation has not originated solely out of bad faith or even outrageously bad judgment on anybody's part. Rather, though exacerbated by current general anxieties about personal political impotence, it has had a source in the presence of the serious and peculiarly modern problems just suggested—problems concerning the assessment of the effectiveness of a person's efforts to communicate in and to a mass society.

The bearing of this upon the thesis of the present paper is as follows: Recognition of such a small but important source of confusion about civil disobedience depends in the end upon our capacity and willingness to distinguish and isolate for special and careful attention the segments of even such a close cluster of accounts as those considered here of the aim or point of civil disobedience—e.g., those suggested in the remarks that civil disobedience is a political act, an act of protest, an act of communication. Thus, even where civil disobedience does have the outward-looking aspect indicated by such characterizations, both actual and potential civil disobedients themselves and persons called upon to respond to them will have further careful and discriminating thinking to do about the aims of civil disobedience. Even then, as should now be clear, such persons will be ill-equipped to talk sensibly about either the effectiveness or the justifiability of civil disobedience until they pay closer attention to precisely how it does or might fit into an ongoing and possibly sustained effort to achieve social and political change, and thus closer attention to how civil disobedients do or might see what they are up to.

IV

The importance of another dimension of concern for what civil disobedients are up to emerges from consideration of the following claim—a claim which, though it hasn't received acceptance so wide as that received by the earlier claims, has nevertheless been influential in some significant quarters:

IV. That civil disobedience is an act of respect rather than of disrespect for law.

Most justifications for the claim cite the characteristically public and open nature of civil disobedience, the subsequent nonresistance to arrest, and the 'acceptance' of normal penalties. They thus perhaps slightly confuse what is the case with what, in the view of the commentators in question, ought to be the case about civil disobedience.³¹ But a more fundamental criticism may be launched by noting the rather limited view of respect and disrespect embodied in the position. The position encourages us to see the contrast between respect and disrespect as clearly revealed in a contrast between behavior that is open and nonresistant and behavior that is neither. But this is a mistake. The sneaky, furtive, evasive, and resistant behavior of a 'common criminal,' instead of clearly revealing disrespect for the law, reveals an important aspect of respect, and one furthermore that is *prima facie* absent in the case of civil disobedience; it is that aspect of respect linked up with heeding, giving serious attention to, believing that one has good reason not to run afoul of, and even fearing the thing respected. Compare the boxer who respects his opponent's left jab. The civil disobedient who so deliberately and openly steps into the path of the full weight of the law may be thought to show *prima facie* the same 'disrespect' for the law that a boxer might show for his opponent by stepping deliberately into the path of the opponent's most earnest blows.

Yet another aspect of respect is even more decisively (i.e., not merely *prima facie*) absent in the case of civil disobedience, at least in part; it is deference to what is respected. It is true that, insofar as the civil disobedient 'accepts' arrest, conviction, and normal punishment, he defers to *these* operations of the legal

---

³¹ The issue depends, for example, on what 'acceptance' of normal penalties amounts to. Though purported civil disobedients do not ordinarily attempt to escape penalties once imposed, they do often enough hire lawyers who plead that imposition of normal penalties for the offense would be either unnecessary or unjust, and, whether or not they have such lawyers, they often enough appear to believe that the penalties imposed (or even impositions of any penalties whatever) are inappropriate or unjust.

system. But there is obviously also something important to which he does not defer. He does not defer to, 'accept,' or 'honor' the guidance or requirements of the very law he deliberately violates.

His failure to defer in this way may not, of course, be inconsistent with his having or showing respect for that very law or for the law generally.[32] But admitting this is a long way from admitting that the violator's failure to defer is itself an act of respect for the law violated or even for the law generally, and the latter claim is the one here being examined. That claim, insofar as it rests only on citation of the openness, and so forth of civil disobedience, remains absurd because it cannot explain how one can at the same time both defer to and violate the law. It is not surprising, therefore, that the claim that civil disobedience is an act of respect rather than of disrespect for the law is suspect and ultimately unconvincing so long as it rests only on these grounds.

Further attempts to explain how violating a law can count as an act of respect for, and even of deference to, law have of course been made by some commentators. The lines of argument are easily sketched. They all involve the claim that violation of *this* (perhaps only purported?) law is an act of deference to *that* law, and the claim that the latter is superior to or more genuine than, and thus overrides or even invalidates (*ab initio?*), the former. These claims are sometimes fancied by the use of distinctions between the letter or 'color' of the law and its spirit or essence, but the claims remain pretty much as they have just been stated.

The prospects for success of these arguments may be ultimately dim. The most basic difficulty is that of preserving a basis for recognizing the prevailing view that civil disobedience does most certainly involve a violation of a law. The distinction threatened is that between civil disobedience and lawful dissent. If, of course, one has no interest in preserving that distinction, then

---

[32] Consider the unexceptionableness of saying: "With all respect, I decline . . . ;" "Though I respect . . . , nevertheless . . . ;" or "I respect . . . , but. . . ." The pattern of argument offered in support of such remarks normally is: 'Though I respect x, something more important is at stake here, viz., y' (where y may be the truth, my integrity, my self-development). If such protestations are to be fully convincing, however, there should be grounds for believing that they are not merely ceremonial and intended only to mollify, placate, and so on. Perhaps that is why a civil disobedient's previous history of obedience or disobedience to the law has come to have the relevance it has.

little stands in the way of the argument. But the distinction has played, at least in modern times, a fundamental role in identifying what civil disobedience is. To give it up is to run the risk of changing the topic so radically as to dissipate the relevance of what one says to persons now attracted to, repelled from, or thoughtful about civil disobedience precisely because they see it as involving a deliberate and solemn violation of a law.

Nevertheless, the issues raised by these arguments are very deep. They extend back into the indecisive treatment within the natural law tradition of commands of civil authorities contrary to natural law. They extend forward to, for example, present controversies about the relationship of national law to the United Nations Charter and to the so-called law of Nuremburg. Under one aspect, the issues center around the relationships of subordinate to superordinate laws, how to tell definitively when and precisely where one set of laws is subordinate to another, whether there can be genuine or only apparent conflicts between the former and the latter, and how and where to draw the line between appeals to superordinate laws and appeals to mere overriding considerations in justifications of departures from conduct required by some specific (purported) law. Under another aspect, the issues center on the situations of persons living within the ambit of laws and on how to describe fairly the act of a person who, though deliberately violating a (purported) law, sees himself nevertheless acting on maxims that should be (or, he believes, are) acceptable to all persons or in the best interests of all persons to accept as their own.

Consider the range of imputations perhaps most congenial to the claim at hand: The civil disobedient, engaged, let us suppose, in a solemn act of conscience, presumably believes that he would be vindicated if judged (correctly) in the appropriate forum. He believes not only that he, though engaging in civil disobedience, would be found guiltless of acting contrary to any of the considerations guiding judgments in that forum, but also that he could not have remained guiltless except by engaging in civil disobedience. He believes, in short, that civil disobedience in his case was required by the—let us say—'law' of the forum. All this can perhaps be admitted about him. It would provide a basis for saying that his act showed deference to and respect for the 'law' of that forum.

But can we accept without complaint the claim that his act

showed deference to and respect for law *simpliciter?* It depends
upon the forum, and upon how the 'law' of that forum is or is
not related to what we commonly and unhesitatingly consider to
be law. And it depends also upon the details concerning how the
'law' of that forum overrides or fails to override, invalidates or
fails to invalidate, the 'law' whose violation made his act genuinely an act of civil disobedience. In the end, we may, for
example, be willing to say only that he thought that his was an
act of deference to law, but that he was mistaken because he was
mistaken in how he resolved one or more of these issues.[33]

Behind the concern leading us into such issues may lie an
assumption that should be gotten into the open—viz., the assumption that if we are to show the civil disobedient worthy of
respect, we must show that he is, at least in intention, steadfastly
law-abiding. This assumption may seem peculiar, especially to
persons who think of being law-abiding as conforming to various
and sundry laws and think of laws as the sort of things inscribed
on legislative rolls and brought into force by executive signa-
tures. It will seem less peculiar to persons who think of being
law-abiding as conforming to something 'higher' and more permanent than merely such enactments of 'King-in-Parliament.' But
even in the latter case, there are significant divergences in possible interpretations of the position. Fidelity to law may mean
fidelity to a constitution, to some allegedly deeper requirements
of a way of social or political life, or to requirements for
maintaining or developing a national, or narrower or broader, cultural or political heritage or character, or to some version of the
permanent interests of mankind either as simply a collection of
secular beings or as creatures of God.

When carried so far, the assumption may in the end amount
only to a demand that the civil disobedient, if he is to be worthy
of respect, be acting in conformity to, or at least with a view to
conforming to requirements set by the interests or aspirations
shared (or sharable) by members of 'his' community (however
extensive that community is considered to be).[34] The thrust of
the demand then appears to be to establish that he is an

---

[33] A man might indeed think he is deferring to law and yet not be doing
so; but it is important also to recognize throughout the present discussion that
he cannot be deferring to law unless he thinks he is doing so.

[34] Thus is exposed yet another (and perhaps the deepest yet) possible
rationale for the "civil" of "civil disobedience."

upholder of community interests and not an 'outlaw'—a matter to be settled in part, perhaps, by discovering something so minimal as that he is acting on maxims that *he* would be willing to see everyone act on, or even believes obligatory for everyone to act on. For the rest, the issue may, depending on the weight others are willing to attach to the above consideration, be settled by deciding that these maxims are (or arguably should be) accepted by other members of 'his' community.

The impact of these considerations on the main thesis of the present paper is as follows: One can notice how the discussion turns (not exclusively, but at least) on various versions of the maxims of the civil disobedient's action, and, in this way, on various versions of what he is up to. The discussion is not unrelated to that in the earlier sections of this paper; indeed, if we return to the segments of the format offered in Section II under 2e, iii and 2e, iv, and to the amplifications of 2e, iii contained in Section III, we can begin to imagine how these imputations might possibly be thought supportive of some of the versions considered here of the maxim of the civil disobedient's action—though we can see also the magnitude of the investigations needed if such suggestions were to be taken seriously. But the discussion here exposes also a new dimension of concern for what civil disobedients are up to, viz., concern for how imputations about the principles or maxims on which a civil disobedient is acting influence descriptions (as in claim IV) of what he is doing. In sorting out some possible variations in these principles or maxims, the discussion has revealed in a new way the need to make discriminations keener than are common in thinking about what civil disobedients are up to. In beginning to make some of these discriminations, we have seen again how the prevalence of over-simple views has helped hide both the richness of the phenomena and the richness of the issues underlying debate about the nature and status of civil disobedience. It is not surprising that, in the face of the prevailing simplisms about these matters, our attention has often been misdirected and we have found ourselves perpetuating unrewarding controversies.

V

The discussion so far hardly exhausts the rewards of studying with more than common care what civil disobedients are up to. Not only should more be done with issues that *have* been raised (e.g., with ramifications of the problems about definiteness of intention just barely mentioned at the end of Section II), but investigations should be made of dimensions of the matter unmentioned so far.

For example, one frequently hears the claim that we give up our 'right' to civil disobedience only at the cost of ceasing to be moral beings.[35] This claim, together with slogans accompanying it—e.g., "Do not let the law become keeper of your conscience," "Do not permit the judgment of the law to be substituted for your own judgment"—appears to express a deep concern for the integrity of individual judgment and character. We should ask very carefully just what social, political, or legal policies we are being advised to adopt in the light of this concern.[36] But we should also probe the concern itself and in particular ask, far more doggedly than has been common, precisely when a person who obeys a law (or disobeys it, for that matter) is *not* acting on his own judgment and in an integrity-damaging way. Surely, here is both another dimension of concern for what civil disobedients are up to and another place where popular assumptions threaten to have been too complacent and over-simple.

Nevertheless, enough has been said above to support the thesis of the paper. When speaking of civil disobedients generally, the range of plausible imputations concerning what they are or might be up to in engaging in civil disobedience has been shown to be significantly large. Furthermore, the steps between one imputation and another, though sometimes seemingly slight, have been seen to be worth noting. These steps bear importantly, as has been seen, upon certain claims concerning the nature

[35] For versions and echoes of this claim, see Gandhi, *op. cit.*, p. 174; and Harold J. Laski, *The State in Theory and Practice* (New York: Viking Press, 1938), p. 66.

[36] Perhaps, for example, we are being advised to adopt some such policy as the following: When a person's convictions (or, merely, judgments) lead him to disapprove of (or even 'regret') (his) conformity to a law, let him violate the law—where "let him" means "don't try to stop him" and this in turn means "don't punish or threaten to punish (or, only, 'blame' or 'disrespect') him for doing this." (Cf. currently popular demands by students for amnesty in cases of 'protest' violations of university regulations.) As is made obvious by the looseness of this formulation, if by nothing else, there is room here for more discriminating approaches.

and limits of civil disobedience—viz., those that find their rationales in connecting the presence or absence of certain features of cases of civil disobedience with the presumed aim or point of the act, as in the claim that civil disobedience is nonviolent; for the challenge of showing the requisite (empirical or conceptual) connections must, we now see, be met somehow—even if only by some reasonably convincing extension—with respect to *each* of the imputed aims and so on within the plausible range (e.g., each of those delineated in the subsections of e, iii and e, iv of the format offered in Section II). It is not enough to show the connections with respect to one, or with respect to each of some more restricted range. Similarly, the steps from one such imputation to another bear importantly upon efforts to assess the effectiveness and the justifiability of civil disobedience; for, if we leave unmarked even certain small and often unnoticed shifts in imputation (as, for example, the shift from imputing an aim of 'witnessing' something to oneself to imputing an aim of 'notifying' others of one's stand), we invite not only confusion about whether and what kind of disobedience will be productive in the achievement of the aims the disobedient has, confusion about what the tests of his success are to be (cf. the discussion of 'notifying' in Section III), and misunderstanding of the dilemmas he may face when his aims are multiple, but also confusion about what further program of aims his action might or might not fit into, and thus confusion about matters of importance in assessing the acceptablility of what he is doing (Section III). Lastly, seemingly small shifts in imputations concerning the maxims or principles on which the civil disobedient is acting, and thus, by this route, concerning what he is up to, bear importantly upon our efforts to think clearly about what, in the end, our total response to civil disobedients should be. Our capacity to see shifts from one to another of these maxims or principles will not only put us in a position to see through some enormously misleading claims about why we should respect (or disrespect) civil disobedients, but will also make a difference in the correctness of our understanding of the forum in which various civil disobedients may be asking to be judged and in which, in all fairness, we ought at least to consider judging them.

It is true of course that the discriminations with which this paper has been concerned are ones that civil disobedients themselves have often not made or made clearly. That is an important fact about civil disobedience and about civil disobedients. We should not overlook it when we consider how to cope intelligently and helpfully with these phenomena.

Earlier versions of parts of this paper were presented at philosophy department colloquia at the University of Minnesota and at Wichita State University. I am grateful for the benefits of the discussions that followed these presentations, as well as for the benefits of a discussion on this general topic several years ago with Robert Rowan.

16

POLITICAL ALIENATION
AND MILITARY SERVICE

MICHAEL WALZER

Despite the conventional claims of the authorities, it is not at all easy to determine the precise extent of the obligations owed by an individual citizen to the modern state. The authorities claim, so far as I can tell, what they have always claimed: that citizens must, if necessary, fight and die for the state. But this view of every citizen as a potential soldier, rushing to arms at his government's call, has its origins in states and societies very different from our own; above all, very much smaller than our own. It was in the polis of ancient Greece and in the medieval commune that the notion of the citizen-soldier was born, and the idea was elaborated by theorists like Rousseau who still thought in terms of small participant communities. The extraordinary transformation in social scale which has occurred in the past

century and a half has created a radically different kind of
political community—one in which relations between individual
and state are so attenuated (at least their moral quality is so
attenuated) as to call into question all the classical and early
democratic theories of obligation and war. The individual has
become a private man, seizing pleasure when he can, alone, or in
the narrow confines of his family. The state has become a distant
power, captured by officials, sometimes benevolent, sometimes
not, never again firmly within the grasp of its citizens. But if this
is so, what do these citizens owe to this state?

In an important sense, only liberal (I mean, chiefly, Lockeian)
theory is capable of answering this question, for only the liberals
have been entirely accepting of the transformation in scale and
of the new individualism it has generated. I want to argue that
the liberal conception of tacit consent provides a key to understanding the new relations between citizens, or rather, some
citizens, and the state. And since the man most often described as
having yielded tacit consent and no more is the resident alien, I
want to examine the (limited) obligations such a man incurs. It
is a commonplace of contemporary social thought that the modern state breeds aliens, whereas older political societies could
only import them. We can learn something about this modern
alienation, I think, if we begin with the older notion of alienage.

All the philosophers of consent have realized what their
critics have in any case told them quickly enough, that the possibility of express consent to a political system—even a democratic system—is rarely available to all men and sometimes is available
only to a few. If consent theory is to be taken seriously, it must
suggest some way of submitting oneself to a government other
than by pledging allegiance to it, taking out naturalization
papers, or becoming an active participant in its politics. Liberal
writers have generally argued that there is such a way; there is a
kind of silence that may be construed as consent. This is the
silence of the unsworn, inactive resident, who enjoys the benefits
conferred by the state and lives amidst its citizens without ever
publicly acknowledging its authority. The acceptance of benefits,
even if their rejection would require such extreme courses of
action as emigration or hermitic retreat, involves, we are told, an
unspoken agreement to maintain the conditions that make the

benefits possible for oneself and others. That means, most importantly, to obey the laws and keep the public peace. This seems to me a reasonable doctrine, and for the purposes of this essay at least I am going to accept it, adding only that the obligations incurred by silence are owed not only to the state but to society as well, that is, to the population in whose midst the resident resides. And they arise not only from the acceptance of benefits but also from the daily round of social activities and the expectations of peaceful conduct which that round inevitably produces in the minds of all the other residents.

The immediate difficulty with this merely tacit consent is, as Locke wrote in his *Second Treatise,* to know "how far it binds." It was Locke's view that any "enjoyment"—of property, lodging, or the bare freedom of the highways—bound a man to an obedience no different in character from that of a full-fledged citizen. A visitor to England or a resident alien was as committed as any "denizen," as any natural-born or legally sworn subject of the king. Tacit consent produced a temporary bond, while express consent made a man "perpetually . . . and unalterably a subject," but the nature of the obligation for the respective durations is, according to Locke, precisely the same.[1] This is a curious view, and since Locke's expression of it is casual and cursory, it need not be taken as an important feature of his political theory. Surely the moral situations of a mere visitor and a long-term resident are different in significant ways, and one might say the same thing about a resident alien and a citizen— especially in a liberal society. The citizen, after all, participates in his government and shares to some degree in the making of decisions about such crucial matters as taxation, conscription, and war. A resident alien does not participate: how far can he be bound to pay taxes, to serve in the army, to risk death in battle?

Before attempting to answer this question, it will be useful to consider an older distinction between temporary and perpetual obligation, made by the common lawyers and summarized in Blackstone's *Commentaries.* Blackstone distinguishes the allegiance owed by a natural-born subject, which "cannot be forfeited, cancelled, or altered by any change of time, place, or circumstance," and the allegiance of an alien and stranger which

---

[1] Locke, *The Second Treatise of Government, paras.* 119–22.

"ceases the instant such a stranger transfers himself from this kindom to another." A natural-born subject can, of course, "transfer himself" as easily as can an alien, but not with the same results. "An Englishman who removes to France, or China, owes the same allegiance to the king of England there as at home and twenty years hence as well as now."[2] This is a view that makes a good deal more sense than Locke's, since it is founded on a whole set of ideas about birth that lend themselves to talk of perpetual obligations. A man does not choose and cannot change his native land as he can choose a political system and later change his mind about its merits. A natural-born subject is like a son or daughter— a comparison implicit in Blackstone's discussion—whose parents are his, willy-nilly, and who has permanent commitments. If this comparison is rejected, as it explicitly is by Locke, it would seem that the notion of perpetual obligation must also be rejected. Perpetuity is an awkward notion when intruded into a consensual universe, for the possibility of reconsideration is inherent if not in the idea of consent itself, then in the idea of government by consent. In the latter phrase both terms refer, I think, to series of acts over time (possibly, in the case of a radical democracy, to the same series), and the two together do not suggest an agreement made at some single moment or for all time. A theorist may reasonably want to make reconsideration a similar series of acts, prescribing some lengthy "due process" for terminating consent and so making the bonds established by consent as firm as he can. But he cannot bar entirely the possibility of a political divorce.

If this is so, then Locke's effort to distinguish tacit and express consent must be called a failure. It is not in the duration of the bond established but in its character for whatever duration that the difference must be sought. In fact, a difference of precisely this kind has been worked out, once again by the lawyers, and it is of enormous relevance to political theory, though it has not, so far as I know, been discussed by political theorists. In the course of the eighteenth and nineteenth centuries, it became a principle of international law that resident aliens were obligated differently from citizens: they were bound to a more narrow range of actions.

[2] Blackwell, *Commentaries on the Laws of England*, Book I, ch. 10.

> Until a foreigner has made himself by his own act a subject of the state into which he has come, he has politically neither the privileges nor the responsibilities of a subject.... He is merely a person who is required to conform himself to the social order of the community in which he finds himself, but who is politically a stranger to it, obliged only to the negative duty of abstaining from acts injurious to its political interests or contrary to its laws.[3]

This is a far-reaching assertion. It suggests that tacit consent produces only "negative" duties, and it might require a political society to include within its territorial confines men whom it could neither tax nor conscript for any public service whatsoever. When stated more concretely, however, the argument is also more limited, and it tends to focus on the issue of military service. The same writer I have quoted above argues that "aliens may be compelled to help maintain social order, provided that the action required of them does not overstep the limits of police, as distinguished from political, action."[4] This is the common distinction: since they enjoy the benefits of social order, aliens may be required to maintain that order, to pay taxes, to serve as police deputies, to join a fire brigade, and so on. But they cannot be bound to fight in either a civil or an international war (unless the country where they live is "threatened by an invasion of savages. . . .") The distinction is nicely illustrated by the behavior of the British government during the American Civil War: "The British government in 1862 [insisted] that as a general principle of international law neutral aliens might not be compelled to perform any military service . . . [but] in 1864 the British government saw no reason to interfere in the case of neutral foreigners . . . enrolled as a local police for New Orleans."[5]

This argument by the international lawyers has a double rationale, only the first part of which is of interest to us,

---

[3] William Edward Hall, *International Law* (Oxford, 1880), p. 43.

[4] *Ibid.*, pp. 171–73; he is following J. C. Bluntschli, *Le Droit international codifié* (Paris, 1874), Sect. 391, but the argument is common to virtually every writer on international law since Vattel.

[5] Francis Wharton, *A Digest of the International Law of the United States* (Washington, 1886), Sect. 202.

though the second may well be of greater interest to them. The resident alien is conceived both as an individual who has made a limited commitment and so incurred only limited obligations, and also as the subject of another state which retains, so to speak, rights in his person. Hence the precise limits of his obligation to the state within whose jurisdiction he resides is often a matter of negotiation between that state and his own (and so not merely of his "own acts").[6] He is protected in his residence here by his citizenship there, and this protection is often confirmed by explicit bilateral treaties. It is important to stress, however, as an American secretary of state did in 1918, that the existence of treaties exempting subjects of the contracting parties from military service abroad does not constitute "evidence of a practise among nations to draft aliens into their forces."[7] The treaties do not, in this regard at least, create a right, but merely protect a right already established. Aliens cannot be compelled to serve (though they can be subjected to considerable pressure to do so, as we shall see). Nor is the condition of a stateless person any different from that of a foreign citizen, though such a person, unprotected by treaty, is all too often treated differently.[8]

The condition of a resident alien in international law suggests two distinctions of major importance to political theory. The first is a distinction between ultimate obligation—the obligation to fight and risk death—and all other, lesser duties. The second is between obligations owed to society and those owed to *political* society or to the state. International law seems to suggest that a man can incur ultimate obligations to society, he can bind himself to defend its population against devastation and destruction even at the risk of his own life, simply by residence and daily

[6] Thus the phrase "neutral aliens" in the statement of the British government cited above; *allied* aliens have often been conscripted with the consent of their governments. See *The Obligations of Allied and Other Foreign Nationals in Great Britain* (London, 1943).

[7] G. H. Hackworth, *Digest of International Law* (Washington, 1942), Vol. III, Sect. 282.

[8] International meetings held before and after World War II attempted to guarantee to stateless persons the status and privileges of neutral aliens. See the *Convention on the Status of Refugees* (1928) and Geneva Convention IV (1949). These are discussed in F. Lafitte, *The Internment of Aliens* (Hammondsworth, England, 1940), p. 221, and Morris Greenspan, *The Modern Law of Land Warfare* (Berkeley, 1959), p. 51.

intercourse. But he cannot commit himself to the polity, he cannot bind himself to risk his life for "ordinary national or political objects," except through those expressions of consent and participation (which may, of course, be variously defined) that make him a citizen. So tacit and express consent have different moral consequences, and the difference suggested by the lawyers, it seems to me, illuminates the precise character of political membership far better than Locke's *Second Treatise.* To be a citizen is to be committed to a political system, not merely to the survival of the society that system organizes, but to the survival of the particular organization and also to all those purposes beyond survival that the organization sets for itself. Residence alone cannot and does not generate such a commitment.

I don't doubt that this is a difficult distinction to apply in practice, for the ordinary purposes of the state are not necessarily political in the narrow sense of that term, that is, concerned with power manipulation and aggrandizement or with the fostering of some secular ideology. One of the purposes of any state is the defense of its society, and it is probably true that certain sorts of societies can only be defended by certain sorts of states. There are likely to be moments, then, when all residents, aliens and citizens alike, are morally obligated to defend the state that defends their everyday social life—against a barbarian invasion, as the lawyers have suggested, and conceivably against any invasion likely to entail serious disruption and devastation. If this is so, it's not difficult to imagine a variety of borderline cases— which I cannot even attempt to resolve here—when the invasion is only threatened and the state takes one or another kind of preventative action. But it is important to stress that the existence of borderline cases does not call the original distinction into question, since it is only by making such distinctions that we know which are the borderline cases. The cases on either side of the line are clear enough.

Since the rights of hospitality and asylum are also established in international law, though not necessarily in the practice of nations, it would appear that the lawyers intend that any given state at any given time include men who have only limited obligations toward its own survival and its "ordinary political objects." And it is not difficult to imagine a state that includes a large number of resident aliens—as Athens, for example, did after the days of Solon. In 434, when the Peloponesian war broke out, Athens had a population of one resident alien for every two citizens; one third of the free men of the city were foreigners. The Athenian case is especially instructive, because citizens and aliens were treated differently with regard to military service: the aliens were organized into separate military units and used only for the defense of the city and its immediate environs.[9] But the condition of Athenian aliens was different from that of aliens in a modern nation-state in that it was virtually impossible for them to become citizens; they constituted something very near an hereditary political caste, with carefully limited rights and duties. The opening up of the possibility of naturalization and the steady pressure of modern governments to establish a uniformity of obligation among their subjects raise moral issues which, so far as I know, never arose in the classical polis. These issues can be seen clearly in the history of conscription in the United States.

Consent theorists have one fundamental problem with the obligation to perform military service: the young men conscripted for that service are often below the age of consent. They are asked not so much to fulfill their obligations as to anticipate them. There are some good reasons for this strange request, beyond its obvious practical reason. Ideally, wars ought to be fought by old men—they might then be less bloody as well as less frequent—but young men perform with markedly greater efficiency and have always been required to serve. And it can be said that these young men have already enjoyed years of peace, as well as all the other benefits their state confers, and moreover that their parents, who are presumed to love and protect them, have had a say in determining the policies of their country. This last cannot be said of the young resident alien, even if he has been resident for all or most of his life. Still, he can only serve when he is young, and if he is exempted now on the grounds of his alienage and later becomes a citizen, as he may well do or try to do, he will have escaped military service altogether.

This is the calculation that led United States officials, beginning in 1863, to require military service of any alien who had

---

[9] There is some disagreement about this among historians. I am following Michel Clerc, *Les métèques athéniens* (Paris, 1893), p. 48; for another view, see H. H. M. Jones, *Athenian Democracy* (New York, 1958), p. 164.

formally declared his intention of becoming a citizen, that is, who had taken out first naturalization papers.[10] This requirement was sharply protested by the treaty nations, on the reasonable grounds that intentions do not make a man a citizen and that many of the draftees were in fact citizens elsewhere and so not liable for conscription in the United States. As a result of these protests, new procedures were adopted which permitted "declarant" aliens (whether citizens of treaty nations or not) to withdraw their declarations, provided they had not exercised political rights under state law and provided also that they left the country within sixty-five days. Both these conditions are of interest. Many states at that time permitted residents of one year to vote in state elections even if they were not yet United States citizens. The federal government claimed the right to draft all persons who had exercised this suffrage and so illustrated nicely the close connection between express consent and military obligation. Clearly, the voting aliens of 1863 were thought to have committed themselves to the United States in some more significant way than other declarant aliens had done. Hence the others could leave rather than serve; the voting aliens were given no option. The requirement that the others leave if they wished to escape service (this did not apply to nondeclarant aliens, who were exempt in the first place) was unusually harsh and so far as I know without precedent. It was not repeated in the World War I regulations, which went through an evolution similar to that just described. Once again, an effort was made to draft all declarant aliens; once again, there were protests from the treaty nations; once again, the United States yielded and established procedures for the discharge or exemption of aliens who withdrew their declarations, with the provision that such men would be "forever . . . debarred from becoming citizens of the United States."[11] They were not, however, required to leave the country. Efforts to bar from future citizenship all nondeclarant aliens who refused military service failed in Congress in 1917. In 1941, however, the distinction between the two kinds of alienage was dropped. After that, no resident aliens were automatically ex-

---

[10] For the following paragraph I am relying chiefly on Wharton, *A Digest*, Sect. 202, and John Houck, "Comment," *Michigan Law Review* 52:265–76.

[11] Hackworth, *Digest*, Sect. 282; amendment of July 9, 1918, to Selective Service Act of May 18, 1917.

empt; they could claim exemption only by foreswearing United States citizenship.

Like the native-born young, then, aliens were required to anticipate their obligations, even though they might not have enjoyed two decades of benefits and even though neither they nor their parents had any political rights. If this seems unfair, however, aliens had one striking advantage over the native-born: they were required to serve only if they hoped one day to become citizens. They could refuse to serve if they were willing to accept a perpetual alienage. This last has never been an option open to the native-born, at least not in their "own" country. If they wish to be aliens, they must go somewhere else.

In 1952, during the Korean War, a law was adopted requiring military service of every male alien admitted to permanent residence (that is, holding an immigrant's visa) and actually resident in the United States for more than one year.[12] The same rule has held during the war in Vietnam. This effectively turns conscription into a kind of enforced naturalization, since it requires an alien to assume the same burdens as a citizen whatever his own hopes and intentions with regard to citizenship. Clearly, it lies within the power of Congress to do this, but it may be argued that it does not lie within its right. Certainly the present legislation represents a sharp break with the established rules of international law and also with the legal traditions of our own country.[13] It is particularly strange and disturbing, though also perhaps revealing of the motives of the legislators, that this dramatic shift should have come during the Korean and Vietnamese wars. For these are precisely the kinds of wars—distant struggles in which the safety of the country and the lives of its inhabitants are not at stake—that the rule against alien service was most clearly intended to bar. Indeed, the bar was first expressed in terms of a simple, no doubt an overly simple distinction between external and internal service—the first (as

---

[12] Houck, "Comment," p. 275.
[13] I have been unable to discover any court cases under the new law. This is probably because it affects so many fewer people than did previous legislation with regard to alien service, the number of resident aliens having fallen sharply during the past thirty years. I should add that many recent immigrants are from Puerto Rico, and they are not regarded as aliens at all. They are, strangely enough, equally subject to conscription at home and in the United States, before and after they have become citizens.

Americans once were more ready to admit than they are today) being likely to have some political motive beyond mere survival. Thus Secretary of State Madison in 1804 said: "Citizens or subjects of one country residing in another, though bound . . . to many common duties, can never be rightfully forced into military service, *particularly external service*". . . .[14]

I want to fasten for a moment on this anomaly: according to international law and American legal tradition, foreign-born residents of the United States can refuse that express consent which provides the only moral basis for conscription, while native-born residents cannot. It would appear that the distinction between tacit and express consent is meaningful only in the life of an alien. But this was surely not the intention of those theorists, like Locke, who originally worked out the idea of tacit consent. For them the alien was only a convenient example of a group of men in fact much larger than the population of aliens, who had yielded nothing more than a silent acquiescence to the polity. And this larger group included native-born men and women. I should think that for Locke it included all those men (the poor and the landless, for example) who were not required to take oaths of allegiance and, if he thought of them at all, it included most women since they also were generally not sworn. And it would include all young men, whatever the economic condition of their families, for a young man below the "age of discretion" clearly cannot be thought to have expressed consent in any binding way and " 'tis evident there is no tie upon him by his father being a subject of this kingdom, nor is he bound up by any compact of his ancestors."[15] For Locke the population that has expressed its consent is thus likely to coincide with the population of adult, male property-owners. Of course, he would almost certainly have conscripted young men without regard to the quality of their consent, since he distinguished the two kinds of consent, as we have seen, in a different way. But this leads him into a very curious position: he requires express consent for taxation, in fact, he requires a double consent, since property-owners are individually sworn

[14] Quoted in Ernst W. Puttkammer, "Alien Friends and Alien Enemies in the U.S.," *Public Policy Pamphlet* No. 39 (Chicago, 1943).

[15] Locke, *Second Treatise*, para. 118.

to the king and then collectively represented in Parliament; but he would require men to fight who are neither sworn nor represented. Perhaps he would have been willing to call this draft what it so obviously is, a simple impressment.[16] In any case, Locke's view of tacit consent suggests the existence of a kind of moral proletariat whose members have nothing to give to the state—neither advice nor consent—except their lives. Such a proletariat did in fact exist in Locke's time. Does it exist in our own?

This is not an easy question to answer, since it requires that one suggest first what consent and citizenship mean or what they ought to be taken to mean in a modern democratic state—a state in which oaths have neither the social currency nor the moral weight that they had in the seventeenth century. It seems to me that the best expression of consent available to the resident of a democratic state is political participation after coming of age. Perhaps I should add meaningful participation, for a man clearly does not incur the obligations of citizenship through actions about whose effectiveness and significance he is deceived. Meaningful is a vague word and one much abused, but for the moment it will have to serve. Just as the oath of allegiance in a monarchy was a pledge to acknowledge and abide by the commands of a sovereign lord, so meaningful participation in a democracy is a kind of pledge to acknowledge and abide by the decisions of the sovereign people. I doubt that this is a pledge often given without some awareness of what is being done. Actual participants in a democratic political process are generally not surprised to be told that they have committed themselves to abide by its results (or to refuse to do so, if they think they must, in a civil fashion, accepting whatever punishment their fellow citizens impose). War is simply one of the possible results and the obligation to fight one of the possible commitments.[17] Surely no one need feel hesitant about telling citizens this if they ever act as if they do not know it.

---

[16] Locke writes explicitly only of the obligation of soldiers, and says nothing of the obligation of citizens or subjects to become soldiers. I am here assuming what seems most likely, that he accepted contemporary recruitment practices. See *Second Treatise,* para. 139.

[17] The argument follows only if the decision to go to war is in fact made democratically; this is obviously not always the case, even in formally democratic systems.

But what of nonparticipants? I think we must say that resident nonparticipants have refused this express consent (and those whose participation is not meaningful have simply failed or been unable to give it) and have yielded only tacit consent to the political system. Though such persons have no legal status, their moral situation is not in any significant way different from that of resident aliens who could, but do not, apply for naturalization papers. The same applies to young men, especially if we assume with Locke that they are not committed by the commitments of their parents (and leave aside the question whether their own political activity can be called meaningful while they are below voting age). Native-born young men are not obviously different from young aliens. Before they are conscripted, then, they ought to be asked, as aliens traditionally were, whether they "intend" to become citizens, that is, whether they intend to exercise their political rights. And if they say no, then we must at least consider the possibility that they be allowed, like aliens again, to avoid the draft and continue their residence, that is, to become *resident aliens at home,* acknowledging their obligation to defend society against destruction, but refusing to defend or aggrandize the state.

Now this may be taken as a monstrous suggestion. Even to talk of resident aliens at home, it may be said, is to misunderstand the meaning of "home." A man has enormous debts to his native land and to his polity. He receives from them both not merely physical security but moral identity. *Extra patria, nullum nomen.*[18] It is surprising how quickly we are back to Blackstone, for arguments of this sort necessarily suggest obligations akin to those we have to our parents. But while I don't want to deny the value of living permanently in one's native land and enjoying a secure political membership there, I do want to deny the relevance of either of these to the question of ultimate obligation to the state. There is more than one reason for arguing irrelevance here, but I think it will be useful to stress a distinction that I have already made: the society into which we are born is not

[18] The psychological importance of "having" a native land is stressed by Sebastian de Grazia, *The Political Community: A Study of Anomie* (Chicago, 1948), but his argument helps to explain only the sense of obligation, not its reality. Exactly what arguments of this sort imply about being as distinct from feeling obligated is unclear to me.

the same entity as the state that governs us, and neither of these is adequately described by the Latin word *patria*. That word blurs the distinction between state and society and is thereby faithful, perhaps, to the world of the polis, but radically divorced from the experiences of modern men. Liberalism from its beginning has emphasized the distinction, not merely in order to subject the state to certain sorts of social control, but also in order to free society and its individual members from the restraints of active citizenship and patriotic fervor. Liberal society is conceived as a voluntary association of private men, egotists and families of egotists, a world not of friends and comrades, but of strangers. And the liberal state, while it permits a limited kind of membership and solidarity, really has another purpose. With its impersonal administration, its equality before the law, its due process, it represents the triumphant solution to the problem of governing a society of strangers. There is a sense, then, in which no one is at home in the modern state; we are all nameless aliens, *extra patria*.

That is an exaggeration, of course, even a gross exaggeration, though just how gross I really don't have to say. The modern liberal state is most often a democratic state, and through the mechanisms of mass self-government it seeks, with some success, to integrate and obligate its citizens. Nevertheless, that vivid sense of cooperating with one's fellows and governing oneself, which is so crucial to democratic legitimacy, has in fact been lost to many of those citizens. And whatever the reasons for that loss, its effects are fairly clear: an indeterminate number of men and women drop out of political life; a larger, but equally indeterminate number never join.[19] It's not the case that they simply don't vote, nor do I believe that nonvoting can be taken as anything but a very rough indication of political withdrawal or nonparticipation. Something more is involved: these people never have "Roman thoughts." They don't join in any of the actions available to democratic citizens; they don't participate in parties, sects, or movements; they don't take part in political debate; they

---

[19] Some people never join because they are prevented from doing so, or from doing so in any meaningful way; they are excluded from citizenship by one or another form of oppression. Oppressed minorities in a democratic state may be regarded as alienated residents, but more needs to be said about them than I can say here.

don't inform themselves on public issues. And in all these ways they refuse or neglect or proclaim their inability to consent to the political system and to the various purposive actions it generates. These are the alienated residents of the modern democratic state, and they are probably far more numerous than are the resident aliens. I should stress that what these people suffer from (or endure or enjoy) is political and not, or not necessarily, moral alienation. They are strangers only to the state, and it does not follow from this logically (it may do so psychologically) that they refuse or neglect the obligations produced by their silence.

Liberal theory knows nothing of an alienation more profound than political alienation, but that is a condition it seems almost designed to specify. The politically alienated man has incurred social obligations by his residence, by the everyday contacts he maintains with other men and women, and by the benefits he accepts. But these obligations do not involve what the ancients called political "friendship" and do not bind him to share the political purposes or the political destiny of his fellow residents, or of those of his fellows who are active in state affairs. He has incurred limited, essentially negative, duties to the state which regulate and protect his social life. He is bound to respect the regulations and to join at critical moments in the protection. But that is all he is bound to do. His only politics is the everyday politics of his personal life.

There is no established right to yield only tacit consent to the state. A resident alien need yield no more, but no state is bound to permit aliens to live permanently or even temporarily under its protection. Even the right of asylum might be qualified by the requirement that all refugees become citizens as soon as the law permits. A declaration of intention to become a citizen might well be made a requirement for admission. But if the legal status of resident alien could thus be eliminated, the moral condition of the alienated resident probably cannot be, at least in the modern state. Nor can alienated residents simply be asked to leave; their condition is, after all, not their own "fault." It is some reflection on the quality of the state in which they find themselves. And yet, so far as I can discover, there are no states

willing to admit the reality of alienation among their inhabitants
or to recognize the alienated resident as a moral person. Just
what this refusal means, what its reasons are, is not entirely clear
to me. There are a number of possibilities. First, the rulers of the
state may be claiming, with Blackstone, that obligation in fact
derives from birth and upbringing and that the voluntary actions
or inactions of adults have no significance in the formation or
destruction of moral bonds. Or, second, they may be assuming
express consent on the part of all native-born men and women in
the absence of express dissent—perhaps on the grounds that such
consent would probably be given were it somehow required,
though the requirement itself would be administratively and
politically difficult to enforce. Or, third, they may be denying
that there is any moral difference between tacit and express
consent and no special value to be assigned to the exercise of
political rights. The first of these reasons is simply a denial of
consent theory, and while I appreciate its consistency and force I
am not going to discuss it here. The second and third quietly
replace the notion that government is legitimized by consent
with another notion: that government is legitimized by the
absence of active and express dissent. People who hold the latter
view would, in effect, force all residents to choose between
full-scale commitment on the one hand and emigration or revolution on the other. And when large numbers of men and women
refuse to choose, as in fact they do, and rest, so to speak, in a
position of tacit consent, they would allow the authorities to
assume the commitment and to act accordingly. But surely this is
to deny to those men and women their moral weight in the
community and to treat them as children, that is, as persons
whose choices are not morally or politically effective.[20]

---

[20] Joseph Tussman has argued that there is no significant difference
between express and tacit consent so far as their moral consequences go. He
does believe, however, that there are many citizens who have not consented at
all: "They are political child-brides who have a status they do not understand
and which they have not acquired by their own consent." *Obligation and the
Body Politic* (New York, 1960), p. 37. I am made uneasy by the presumption
here that large numbers of adults can be passed off as children, and I doubt
very much that these people have no understanding at all of their status,
though they may have a different understanding of it than Professor Tussman
does. I should add that Professor Tussman is by no means content with his
child-brides; he would prefer adult marriages. But what if the adults fight
shy?

But how might the force of tacit consent be recognized? It would of course be possible, as I have suggested, to allow native-born young men the same choice that young aliens have, or have had in the past. They could be invited at age nineteen or twenty either to declare their intention of becoming a citizen, thereby accepting conscription, or to become resident aliens at home, losing forever their political rights and avoiding military service except in specified conditions of social emergency. There are, however, obvious objections to this. It imposes a very difficult choice on very young men. And while it is true that we do this already, and by denying the possibility of voluntary alienage at home make the choice even more difficult, that does not make it a good thing to do. There is nothing necessarily wrong with forcing young men to make hard choices, but forcing them to make permanent choices, with no possibility of reconsideration, places a burden on them that is clearly unjustified. On the other hand, the possibility that if reconsideration were permitted, few men would choose citizenship until they were past the age for military service may be sufficiently strong to warrant the harshness of perpetual alienage. If this is so, the second objection follows: perpetual alienage means the division of the members of state and society into two classes, with different rights and obligations. But the whole tendency of modern legislation and of contemporary social struggle is to establish a single class of citizens with precisely equal rights and obligations. A two-class system is not necessarily incompatible with democratic government, as the Athenian case demonstrates, but there is something repugnant in the spectacle of a group of men denied political rights because of a decision made in their late adolescence or very early manhood. The spectacle becomes especially repugnant when it is realized that not all men will face the same choice when it comes their turn to decide. Women will presumably not have to decide at all, nor will men who reach the age of military service during years when conscription is not thought necessary, and the choices of men in peacetime and wartime will be radically different. So the division of the classes will be as arbitrary and unjust as such divisions have always been in the past.

It seems clear to me that tacit and express consent must be regarded as producing different degrees of obligation, and yet it seems equally clear that any legal recognition of these differences, or rather any recognition that makes them permanent, is undesirable. There is one way out of this dilemma, and that is to suggest that the state, while not legally establishing or perpetuating the differences, must do nothing to override them. That means, above all, that it cannot simply assume the express consent of its citizens and press them into its service, as it does today. For some of its citizens at least, and perhaps many of its citizens, have never yielded or will never yield such consent. For them conscription, except in cases of social emergency, is nothing more than impressment; it has no moral basis at all. But the group of alienated residents or silent citizens neither has nor ought to have any determinate membership. There are degrees of alienation, and even were the state determined to recognize and measure these degrees, it is hard to see how it could do so. Nor does the group of alienated residents have a stable membership. In a democracy, at least, there is always the possibility of rejoining the polity. Individuals move, and should certainly be allowed to move, in and out of the political system.[21] Hence the principle "respect the differences between tacit and express consent" must establish a presumption against any conscription at all, except when the country as a whole or some part of it is threatened with devastation.

I am inclined to think that the presumption is very strong indeed and that military conscription at any other time or for any other purpose—for political crusades, foreign interventions, colonial repressions, or international police actions—is virtually certain to be unjust to many individuals, even if the war itself is entirely justified. Conscription, then, is morally appropriate only when it is used on behalf of, and is necessary to the safety of, society as a whole, for then the nature of the obligation and the identity of the obligated persons are both reasonably clear. But the state must rely on volunteers and can only hope (a genuine

[21] But note Rousseau's qualification: commenting on the conventional contractarian argument that a man can always withdraw his consent by leaving the country, he adds, "Providing, of course, he does not leave to escape his obligations and avoid having to serve his country in the hour of need." *The Social Contract*, translated by G. D. H. Cole, Book III, ch. XVIII. The same can be said of any internal withdrawal; it is generally easier to incur obligations than to renounce them.

and vital democracy could expect) that committed men, whether they can readily be identified or not, will choose to come forward.[22]

The myths of common citizenship and common obligation are very important to the modern state, and perhaps even generally useful to its inhabitants, but they are myths nonetheless and cannot be allowed to determine the actual commitments of actual men and women. These commitments depend upon their own actions, and their actions, presumably, upon their previous moral experience: both actions and commitments are bound to be diverse in character. If the whole gamut of possible commitments cannot be specified in law, it can be understood in theory, and law can be adjusted on the basis of that understanding. I have argued that the notion of alienage provides a useful theoretical parallel to the moral experience of alienation and to the commitment or lack of commitment that follows from that experience. It suggests a way of recognizing the political strangers among us and of doing them justice as moral persons. I don't mean, once again, that justice will or can be done by assigning a legal status or creating a determinate class of individuals exempt from certain obligations and deprived of certain rights. So far is this from being the case, that whenever conscription is enforced in the absence of social emergency, alienated residents (or those of them sufficiently self-aware to make claims on account of their alienation) should probably be treated as conscientious objectors are at present—exempted but not deprived, so as not to create a second-class citizenship. Perpetual alienage would be almost as bad as permanent exile, the only alternative to conscription available today to these same people. It can be argued, of course, that estrangement from the day-to-day self-government of society ought not to be tolerated in a democracy, for in the long run it undermines the sense of political obligation altogether and en-

---

[22] There is one way of making this distinction in law that I want to notice, but not necessarily to endorse. In Australia during World War II, young men were conscripted for home service, while only volunteers were sent overseas. It's not the case, of course, that the defense of Australian (or any other) society could never require overseas service. Still, this is a rough and often acceptable way of guaranteeing that conscripts never be forced to wage a political war.

dangers the everyday mutuality and peacefulness of social life. Alienation is not a desirable human condition. That is no reason, however, for refusing recognition to those men and women whose condition it is.

17

POLITICAL CHANGE THROUGH CIVIL DISOBEDIENCE IN THE USSR AND EASTERN EUROPE

ALFRED G. MEYER

The communist states of Soviet Russia and Eastern Europe have undergone significant, at times dramatic, political transformations within the last two decades; and since each of these systems has changed at its own pace and in its own direction, the universe of European communist systems by now is quite heterogeneous. Nonetheless, it may be possible to make a few generalizations that will still apply to all of them.

I

Communist regimes come to power, not necessarily by revolution, but with the aim of carrying out a revolution, that is, a thorough change of the entire social, economic, and political system. This involves destruction of established institutions and the erection of new ones—a phrase written lightly, even though it implies gigantic efforts, conflicts, convulsions, and hardships. The methods used by communist regimes in their attempts to effect such revolutions-from-above (to use Stalin's phrase) are well-known. They include the attempt to subject the entire organizational and associational life of the society to control by the ruling party; the thorough reeducation of the population in the spirit of the party's ideology, which seeks to establish its authority in all areas of human thought; and the marshaling and mobilization of all material and human resources for the tasks to which these regimes give top priority—national defense, political stability, and rapid industrial growth. The form of the resulting polity is bureaucratic; its style, paternalistic, with the father figures shifting from moralistic sermonizing to vengeful, punitive coerciveness, to grudging offers of rewards for good performance.

The theoretical justification for this paternalism is provided in the communist theory of state, elaborated by Lenin, Stalin, and their successors, and codified in the textbooks on Marxism-Leninism. According to this doctrine, the communist state is just and rational; it therefore is entitled to obedience by all citizens. It has these qualities because it is ruled by the Communist party; and this party asserts as axiomatic truth that it fully and truly represents the interests of all the people. Therefore, there neither is nor can be any conflict between the rulers and the ruled, and all authority is by definition self-imposed. Since the communist state is a state of all the people and for all the people, any work done or sacrifice made for it by the individual is in the interest of that individual. Indeed, there can be conflicts between individual and public interests only in the false imagination of unenlightened or immoral citizens.

The image sketched here obviously implies a system that tolerates neither deviant behavior nor deviant thoughts. Indeed, it frowns on any yearning for privacy or escape; and its architects have a compulsive need for assurances that their society is obedient, disciplined, and fully united behind its leaders. Manifestations of heterogeneity, not to mention conflict, are regarded as disturbances.

Strains nevertheless appear in all communist societies. The old order cannot be destroyed and replaced at will; instead, it fights for survival. The peasantry resists collectivization, actively or passively; national sentiments remain alive; scientists assert their knowledge against party ideologists; religious practices survive. In short, the national culture offers resistance to the bureaucratic revolution-from-above. Within the ruling bureaucracy, meanwhile, the in-fighting and internal politicking that troubles all giant organizations inevitably appear, together with such age-old phenomena as inefficiency, corruption, and the abuse of authority—all causing pain to both the political elite and the masses of the population. Further strains arise from the fact that communist societies develop a class structure or a stratification pattern or, if the expression be preferred, pyramids of rank, authority, affluence, power, status, and so forth, in which competition for advancement is sharp, and those not rising as high as they think they should may come to regard the entire social order as inequitable. Strains and growing pains notwithstanding, communist regimes may nonetheless reach their immediate goal, which is the industrialization and modernization of their relatively underdeveloped societies. When they do this, the Communist parties that have hitherto manipulated their societies with relative abandon (subject to the reservations expressed above) gradually find themselves confronted by complex, heterogeneous societies, sensitive to arbitrary tinkering, but sometimes unresponsive and at other times nervously overresponsive to coercion, highhandedness, and other paternalistic methods; societies containing many professional elites with intellectual conventions and ethical codes of their own and with strong ties to professional colleagues across the ideological borders. It is obvious that all the strains I have listed engender dissent as well as pressure for change. But the confrontation of modern industrial society with a political elite of the Stalinist type generates by far the strongest of these urges. In this case the pressure is for political change, for restructuring the political system from system-building to system-management, from bureaucratic revolutionism to liberal conservatism, from command to interest aggregation.

The communist systems of the USSR and Eastern Europe have felt pressures in this direction to a greater or lesser extent for the last fifteen years or more. But the counterpressures have also been very strong. Resistance to the changes that seem necessary are of various types. One of them is ideological, which means nothing else than that the practices of Stalinism were codified into a doctrinal catechism and thus elevated to solemn dogmas. Although the figure of Stalin has been removed from its pedestal, and his body from its resting place *ad dexteram patris,* the forms and institutions and style of his rule have lingered on persistently, partly because they were deeply engraved in the ruling ideology. The ideology, in turn, is reaffirmed with stubborn persistence by the established political elite, which is a product of the Stalinist era, learned how to rule under it, is not likely to retrain itself for the rather different functions that seem called for today, and regards all and any pressures for reform as threats to itself and to the entire system. One might add that bureaucratic establishments in general tend to become immobilistic; or one could argue that bureaucratic rulers as well as paternalistic authoritarians harbor deep suspicions against all manifestations of "spontaneity," i.e., all activities they themselves have not organized and inspired. Change, and indeed all policy and activity, is to be initiated at the top, not at the bottom or even in the middle layers, of the system. Hence in the communist polities being examined here politics is repressed and muted; debate is not quite legitimate, because, theoretically, all intellectual problems are supposed to be solved by reference to codified authority. Pressures for change are totally illegitimate; and individual or group claims against the system are not allowable either. Against abuses the individual may and indeed should complain; and for the relief of undue hardships or inequities the system provides numerous safety valves. Moreover, each citizen and every conceivable collective body is expected to show initiative in carrying out their many assignments. On the whole, however, dissent and the expression of interests, to say nothing of pressure for political change, are severely discouraged. Moreover, the *range* of permissible action is more restricted than, say, in the United States, almost as if the guiding rule were, "Whatever is not expressly permitted is forbidden." To state this formally, in addition to a codified legal framework of rights, duties, and prohibitions, the European communist systems operate with a restrictive framework of custom, usually referred to as socialist morality, which they enforce with the help of both peer group constraint and political authority. To the American academic observer the difference between communist and Western systems seems to be very great, although it may well be that the American ghetto dweller, the migrant farm-worker, or the long-haired youth holding "straight" values in contempt finds unwritten law as restrictive and as harshly and capriciously enforced as socialist morality in the USSR.

Having noticed the constrictive framework of communist countries, in which the authorities seek to endow all human endeavors with political significance, so that all life activities become matters of public policy, one may be surprised by the variety of ways in which the citizens of these countries do express dissent or dissatisfaction and may even seek to bring about changes. (I will leave aside for the moment the question which, if any, of these actions fall within the fabric of "civil disobedience.") The observer may be even more astonished to find that some of these methods have been in use throughout the history of these societies, even during the reign of Stalin. Libermanism was voiced by some economists as early as the 1940s. A play sharply critical of the Soviet military establishment was written and staged during World War II (*The Front* by Korneichuk). György Lukács never quite ceased arguing in favor of a turn toward enlightenment and intellectual tolerance.[1] We have dim knowledge of strikes and demonstrations through most periods of these countries' history. Pasternak wrote his passionately antirevolutionary novel during the chilliest years of the Stalinist ice age. Indeed, the years 1946-48 in the USSR, and the years 1952-53 in Hungary and Poland were periods of profound, prolonged, and widespread stirrings of dissent. With full information we would doubtless learn that there has been change in the frequency with which such sentiments were expressed. But relative acquiescence reigned only during a few brief periods when sharp repression temporarily shocked the people into silence. In the USSR, these years of almost total absence of dissent might be 1935-39, 1948-49, and 1951-52; in Eastern Europe (except for Yugoslavia), the only period of this kind was 1949-52.

An exhaustive list of all kinds of deviant behavior manifested in communist countries would have to include various actions that are of no interest to us here, such as corruption; the

---

[1] His article written on the 170th anniversary of Lessing's death and published in *Szabad Nép*, February 15, 1951, veils this message only very thinly.

systematic and deliberate violation of legal or other rules practiced by administrators, managers, and other people wielding public authority for the purpose of fulfilling their assignment or doing their job well; or, more broadly, the ever-present tendencies toward informal organization and informal behavior which are familiar to all students of complex organizations and bureaucratic management. These well-known patterns of rule-breaking, without which large administrative structures could not function, are mentioned only in order to show that underneath the façade of purposeful orderliness there is plenty of individual or group autonomy, initiative, competition, and at times even pressure for change. The boundary between the evasive tactics of bureaucratic officials and instances of civil disobedience may be very unclear. Another type of behavior outside the scope of this chapter is the clever use of existing rules and frameworks for ends not intended by the regime, as the use of grain for feed by collective farms in periods when the price difference between grain and livestock makes this profitable for them, as happened in the USSR in 1953-54. This practice contributed to a grain shortage which in turn was one of the reasons for Khrushchev's campaign to till the virgin lands of Kazakhstan. Yet another kind of deviancy of little interest here is criminality and asocial behavior such as juvenile delinquency, alcoholism, absenteeism, and disrespect for authorities,[2] even though a sharp increase in the frequency of any such behavior is likely to be interpreted by party leaders as a sign of protest and a symptom of political crisis or unrest, hence as some sort of public desire for change. Still, these many types of deviancy will be neglected here because our concern is for deliberate expressions of dissent and dissatisfaction and deliberate moves for some alteration in the system.

I shall make a list of typical forms of deliberate dissent, ordered somewhat roughly according to the degree of their severity or illegality. They range from clearly legal and permitted acts through words or deeds that may be legal, but violate socialist morality or party discipline, to clearly illegal statements or activities. The lines of demarcation here too are not rigid, and

[2] A most surprising token of contempt for authority I myself observed in a Soviet city some years ago was the attempt of a police officer to detain a young lady for some offense. The girl resisted arrest and managed to escape because bystanders in large numbers came to her aid.

depend on changes in the political climate. What is permitted today may have been illegal a few years ago; what is beyond acceptable behavior in Poland may today be quite proper in Hungary. Indeed, what can be done quite openly in Science City may lead to immediate arrest in Novosibirsk, a few miles away. In displaying such variety of legal and moral frameworks, the communist world is no different from ours.

Individual citizens, who feel they have cause for complaint against officials or agencies (of a relative subordinate rank), can and do write to a wide choice of authorities in the party, the press, the parliament, or other representative assemblies, and to law enforcement agencies or inspectorates to call attention to the alleged misdeeds; and it is clear from all the evidence we possess that such complaints are investigated. This channel of complaint is perfectly legal, widely used, and often not very effective, because the deeper causes of dissatisfaction are immune to such complaints either because they are related to policies to which the regime is firmly committed or because they are imbued with an authority which the complainant dare not touch.[3]

A slightly more daring and also more effective way of resisting authority is the maintenance of behavior patterns and the expression of ideas that do not entirely fit into the mold of the "socialist man," or the good communist. As I have hinted above, communist societies harbor subcultures that have resisted assimilation, and whose members continue to live according to patterns not entirely liked or approved of by the parties. Some of these are traditional in origin, such as ethnic groups or religious communities; and these have maintained their own way of life with surprising success. At times they resist assimilation or destruction openly and boldly: gypsies still refuse to settle down or give up their unproductive work; believers may openly wear religious symbols or demonstratively attend services. In 1966, some of the celebrations of the Polish millennium turned into

[3] It is generally understood that a substantial portion of complaints voiced through these and other safety valves provided by communist regimes is in fact inspired, suggested, or planted by the party authorities themselves. This is most obvious in the case of official humor magazines (*Krokodil, Szpilki, Eulenspiegel,* and others), that point the arrows of their satire at those abuses or failures which the party wishes to eliminate. Yet some of these magazines have come under fire because they overstepped the limits of permissible criticism. Cf. the 1947 denunciation of Zoshchenko and the criticism leveled ten years later at the editors of *Eulenspiegel.*

mass demonstrations of loyalty to the Roman Catholic Church. Other subcultures are of more recent origin; for instance, the many professional and scientific elites loyal to their own professional ethics, or the new youth culture which renounces the values of a careerist, "straight" society, and dares to show signs of such renunciation. We know of numerous other ways of showing dissatisfaction with what the regime offers: consumer strikes against shoddy goods; readers' boycotts of officially approved literature; or those subtle but unmistakable demonstrations that take the form of applauding, booing, or remaining silent at the wrong places during a public performance of some kind, be it a play by Schiller or the oratory of someone cloaked with authority.

When this is done by party members it can be a serious offense against party discipline. For there are occasions when the party expects every loyal member to speak up, be it for the purpose of self-criticism or for the purpose of denouncing someone whom the party condemns. In 1947 it took several months of pressure before Varga's colleagues publicly rejected his views. And when Pasternak was publicly repudiated, hardly any major Soviet writer joined in the ritual.

The various professional subcultures seem to have an intensive intellectual and social underlife, if we can generalize from what we know about the culture of artists, writers, and scientists in these countries. These professions are deeply divided into factions according to their commitment to, or rejection of, establishment ideas and policies. The dissenters or radicals know that they face a variety of publics which can at times be manipulated. They may form protective alliances with like-minded people in other subcultures or become their clients, as for instance the artists who create in nonofficial styles and survive in the USSR because the scientific elite buys their works and in this fashion sponsors them. For this reason, Soviet graphic art, which can be sold for lower prices than canvasses, seems to be more avant-garde than painting; while sculpture remains the most traditional art form. In Eastern Europe I made friends with an artist whose statues were done in Stalinist style, but his pastels were unorthodox in both style and content.

The liberal-radical subculture I am talking about seems well organized even though split into wings and cliques. It behaves like a clique against the outside world of officialdom, even though it also has multiple and close connections with it. Its various factions may have their own hangouts and, in periods of relative freedom, their own journals, even if they are only obscure journals published in provincial towns. In 1956 57, the Polish radicals had *Po Prostu;* the radical liberals wrote for *Przegląd Kulturalny;* for the establishment liberals the party created *Polityka;* the party itself spoke through many other newspapers and journals; and the far right spoke through the Soviet publications *Pravda, Kommunist,* and *Voprosy Filosofii.* Today, the radical right need not publish abroad, but the radical left does in *Borba* (Belgrade), *Kultura* (Paris), *Grani* (Frankfurt) and many other outlets.

Among the institutions serving the liberal-radical community, there is an intensely active black market in books and works of art; equally active circulation of unpublished manuscripts, unauthorized, semiprivate concerts, readings, or exhibits; and, most illegally, the circulation of mimeographed agitational material. At the time of the Siniavsky-Daniel trial in the Soviet Union, an entire White Book, prepared by people friendly to the defendants, circulated widely and was finally published abroad. It contained letters that had been written to, but not printed by *Izvestiia* and *Literaturnaia Gazeta,* summaries of defense testimonies before the court, and unpublished letters to the party Central Committee, the court, and other authorities. In the wake of this much-publicized trial there has been a series of other cases before Soviet courts as well as punitive administrative actions, all dealing with a continuing wave (or wavelet) of dissenting and protesting activities, including public protests against the Soviet military intervention in Czechoslovakia in August 1968.

There is thus vivid traffic in information and ideas, including open protest; much of this traffic doubtless flows up into the highest circles of the party leadership. Of all this the Western observers receive only occasional samples; some material leaked out by the liberal or radical community through its friends abroad, some of it from the party press itself, for instance, in reports about scientific or professional congresses, or in some derogatory remarks made by a party leader.[4]

[4] An impressive collection of such documents can be found in *Problems of Communism*, vol. XVII, no. 4, pp. 31-114, and vol. XVII, no. 5, pp. 24-112; the latter issue includes interesting samples of protest poetry, fiction, and criticism.

Incidentally, the liberal-radical subculture seems to have its special heroes. These are the victims of administrative reprisals, alumni of concentration camps and torture rooms. Some of these victims of Stalinism, according to recent observers, seem to enjoy an almost saintly prestige, are respected even by the authorities, and apparently enjoy a certain measure of fools' freedom. They are in the forefront of dissent and reform movements. It is even more remarkable to observe how many top-ranking party leaders owe their rise and their initial popularity or charisma to the fact that they have done time in the jails of Stalin or the little Stalins of Eastern Europe. This is true of several people in the highest councils of the Czech, Hungarian, and Polish parties.

The respect and relative permissiveness with which the party tends to treat these heroes of the liberal and radical communities, even when they are no longer in positions of authority, indicate that these subcultures must be examined in their interaction with the establishment. The first observation to be made here is that the liberal intelligentsia and the officialdom test each other continually, the liberals seeking to stretch, and the party bureaucrats to restrict the bounds of permissible behavior. The radical subculture lives a more pronounced underground existence, even though technically many of its activities are not illegal either. After a few dadaist "happenings" in Budapest, in 1967, the participants, or some of them, were taken to police headquarters and warned not to stage any more, so that the next happening was already an act of defiance, although still not clearly illegal.[5] Neither is it illegal to resign from the Communist party, a step taken by a number of leading Polish writers in the fall of 1957 and by several other groups in Eastern Europe since then. But it is rightly regarded as a slap in the face of the establishment, almost as embarrassing to the regime as suicide. It is amazing how sensitive communist elites are to suicide on the part of their leading citizens, and how suicide therefore becomes a mode of civil disobedience, seemingly more shocking to communist leaders than the ritual self-immolation of Vietnamese or American dissenters is to their political leaders.

Less destructive means of protest include strikes and work

---

[5] This statement is based on several informants who participated in these "happenings."

stoppages. The almost total cessation of Soviet, Hungarian, and Bulgarian writers to submit manuscripts in the late months of 1957 was a silence strike which seems to have been well organized and to have hit the party very hard. People can strike by not showing up at compulsory meetings, as the students of Humboldt University did in the summer of 1957 when the new State Secretary in the Ministry of Education, recently appointed to tighten control over the universities, came to address them and faced a hall full of empty benches.[6] Or people can show up where they are not supposed to, as the townspeople of Turza (Upper Silesia), whose parish priest the party threatened to replace by another; the people came out in a protest demonstration, and the priest stayed.[7] Authorized meetings can be used for unauthorized purposes, like the famous celebration of the tenth anniversary of the "Polish October" which took place at the University of Warsaw in October 1966. At this meeting, another interesting variant of showing dissent was practiced when mimeographed copies of Gomulka's programmatic speech of ten years before were distributed, only to be seized by the authorities as, presumably, a subversive document. Needless to say, it would be equally subversive to quote some of Mao's writing today, just as it would at least be tactless today to quote Lyndon B. Johnson's 1964 election speeches dealing with United States policy in Asia. And, of course, it would be even more subversive in the communist world to take Marxism seriously. For that offense, Kuron and Modzelewski today are in jail.

The most ludicrous example of illicit behavior doubtless is the offense of doing good deeds without prior authorization, not so much because it implies criticism of the establishment, but far more because it is a manifestation of spontaneity. A nice example is furnished by the eager beavers of the Tashkent Komsomol who, bored with the routine activities of their organization, decided to show their enthusiasm and their commitment to communist morality by undertaking a variety of constructive community projects. A suspicious public prosecutor, possibly sensing a conspiracy, began to investigate. Some arrests were

---

[6] See F. L. Carsten, "East Germany's Intellectuals," *Problems of Communism*, VI:6, (1955), 50.

[7] M. K. Dziewanowski, "Communist Poland and the Catholic Church," *Problems of Communism*, vol. V, no. 3 (September-October 1954), 7.

made. In the end the suspects were released. But the Komsomol authorities expressed their fury at the impudence of these young people's independent activity.[8]

For the sake of completeness, let me briefly mention the recurrent instances of mob action and violence in the communist countries. With the possible exception of the riots in Soviet labor camps, 1952–54, all violent upheavals known to me began as unplanned and peaceful demonstrations and were turned into bloody uprisings only by the repressive acts of the police or (in the case of Hungary) intervention forces. This applies to the working-class riots of Berlin, Plzen, and Poznan as well as to the violent Polish riots in October 1957, after *Po Prostu* was closed down. The case of Hungary in 1956 is somewhat more complex. Here a genuine revolutionary situation developed as soon as the Hungarian troops refused to open fire on the demonstrators. Had the Soviet troops not interfered, the disorders would most probably have led to an overthrow of the communist regime. In some of the labor-camp revolts, as well as in Hungary, and also in Poland in October 1956, unarmed demonstrations and police violence were followed by the emergence of participatory democracy, taking the form of action committees (soviets).

In surveying the entire phenomenon of dissent and pressure for change in these countries, one is struck by the great fluidity of the limits between permitted and forbidden modes of expressing dissatisfaction or criticism. The capriciousness with which official humor (humor magazines, cabaret, circus clowns) is treated by the party is a token of its ambivalence in this respect. Even more telling instances of insecurity and ambiguity are the frequent disagreements in high circles, or the sudden changes in judgment: a book highly praised by *Izvestiia* may be condemned by *Pravda* on the same day. Such things happened even under Stalin.

The overall impression is that people no longer quite know what is and what is not proper to say. Kuron and Modzelewski are in jail for making statements that are far less provocative than the editorials of *Po Prostu* or even *Trybuna Ludu* ten years earlier. Adam Schaff has been fired for saying things that some years before were considered establishment ideology. When

---

[8] The incident is discussed in *Komsomolskaia Pravda*, November 10, 1956, p. 2.

Mihajlov went to jail the first time, it was for expressing sentiments that were less radical than those printed in *Praxis* at the same time. What Tarsis, Siniavsky, and Daniel have written is no more radical than the works of Wazyk, Dudintsev, or Solzhenitsyn, or of Bulgakov, whose books are now being published in only slightly censored versions. One gets the impression that communist leaders often are more shocked by what is said than what is done, that they fear words more than actions, and thus will tolerate many an unorthodox practice as long as no one calls attention to it. Sanctions are imposed not on what is illegal but on what the bureaucrats feel to be threatening—threatening to them, or to the establishment, or to the moral, cultural, and political stereotypes by which the establishment lives. Similar fluidities in the boundaries between permitted and intolerable behavior may exist in many other societies.

II

I shall now comment on what I have written so far by asking which of these manifestations of dissent, if any, ought to be regarded as acts of civil disobedience. I shall then conclude with an attempt to assess the effectiveness of any such acts, that is, with some remarks about the place of civil disobedience in the communist societies of Russia and Eastern Europe.

In his recent encyclopedia article on the subject, Christian Bay defines civil disobedience as an act of public defiance of a law or policy enforced by established government authority.[9] The defiance should be premeditated, open, and ought to be conceived as an example that others might follow. It should be known by the perpetrators of the act to be illegal or of contested legality. Bay emphasizes the care and deliberation with which practitioners of civil disobedience must limit both the ends and the means of their acts. He sees the principal aim of such defiance as educational: civil disobedience strives to change public and official perceptions about what is and what is not illegitimate. Moreover, he argues that the aim of such defiance should always be conciliatory, never divisive.

[9] Christian Bay, "Civil Disobedience," *International Encyclopedia of the Social Sciences*, vol. II, pp. 473-87.

The emphasis here is on a meticulous adherence to moral precepts, and the outlook for success appears very gloomy. Civil disobedience, according to Bay, results from a painful weighing of evils against each other (disobedience versus violence; personal defeat versus the sin of inflicting harm). The mood is one of existential despair; typically it is Camus who becomes the major spokesman of the philosophy of civil disobedience. Indeed, the wish not to win seems at times to motivate Bay:

> Countless individuals in the course of history have chosen to shed their blood rather than compromise in matters of faith or conviction. It is arguable, however, how many among them should be considered spokesmen for civil disobedience. Their acts of defiance may in many cases have been instinctual; even visceral, rather than premeditated; their goals may at times have been unlimited—say the salvation of mankind; and their means may have not always been *chosen*. . . . Not every brave and for the time being nonviolent true believer is practicing civil disobedience when defying the law of the government; one would at the least require of him a reasoned determination not to repay injustice suffered with new injustice inflicted once victory has been won.[10]

As if a victory, once won, did not have to be secured! The pessimism inherent in this interpretation seems to be based on the assumption that morally intolerable political systems cannot be reformed without violence, but that violence must under all circumstances be foresworn. By itself, the first assumption would convert its adherent into a revolutionary. But the revolutionary sentiment is turned into existentialist pessimism by a concentration on the means-ends dilemma. This dilemma then turns into the axiom that reforms are impossible as long as they are necessary, it being understood that they become unnecessary should they ever become possible. Meanwhile, one must try the seemingly impossible, which is moral suasion through demonstrative self-sacrifice or carefully chosen acts of defiance. The rejection of revolution as an alternative,

10 *Ibid.*, p. 475.

moreover, is derived not only from the means-ends dilemma, but perhaps even more from an important if residual commitment to the given system: some of its details may be evil, but its basic structure, or at least the principles by which it allegedly operates, are accepted, and a totally different system is either not desired at all or is considered unattainable under the given circumstances. Hence civil disobedience is loyal opposition in a system which is reluctant to tolerate any opposition and manifests no great willingness of change itself. One of the reasons why the prospect of success for this kind of opposition is so gloomy is its dependence on publicity. Yet many courageous acts of defiance are either given the silent treatment or are distorted into violent, subversive acts by the establishment media. Many of the protests voiced in the communist world reach us despite the authorities because they somehow find their way into the foreign press, though the Soviet public at large is not informed about them. Civil disobedience nonetheless does work under some circumstances; there are occasions when one can work on the enemy's conscience. There may be forces within the society (interest groups, classes, factions within the political elite) that can be aroused by acts of civil disobedience; finally; there may be cases in which the authorities lose little by giving in, or when it would be more costly for them to suppress civil disobedience than to yield to it.[11]

In trying to match acts of defiance in the USSR and Eastern Europe with this definition of civil disobedience, I was surprised at how many of the activities summarized above fit this definition, and how neatly Christian Bay's specifications apply to the situation of dissatisfied elements in these countries. First, it should be stated that, to a limited degree, the ruling elites of communist countries have become sensitive to moral suasion. These are political systems committed to a systematic ideology, over the interpretation of which they seek to exercise most rigid control; but they have not quite succeeded. Not that their vulnerability in this regard ought to be overstated. More important, the existentialist mood of civil disobedience, in which evil is carefully and painfully weighed against evil, in which whatever

---

[11] See the discussion of *ahimsa* in E. Victor Wolfenstein, *The Revolutionary Personality* (Princeton, N.J.: Princeton University Press, 1967), p. 288.

you do gets you into trouble, so that at times the only thing that still counts is the morally correct stance—this mood seems to be an apt portrayal of the perception which dissenting intellectuals have of their own communist systems. The moral tone of political discourse, especially after Khruschev's so-called secret speech of 1956 had torn the mask off Stalinism and exposed its moral bankruptcy, forcibly strikes anyone surveying the rise and fall of reform movements in communist countries. The only circles in which one finds a similar preoccupation with morality in politics in the Western world are the radical student movements of today. One must add that the radical and liberal intelligentsia in the communist world have been thoroughly politicized, and they try to calculate finely the remotest consequences of their actions. Nowhere in the world does dissenting political activity seem to be so self-conscious and deliberate as in these countries. Furthermore, these spokesmen for reform usually are very careful to limit their demands; their opposition indeed is loyal most of the time, and they try hard to push for reform without provoking the authorities into retaliatory action. More and more they appeal to the rights granted them by the constitutions allegedly guiding their political systems. Like the civil rights movement, which began by asserting rights which full citizens take for granted (like being served a bowl of soup at a drugstore lunch counter), the liberal-radical protest movement (if one can speak of a movement) in the communist world has begun to insist on the actual exercise of rights formally granted by existing laws. Indeed, the appeal to formal norms of the polity, the insistence on adherence to rules, laws, and constitutions, in short, the legalism and constitutionalism of the dissenters is the trait in the pattern of Soviet and East-European protest phenomena most likely to impress the foreign observer.

The care with which dissenters in the communist world have limited their demands is one argument in favor of classifying their activities as civil disobedience, as defined by Bay. One might object that it is fear rather than a moral calculus which defines the limits of dissent in authoritarian societies. But this objection is unconvincing because of the spectacular growth of courage, the conquest of fear, shown by increasing numbers of dissenters in that part of the world. This new spirit of defiance and fearlessness, manifested in words and deeds, gives the protest movement in the communist world a profoundly moral character and in this sense, too, renders Bay's definition of civil disobedience applicable to their activities. The people I have discussed do not fight for narrow personal gain nor group advantages. Theirs is an activity of self-abnegation. They are imperiling their careers, their comfort, and their liberty for a purpose they see defined in highly moral terms. They speak for the nation or even for mankind rather than for a group or a class; or at least they think they do. Clearly we are discussing people who are bearing witness to their ideals.

The success of all this pressure seems, at first glance, to have been tremendous. The extension of freedom, or more exactly the widening of the range of permissible behavior, over the last fifteen years has gone much beyond anything that most Western students of communist societies would have dared to imagine. There have been serious setbacks, and the pace of liberalization differs markedly from one country to another or even from one realm of human endeavor to another. Still, the overall change has been dramatic The boundaries of permissible or tolerated behavior have been stretched perceptibly in life styles, entertainment, art, and science; in contact with foreign countries and the absorption of Western influence, even in such sensitive fields as philosophy and social science; in the critical examination of the past and even the present; in economic relationships; and, in Yugoslavia and Czechoslovakia, even in political life.

The list could be extended at will, to include the dismantling of much of the police apparatus, the decollectivization of agriculture in Poland, the greater emphasis placed by economic planners on consumer satisfaction, changes in the Polish, Hungarian, and Czech regimes, Khrushchev's de-Stalinization campaigns, and the alleviation of some of the worst conditions in forced labor camps in the wake of riots, honors paid by the authorities to victims of their own policies and indeed to the rebels against this oppression. The successes have indeed been remarkable.

It is impossible, however, to determine which of these changes are the result of conscious and deliberate pressures for reform and which of them might have come about in any event, without pressure. It seems safe to say that all meaningful reform has come about only when dissent and civil disobedience found a responsive echo in some strategic force within the society, be it a significant group like the scientific community, an entire class like the workers, or a faction within the ruling party. At the same time, when change has resulted from demands made more spontaneously and inarticulately by broader masses of the population, it is doubtful whether we can examine with sufficient exactness what role civil disobedience or intellectual rebellion played in triggering reform. Some day, perhaps, monographs may be written about some specific reform in which the relationship between grassroots demands and articulation of conscious interest can be examined. The material now available is not sufficient for this.

The argument up to this point about the success of civil disobedience and its functional equivalents in the USSR and Eastern Europe might seem to place me among those specialists who foresee continued liberalization in this area of the world. Indeed, strong arguments may be advanced to support this view. The simplest argument is that the wheel of reform cannot easily be reversed, that a society once freed from excesses of repression will not submit to it again. A more sophisticated argument is that a modern industrial society is too complex to be run by command and repression. Repression is regarded as dysfunctional to modern society. Its sharpest manifestation, terror, is often interpreted as a primitive but effective mobilization device for societies in which other means for mobilizing inert populations and resources are scarce. But it becomes counterproductive after a certain level of modernization has been reached. In turn, this interpretation of the functions of terror is related to widely accepted theories of progress (usually called development or modernization), according to which economic development leads to a more and more stable social and political equilibrium of the modernizing society.

These arguments do not convince me, however, and I cannot therefore commit myself to this view. In fact, recent developments in various parts of the world, including our own, but most spectacularly the Soviet intervention in Czechoslovakia (August, 1968), suggest that this view may be too facile and optimistic. Terror, authoritarianism, and repression may have important functions even in mature industrial societies, long after the mobilization phase is over. Or, if indeed they are counterproductive, that may not necessarily imply an inevitable trend toward liberalization. Dissent and heterogeneity may be more unsettling and threatening in mature industrial societies than they are in modernizing ones; the need to preserve law and order may become so overwhelming that strong repression becomes routine. In the communist polities of the Soviet Union and Eastern Europe, such a reassertion of authoritarianism does not even require political change; instead, it would merely mean a continuation of the political legacy of Stalinism. What I have argued, however, is that even in such authoritarian regimes dissatisfied groups can find means short of violence, and involving appeals to moral principles, that may have long-range effect.

18

GANDHI'S SYNTHESIS
OF INDIAN SPIRITUALITY
AND WESTERN POLITICS

WAYNE A. R. LEYS and P. S. S. RAMA RAO

Gandhi's statements about obligations were, for the most part, performatory utterances, made under varying circumstances during a long life of political activity. They were never fitted neatly into a systematic theory. Some of his opinions were borrowed from European and American writers. Others were echoes of ancient Indian scriptures. Gandhi achieved a unique synthesis of these borrowings and it is obvious that men in other times and places have tried to be guided by what he said. His eclecticism, however, and the occasional nature of his teachings make for a great deal of misinterpretation. While misinterpreted doctrines are often useful, it is our purpose here to set some of the record as straight as we can. In this chapter we shall attempt to explain how Gandhi treated political obligations, indicating the beliefs he found essential to nonviolent disobedience and identifying some of the difficulties that he encountered in subordinating political obligations to moral obligations.

I

Gandhi's political views can be placed in the spectrum of occidental political philosophy as one more attempt to reconcile legal and political authority, on the one hand, and respect for individual freedom and conscience, on the other. As usually interpreted, philosophers like Plato, Hegel, and Marx are near one end of the spectrum, in various ways subordinating individual conscience. The liberal tradition represented by men like Locke and Mill are on the other side, arguing for limits to legal and political authority. Though the "liberals" objected to political absolutism, they did not quite maintain that the individual is supreme against the state. The extreme position in the spectrum is the point of view stressed by the anarchists who argue that the individual conscience defeats all claims of the state.

Gandhi's concept of political obligation can be interpreted as a peculiar blending of each of these elements. In line with the Marxists, he says that "unrestricted individualism is the law of the beast of the jungle."[1] Along with the democrats, he says: "I claim to be a democrat both by instinct and training."[2] And he joined hands with the anarchists when he advocated a state of "enlightened anarchy" where "every one is his own ruler."[3] Professor Bondurant finds some similarities between Gandhi and T. H. Green, but, as she herself points out, "he was all these and none of them for he never lost his profoundly revolutionary character."[4]

Although elements of socialism, liberalism, and anarchism are

[1] M. K. Gandhi, *All Men Are Brothers* (New York: Columbia University Press, 1958), p. 143. There are numerous collections of Gandhi's editorials and speeches, including the *Collected Works of Mahatma Gandhi*, a hundred-volume work being published by the Government of India. For convenience, most of our citations will be to two collections that are currently available in the United States.

[2] *Ibid.*, p. 142.

[3] *Ibid.*, p. 140.

[4] Joan V. Bondurant, *Conquest of Violence* (Berkeley: University of California Press, 1965), p. 188.

found in Gandhi's notion of political obligation, in the ultimate analysis, however, the anarchist elements dominate his thinking. In the context of political authority, Gandhi was led to this position because he abhorred all violence and destruction of individuality by the state. The state, for him, "represents violence in a concentrated and organized form. The individual has a soul, but the State is a soulless machine, it can never be weaned from violence to which it owes its very existence."[5] Elsewhere he says: "I look upon an increase of the power of the State with the greatest fear, because, although while [sic] apparently doing good by minimizing exploitation, it does the greatest harm to mankind by destroying individuality which lies at the root of all progress."[6] Now to say that the individual counts more than the state in Gandhian thought does not mean that Gandhi advocates laissez faire or that he pits the individual against the society. In the Gandhian conception, the individual is subject to social restraints and social obligations, but these restraints are self-imposed for the sake of the well-being of the society. In fact, Gandhi considers that voluntary restraints on the part of the individual enrich both the individual and the society. Individuality should not be mistaken for individualism or egoism. That is why Gandhi calls his conception "*enlightened* anarchy" where "the individual rules himself in such a manner that he is never a hindrance to his neighbor. In the ideal State, therefore, there is no political power because there is no State. But the ideal is never fully realized in life. Hence the classical statement of Thoreau that that government is best which governs the least."[7]

II

The difficulty in classifying Gandhi in any of the Western political philosophies is that the Western-sounding foreground of political doctrine has a background of Indian philosophy. His belief in the possibility of individuality without political individualism is found in comments like the following:

---

[5] M. K. Gandhi, *All Men Are Brothers*, p. 148.
[6] Quoted in M. S. Patel, *The Educational Philosophy of Mahatma Gandhi* (Ahmedabad: Navajivan Publishing House, 1956), pp. 51–52.
[7] M. K. Gandhi, *All Men Are Brothers*, p. 140.

I do not believe that an individual may gain spirituality and those that surround him suffer. I believe in *advaita*. I believe in the essential unity of man and for that matter of all that lives. Therefore I believe that if one man gains spiritually, the whole world gains with him and, if one man falls, the whole world falls to that extent.[8]

This contention will be better understood if we bear in mind the Indian metaphysics of *advaita* to which Gandhi referred. Advaita holds that man in his innermost depths is nothing other than the Universal Spirit. And Gandhi says that "to see the universal and all-pervading Spirit of Truth face to face one must be able to love the meanest of creation as oneself. And a man who aspires after that cannot afford to keep out of any field of life. That is why my devotion to truth has drawn me into the field of politics. . . . "[9] For Gandhi, therefore, an individual is essentially a soul or spirit.

The individual is, for him, a moral person whose duty is to pursue truth. But what is truth?

The word *Satya* (Truth) is derived from *Sat,* which means "being." Nothing is or exists in reality except Truth. That is why *Sat* or Truth is perhaps the most important name of God. In fact it is more correct to say that Truth is God, than to say that God is Truth.[10]

And he goes on to say:

Devotion to this Truth is the sole justification for our existence. All our activities should be centered in Truth. Truth should be the very breath of our life. When once this stage in the pilgrim's progress is reached, all other rules of correct living will come without effort, and obedience to them will be instinctive. But without Truth it would be impossible to observe any principles or rules in life.[11]

[8] *Ibid.*, p. 118.
[9] *Ibid.*, p. 58.
[10] M. K. Gandhi, *Non-Violent Resistance (Satyagraha)* (New York: Schocken Books, 1961), p. 38.
[11] *Ibid.*, pp. 38–39.

Holding on to truth is what Gandhi calls *Satyagraha.* "Satyagraha is literally holding on to Truth and it means, therefore,
Truth-force. Truth is soul or spirit. It is, therefore, known as
soul-force."[12] Though the justification of our existence lies in
our devotion to truth, "it is impossible for us to realize perfect
Truth so long as we are imprisoned in this mortal frame."[13]

The way leading to truth lies in *ahimsa* or nonviolence.
Ahimsa, for Gandhi, has positive and negative connotations. In
its positive connotation, it means unbounded love, affection, and
sympathy, and in its negative aspect, it means noninjury to any
living creature in thought, word, and deed. Therefore he points
out that

> without *ahimsa* it is not possible to seek and find Truth.
> *Ahimsa* and Truth are so intertwined that it is practically
> impossible to disentangle and separate them. They are like
> the two sides of a coin, or rather of a smooth unstamped
> metallic disc. Who can say, which is the obverse, and which
> is the reverse? Nevertheless *ahimsa* is the means; Truth is
> the end. Means to be means must always be within our
> reach, and so *ahimsa* is our supreme duty.[14]

Gandhi further asserts that "means and end are convertible
terms in my philosophy of life."[15] The means are given to us to
a limited extent, but never the end, and it is therefore all the
more incumbent on us to adhere strictly to the purity of means.
Like walking on a razor's edge, the pursuit of truth is no easy
matter. The seeker after truth has to be firmly committed to
nonviolence and has to overcome many an obstacle and conquer
many an evil in his pursuits, "for the quest of Truth involves
tapas—self-suffering, sometimes even unto death. There can be
no place in it for even a trace of self-interest."[16] Apart from a
commitment to truth and nonviolence, and a preparedness for
self-suffering, a perfect *Satyagrahi* (seeker after truth) has to
fulfill, according to Gandhi, a number of other qualifications like

[12] *Ibid.,* p. 1. In ordinary parlance, however, any public protest has come to
be associated with the word *Satyagraha* in India for the past two decades.

[13] M. K. Gandhi, *All Men Are Brothers,* p. 75.

[14] M. K. Gandhi, *Non-Violent Resistance,* p. 42.

[15] M. K. Gandhi, *All Men Are Brothers,* p. 81.

[16] M. K. Gandhi, *Non-Violent Resistance,* p. 39.

being a teetotaller, controlling his palate, regulating his sexual urges, leading a simple life, having courage and fearlessness, possessing no material goods, and so on; with the result that a perfect Satyagrahi almost has to be a perfect man.

To a casual observer all these rules seem to be more in consonance with the life in a monastery than in the political arena. This is in a sense true, for Gandhi was trying to "spiritualize" politics. He says: "For me, politics bereft of religion are absolute dirt, ever to be shunned. Politics concern nations and that which concerns the welfare of nations must be one of the concerns of a man who is religiously inclined, in other words, a seeker after God and Truth."[17]

An unwary reader might complain that mystery still surrounds the entire notion of Satyagraha. What does it mean to say that we should hold on to truth? But the notion is not as mysterious as Gandhi's writings sometimes suggest. The man in action is sometimes more easily understood than the words in which he formulates his doctrines. Gandhi's own application of Satyagraha points to two related things. Negatively, it enjoins upon man the duty to eradicate evil, and positively, it reminds him of his obligation to serve the community. Thus, throughout his life Gandhi was striving to root out evil practices and age-old prejudices like the inequality of men, racial and communal hatred, the practice of untouchability, and so on. Positively, his constructive program includes experiments in "Basic Education," promotion of *khadi* (hand-spun cloth) and village industries, including a sense of self-respect in the oppressed and downtrodden people, and so on. Shorn of all the mystical vocabulary, Satyagraha may be viewed (1) as a way of life exemplified by Gandhi himself, and (2) as a technique of domestic, social and political action with a view to bringing about desired change, through peaceful means, for the common good. Satyagraha is not simply resistance to injustice, but also is the promotion of common good in a peaceful and constructive way. Many questions, of course, arise as to what is evil, and who is to determine that a practice is evil, the kind of program one has to undertake in his social reconstruction work, and so on. All these belong to what we call the "logistics" of Satyagraha, a consideration of which is beyond the scope of the chapter.

[17] M. K. Gandhi, *All Men Are Brothers*, p. 69.

Satyagraha, when it descends from the metaphysical to the political realm, consists in the opposition to unjust laws, since such opposition is essentially a resistance to evil. Gandhi therefore points out: "But on the political field the struggle on behalf of the people mostly consists in opposing error in the shape of unjust laws. . . . Hence Satyagraha largely appears to the public as Civil Disobedience or Civil Resistance."[18]

III

Gandhi borrowed the phrase civil disobedience from the famous essay by Henry David Thoreau some years after he had gotten the idea of Satyagraha and, from time to time, he made various distinctions between the practices that he called civil disobedience and practices that he considered less worthy. Civil disobedience is treated as a species of an essentially spiritual principle, Satyagraha, "the exercise of the purest soul force in its perfect form. . . . For this exercise, prolonged training of the individual is an absolute necessity, so that a perfect Satyagrahi has to be almost, if not entirely, a perfect man."[19] Satyagraha as applied in the political structure of a community manifests itself, then, as civil disobedience, and Gandhi defines it as "the civil breach of unmoral statutory enactments."[20] In contrast to the Thomistic tradition, which contends that an unjust law is no law at all, Gandhi does not seem to doubt the legal status of the disputed orders, but only their justness or morality.

Civil disobedience is essentially a dynamic concept and involves active resistance to the unjust laws. It is not passive resistance.

> Passive Resistance is used in the orthodox English sense and covers the suffragette movement as well as the resistance of the non-conformists. Passive resistance has been conceived and is regarded as a weapon of the weak. Whilst it avoids violence, being not open to the weak [sic] it does

[18] M. K. Gandhi, *Non-Violent Resistance*, p. 6-7.
[19] *Ibid.*, p. 35.
[20] *Ibid.*, p. 1.

not exclude its use if, in the opinion of the passive resister, the occasion demands it.[21]

Civil disobedience, on the other hand, is for Gandhi, by definition, nonviolent. It is civil in the sense it is not criminal. And being civil, no action is attempted and no move is made in secrecy. Just as a criminal is one who is not in the habit of obeying laws, a civil resister is one who is generally a law-abiding citizen. In order, therefore, to undertake civil disobedience, one should have qualified himself as a law-abiding citizen. Moreover, "disobedience to be civil must be sincere, respectful, restrained, never defiant, must be based upon some well-understood principle, must not be capricious and above all, must have no ill-will or hatred behind it."[22] Civil disobedience may be undertaken either individually or collectively. Since there is always the possibility of a mass civil disobedience becoming violent, Gandhi sometimes advocates that it should be restricted to the Satyagrahis, who are well-disciplined morally and spiritually. Sometimes, however, Gandhi admits the desirability of mass civil disobedience, assuming that the people are guided by suitable leaders.

While Gandhi does not, in general, seem to favor mass civil disobedience, (unless the people are firmly committed to nonviolence and are pledged to accept suffering), he regards as feasible mass noncooperation. "Non-co-operation predominantly implies withdrawing of co-operation from the State that in the non-co-operator's view has become corrupt and excludes Civil Disobedience of the fierce type described above. By its very nature, non-co-operation is even open to children of understanding and can be safely practiced by the masses."[23] While civil disobedience involves the active breaking of laws, noncooperation need not do so. There was no law which demanded buying of foreign goods, and the people of India were breaching no law when they boycotted British goods during their independence movement. Other instances of noncooperation as practiced in India were the surrendering of titles, honors, and the like conferred by government; boycotting administrative office, judicial courts, schools;

[21] *Ibid.*
[22] M. K. Gandhi, *All Men Are Brothers*, p. 99.
[23] M. K. Gandhi, *Non-Violent Resistance*, p. 4.

resigning from police, military, and other administrative and executive positions; *hartal*, i.e., closing of shops and other business establishments; picketing; and so on.

The effectiveness of noncooperation comes from the dependence of any government, however tyrannical, on the consent of the governed. A large-scale noncooperation can paralyze the regime and bring down the government through peaceful means. Gandhi believed that a constructive program also has to be formulated for any noncooperation movement to be successful.

Although Gandhi tried to avoid certain difficulties with his distinction between civil disobedience and noncooperation, the distinction disappears in practice, for most noncooperation movements sooner or later violate some law. This is sure to happen if the authorities ban organized picketing or if a boycott is declared to be a conspiracy.

Gandhi, therefore, says on another occasion:

> A little reflection will show that civil disobedience is a necessary part of non-cooperation. You assist an administration most effectively by obeying its orders and decrees. An evil administration never deserves such allegiance. Allegiance to it means partaking of the evil. A good man will therefore resist an evil system or administration with his whole soul. Disobedience of the laws of an evil State is therefore a duty.[24]

Civil disobedience and noncooperation being offshoots of the genre Satyagraha, some of the conditions that Gandhi prescribes for Satyagraha, like strict adherence to nonviolence, respect for the opponent, and so on, are applicable to noncooperation as well as to civil disobedience. Gandhi himself does not use these terms consistently, and it is not always easy to say whether a particular action has been performed in the spirit of civil disobedience, passive resistance, noncooperation, or Satyagraha.

IV

Gandhi's distinction as a political thinker does not lie just in the enunciation of the familiar doctrine that evil and unjust laws

[24] *Ibid.*, p. 238.

ought to be disobeyed. Distinctive in his thinking, however, are the revolutionary implications that his doctrine involves. We have seen that the proposition that man should pursue and realize truth is a categorical imperative for him. From this it follows that anything which is an impediment to the pursuit of truth should be overcome. Evil is an impediment to truth. Therefore, evil should be overcome. The overcoming of evil may be by the infliction of suffering on others, but this increases evil and does not decrease it. Therefore, the infliction of suffering must be on oneself, and Gandhi is emphatic in asserting that the pursuit of truth necessarily involves suffering on the part of the pursuer. "Satyagraha means readiness to suffer and a faith that the more innocent and pure the suffering the more potent will it be in its effect."[25]

Unjust laws being necessarily evil, a seeker after truth has the *duty* to resist unjust laws. Gandhi speaks of civil disobedience as both the right of a citizen and his duty. Thus he says: "I wish I could persuade everybody that civil disobedience is the inherent right of a citizen. He dare not give it up without ceasing to be a man."[26] And he goes on to say: "Civil disobedience therefore becomes a sacred duty when the State has become lawless, or which is the same thing, corrupt. And a citizen that barters with such a State shares its corruption or lawlessness."[27] When Gandhi uses such phrases as "inherent right" and "birthright," concerning civil disobedience, he seems to mean something like the natural rights of Western political theory. But when he speaks about the "duty" of civil disobedience, he means it as a moral duty. Here, again, is an instance of the intersection of politics and morality in Gandhi's thought.

One has a duty to resist an unjust law, because it is a hindrance to the pursuit of truth not only for the resister but also for the legislator or oppressor. Resistance to an unjust law is a self-regarding moral duty, but it is also an other-regarding moral duty. The consequence of this line of reasoning is that one disobeys an unjust law out of a reverence for the moral personality of the opponent. The unjust law is an evil, but the person who enacted the law is inherently good. "Man and his deed are two distinct things. It is quite proper to resist and attack a

[25] *Ibid.*, p. 294.
[26] *Ibid.*, p. 174.
[27] *Ibid.*

system, but to resist and attack its author is tantamount to resisting and attacking oneself."[28] Gandhi also frequently speaks of the "trust" a civil resister should place in the oppressor's potential goodness; in the "conversion" of the wrongdoer; in the "weaning away" of one's opponent from error.

Second, the fact that Gandhi uses such language as "conversion," "weaning away," and so on, should not lead us to infer that he takes for granted the self-righteousness of the civil resister and the wickedness of the opponent. He frequently argues that a civil resister should view the disputed subject objectively with a detached mind, and that he should give the fullest consideration to all the points of view. "Three-fourths of the miseries and misunderstandings in the world will disappear, if we step into the shoes of our adversaries and understand their standpoint. We will then agree with our adversaries quickly or think of them charitably."[29] Moreover, Gandhi recognizes that though truth itself is absolute, our notions of truth are sometimes relative and therefore there should be room for discussion, negotiation, persuasion, and reconciliation in our dealings with our opponent. Thus he says: "All my life through, the very insistence on truth has taught me to appreciate the beauty of compromise. I saw later in life that this spirit was an essential part of Satyagraha."[30]

Compromise should be based on give and take, but there should be no compromise on fundamental principles. What, moreover, is implied in the admission of fallibility is the willingness of the Satyagrahi to suffer.

Q. (Sir Chimanlal) : However honestly a man may strive in his search for truth his notions of truth may be different from the notions of others. Who then is to determine the truth?

A. (M. K. Gandhi) : The individual himself would determine that.

Q. Different individuals would have different views as to truth. Would that not lead to confusion?

---

28 M. K. Gandhi, *All Men Are Brothers*, p. 88.
29 M. K. Gandhi, *Non-Violent Resistance*, pp. 193–94.
30 M. K. Gandhi, *Autobiography or The Story of My Experiments with Truth* (Washington, D. C.: Public Affairs Press, 1948), p. 184.

A. I do not think so.

Q. Honestly striving after truth is different in every case.

A. That is why the non-violence part was a necessary corollary. Without that there would be confusion and worse.[31]

Therefore, whatever may be the form of Satyagraha that one undertakes, nonviolence is a *sine qua non*. Violent civil resistance cannot be justified because it is not morally superior to the position of the state which seeks to impose its laws forcibly.

Third, the fact that a civil resister who breaks a law is willing to undergo punishment cheerfully does not weaken the political structure of the community, but, in fact, will strengthen it. "Civil disobedience is never followed by anarchy. Criminal disobedience can lead to it. Every State puts down criminal disobedience by force. It perishes, if it does not. But to put down civil disobedience is to attempt to imprison conscience. Civil disobedience can only lead to strength and purity."[32] Again, Gandhi points out that "the real meaning of the statement that we are a law-abiding nation is that we are passive resisters."[33] Showing that he had understood English law, Gandhi remarks that the law does not say "You must do such a thing"; it says "If you do not do it, we will punish you."[34] To disobey a law and suffer the penalty attached to the violation is perfectly legal, and therefore, we may say that a civil resister obeys the law by disobeying it!

Fourth, Gandhi insists that Satyagraha should never be undertaken for purely selfish ends and personal gain; otherwise, "there would be no end of scoundrels blackmailing people by resorting to the means."[35] Nor should it be undertaken out of utilitarian considerations. "A votary of *ahimsa* cannot subscribe to the utilitarian formula (of the greatest good of the greatest number). He will strive for the greatest good of all and die in the

---

[31] M. K. Gandhi, *Non-Violent Resistance*, p. 29.

[32] *Ibid.*, p. 174. Cf. H. L. A. Hart: "If we are ready to go to prison rather than obey our attitudes might very well strengthen the system as a whole and not weaken it." "Legal and Moral Obligation," in A. I. Melden (ed.), *Essays in Moral Philosophy* (Seattle: University of Washington Press, 1958), p. 105.

[33] *Ibid.*, p. 18.

[34] *Ibid.*

[35] *Ibid.*, p. 313.

attempt to realize the ideal. .... The utilitarian to be logical will never sacrifice himself. The absolutist will even sacrifice himself."[36]

Nor should there be any "game" of Satyagraha, using it as an expedient and hitting the opponent when one finds him weak. On this account Gandhi was often criticized that he did not play *realpolitik*. The result, his critics contended, was a record of "missed opportunities."[37] For example, when the British strength was deployed and dissipated during World War II, Gandhi could have intensified his Satyagraha campaigns in India, making the British presence impossible. But he refused to do so saying: "It is absurd to launch civil disobedience today for independence. How are we to fight for independence with those whose own independence is in grave peril? Even if independence can be given by one nation to another, it is not possible for the English. Those who are themselves in peril cannot save others. But if they fight unto death for their freedom and they are at all reasonable, they must recognize our right of free speech."[38] Gandhi's career is molded by many such instances and, as Arne Naess points out, "by not exploiting their advantageous position, Gandhi's supporters remained true to his and their own aim, which was future cooperation with those who were then their opponents."[39]

Because of Gandhi's reputation as a shrewd bargainer and game-player, his denials that Satyagraha is a game have fallen on deaf ears. Some of the participants in civil disobedience campaigns have obviously looked upon their own actions, as they are usually viewed by officials, as a kind of bargaining, tactics being selected because of their nuisance value. This misinterpretation is widespread in the United States, where the nullification tradition is strong and the dominant conception of politics is the idea of agreement on *quid pro quo*.

[36] M. K. Gandhi, *All Men Are Brothers*, pp. 89–90.

[37] See, for example, Sasadhar Sinha, *Indian Independence in Perspective* (New York: Asia Publishing House, 1960).

[38] Quoted in Hiren Mukherjee, *Gandhiji: A Study* (Calcutta: National Book Agency Ltd., 1958), p. 134.

[39] Arne Naess, *Gandhi and the Nuclear Age* (Totowa, N.J.: The Bedminster Press, 1965), p. 13. Arne Naess gives a number of such examples from Gandhi's life.

V

It is sometimes said that Gandhi's doctrine of Satyagraha can only be enunciated from the point of view of an agitator, that it is incompatible with the duties of an administrator. It is true that Gandhi was, throughout his life, an agitator. But this criticism may be discounted in so far as it presupposes a *realpolitik* where there is a confrontation between the "interests" of the agitator and the administrator, and the result of such a confrontation is either an uneasy compromise or suppression depending upon respective strengths. This is not the spirit in which Gandhi worked. For him, there are no "interests" apart from common interests. He did not aim at any uneasy compromise, but always aimed at real transformation of one party by the other. Moreover, as we have already pointed out, Gandhi like Kant insisted on the universalisability of a maxim. In his evidence before the Hunter Committee, Gandhi made this clear.

Q. (LORD HUNTER) : I ask you to look at it from the point of view of the Government. If you were a Governor yourself, what would you say to a movement that was started with the object of breaking those laws which your Committee determined?

A. (M. K. GANDHI) : That would not be stating the whole case of the Satyagraha doctrine. If I were in charge of the Government and brought face to face with a body who, entirely in search of truth, were determined to seek redress from unjust laws without inflicting violence, I would welcome it and would consider that they were the best constitutionalists, and, as a Governor I would take them by my side as advisers who would keep me on the right path.[40]

A variant of the above criticism is the reminder that Gandhi was opposing an alien government throughout his life, and that his doctrines would have been different had it been a representative democratic government. Gandhi, however, points out that "in England it often happens that ministers can continue in the executive even though they lose all the confidence of the public. The same thing may happen here too and therefore I can

---

[40] M. K. Gandhi, *Non-Violent Resistance*, p. 20.

imagine a state of things in this country which would need Satyagraha even under Home Rule."[41] Elsewhere he says: "The real *Swaraj* (political self-government) will come not by the acquisition of authority by a few but by the acquisition of the capacity by all to resist authority when abused. In other words, *swaraj* has to be obtained by educating the masses to a sense of their capacity to regulate and control authority."[42]

Therefore, the right to resist authority and the duty to disobey unjust laws remain with the people even in a democracy. Gandhi nevertheless concedes that in a democratic form of government there will be fewer occasions for people to resort to civil disobedience. He says:

> I would be deeply distressed if on every conceivable occasion each one of us was to be a law unto himself and to scrutinize in golden scales every action of our future National Assembly. I would surrender my judgment in most matters to national representatives, taking particular care in making my choice of such representatives. I know that in no other manner would a democratic government be possible for one single day.[43]

At times Gandhi made sweeping claims for the practicability of a social order in which moral obligations take precedence over ordinary political and legal obligations. At other times, Gandhi laid stress on the improbability that very many human beings could discipline themselves sufficiently to carry out a program of active civil disobedience. As is well known, he was extremely frustrated after Indian independence had been achieved at the price of partition with subsequent rioting by Hindu and Moslem mobs.

It cannot be shown, at this time, that Gandhi succeeded in developing a new way to solve political problems. It can be said, however, that he did succeed in showing how a man with a conscience can participate in politics. So far as the state is concerned, there still seems to be a puzzling relationship between

---

[41] *Ibid.*, p. 34.
[42] M. K. Gandhi, *All Men Are Brothers*, p. 140.
[43] C. F. Andrews, *Mahatama Gandhi's Ideas* (New York: Macmillan, 1930), p. 144.

moral and political obligations. From the standpoint of individuals and like-minded groups, Gandhi worked out a new way to relate the two kinds of obligations.

It may be pointed out in conclusion that we have only endeavored here to expound and bring out some of the distinctive characteristics of Gandhian thought on civil disobedience, without pretending that we have thereby formulated a complete political theory.[44] Gandhi was essentially an activist with a tempestuous public life of half a century. Not being an abstract thinker, he sometimes lacks the clarity and analytic precision that characterize philosophical writings. One can point out many apparent contradictions in Gandhi's thought. Gandhi himself was not unaware of these difficulties. "At the time of writing," he said,

> I never think of what I have said before. My aim is not to be consistent with my previous statements on a given question, but to be consistent with truth, as it may present itself to me at a given moment. The result has been that I have grown from truth to truth; I have saved my memory an undue strain; and what is more, whenever I have been obliged to compare my writing even fifteen years ago with the latest, I have discovered no inconsistency between the two."[45]

What we have tried here is to bring out the consistency with which Gandhi found a spiritual meaning and a moral obligation in the conflicts of political life.

---

[44] Some of Gandhi's difficulties in the theory of organization and leadership are discussed in our book, *Gandhi and America's Educational Future* (Carbondale, Ill.: Southern Illinois University Press, 1969).

[45] M. K. Gandhi, *All Men Are Brothers*, p. 170.